THE AFRICAN WRITERS' HANDBOOK

Other publishing resource titles published by
African Books Collective Ltd

African Publishers Networking Directory 1999/2000 3rd edition
Compiled by African Books Collective

The Electronic African Bookworm: A Web Navigator
Print version, compiled by Hans M Zell

A Handbook of Good Practice in Journal Publishing 2nd edition
by Hans M Zell
Published jointly with the International African Institute

Women in Publishing and the Book Trade in Africa:
An Annotated Directory
Compiled by African Books Collective

The African Writers' Handbook

Edited by

James Gibbs and Jack Mapanje

Associate Editor: Flora Rees

African Books Collective Ltd • Oxford

in association with the Dag Hammarskjöld Foundation • Uppsala

First published 1999 by African Books Collective Ltd, Oxford
in association with the Dag Hammarskjöld Foundation, Uppsala, Sweden.

The concept of this book follows *A Handbook for African Writers*
edited by James Gibbs (Oxford: Hans Zell Publishers, 1986).

African Books Collective Ltd
The Jam Factory, 27 Park End Street
Oxford OX1 1HU, UK

British Library Cataloguing in Publication Data
The African writers' handbook
    1. Authorship – Handbooks, manuals, etc. 2. Publishers and
    publishing – Directories 3. Authors, African
    I. Gibbs, James II. Mapanje, Jack
    808'.02'08996

    ISBN 0 9521269 6 6

Cover illustration by James Gayo

Designed, typeset from disk and produced for ABC by
Chase Production Services, Chadlington, Oxfordshire OX7 3LN
Printed in the EU

Contents

Perspectives on Publishing in Africa

PART TWO

Arusha III and Beyond

Getting Started

Getting Together

Getting Published

Getting on with the State

Getting on with the Law

Getting on with the Book Trade

The Author's Bookshelf   362

Publishers' Preface

A thriving, autonomous publishing industry in Africa is an indispensable part of the cultural development and renaissance of the continent. And cultural development is an integral part of development in its true sense – with all its implications for human beings. It is within this context that African Books Collective (ABC) and the Dag Hammarskjöld Foundation, came together to hold a seminar on African writer–publisher relations in Tanzania in 1998, and to publish this Handbook.

A Handbook for African Writers, edited by James Gibbs, and published by Hans Zell Publishers in 1986, arose out of a conference in London in 1984 on 'New Writing in Africa'. That same year, the Foundation held a seminal conference – now known as Arusha I – in Tanzania on 'The Development of Autonomous Capacity in Publishing in Africa'. Although not linked, there was much common ground between the two initiatives: the 1986 *Handbook* came down strongly on the side of local publishers as the first stop for the author with a manuscript, whilst Arusha I called for 'autonomous indigenous publishing (houses) ... owned and controlled by Africans themselves ...'.

In the next decade, in 1996, the Dag Hammarskjöld Foundation held a re-assessment seminar, known as 'Arusha II', on 'The Future of Indigenous Publishing in Africa'. Arusha II strongly supported a call by Walter Bgoya, Co-Director of Arushas I and II, and Publisher Director of Arusha III, to hold a conference of African writers and publishers with the aim of arriving at a 'New Deal' between the two professions and agreeing on common approaches to the imperative task of enhancing the role of literature and publishing in the continent. Arusha II called on African governments to designate publishing as a strategic industry in development, for cultural autonomy and pride are integral to development.

And so it was that Arusha III was held at Tarangire Sopa Lodge, Arusha, in Tanzania in February 1998, organised by ABC and the Foundation. It brought together a major representative group of Africa's most active and engaged writers and publishers to discuss, debate and argue about their respective relations, rights, and responsibilities. Linked to and informed by the seminar, but not directly arising from it, this wholly new Handbook has been developed. The two projects are part of a whole: contributions to the essential strengthening of autonomous African publishing.

A pilot edition of the Handbook was discussed at Arusha III, and has been further developed and refined in the light of those discussions. It is intended primarily as a resource for the aspiring or not yet widely published African writer. It does not claim to be definitive but rather a starting-off-point guide, and is complementary to other sources cited in 'The Author's Bookshelf'. It has been an encouragement that so many distinguished writers and publishers agreed to share their experiences by contributing to the Handbook.

'A Social Contract for Books' by Paul Tiyambe Zeleza provides the context for the book, reflecting the concerns which led ABC and the Foundation to organise Arusha III and publish this Handbook. It is such a deeply informed, balanced and far-sighted exposition of the issues by one of Africa's most engaged and pre-eminent writers and scholars, that it stands as the scene-setter for other contributions.

As the publishers, we are happy to take this opportunity to express our thanks to all those who have helped us in shaping this book. The planning group included Walter Bgoya, the Publisher Director, and Niyi Osundare, the Writer Director, of Arusha III. We are extremely fortunate to have had the benefit of the knowledge, experience and wisdom of our two friends: qualities made real and relevant by their great intellectual engagement, their passionate concerns for the cultural future of Africa, and their intense energy in pursuing that future. We have benefited throughout from their advice, friendship and support.

Of the many people who have given information or advice, we would like in particular to thank Hans Zell, a member of the planning group who has provided his expertise at many levels in shaping the book, and has contributed an article on Internet resources, 'The Author's Bookshelf', and much information and research guidance for the directory sections. We owe a great debt to Flora Rees, Associate Editor, over and above any conventional thanks. Her editing and research skills and her enthusiasm for the book have been essential in bringing it to fruition.

The views expressed in this book are not necessarily those of the publishers. And that brings us to its editor, James Gibbs. Assisted by his co-editor, Jack Mapanje, he has worked long and hard amidst many other commitments, drawing on his knowledge and long-standing engagement with African literature and writing, and for a modest honorarium. It has been therefore largely a labour of love. It might be seen as somewhat odd for publishers to advertise what might seem like exploitation of an author, and somewhat ironic in the light of the genesis and subject-matter of the book. But neither ABC nor the Dag Hammarskjöld Foundation are commercial organisations, and the editor, others in the planning group, and contributors to the book have worked together in a spirit of partnership to make what we hope will be a contribution to the health of creative writing and publishing in Africa. It would not have been possible at all without the financial support of the Swedish International Development Cooperation Agency (Sida) who supported the Arusha I seminar, and the publication of this Handbook as part of a long-term commitment to African cultural development by Swedish aid institutions. With this support, copies of the Handbook will be distributed free of charge to African writers, writers' organisations, and the wider African book communities. We are pleased to record our very real appreciation to Sida for their interest and financial support.

Mary Jay, African Books Collective Ltd
Olle Nordberg, Dag Hammarskjöld Foundation

Acknowledgements

This volume repeatedly insists that producing a book requires the contributions of many people, and it is appropriate that the editors owe debts of gratitude to a particularly large number. Some are named below, and the help of many others can be inferred both from comments in the text, and from the material by diverse hands that enriches the volume. We have not listed below the names of those 'diverse hands', the contributors to this Handbook named on the Contents page. Part of the book is theirs; the book is partly theirs. We are simply happy and grateful that they shared their ideas in this forum.

Those who attended the Tarangire seminar at which the 'New Deal', which stands as the focus of this Handbook, was beaten into shape have, likewise, not been mentioned in this section. They know how much they shared at Sopa Lodge, how much was contributed to the important new thinking that pulses through the 'New Deal' statement, how their ideas influence the shaping – and the detail – of this book. All the names can be found at the end of the 'New Deal' statement. Exception must, however, be made for the Seminar Directors, Walter Bgoya and Niyi Osundare, and those from the Dag Hammarskjöld Foundation who were present: Olle Nordberg and Sven Hamrell. The Directors guided discussions with discretion and strength borne of experience. Through its representatives, the Foundation supported the gathering, and the present volume, with enthusiasm, insight and generosity, and without interfering in any way.

As supportive creators of opportunities, Bgoya and Osundare, Nordberg and Hamrell have been matched by the staff at the African Books Collective in Oxford, particularly by those who were deeply involved in 'the Handbook project'. That is to say by the patient, persistent Mary Jay and by Flora, who was transformed from 'Flora Lucas, Seminar Assistant' at Tarangire to 'Flora Rees, Associate Editor' in Oxford. As part of the core team, they sustained this project over the months it took to bring it to fruition, and their contributions are much appreciated.

There is no space to thank individually all those who responded to enquiries. But it is appropriate to write out the names of those who earned our gratitude by going the second, third, or more miles, those who, by their support, through responding to follow-up enquiries, by making contacts or establishing links, alerted the editors to important material they were likely to miss. We would like to thank in particular Ama Ata Aidoo; Diana Bailey; Greefield K. Cholong; Steven and Moira Chimombo; Monica Cromhout; Chris Dunton; Gordon Fielden; Kessie Govender; Abdulrazak Gurnah; Jane Katjavivi; Ruth Kumpmann; Charles and Roberta Larson; Bernth and Judy Lindfors; Margaret Ling; Don Long; Akberali Manji; Alastair Niven; Chikwenye Okonjo Ogunyemi; Christine Pagnoulle; Carol Priestley; Peter Ripken; Diana Rosenberg; Tijan M. Sallah; Katherine Salahi; Raks Seakhoa; Lynn Taylor; Per Wästberg; and Jan Kees van de Werk.

The volume they have helped us put together is a successor to *A Handbook for African Writers* that Hans Zell, to whom many thanks are due, published in 1986. One of those who wrote in after reading the Handbook was Duma Uthman, an aspiring short-story writer from Eldoret, Kenya. Uthman's letter concluded: 'I'm kindly asking you to give more idea how I can become a known writer, and how my stories can be printed and/or published.' It has taken some time, but the editors hope the wait for this much enlarged, this wider-ranging volume, has been worth it. We hope it will give 'more idea'. For any inadequacies and inaccuracies the editors take responsibility.

James Gibbs

Jack Mapanje

The publishers and editors acknowledge with thanks permission to reproduce the following materials:

Paul Tiyambe Zeleza 'A Social Contract for Books'. *African Book Publishing Record*, Vol. 22 no. 4, 1996, 251-55.

Cyprian Ekwensi 'Random Thoughts on Clocking Sixty-five'. *The Essential Ekwensi*. Ernest Emenoyou, ed. Ibadan: Heinemann Educational Books (Nigeria) Plc, 1987.

Walter Bgoya 'Publishing in Africa: Culture and Development'. *The Muse of Modernity: Essays on Culture as Development in Africa.* Philip G Altbach and Salah M Hassan, eds. Trenton, NJ: Africa World Press, 1996.

Henry Chakava 'An Autonomous African Publishing House: A Model'. *Development Dialogue,* nos. 1-2, 1984, 123-31. Reprinted in *Publishing in Africa: One Man's Perspective.* Boston: Bellagio Publishing Network, Bellagio Studies in Publishing, 6; and Nairobi: East African Educational Publishers Ltd, 1996.

Hans Zell 'African Publishers – "Mostly Liars and Cheats"?' *African Publishing Review*, Vol. 4 no. 3, May/June 1995, 14-16.

Ken Saro-Wiwa 'Notes of a Reluctant Publisher'. *African Book Publishing Record*, Vol. 22 no. 4, 1996, 257-59.

Henry Chakava 'Publishing Ngugi: The Challenge, the Risk and the Reward'. *African Publishing Review,* Vol. 3 no. 4, July/August 1994, 10-14. Reprinted in *Publishing in Africa: One Man's Perspective.* Boston: Bellagio Publishing Network, Bellagio Studies in Publishing, 6; and Nairobi: East African Educational Publishers Ltd, 1996.

Omowunmi Segun 'Writing Against Repression'. An interview with Niyi Osundare. C^2 the campaigning magazine of Amnesty International, January 1999, 18-19.

For permission to use extracts from listings, and excerpts from descriptive information, for the two sections on 'Prizes, Awards and Contests', and 'Book Fairs', from *Book Marketing and Promotion: A Handbook of Good Practice* (forthcoming, 1999), we are grateful to Hans M Zell and the International Network for the Availability of Scientific Publications (INASP).

Material for the directory sections:

Writers and Scholars International Ltd. 'Freedom of Expression Organisations'. *Index on Censorship* Vol. 27 no. 3, May/June 1998 Issue 182, 130-32.
African Books Collective. *African Publishers Networking Directory 1999/ 2000*. Oxford: African Books Collective Ltd, 1999.

Editors and Contributors

About the Editors

James Gibbs was the Editor of *A Handbook for African Writers*, from which this Handbook follows. He has taught in Ghana, Malawi, Nigeria, and Belgium and is currently at the University of the West of England, in Bristol. He has published on African literature, particularly drama, in English, and has been working, with Kofi Anyidoho. on an issue of *Matatu* devoted to the Performing Arts in Ghana. He is a co-editor of a new, annual publication *African Theatre* (James Currey Publishers).

Jack Mapanje, Malawian poet, linguist, and academic, was detained by Hastings Banda's security forces while heading the Department of English, University of Malawi. Since his release, after three-and-a-half years' imprisonment, he has been teaching, lecturing, and writing in the United Kingdom. His latest book of poems is *Skipping without Ropes* (Bloodaxe, 1998). He is currently visiting research fellow at the School of English, University of Leeds.

About the Contributors

All of the African writer contributors are published authors, and many of them are recipients of awards and prizes, not all of which are listed below.

Dapo Adeniyi is a vastly experienced journalist, and currently the Editor of *Glendora Review: African Quarterly on the Arts*, which, with its stable-mate, *Glendora Books Supplement*, is providing an invaluable platform for discussion of artistic issues in Africa.

Walter Bgoya was General Manager of the Tanzania Publishing House from 1972 to 1989, when he formed his own company, Mkuki na Nyota Publishers. He was Co-director of Arusha I and II, and Publisher Director of Arusha III. He is a founder member, and member of the Council of Management of African Books Collective (ABC); Chairman of the Managing Committee (the jury) of the Noma Award for Publishing in Africa; and is a founding member and on the General Council of the African Publishers' Network (APNET).

Henry Chakava is the Managing Director of East African Educational Publishers, Nairobi, formerly Heinemann Kenya. He led the company to full Kenyan ownership. A former Chairman of the Kenya Publishers' Association, he is a founder member, and member of the Council of Management of African Books Collective (ABC). He is a founding member and on the General Council of the African Publishers' Network (APNET).

James Currey worked with David Philip at the Oxford University Press in Cape Town (1959-64) and then took over Rex Collings' Africa list at the Oxford University Press in London (1964-67). He went to Heinemann to develop their African academic and school list and added some 250 titles to the African Writers Series. He started his own imprint, James Currey Publishers, in 1995.

Mary Jay has been a Consultant at African Books Collective (ABC) since 1989, and the Senior Consultant since 1996. She is Secretary to the Managing Committee (the jury) of the Noma Award for Publishing in Africa. She was previously deputy to the publisher at Hans Zell Publishers, and Deputy Editor of *The African Book Publishing Record*.

Regina Jere-Malanda is a freelance writer on issues of freedom of expression in Africa, and a contributor to *Index on Censorship*.

Taban lo Liyong, a prolific Sudanese writer, has held a succession of academic posts in East Africa, and is currently Director of the Centre for African Studies at the University of the North in South Africa.

MM Mulokozi is a Tanzanian writer within the tradition of Swahili culture. He has published works in Eastern Africa in Kiswahili and English, and is active in writers' issues and organisation within Tanzania. He is a researcher at the Institute of Kiswahili Research in Dar es Salaam.

Michael Norton is the founder and former Director of the Directory of Social Change which provides information and training to the UK voluntary sector, and has a large publishing programme. He founded Books for Change, a development publishing initiative based in Bangalore, and a village publishing programme in Andhrapradesh. He runs occasional workshops on publishing and communications skills for development organisations.

Kole Omotoso is a prize-winning Nigerian novelist, playwright, critic and scholar. He has published widely within Africa, and in the UK, and is a member of the Managing Committee (the jury) of the Noma Award for Publishing in Africa. He has taught literature at the

Universities of Ibadan and Ile-Ife, and is currently Professor of Literature at the University of the Western Cape in South Africa.

Onsonye Tess Onwueme is a Nigerian playwright, formerly teaching at the University of Ibadan. She was active in the establishment of Africana Legacy Press, and is currently Distinguished Professor of Cultural Diversity, and Professor of English, at the University of Wisconsin-Eau Clare in the US.

Femi Osofisan is a Nigerian playwright, scholar, critic and actor. He has been widely published within Africa, and has held a number of university appointments, and visiting fellowships. He currently combines the post of Professor of Theatre Arts at the University of Ibadan, with international commitments to directing Nigerian plays, most recently in Ghana and the US.

Niyi Osundare is a Nigerian poet and scholar, winner of the Noma Award for Publishing in Africa 1991, the Commonwealth Poetry Prize 1996, and the Fonlon-Nichols Award 1996. He was Writer Director of Arusha III, has taught at the University of Ibadan, and is currently Professor of English at the University of New Orleans.

Yvonne Vera is a Zimbabwean novelist. She was awarded The Voice of Africa 1999, the Swedish literary award; and won the best book Africa Region 1997 Commonwealth Writers Prize. She has taught at the University of Trent in Canada, and is currently Director of the National Gallery in Bulawayo.

Paul Tiyambe Zeleza is a historian and creative writer, and winner of the Noma Award for Publishing in Africa 1994. He has written widely about the role and interaction of research, writing and publishing in Africa. He has taught at the University of York, Canada, and is currently the Director of the Center for African Studies, University of Illinois at Urbana-Champaign.

Hans M Zell is a publishing consultant and was the founder of the Hans Zell Publishers imprint. He has written extensively on many aspects of publishing and book development in Africa. He is the author of several reference works on the African book trade, African literature and African studies, and has been Editor of *The African Book Publishing Record* since 1975.

Introduction

Niyi Osundare

On page 277 of this book, James Gibbs captures the sour state of the relationship between African writers and African publishers with a graphic account of his recent experience in Ghana:

> ... bringing writers and publishers together is far from simple. The Ghana International Book Fair in Accra in November 1996 was remarkable for the lack of contact between the representatives of the groups present in the Ghanaian capital. Sadly, while African publishers met at the SSNIT Guest House for a series of discussions, the Pan African Writers Association (PAWA) hosted a lively series of events at their base, PAWA House. Book Fairs would seem to be obvious occasions at which all those involved with books and the book trade can come together, but clearly organisation and goodwill are required to bridge gaps.

Hans Zell appeared to be foreshadowing the above observation when, the year before, and in an article provocatively titled 'African Publishers – "Mostly Liars and Cheats"?', he reached the following conclusion:

> So there is an urgent need to bring together African writers and publishers, and start a dialogue to foster a better understanding of the publishing process and how publishers work, and which might then lead to improved author–publisher relationships. (p. 94)

These words are too precious to fall on deaf ears. And so, on February 23 to 26, 1998, twenty African writers and publishers and ten resource persons with a background in publishing met at Tarangire Sopa Lodge, Arusha for an 'African Writers–Publishers Seminar'. Directed by Walter Bgoya (publisher) and Niyi Osundare (writer), and organised by the Dag Hammarskjöld Foundation and the African Books Collective (ABC), the seminar emerged with a ' "New Deal" between writers and publishers in Africa in their struggle to strengthen African literature and culture'. As can be expected, that 'Deal' did not come the easy way. Each group came with its own trunkload of views and grievances, and there were passionate accusations and spirited defences on both sides. But in the end, a fruitful agreement was reached on vital areas such as (a) the role of the writer and the publisher's expectations, (b) contractual issues and writer–publisher relations, (c) African values and African writing (Davies, pp. 126-30).

Without doubt, the Tarangire (Arusha III) Agreement marked an historic development in writer–publisher relations in Africa. For the first time, both groups came face-to-face, mind-to-mind in a remote African setting and deliberated vigorously on the present state and future of writing, publishing, and culture in Africa. It is too early in the day to declare with magisterial certainty that Arusha III constitutes a turning-point in the hitherto problematic relations between African writers and African publishers, but there is no doubt that some progress has been made. The 'New Deal' hammered out in Tarangire in 1998 remains today a reference point; it is the duty of all concerned with the future of the book in Africa to help it become a positive point of departure. It is also the beginning of a dialogue whose flame must be kept perpetually burning.

Thus it is no exaggeration to say that the present Handbook is informed and energised by the spirit of Arusha III and the 'New Deal'. It is not just the site for the articulation of that 'Deal'; it is also its continuation, a medium which commits it to permanence and which provides it with the power to travel. True to its name, it is a Handbook; a companion of a kind, a thesaurus of ideas – and ideals. It is, therefore, both academic and pragmatic, idealistic and utilitarian. Its contents are diverse in perspective, assorted in approach, divergent in opinions. But from it all emerges a configuration of ideas and visions, helped by a 'common backcloth', shared anxiety, and collective hope.

The Handbook is organised in two different but related parts. Part 1 has two sections, the first comprising mainly views and opinions of writers, the second those of the publishers. But as readers would realise in their journey through the terrain of this text, the wall between the two is, indeed, porous enough to allow a reasonable amount of mutual seepage. For instance, both Ken Saro-Wiwa and Dapo Adeniyi, who appear on the publishers' side here, are writers in their own right, whose viewpoints move back and forth on the bridge between the two groups, while the correspondence between Paul Tiyambe Zeleza's 'A Social Contract for Books' and Walter Bgoya's 'Publishing in Africa: Culture and Development', two eminently seminal contributions to this book, is too striking to be dismissed as merely coincidental.

Thus, although the pieces which constitute Part 1 of this book were written by different people in different places on different occasions on different topics in different styles, there are common strands running through the tapestry of the discourse. First the writers' side: Cyprian

Ekwensi's 'random thoughts' correspond in parts with those of Taban lo Liyong who, in his own words, is 'the most remaindered author in London and Nairobi', in their evocation of the good old days when the African writer suffered less, and the profession carried more honour than danger. In Femi Osofisan's 'An Experience of Publishing in Africa' and Kole Omotoso's 'Is There an African Writer Out There to Address ... ?' we encounter a narrative of disillusionment after the bubbling nationalism of the 1970s when radical Nigerian writers shunned foreign publishers, casting their lot instead with their indigenous counterparts. It has been a tale of woe and betrayal, but all is not lost: Osofisan's piece ends with a glimmer of hope, while Omotoso's is addressed to his daughter, to the future.

Tess Onwueme's 'To the Would-be African Female Writer: Husband Yourself First!' is also an address, but this one is to the African female writer 'eaten not only by the voracious male critic, but even by other female writers ...'. The injunctions in her 'Art of Human Management' (Never quarrel with your publisher, bookseller, agent ...) sound quite conciliatory and well-intentioned, though they would require more than missionary forbearance given the present writer–publisher relations in Africa. Our ideal writer–publisher bonding emerges in the account of Yvonne Vera who has discovered 'the beauty of publishing at home' with Baobab Books of Zimbabwe and the creative editorial collaboration of Irene Staunton. In many ways, Paul Tiyambe Zeleza's 'A Social Contract for Books' is a bridge-crosser. Starting off from the premise that 'books are indispensable for development', Zeleza goes on to identify six stakeholders of the book industry: the state, publishers, writers, educational institutions, libraries, and the reading public, with emphasis on the 'social contract that needs to be forged' between them to ensure a fruitful production, dissemination, and consumption of knowledge. There is no doubt that this contract has never worked properly in Africa, which is why the continent lags grossly behind in 'the international political economy of knowledge production'. What do African publishers have to say about their own part of the contract?

Walter Bgoya's 'Publishing in Africa: Culture and Development' answers this question – and others – with remarkable erudition and commitment. The book, the author declares, is not a neutral object; neither are the processes of its production and distribution. Complementing Zeleza's point about the indispensability of the book in development, Bgoya sees publishing not only as an industry but also as a mission with far-reaching implications for racial, gender, and class issues. Bgoya situates publishing within the dynamics of culture, history, and political economy, stressing its vital role in the overall liberation of the continent. In two separate but related pieces, Henry Chakava enriches

xxii   NIYI OSUNDARE

this book with his manifold experiences as one of the veterans in African publishing enterprise. The first, 'An Autonomous African Publishing House: A Model', provides helpful advice on how to run an African publishing enterprise and remain in business, while the second, 'Publishing Ngugi: The Challenge, the Risk, and the Reward', is an engaging account of the kind of ideal writer–publisher relation described earlier on by Yvonne Vera. In addition to providing useful information about Ngugi the writer, and his travails in the hands of Kenyan authorities, this article also reveals so much about the relationship between curricular shift and publishing considerations.

If Chakava's first piece advises publishers on how to stay in business, Dapo Adeniyi's 'Before Your Text Goes Into a State of Permanence' counsels the budding writer on the perils of the trade: a rejection slip is not a death sentence but an opportunity for 'creative reconsideration and re-examination'. But a writer, if he or she has the means, may slam the door against rejection slips for ever by deciding to become a self-publisher. Ken Saro-Wiwa's 'Notes of a Reluctant Publisher' gives a fascinating account of the challenges of a writer who decides to become his own publisher.

No matter how good the book or how beautifully published, what is its worth if it is unable to reach its ultimate goal, the reader? In 'African Books Collective and Creative Writing and Publishing in Africa', the indefatigable Mary Jay lets us into the inner working of the African Books Collective (ABC), undoubtedly the most effective collective 'window on the world' for African publishers – and writers. For about a decade, ABC has served not just as a distribution centre for African books, but also as a resource centre and catalyst for the publishing industry in Africa, playing its role in Africa's 'second liberation', contributing its quota to 'cultural renaissance of the Continent'. Part 1 concludes with Hans Zell's 'African Publishers – "Mostly Liars and Cheats"?', an article which lays bare the myths and fallacies plaguing writer–publisher relations in Africa, stressing the need for both sides to come to a more honest understanding of each other's position.

In many ways, Part 2 of this book is the real 'Handbook'. Thronged, heterogeneous, and detailed, its unifying force is its utilitarianism and singleness of purpose coupled with the meticulous assiduity of James Gibbs and his near Herculean task of throwing light on some of the most problematic, most confusing areas of writing and publishing. His broad preoccupation takes him to the esoteric province of the Law, the frenetic world of the literary agent, the detailed list of available literary prizes, directories of African publishers and African magazines – valuable information which makes the Handbook a treasure-trove for aspiring and budding writers, and a useful reference source for all.

Gibbs weaves in and out of the discourse in this section of the book. Particularly remarkable is the 'Arusha Report', a piece drawing on an article by Gibbs previously published in Malawi, whose significance surely goes beyond its original audience; 'Language' where Gibbs makes a well-informed contribution to the language debate in African writing; and 'What Conditions Favour Writers' which examines the socio-economic circumstances of writing and writers in Africa. Gibbs ranges over the world for examples of conditions which correspond to or contrast with the African situation, combining anecdote with analysis, annotation with parable, fact with fiction.

However, a few guest writers' make a significant entry in this section. James Currey's 'Co-Publishing: A Model' provides useful information about the sometimes complicated act of co-publishing, while highlighting its advantages to the African author – and by extension the African reading public. Michael Norton drops valuable hints on 'How to Publish Your Own Book', drawing heavily on his own personal experience as a self-publisher (though unlike Ken Saro-Wiwa above, he is not in any way 'reluctant' about his project). Two other writers concentrate on censorship: Regina Jere-Malanda, in 'Censorship: Nothing Has Changed', discusses the 'travails of African writers and the media in general' at the hands of Africa's resurgent dictators, while Niyi Osundare, in an interview titled 'Writing Against Repression', focuses on the role of writers in the struggle against tyranny with particular reference to Nigeria under Abacha.

In both its contemplative Part 1 and pragmatic Part 2, *The African Writers' Handbook* demonstrates a clear grasp of the interplay between the cultural and socio-economic circumstances of Africa and its knowledge industry. Virtually all the contributors note how the bubbling hopes of the 1970s and early 1980s collapsed years later with the advent of the Structural Adjustment Programme (SAP), a socio-economic imposition which, true to its acronym, has *sapped* Africa's energy, triggered political instability, massive devaluation of its currencies, the weakening of its burgeoning industrial base, the pauperisation of the majority of its people, and the resurgence of illiteracy. The challenge in the past two decades, therefore, has been how to survive as a writer or publisher in what Paul Tiyambe Zeleza has aptly described as a 'structurally misadjusted Africa'. Every contributor recognises the book as an indispensable factor in development; and as Arusha III's 'New Deal' has made abundantly clear, writers and publishers must regard themselves as partners in business if Africa is to win its battle for the book.

Without a doubt, *The African Writers' Handbook* is a significant contribution to the on-going dialogue on the destiny of the book in

Africa, but we are modest enough to admit that it does not represent the voices of *all* African writers and publishers from all African regions, and in all languages on the continent. For instance, the voices of writers in indigenous languages are not directly heard here (though a powerful case is made in their defence); nor are those of writers and publishers from Arabic, Francophone, and Lusophone areas. This limitation should not be construed as an oversight or disregard for our counterparts from these areas. It is our hope that the dialogue of the future would be broader and more multilingual. In the meantime we take refuge in the essential commonality of the African experience, and the fact that the issues discussed in this book are applicable to other languages and other regions of Africa. The 'New Deal' whose spirit informs these pages provides a new response to old problems while pointing the way to a better future.

Niyi Osundare
Writer–Director, Arusha III
23 April 1999

PART ONE

A Social Contract for Books

Paul Tiyambe Zeleza

This essay was first presented as a keynote address at the Zimbabwe International Book Fair Indaba '96 on 'National Book Policy: the Key to Long-term Development', Harare, Zimbabwe, 26-27 July 1996. The text published here is a reprint from a slightly edited version which was published in The African Book Publishing Record, *Vol. 20, no. 4, 1996. It was also published in* National Book Policies for Africa: the Key to Long-term Development, *the complete proceedings of the Indaba published by the Zimbabwe International Book Fair Trust. (Harare: ZIBFT, 1997, $16.00/£8.95. Distributed outside Africa by African Books Collective Ltd, The Jam Factory, 27 Park End Street, Oxford OX1 1HU, UK.)*

Introduction

I was asked to speak on 'National Book Policy as a Continuous Process of Dialogue, Collaboration and Implementation'. Initially, I was not quite sure what I would say, for I am neither a politician nor a publisher, both of whom I am usually wary of, although for different reasons. But I read books, indeed, I derive my living from teaching and prescribing books, and in the publish-or-perish world of academia I am expected to write them as well. So it began to occur to me that the topic is actually close to my heart and livelihood, that all of us, indeed, have a stake in the development of a vibrant book industry. And so I decided to entitle my address 'A Social Contract for Books', for what is needed is a social contract among the major stakeholders of the book industry. I have identified, and will discuss, six: the state, publishers, writers, educational institutions, libraries, and the reading public.

In African discourse, the value of a project, of an idea, has to be justified in terms of development if it is to be taken seriously, so let me state at the outset that books are indispensable for development. They are not a luxury in so far as the development process is underpinned by human thought, visions, planning, and organisation, all of which require material and intellectual resources. The culture of reading is, of course, central to our contemporary world, to the information age in which we apparently live, an age that imprisons and impoverishes through illiteracy and ignorance. This is an era when the open intimacies and prejudices of the village are possible as the boundaries of national isolation and intellectual provincialism wither away. Africa's position in the global village of book publishing is weak: whereas nearly 800 book titles are published per million inhabitants in Europe, in Africa the figure is a miserable one: fewer than 20.[1] The case for developing the book industry, devising policies that promote a reading culture is, therefore, imperative. The risks of not doing so are greater intellectual and economic marginalisation for the continent: we will be reduced to exposed pedestrians on the information highway as others, driving on the backs of powerful and prestigious publishing systems and academic enterprises of the industrialised North, who already churn out the bulk of the world's books, journals, databases, computers and software and other information technologies, and dictate international copyright and intellectual property laws, whizz past us, arrogantly splashing mud at our vulnerable cultures.

Where does Africa fit in the international political economy of knowledge production, dissemination, and consumption? How can our various countries and communities ensure that they are not condemned to eternal information dependency, always importing their knowledge of the world, and sometimes of themselves: from others, knowledges of history and humanity, society and science, nature and culture, and the paradigms and prescriptions of development and modernity, governance and democracy – which are often distorted and even destructive, for they are almost solely derived from Western experiences and fantasies – instead of producing and sharing and, indeed, exporting our own? To answer these questions we need to assess the development and state of the continent's basic infrastructures of knowledge development and dissemination, namely, the availability of publishing houses, technical expertise, printing facilities, electronic technologies, libraries, and bodies of capable writers. Knowledge and information, whether in the form of books and newspapers, television and cinema are, of course, not created in a vacuum but in concrete contexts conditioned by economics and politics and the traditions of intellectual and cultural production. And each medium has its specific structures of production and distribution, its mode of organising and articulating the interests of the stakeholders.

In this presentation, then, I focus, first, on the political and cultural economies of the African book industry, and second, the social contract that needs to be forged between the identified six stakeholders. I hope you will forgive me for being rather too general and prescriptive in my remarks. I am only too aware that conditions in Africa vary enormously, that the levels of book development and underdevelopment are quite uneven, that the space between prescription and implementation is filled with complex and protracted social struggles, and that, in fact, Africa has perhaps suffered more than most from cheap and careless prescriptive advice, most glaringly in recent years in the form of ill-conceived structural adjustment programmes, which have wreaked havoc on African productive economies, enterprises, and energies, including the book industry. The excuse for the generality and brevity of my remarks is time. More importantly, most of you gathered here know far more about the African book trade than I do and will, indeed, be exploring its growth, constraints, and possibilities in the next two days.

The Cultural Economy of African Books

Books constitute crucial repositories of social memories and imaginations, containing the accumulated cultural capital of society, of its accomplishments, agonies, and aspirations. Books, therefore, are not and cannot be a luxury, a dispensable dessert on the menu of development, nationhood, or human progress. They are an essential component of these processes – indeed, their intellectual salt, spice, and starch Through books the past is remembered, the present understood, and the future created; knowledge is codified, contested, and consumed; and communities separated by the yawning divisions of time, space, and status can, and often do, converse with each other, in the process of which ideas, images, and inspirations are sometimes exchanged. Thus, reading offers a singular opportunity not only to acquire the formal knowledge of the academic disciplines and the practical skills of technical know-how, it is also a means of sharing and sampling the cultural sensibilities of other times and traditions, places and peoples, countries and classes. To read is in a large sense to partake in collective intellectual conversation crystallised over many generations to claim, and perhaps to contribute to, the immense heritage of human social thought. That is why illiteracy is so debilitating, so destructive, so dehumanising: the illiterate, whatever their abilities and ambitions, wiles and wisdom are cut off from the written dialogues and endowment of humanity.

The written word has a complex and varied history in Africa. It has ancient roots in some of continent's early civilisations, especially those of the Nile Valley, including Egypt, Ethiopia and the Sudan, and the later ones of western and coastal eastern Africa. In these civilisations literacy was often confined to the state, commercial, and religious elite, whether Christian or Islamic. This was, of course, not peculiar to Africa. Almost everywhere in the world, mass literacy is a relatively recent historical phenomenon, a product of the industrialisation and democratisation of social life. In many parts of Africa the written word arrived with European colonialism, although in most cases mass literacy only came with independence. In 1960, the putative year of African independence, only 9 per cent of the African population was literate. Thirty years later the figure had jumped to almost 50 per cent. This suggests that it is only in the period after independence that the basis for a viable book industry was established in most African countries.

But the infrastructures of the industry continued to carry a heavy colonial imprint either because of benign neglect, or the promiscuous borrowing of models from the developed countries which were often imposed without domesticating them to the local cultural and demographic realities. Consumed as they were by the economics of development and the politics of nation-building, cultural development in general and book development in particular remained low on the policy totem pole of many African governments. Legislation affecting the book industry was either inadequate, inappropriate, or outdated. Further undermining book development were permissive or unimaginative tariff and taxation policies which either unnecessarily raised the local costs of book production or made it difficult for local publishers to compete with large, foreign, multinational publishing companies. Most importantly, perhaps, state authoritarianism bred the silences of censorship, in which critical voices were stifled, and the performances of ostentatious power, whereby 'traditional dances' and other forms of public culture were turned into vulgar celebrations of undemocratic power.

Also unhelpful in some countries was the monopolisation of critical segments of the publishing market by state-owned publishing houses for whom propaganda mattered more than probity, conformity more than creativity, the exaltation of banal power more than the efficiency of book production. In some cases the state publishing firms were established to 'indigenise' the publishing industry, to supplant the foreign-owned publishing companies whose institutional loyalties, editorial networks, and re-investment outlets lay overseas, and whose commitment to local publishing often swung with the foreign exchange rates and regulations. For example, when Tanzania entered a period of financial crisis in the 1980s the multinational publishing companies left, only for some of them to return later when they learned that there would be an allocation of US$60 million from the World Bank for educational supplies (Mcharazo 1995, 245). For their part, private indigenous publishers, usually buffeted between the heavily-subsidised parastatal publishers and well-resourced multinational publishing houses, found themselves further handicapped by shortages of monetary and material capital, editorial, production, promotion and marketing skills, and limited markets. They also proved less attractive to writers who could access the major publishers because they were less able, or willing, to pay royalties and stroke their authors' egos.

Many African authors, brought up on a fulsome diet of colonial and Eurocentric education, displayed a marked preference for overseas publishing or with local subsidiaries of multinational firms, not only because of the pecuniary attractions of foreign exchange royalties, but also the reputational rewards of international renown: speaking tours, conference invitations, visiting appointments abroad, and so on. The relative devaluation of local publishing, certainly among academics, with whom I am most familiar, reflected the historical and prevailing relations of domination and dependency between Africa and the West, and the fact that the intellectual structures of reference, attitude, and legitimation internationally and within African universities themselves continued to be determined by Western standards and epistemologies.[2] I remember in 1989 being denied appointment as Senior Lecturer both at the University of Zimbabwe and the University of Botswana, a position I already held at Kenyatta University in Nairobi, because most of my publications were in African rather than the so-called 'international' journals. Ironically, the same publications earned me an appointment in Canada at the beginning of 1990.

Universities and schools constitute the fourth group of stakeholders in the book trade. Book sales to schools, colleges, and universities most likely provide the largest market for books in most African countries. Therefore, the content of curricula and canon, the composition of syllabuses and examinations, matter a great deal, for they determine the books that will be sought out by schools and students, the titles that will rake in the profits to subsidise the less commercially viable, but equally important, publications. There seem to be three main methods in which textbooks are prepared, published, and prescribed in African schools.[3] In some countries the books are specifically prepared and published by the government itself. In such cases the writers are selected by the ministry of education from within or outside the ministry. In other countries, while the authors are not officially chosen, the ministry selects and recommends certain texts that meet the established pedagogical criteria. Finally, there are countries where books published by private and state-owned companies, commissioned and non-commissioned books, compete for the hearts and minds of teachers and students. In general, ministries of education wield enormous power and dictate the shape of the playing field. Since they can literally make or break the fortunes of publishers, especially the smaller ones, the way that power is constituted and exercised is of utmost importance.

Libraries constitute another identifiable 'captive' market for books. School and university libraries are obviously critical. Certainly they constitute the backbone of scholarly publishing. Even in the industrialised countries, where personal incomes are relatively high, libraries provide the major market for scholarly products, especially journals, which derive as much as 90 per cent or more of their income from library subscriptions. Library systems in Africa expanded rapidly on the heels of the explosive growth in education after independence, but since the onset of the economic crisis and structural maladjustment in the 1980s in many countries, funding for education in general and libraries in particular has declined sharply, necessitating severe cuts in the acquisitions of books, journals, and other materials for libraries. For example, all but three out of 31 African university and research libraries surveyed in 1993 reported a drastic and depressing drop in their journal subscriptions from the mid-1980s, with some cancelling all their subscriptions (Levey 1993). That is intellectual suicide. One response to the library crisis has been growing reliance on gifts and donations of books and journals from charitable institutions and individuals, mostly in the developed countries. But much of this 'book aid' is episodic and library aid, like all aid, has strings attached, and it reinforces Africa's dependency on Western intellectual paradigms, problems, and preoccupations. It has been suggested, a little cheekily, that 'many of the donations that do arrive would be far better if they were pulped. This might at least provide some new paper, a basic resource which Africa needs more urgently than other countries' cast-off books' (Sturges and Neil 1990, 79).

The last, but by no means least important, group of stakeholders for the book industry consists of the general reading public, or rather publics, for readers are quite diverse in their tastes and tendencies. The potential general reading public is, of course, made up of products of the educational system. Whether or not they become regular readers depends on many factors, including their incomes and interests, occupations and orientations. Much has been said about few reading for pleasure, a view based more on anecdotal evidence than extensive research. A recent research study on Kenya revealed that a majority 39 per cent of consumers bought because of a love of reading (Nyariki and Makotsi 1995, 11). The distinction between reading for pleasure and reading for a purpose is, in fact, quite problematic. In a sense, all reading is utilitarian, it is purposeful: it can be for immediate aesthetic pleasure or the delayed practical satisfaction of job training. In short, people read for different reasons, none of which is intrinsically superior to the others. The question that African writers and publishers should be asking themselves is how to make their books more attractive and competitive, how they can meet the diverse interests of African reading publics, from creative fiction to computer manuals. Why, for example, is Western pulp fiction so popular among many readers in African cities? Clearly, there is a need that is not being met by our writers, for some of whom rural life is the only subject worthy of focus for they believe it represents African cultural authenticity. That is writing out the experiences of a third of the African people who live in cities.

Towards a Social Contract for Reading

Each of the stakeholders identified – the state, publishers, writers, educational institutions, libraries, and the reading public – has a critical role to play in the development of vibrant reading cultures and dynamic book industries. The challenges are daunting, made more so since the 1980s by the harsh economic conditions confronting many African countries, and compounded by reactionary structural adjustment programmes imposed by the Bretton Woods twins, the World Bank and the IMF. These programmes, which call for massive cuts in government expenditures, trade liberalisation, currency devaluation, and indiscriminate privatisation, all in the almighty name of the market, have wreaked havoc on education and employment, among many other sectors, that generate the literacy levels and purchasing power essential for an expanding and sustainable book trade. Currency devaluations have raised the domestic prices of imported machinery and inputs, such as paper, and thus increased the costs of local book production.

But as with all difficult historical moments, the present conjuncture is pregnant with contradictions and the possibilities of positive change. The winds of democratisation which have been sweeping throughout Africa, from Algeria to South Africa, Djibouti to Senegal, partly spawned by the struggles of rural and urban civil societies against the frustrations and failures of postcolonial developmentalism and the discontents of structural maladjustment programmes, are generating more favourable conditions for discursive freedoms, for liberating the written word from silence. As the state monopolies of politics and production are curtailed, and as the censorship boards lose their omniscient powers and the parastatal publishers their privileges, the playing field is levelled so that the pens of committed writers and the presses of independent publishers can roll with new energies.

The social contract for books, for the development of a vigorous reading culture, requires specific commitments and contributions from each of the stakeholders. African states have three primary responsibilities. First, increased state investment in education, which includes promotion of adult literacy programmes and the expansion or establishment of extensive public library systems in both the urban and rural areas, is essential. Second, reading needs to be made less costly by lowering taxation on books and materials needed for publishing. Third, civil liberties and freedoms, including freedom of expression, need to be upheld. These freedoms are not commodities whose value shifts according to the fluctuations of cultural currency: they are fundamental human rights.

For their part, educational institutions, at all levels, from primary school to university, need to devise pedagogical practices that encourage and reward extensive reading rather than empty regurgitation, critical inquiry not conformist inertia, intellectual curiosity not indolence. All too often, school education and its regulated culture of reading are regarded as terminal, rather than as stages in a continuous process of learning and living, of personal and social development, individual and collective enlightenment. As a part of this agenda, local publishing by school and university teachers should be sanctioned not censured.

As for libraries, they must aggressively and systematically collect books and materials published within their countries and the continent at large, instead of concentrating on acquiring them from Europe or North America. Research libraries need to procure the latest information technologies, such as CD-ROM capability and electronic networking, for not to do so would be to reinforce Africa's intellectual marginalisation. These technologies, of course, do not come cheap. Besides the high costs of equipment and training, there are the recurrent costs of subscription to databases. Also, in so far as most of the existing databases contain Northern scholarship, not scholarship from the South, let alone Africa, the challenge is not simply one of importing electronic technologies, but of producing national, regional and continental databases in electronic format. This requires extensive scholarly, marketing, and technical support networks which can only be built by forging inter-regional and international library linkages.

Without publishers and writers, of course, there would be no books and other materials to read. Publishers, especially the small indigenous ones, need to improve their promotional and marketing activities by employing trained staff, and to professionalise their dealings with authors by paying them royalties at agreed and regular intervals, for example, and involving them in the publicity campaigns of their books, for without that they will be unable to attract or retain the best and brightest writers. All too often, publishers concentrate their energies on the captive school textbook market to the detriment of other areas of publishing, such as scholarly and popular books. This excessively narrow base does little to promote the book industry; in fact, it reinforces dependency on foreign publications in the under-published areas. In short, African publishers need to spread their eggs into several publishing baskets. And foreign publishers operating in African countries have a responsibility to reinvest their profits locally and can assist in building local publishing infrastructures and intellectual traditions by using domestic resources for editing and reviewing manuscripts. Reliance on external reviewers based in Europe or North America, often justified in the dubious name of international standards, holds African authors hostage to conventions, conceptions, and concerns that may have little relevance or that encourage shallow analyses and stereotypical images of African societies, cultures, and realities.

The heavy devaluation of many African currencies in the last decade has made imports of books from abroad very expensive, including those published by African authors. Recently while attending Malawi's first literary festival to celebrate the demise of Banda's dictatorship and the dawn of a more democratic order, it was quite saddening to find that the books published abroad by Malawian writers exiled during the Banda years, such as Jack Mapanje, Frank Chipasula, and myself, were simply unaffordable. My novel, *Smouldering Charcoal*, published by Heinemann, sells for MK350, well above the minimum wage. 'At that price,' commented one literary critic (Chirambo 1996, 9) in a paper given at the festival, 'that book is as [good as] banned'. Locally produced books are not necessarily cheaper, indeed, they may be more expensive in situations where most of the inputs are imported and economies of scale do not apply. However, the 'famine' of imported books offers local publishers reduced competition and an opportunity to forge creative and mutually beneficial co-publishing and marketing arrangements with multinational or foreign publishers. There is a need to market African books aggressively not only within Africa itself, but also abroad, for what is at stake is Africa's capacity to define and describe itself to itself and to the rest of the world, and to see that world through its own eyes, not the warped lenses and fantasies of others. This is why the efforts by the African Books Collective (ABC) to undertake the joint promotion and distribution of African books outside the continent, and the African Publishers Network (APNET) to encourage intra-African publishing and trade in books, must be applauded and supported.

Book reviewing is an important component of the publishing enterprise and the reading culture. Reviews, even bad ones, advertise books, and mediate the critical consumption of texts by the reading public. The publishing industry, therefore, working together with the mass media, needs to promote reviews in newspapers, and book discussion programmes on radio and television. Also deserving support are review publications for the scholarly and general public. In this region one can mention *The Southern African Review of Books* and *The Zimbabwean Review*, and on the continental level there are APNET's *African Publishing Review* and the British-based *The African Book Publishing Record*. There is room for many more of such review outlets aimed at different segments of the reading public of African books. Currently, the Center for African Studies at the University of Illinois, where I teach, is planning to launch, in collaboration with the Dakar-based Council for the Development of Social Science Research in Africa (CODESRIA), *The African Review of Books*, in tabloid format, to be published jointly and simultaneously in Urbana-Champaign and Dakar for the overseas and African markets, respectively. Through this outlet we hope to give African books greater exposure to the North American market, one of the largest in the world for Africana materials; and to facilitate the review of books written by Western Africanists and by African scholars based in the continent, in order to promote serious transatlantic intellectual conversation between Africanist and African scholars and break the tendency towards self-referential solitude among them.

This brings us to the role of writers. Besides writing, what else can they do to promote the book industry in their respective countries and the continent as a whole? Serious writers have a responsibility to be subversive, that is, to prick the public conscience, not to pacify it, to say so when the emperors are naked not to cover them with the flowery verbiage of lies, to denounce the tyranny of state power as well as the terrors of civil society, not to give succour to the violations and violence of the intolerant chauvinisms of race, nationality, ethnicity, gender, class, religion, and sexuality, but to imagine more generous conditions of being human. Outside the often intensely lonely writing process, in the public market of ideas and subsistence, writers need the protection of collective organisation against state authoritarianism and sometimes exploitation by, can one dare say, publishers.

As cultural artifacts books play an important role in the development of the cultural identities and expressive capacities of peoples, societies, and groups. In this context, the question of the language in which books are written is obviously critical, especially in Africa, where with the exception of Arab North Africa and to a smaller extent

Ethiopia and Tanzania, the European languages introduced through colonialism remain the languages of *national* culture, government, business, and intellectual production. It is, of course, simplistic to assume that writing in the indigenous languages is intrinsically progressive: tyranny can be articulated in a native tongue, oppression can wear the expressions of tradition. And it may be historically too late to wish the colonial languages away. That does not mean they cannot be domesticated, given local accents, which, in fact, has already been happening and will continue to be the case. But neither can the need to promote writing in indigenous languages be swept aside. Can people really enjoy their democratic rights in countries where official languages are spoken by a small educated minority, and the vast majority of the population are excluded from effective participation in any official business and communication, when they cannot read, write or speak the language in which laws are inscribed and political discourse is conducted? What is the cost in terms of the development of education and a reading culture when formal education is offered in a language foreign to the child? African governments, publishers, educators, and writers need to take the question of language seriously, for linguistic rights and development are an essential part of human rights and development. As Nguessan (1996, 12) states, there is not a single country in the world that has developed 'with a language that is foreign to the land and is unknown to the vast majority of its citizens'.[4]

The reading public has an interest in all these matters, and responsibility to patronise and promote African books. Without readers, books, however profound their contents and impressive their covers, gather dust on library or booksellers' shelves as monuments to irrelevance. Only a voracious and discriminating reading public can ensure that Africa produces not only more books, but good books, those that enlighten and enrich our lives, not debase our sensibilities. The privileged few can, and ought, to do more than simply buy and read books. Africa's wealthy capitalists could support cultural production as a whole, and the book industry in particular, by sponsoring literary prizes and arts grants. It is shameful that there is no African-sponsored equivalent of the Noma Award for Publishing in Africa or the Commonwealth Writers Prize. Culture and books are too serious to be left to sympathetic foreigners or governments. All of us have a stake in them, for they embody our values, practices and possibilities, dreams and destiny, pasts and futures, our investment in a reflective, critical, and tolerant humanity.

Notes

This essay was specially written for presentation at the Zimbabwe International Book Fair Indaba '96 'National Book Policy: The Key to Long-term Development', Harare, 26-27 July 1996.

1 For the industrialised countries as a whole the figure is about 520 and for the Third World it is about 40. See Jessica Barry 1996, 4.
2 See Chapters 3 and 4 of my *Manufacturing African Studies and Crises*, 1998.
3 See Chapter 8 of *Manufacturing African Studies and Crises*.
4 The OAU Heads of State and Government adopted the Language Plan of Action in 1987, but as with most OAU resolutions, not much has been done to implement it. See Mateene 1996.

References

Barry, J. 'Digging For Gems in a Book Lover's Paradise'. *The Herald* (Harare), 24 July 1996, 4.

Chirambo, RM. 'Malawian Literature Under Dr Kamuzu Banda and Its Place in the New Democratic Malawi'. Symposium on Malawian Literature at the Malawi Literacy Festival, Blantyre, 15-20 July 1996.

Levey, LA, ed. *A Profile of Research Libraries in Sub-Saharan Africa: Acquisition, Outreach, and Infrastructure.* Washington: America Association for the Advancement of Science, 1993.

Mateene, K. 'OAU's Resolutions on African Languages and the State of Their Implementation'. Paper presented at the Colloquium on Language Legislation and Linguistic Rights, University of Illinois at Urbana-Champaign, 21-23 March 1996.

Mcharazo, AAS. Summary of S Arunachalam's 'Accessing Information Published in the Third World: Should Spreading the Word from the Third World Always Be Like Swimming Against the Current'. Review of *Workshop on Access to Third World Journals. African Book Publishing Record*, Vol. 20 no. 4, 1995, 245-46.

Nguessan, M. 'Language and Human Rights in Africa'. Paper presented at the Colloquium on Language Legislation and Linguistic Rights, University of Illinois at Urbana-Champaign, 21-23 March 1996.

Nyariki, L and R Makotsi. 'Problems of Book Marketing and Distribution in Kenya'. *African Publishing Review*, Vol. 4 no. 2, 1995, 10-11.

Sturges, P and R Neil. *The Quiet Struggle: Libraries and Information for Africa.* London: Mansell, 1990.

Zeleza, PT. *Manufacturing African Studies and Crises.* Dakar: CODESRIA, 1998.

African Writers:
The Publishing Experience

The Publisher and the Poet

Niyi Osundare

The genre I practise provokes goose pimples in publishing circles. At the mere mention of poetry, prospective publishers grab their hats and dash for the nearest exit. 'Why don't you write prose?' I have been asked several times. 'Prose of any variety, particularly romance and thrillers ... the type that moves fast in supermarkets and airports? No reasonable publisher would tie down hard-earned money on poetry, you know. There are bank loans to clear, staff to pay, etc. etc., the warehouse has no space for static stock ... Why don't you write a textbook, the type that can be lobbied into the government-approved reading list for schools? Make money and say a resounding "farewell" to poverty ...' A publisher (who is also a personal friend) once said, half-jokingly, 'Come on, write something I can crow about. You're too nice to be a mere poet.'

Everywhere I go, publishers complain that poetry does not sell (though very little attempt is being made to sell poetry). Some literary commentators have even pontificated that ours is the age of punk, cable television, video, Stephen Spielberg and other post-modernisms. The only poetry that sells today is the tendentious clarion of the advertiser's jingles or the metallic thrill of Ninja Turtle. So I would be only a little surprised if, in the not-too-distant future, someone did a post-modernist treatise on 'The Death of Poetry'.

I see a lot around me in Nigeria, in Africa, which contradicts that morbid prognostication – and the publishers' pessimism. Poetry remains the most widely practised of all the literary genres. In my personal capacity I receive, or am consulted on, an average of two poetry manuscripts/books a month. And, as an editorial consultant to Heinemann Educational Books (Nigeria) Ltd, I have been inundated by tomes and tomes in verse. It is now common knowledge that about half of the entries for the Association of Nigerian Authors (ANA) annual prizes in all categories come from the poetic genre. This is hardly surprising, given the fact that Africa still remains a largely oral culture with emphasis on the sanctity and answerability of the word, a place where the proverb still transmits loric wisdom from lip to lip. In this yet un-'post-industrial' portion of the world, the lyric of the river, the tall anthem of the mountain, the moon's nomadic glide on the tarmac of the sky ... are all part of a flow and rhythm which summon a thousand songs into being. Every occasion, every event, provokes a song. Every occasion: birth, death, marriage, the commissioning of a new development project, the First Lady's goitre, the gory legacies of the continent's military dictators and civilian presidents-for-life. Any wonder, then, that in Africa's transition from oral to scribal culture, poetry continues to play a significant role?

But this question only resolves itself in curious contradictions – and further questions. If Africa thrives so healthily on oral poetry, why does so little poetry get published? Why is the 'poetry market' so narrow and so precarious? If the poetic genre is endowed with so many practitioners, why does published poetry remain unpurchased? What is responsible for the popularity of oral poetry and the unpopularity of the written? Why are publishers so scared of poetry? To many observers, the questions above should not really concern me. Neither should the anxieties generated by them, After all, I have had different volumes of poetry published by eight different publishers – between 1983 and 1997 – a time-span of only fourteen years! And unlike many writers of my generation and the one after it, I do not have a file full of rejection slips to display the way a worsted warrior parades his plague of scars. So, as I was told in 1988 by a colleague in the Department of English, University of Nigeria, Nsukka (shortly before my reading at the Anthills), I am indeed a 'lucky' person. However, that luck is relative. For although my interactions with my publishers have been largely pleasant, they have not been consistently problem-free. But let me step out on the positive foot.

New Horn Press was my first publisher. New Horn, founded and managed by Abiola Irele, the renowned scholar-critic. True to the spirit of its predecessor, *The Horn*, which provided the starting-point for modern Nigerian literature, New Horn Press had a bias for poetry and was impressively enthusiastic about providing a much-needed outlet for new Nigerian writing. So, when I completed my very first collection of poems in 1981, New Horn was my natural first choice. (The press had then just released *Shadows and Dreams*, a beautifully produced poetry collection by Harry Garuba.) Abiola Irele received my manuscript in the morning one day, and in the afternoon of the next, he lifted my spirit by describing it as 'terrific', and wondering if I wouldn't mind giving it to New Horn. Of course, New Horn got the manuscript. A few weeks later, on the experienced counsel of Abiola Irele, the title was changed from *I Sing of Change* to *Songs of the Marketplace*, the latter title being the product of Irele's initiative and creativity. Thus I was lucky to have started off with a professor/publisher who knew what to do with the manuscript in his hand.

My second experience was with Heinemann Educational Books, Nigeria. It all began in 1984 in an author-sourcing act that I consider rare in Nigeria. I was in my office one bright afternoon when one of Heinemann's editors walked in with a personal invitation from the Chairman, Aigboje Higo. I was pleasantly surprised when, on my visit to his office the following day, Higo looked straight into my eyes and said without mincing his words: 'We want to be your publisher.' I must confess that that invitation gave me a lot to chew upon. For, some of us in the second generation of Nigerian writers, in the true spirit of decolonising African letters, had pledged total loyalty to indigenous publishers, and turned our back on the multinational publishing houses which we saw as active agents in the West's exploitation of Africa. Heinemann was one of those multinationals. But when I considered the 'local content' of Heinemann's publication list, and the zeal and hope Heinemann Nigeria was investing in its then new Frontliner Series, I decided to give Heinemann a try.

Three weeks later, the manuscript of *The Eye of the Earth* landed on Higo's desk. Exactly two days later, he sent for me again. 'I have read this', he said, holding my manuscript. 'It is a unique voice in Nigerian poetry. But why don't you consider a "Preface" or "Foreword" to it? It will enrich the text and put the poems in context.' From this initiative was the 'Foreword' to *The Eye of the Earth* conceived and born. The 'Foreword' did not only enrich the volume, it also turned out to be the poem before the poems! *The Eye of the Earth* won the 1986 Association of Nigerian Authors (ANA) Poetry prize and was overall joint-winner of the Commonwealth Poetry Prize for the same year. When congratulatory messages started pouring in, I kept on saying that the honour must be evenly shared between the author and the publisher. The success of *The Eye of the Earth* was a good starting-point with Heinemann Nigeria which has since published two other poetry volumes of mine (with another one in press). So when, in 1993, those publishers appointed me Editorial Consultant, it was an assignment I accepted with a clear sense of purpose, a rare opportunity to contribute my own effort to its growing Frontliner Series.

* * *

Now the other side of the coin. Of course, it is not often that I have been 'lucky' enough to have my manuscripts handled by professor/publishers or publishers who are also poets – publishers who can feel poetry from the inside, keenly aware of its power and promise beyond its market value. I have also encountered publishers who consider publishing poetry an unreasonable risk unless the poems are guaranteed a place in the school reading list. There are also publishers who run away from individual collections/volumes, preferring to stake their resources on poetry anthologies through which they can use one stone to kill many birds. This is certainly better than nothing, but some of the anthologies are hardly representative of the comprehensiveness and diversity of the offerings of the individual contributing poets. In most cases, the reader is given nothing more than 'sound bites' from an otherwise rich orchestra. But, in our peculiar circumstances in Africa today, many consider this half-voice to be better than silence.

Getting one's manuscript accepted by the publisher is one problem: but seeing it published beautifully and efficiently is quite another. In Africa today, the journey between the manuscript and the book is snared by enormous problems. The headache begins with the half-literate printer and the uninformed typesetter, and degenerates into full-blown migraine with the incompetent editor. In Nigeria, over the years, I have worked with extremely bright and imaginative editors; but, alas, I have also seen many of my galley proofs mangled by 'Editors' (the quotation marks are deliberate!) who simply do not know the difference between the stylistic and graphological imperatives of poetry and those of prose. In addition to the interminable quarrels over spelling, there are running feuds over lineation, indentation, spacing and spacial foregrounding, stanza arrangement, appropriate use of italics and glossing of words and expressions derived from indigenous languages and cultures. Let me give a short illustration. While reading the proofs of one of my volumes a couple of years ago, I had a half-page of poetry and a half-page of prose. When I checked my manuscript, I saw that the words in the proof were correctly printed, but the lines and stanzas had been stripped of their graphological integrity and reduced to run-on, continuous prose. When I asked for an explanation, I was told that it was done so as to economise on space.

I must admit that my kind of poetry may not be the easiest to get into print. I explore and exploit the blank page the way a painter engages the canvas. For me the meaning of a poem begins from its appearance on the printed page. I frequently assault the morphology of the word to make it mean more than itself. Only well-educated, sensitive editors can recognise these practices as deliberate transgressions, and not atrocious errors begging to be knocked back to 'normality' with red ink. And what's worse, this self-confessed transgressor is also incurably fastidious. I read and corrected the proofs of one of my recent poetry books five times! But even then ...

Patient, persevering editors I have encountered everywhere my book has been published in Nigeria – budding professionals who would have brought great credit to the publishing enterprise if only they had had access to better education and training. And better remuneration. As things stand now, the better-educated, better-trained, but poorly remunerated editors are frequently lured off to 'greener pastures'. The not-so-competent ones who stay on cannot perform. This unwholesome combination of 'brain-drain' and frequent personnel turnover makes it difficult for an author to develop a long working relationship with an editor, a relationship which would enable them to understand each other's habits and stylistic idiosyncrasies, one that would make it possible for publishing houses to develop and sustain a *tradition* of professional excellence. I once had a manuscript which went through the hands of three successive editors (in the same establishment) on its way to publication. Of course, each editor left the house without preparing any 'hand-over notes'. So with each editor, I had to 'begin again'.

Without doubt, it is in the area of author promotion that I have had the worst deal from my publishers. To be sure, one of them has been very supportive in the provision of local transportation and other facilities which aid my frequent travels; another has been a tremendous help in the transmission of my mail. With these two, a relationship has developed which transcends the formality of the publishing house. But my books are not being displayed in places where they can be *seen*, where they can woo their way into the hands (and pockets!) of reluctant buyers. Quite frequently I receive letters from prospective buyers (especially students) asking me where on earth my books, even those published in Nigeria, can be acquired. In nearly all cases, the answer is: 'My publisher's warehouse.' Which publisher in Nigeria talks about packaging the author, organising literary luncheons, readings within publishing premises, autograph sessions, 'grounding' with literary journalists? When news broke last year that the East African Educational Publishers had committed so much of their resources to inviting me to Kenya for the promotion of its New Poets of Africa series, many people in Nigeria (writers and publishers alike) received the news with incredulity.

And royalties? One could write a whole book on that issue. Of my eight publishers, two (one of them UK-based) send me returns on a regular basis, two on a sporadic basis; the remaining four have never said a word about how my books are doing, or paid me a penny. And not one of all my Nigerian publishers has declared how many copies of my books they have been selling outside Nigeria, and how much has accrued from the sales.

And yet the author is the proverbial goose that lays the golden egg. If the publisher allows the goose to die through cheating and neglect, where will the next golden egg come from? Surely, 'The time has come for a "New Deal" between writers and publishers in Africa.'

The Experience of Being a Writer in Tanzania

MM Mulokozi

I was born in a traditional village in Bukoba in the then Tanganyika Territory in 1950. I lived in the village until I completed Standard IV, when I had to go to a mission boarding school. That was in 1962. From that time until I completed my first degree at the University of Dar es Salaam in 1975, I was virtually a captive of the 'boarding school' world and mentality, characterised as it was by an élitist, secluded, protected mode of existence, and a British-oriented literary-artistic culture. That environment had a lasting impact on my character and must have influenced my decision to become a writer.

My formative years were shaped during the final phase of colonialism and the early years of independence. It was a period of upheavals, revolt, African awakening, and optimism. That also was to have a lasting impact on my outlook and my writings.

While in primary and middle school, I read most of the Swahili titles, fiction and non-fiction, available in the school library. They included translations of such world classics as *Alfu-Lela-Ulela*, and the colonial classics such as *Treasure Island*, *Robinson Crusoe*, *King Solomon's Mines*, *Allan Quatermaine*, plus the few locally written titles then available, especially the poetry and fiction of Shaaban Robert (1909-62). I was fascinated by such tales, and was gradually but unconsciously turning into a bookworm. By the final years of middle school, I had mustered enough English to be able to read many of the simplified English readers then available. It was my first introduction to English literature in the original, and I was enthralled. I read Charles Dickens, Sir Walter Scott, Shakespeare stories, and many other interesting authors, plus poets such as Coleridge. I still recall how I was enraptured by Coleridge's *The Rime of the Ancient Mariner* which I later translated into Kiswahili. Thus by the time I entered Kahororo Secondary School at Bukoba in 1966, I was already inclined towards literature and writing, mainly because of my out-of-class reading rather than my classroom experience. Fortunately, in the secondary school there were more and better books to which, since I was the school librarian, I had unlimited access.

Three other factors helped to shape my literary career while in secondary school. These were: the poets' club, the encouragement of my English teachers, and writing competitions. The poets' club was an extra-curricular activity which students interested in poetry could join. There were other clubs for those not so inclined, for instance boxing, singing, book binding, and debating clubs. Needless to say, I joined the poets' club during my first year at the school. Club members used to write poems which were read and discussed at their weekly meetings. Sometimes some of the better poems would be recited during school festivals. We wrote in both Kiswahili and English, but all my first poems were in English. Later, I was to opt for Kiswahili for reasons that I cannot go into here. In the club, one had an opportunity to meet and get to know fellow aspiring poets, and many lifelong friendships were forged through the club. One of the people I met through the club in 1967, who later became my lifelong writing partner and personal friend, is KK Kahigi, the distingished poet and scholar.

The interest and encouragement of my teachers was very crucial during these formative years. Our poets' club had a staff advisor, who attended our discussion meetings and guided us in our artistic work. My two American, English language teachers apparently felt that I was a potential writer, and encouraged me to read and read and read, and to write as much and as often as possible. They lent me books and reviewed and corrected drafts of my poems, stories, plays, essays etc. Without this encouragement and partnership I probably would not have developed into a writer.

In these days there were writing competitions for school pupils. One such competition was the Brooke Bond Tea essay-writing competition, apparently organised from Nairobi. When I was in Form II, I took part in that competition and, to my surprise, won one of the prizes – a copy of *Roget's Thesaurus*. It was the first time I had won a writing prize, and I treasured the book greatly. Moreover, it was the first time I had come across a thesaurus, and I soon discovered that it was a very useful tool for a writer. I still have the book, and still refer to it often. While in Form IV, I participated in the 'Expo 70' essay-writing competition organised by Japan. I entered as a junior, but when the results were announced, I had won the second prize among the seniors! This time I received a huge radiogram for which I had no use as I was still in school; and at home in the village the gadget was useless because there was no electricity, and I had to sell it at a give-away price. I used some of the proceeds to buy what I needed most – a used manual typewriter!

By the time I was in Form III, I was already becoming, and probably behaving like, a writer. I mostly wrote at night – I would wake up at about 3 am, go to a classroom, switch on the lights, and work on a manuscript until 6 am. I would be alone, and all would be quiet, since all the other students would be in bed, unless it was near examination time, when many students would be up early or stay up late to do their revision. Before the end of 1968, I had completed two manuscripts: a novel in Kiswahili, which I submitted to a novel-writing competition which, I think, was organised by the East African Publishing House (EAPH) in Nairobi, and a play. The novel was historical: it was about the Mombassa uprising of 1631-32 against the Portuguese. It did not win a prize but was returned to me. Unfortunately, the manuscript was either burnt or thrown away by a fastidious stepmother when I left it at home to go to high school in 1970.

The other manuscript was a historical drama, in English, on the Hehe king, Mukwava, who resisted German colonisation between 1891 and 1898. It was my History and English teacher, Mr Tracy Harrington, an American, who suggested to me the idea of writing a play on Mukwava, promising to stage it if it turned out to be suitable. I wrote the play as asked and named it *The Tragedy of Mkwawa*. Mr Harrington read it, corrected the errors and typed it. He then directed the staging of the play by a combined drama group of our school and a nearby girls' secondary school. The play was so successful that the group was later transported to the capital city, Dar es Salaam, to perform it for President Nyerere. I did not accompany the group to Dar es Salaam, as I had then temporarily left the school, having quarrelled with some of the teachers (but that is a different story).

In those days we used to read some of the titles from Heinemann's African Writers Series in our literature course, and we were impressed by the fact that those books were written by fellow Africans. Hence those of us who were writers aspired to be published one day in that prestigious series. Thus, when the manuscript of my Mkwawa tragedy was ready, I wanted to send it to Heinemann for possible publication. However, my teacher, Mr Harrington, advised me against the idea; he probably felt that it did not stand much chance of getting published by such a prestigious multinational. Instead, he advised me to try EAPH in Nairobi. It was unfortunate advice, as I will show later. Nevertheless, it ushered me into the devious and devilish world of East African publishing.

My introduction to the world of publishing was harsh and disconcerting. The revised English version of my Mkwawa play was submitted to EAPH in 1969. They acknowledged the receipt but said no more. The book was never published and I never saw the manuscript again. In 1973, I sent them a Kiswahili translation of the play. Again they acknowledged the receipt and kept mum. A year later they informed me that they were going to publish it and sent me the contract forms for signature. I was of course very happy. In 1977, I received the galley proofs of the Kiswahili version. In 1979, the Kiswahili version came out. It was immediately selected as a school reader in O-Level Kiswahili literature in Kenya. The book was on the list for about eight years, until around 1988. It was reprinted many times and sold thousands of copies. Throughout the period, I never received a statement of sales, not to mention a royalty cheque.

In 1986, after a gruelling day-long journey by bus from Dar es Salaam, I went to EAPH's offices in Nairobi for the first time. They were obviously surprised and embarrassed to see me. The publishing manager showed me a statement of sales of my book. It showed that EAPH owed me more than 50,000 Kenyan shillings in royalties, probably about US$10,000 at the current exchange rate. With that money one could build or buy a big bungalow in Tanzania at that time. The publishing manager 'apologised' to me for their failure to communicate with me, and informed me that they were now in the process of finalising the accounts after which they were going to pay all the authors. He then invited me for a sumptuous lunch at a plush hotel, after which he wrote me a cheque for 5,000 Kenyan shillings to cover my bus travel, hotel and subsistence cost for the seven days I was in Nairobi. He promised me that my cheque would be posted to me in Tanzania in about a month's time. I returned to Dar es Salaam greatly overjoyed. But the cheque never came, and in 1987 I read in a newspaper that EAPH had gone into receivership. The management had succeeded in plundering the company to its death. I rushed to Nairobi to see if I could salvage anything from my accumulated royalties and find unsold copies of my book. An official of the liquidators told me that there was no way they could pay the authors their royalties. They were going to sell the assets and see if they could pay the bigger creditors, i.e. the banks, printers, etc., not minor folk like authors. He promised however to sell me copies of my book at 20 per cent of the market price if I was interested. He then took me to a huge godown in the industrial area packed to the brim with EAPH books, and assured me that all the books would either be burned or shredded to make toilet paper unless a buyer was found soon. I had no money, yet I could not stand by and let such good books be burned while schools in Tanzania were operating without books. I therefore returned to Dar es Salaam post-haste and contacted one Western donor agency whose director I knew to be sympathetic to literature. After I had explained the situation to him, he agreed to offer US $5000 for purchase and transportation of some of the books to Tanzania.

I wrote five other manuscripts between 1970 and 1975 – two plays, a collection of short stories, a long epic, and a translation of *The Rime of the Ancient Mariner*, but all of them were rejected by publishers, among whom were Tanzania Publishing House (TPH), Oxford University Press (Dar es Salaam) and the East African Literature Bureau (EALB). I was quite depressed, and I remember tearing up one of the manuscripts in anger when it was returned by a publisher. Unfortunately I did not have another copy. That was in 1971.

Fortunately, a collection of poetry, *Mashairi ya Kisasa* (prepared with KK Kahigi) was submitted to TPH in the same year. Some of the readers advised the publisher against publishing it because it did not adhere to the rigid traditional prosodic rules. However, TPH happened to have a far-sighted editor, Mr I Mbenna, who felt that the book should be given a chance. Hence the collection was published by them in 1975. That small book made history in the sense that it was one of the first books to contain poetry that did not adhere to the traditional prosodic system. It was therefore attacked from all sides, and was at the centre of the now famous debate on Swahili poetry that raged in Tanzania and Kenya from about 1974 to the late 1980s. The book remained in print for some twenty years; and the annual royalties were consistently, if not promptly, paid without failure until the early 1990s, when payments became more intermittent and hard to get.

Another collection of our poetry *Malenga wa Bara* was submitted to Oxford University Press, Nairobi, in 1972 or thereabouts and returned to us with regrets. We then sent it to EALB who after a while agreed to publish it. The contract forms stated that the authors would be paid a 20 per cent royalty on the net price. On publication in 1976, we were paid an advance on royalties of 200 Tanzania shillings and the book became a school reader. In no time the first edition of about 3,000 copies was sold out. Before it could be reprinted, the East African Community broke up amidst political wrangling, and the EALB was dismembered into three 'national' companies. The Tanzanian EALB became East African Publications Ltd (EAPL), who failed to reprint the book, although it was needed in schools, and, of course, never paid us any royalties. More recently (1996), the book has been issued again by Dar es Salaam University Press (DUP). Another collection of the verses of Kahigi and myself that arose out of the debate on poetry is *Kunga za Ushairi na Diwani Yetu*. It was published by TPH in 1982 and has been in print to date. The royalties were paid regularly until the early 1990s when TPH was put up for sale.

I wrote a lot while a student at the University of Dar es Salaam between 1972 and 1975. The University of Dar es Salaam had excellent literature courses, in both Kiswahili and English, and a number of clubs and associations for would-be writers. I was a member of several of those. One informal poets' club used to meet in the evenings and included among its members Marjorie Oludhe Macgoye, the then university bookshop manager, now a widely published Kenyan novelist. The poet, Yusufu M Kassam, was also in the group.

In the 1980s, I did not engage in much creative writing as I was more involved in academic work. In 1991, a Children's Book Project (CBP) was established in Tanzania with the objective of supporting production and supply of books for children. I was involved in the project from the beginning, and wrote four books for the project between 1991 and 1997, three of which were historical novels for young people, and the fourth a long historical poem. Publishing under the project was a new and exhilarating experience for me and other writers in that for the first time our books were published quickly (usually within a year from the time of submission of the manuscript) and the royalties were paid immediately upon publication. The CBP made the Tanzanian writer taste, for the first time, what writers in other countries (outside Africa of course) have enjoyed for generations and now take for granted, i.e. respect and remuneration.

Here ends the story of my adventures with a pen; my bitter-sweet experience at the hands of publishers. It is clear from the narration that a crucial factor for me was the opportunity to read a variety of books accorded to me at my boarding school. I believe that if I had not had that much access to books I probably would not have become a writer, for a writer is by definition an assiduous reader. A writer who does not read fellow writers has no right to expect or demand to be read by others. Unfortunately, modern Tanzanian pupils lack the opportunity to access books, since there are no libraries in most of our primary and secondary schools. This being the case, it is idealistic to expect our current schools to produce many writers. Apart from access to good, and many, books, my evolution as a writer was assisted by the school environment (poets' club) and the encouragement I received from my teachers. Neither of these elements is now found in most of our schools. The final factor, motivation through competitions and awards, is likewise no longer common, though some essay-writing competitions are still occasionally held. It may be a good idea to revive these contests if we really want to have a new generation of writers.

Revelations and Reversals: Writing Inside the Continent

Yvonne Vera

Each time I publish a novel I learn something new about a paragraph, about interpretations concerning the text I have just finished, about the nation for which I have composed it. Writing is about revelations and reversals.

When it comes to the spectrum of experiences so much seems to happen in so little time. Nothing is ever stable in writing, and often, I reverse my earliest convictions about narrative, and about publication. Only a few truths remain my own, especially the passion for writing, and for that, each writer has to define and secure. Such truths belong to those inexplicable moments sheltered by our intrinsic feeling and the treasures we dare believe necessary to share.

I am not sure which is more important, practical wisdom in publishing or just writing. At this moment, I know far less about publishing, and much more about my own motivation for composition. There are a lot of young writers in Zimbabwe interested in solutions to publishing and less so in solutions to writing – I think these are sometimes related but separate values. Sometimes there is too little reading. A love of writing must be matched, if not exceeded, by a love of reading. To write must also be to imagine a book being read. The two acts are a unity.

At times, the relationship between an author and a publisher can be special and crucial to the development of both. I first published in Canada in 1992. It took two years before that book was read in Zimbabwe. The book was about Zimbabweans.

Then, I was still trying to find my identity as a writer, to decide perhaps, if I wanted to write at all. My link to the Zimbabwean community felt necessary to that growth, and I was restless. I needed certain contours, a prism. I needed a landscape. I needed some totally familiar horizon, then I would be whole. I moved to Zimbabwe in 1995, to Bulawayo. This is where I was born and raised.

I knew, by 1993, that my book on Nehanda, a revered figure in the national consciousness of Zimbabweans, had to be published first in

Zimbabwe. Nehanda dominates much of the religious and political activity in this nation. It would be my first novel. The publication of *Nehanda* coincided with the celebration of 100 years since the first Chimurenga, Zimbabwe's armed resistance which Nehanda, as spirit medium, had launched. This woman, the main force behind that first resistance to occupation, represented for me our pre-colonial link with land, death, time, and all our philosophies of identity. When the book was accepted and published by Baobab Books that marked for me the beginning of my career, properly, as a writer. That first publication had been important, but I felt at sea somehow, and lacked a certain immediacy to subject matter, to theme. I needed to be a witness, a participant.

With Baobab was Irene Staunton. We rose into each other's worlds with an immediate sisterly affection in her office in 1993. I was charmed by her entire being, her acute intelligence. She had such a belief in *Nehanda*, and treasured and protected it. Even today, as publisher and editor, when she offers a suggestion I feel immediately that she is protecting my book from harm, that it is her book. I have often been asked, 'Are you writing a book for Irene?' I am not often asked, 'Are you writing?' Perhaps this is because after that, I would indeed say 'I am writing a book for Staunton. I hope she likes it.' Before I wrote *Without a Name*, I told her the story first. Her response enabled me to write it. She was enthusiastic and seemed to identify the core of the narrative and make it hers, even while it was only a seed in my own mind, a little more than an intuition. She has always been fair, honest and very close to my text. I treasure this. She has understood and respected my style and method. We are friends. I know the relationship we have is rare, and I have stayed with Baobab since. A publisher can shape your sense of stability and family, which to me was important. Some writers do not need any kind of anchor. I am the sort who needs to phone the publisher and say, 'What do you think of this idea for a novel?' Even when I am already convinced. If I have had a reader as I write, it has often been my publisher.

Publishing in Zimbabwe was important for another reason, to control the availability and cost of books to local readers. The books which are imported into Zimbabwe usually cost a lot more than those produced locally. I wanted to contribute to a situation in which Zimbabwean readers have easy and immediate access to their own authors, to their own cultural product, rather than wait for import or the negotiation of contracts with publishers abroad. This is a delayed process.

In the rituals of launching books and celebration in Zimbabwe, local authors meet communicate and share ideas. *Nehanda* was

launched by Zimbabwean author Chenjerai Hove, and he spoke in
words which evoked an ancestral heritage, and this suited my own
mood, and he set the book free, as he said it, like the ancestral bird
Shirichena, which is our beginning, into the sky. This was a spiritual
setting off, which many local people in the Harare Gardens, understood on that occasion. This was an appropriate reception for
Nehanda.

We have a community of authors to whom the publication,
circulation, and celebration of any single book is a shared activity.
Zimbabwe is like that. We discuss covers and reviews, we discuss
prizes. We laugh, we create.

This is not to say international publication is unimportant to us. In
fact, it is crucial to the cultural exchanges which widen our readership,
to the spread of our literature and cultural product. The successful
translation of a book furthers understanding of our cultures and
histories, and demonstrates the influences on the conventions of the
novel which, rising from our own backgrounds and traditions, we have
been able to generate. As African writers we feel initiated into an
international culture of art and reading; the activity becomes less
personal and solitary, and moves beyond nation. Often we discover
that the challenges to writing, to the creative act itself, are identical.
The passion for insight and discovery, and the desire for an appropriate form and language to capture every possible inspiration. The
struggle for writing is the struggle for expression.

In publishing at home, one felt part of the swing of things, and as
our own literature is young and growing, the contribution seemed
more direct, more committed and engaged. You watched the interest
grow, and in my case, the necessity for a literature that grows out of
women's experiences, a literature that suggests transformation and a
challenge to taboo, that invents a language to banish women's
silences. *Nervous Conditions* was the first novel in English by a
Zimbabwean woman writer; *Nehanda* was the second. *Nervous
Conditions* was published abroad before appearing in Zimbabwe; this
had not been the author's first impulse.

Zimbabwean women are working hard to establish a national
literature in which their experiences are accommodated. I can only
hope that what I have done, so far, gives Zimbabwean women hope
and confidence that they can pursue a career in writing, and that it is
necessary for them to describe the worlds in which women often
discover themselves – sometimes shattering, sometimes ennobling.

The publication of *Butterfly Burning* (1998), for example, was a
high moment in my own motivation to return home. I found a final
fulfilment and realisation of that impulse I had carried through in

1995. I wanted to write on Bulawayo, a city where I was born and where I currently live. While growing up, I wished to read a novel set in Bulawayo, among the streets in which I grew up, in the township, and the people there. I wanted to capture their fears, their style, their survival. I wanted to celebrate the love of music and the harmony of it all. It was a unique moment for me to be in Bulawayo, living on one of these same streets, and writing *Butterfly Burning*. I was happy to publish this novel first in Zimbabwe. Each novelist should encounter a familiar street in the folds of a book. It is a wonderful feeling.

There are many reasons why some of what I describe might change; Baobab is currently for sale and might change hands. The cost of books, even when published locally, has escalated due to the devaluation of our dollar. The Zimbabwean public cannot afford books as well as other immediate needs. The education system is transforming rapidly, there is so much more to think of. And for me, as a writer, only one truth – to travel into that unbounded space, the imagination.

An Experience of Publishing in Africa

Femi Osofisan

On the subject of publishing, I should indeed have a lot to say. After all, apart from possibly Cyprian Ekwensi, I am the most published author in Nigeria. Since 1968, when I began my career in the theatre, I have published with no fewer than thirteen publishers in Nigeria,[1] (a record that even Ekwensi has not equalled). This would seem to indicate, at first sight, a story of astonishing success. At a second look, however, the question must arise – why this wayward and erratic shift of allegiances? Why is it that, virtually every year, I have had to turn to a different publisher for my works?

A facile explanation would be that, in the egregiously virgin space of Nigerian book publishing, new houses are constantly being born, and these naturally turn first to those they consider successful authors for manuscripts. Every three to four months, more or less, I am besieged by some aspiring publisher looking for some new work, and promising the whole heaven in remuneration. Foolishly, I succumb to these pressures, and of course, as time passes, the promises collapse; and I turn away, ready to be plucked by the next sweet-tongued adventurer. But the reasons for this unusual publishing drama go deeper than this. It is a subject on which I have written quite copiously, especially in my columns in Nigerian newspapers, first in the *Guardian*, and later in the *Sunday Times*. But since these papers may not have been accessible to readers outside the country, I am going to take the risk of repeating them here in this article.

I believe it is common knowledge now that I began as a member of a small group of aspirant writers who met in Ibadan in 1973, and decided for a number of reasons to publish and promote our works uniquely in Nigeria. We took this decision because first, we believed that writing had, or ought to have, a direct political purpose, and therefore that publishing outside the country would divert us from this noble purpose. The foreign publisher, we reasoned, would be obliged to ask the author to tame his or her work for foreign readers, whose concerns, naturally, would not be the same as those of our people.

Already we felt that this kind of pressure was responsible for the orientation in the African books of the time towards exoticism, for the preponderance of the theme of cultural alienation, rather than the more urgent problems of our society's political and economic development. We saw that our nation was under the threat of disintegration into a bloody civil war, through military *coups d'état*, corrupt leadership, economic clientilism, and such woes; whereas our authors were writing about ethnographic customs and rituals, and being celebrated for these in the Western presses.

Hence, to avoid this danger of irrelevance, of exotic (self-)indulgence, we thought it best to shun the foreign publishers, and cultivate our own audience at home. Of course, there would be many problems with this decision, as we were well aware. One, for instance, was the lack of publishing houses. But for us, this was just another area of lack that we thought it our duty to repair. Our work, we argued, should provide the incentive for the establishment of good publishing houses. For, after all, how would publishing houses be born if we all sent our manuscripts abroad to publish? Moreover, how would a local readership develop unless there was an indigenous publishing industry to nurture and encourage it? And finally, related to this, was the question of the availability of the books. Foreign publishing meant that many of the known texts of the time were just not available in the local market. They had to be imported first, by merchants whose priorities were often distant from the promotion of intellectual enlightenment.

These were among our brave, idealistic reasons. But after two decades in practice, the result, to my horror, was just the opposite of what we had expected! Instead of a thriving book industry, for instance, what we had was a literal graveyard, where the imminent death of the book was the most urgent peril! From a personal perspective, I was ending up not with credit, but an acute loss. I had published so many books with so many publishers, but these books were, like those of my other colleagues, nowhere to be found on the bookshelves. Few of those that were published were of any acceptable standard anyway – with unattractive covers, poor formatting, poor inking, jejune illustrations, the cheapest available newsprint. Even after assiduous correcting by the author, which of course nobody paid for, the books would still come out riddled all over with avoidable typographical errors. Furthermore, there would be no promotion whatsoever for the book. Not even when it was a play that had had a successful run, and for which readers were eagerly waiting. Hence, not surprisingly, royalties were laughably meagre and infrequent: with the annual money from all the books altogether, I could not replace one of the tyres for my car!

But the worst of the wounds really was this unavailability of the books. Students and other interested readers would keep plaguing us with complaints about not finding our books to buy. Yet when you complained to the publisher, he or she would tell you angrily that the books were not in the bookstore because nobody was asking for them! At one time, some of us hit upon what we thought would be a solution to this. We resorted to going to the warehouses ourselves to buy our books, so as to market them ourselves. But it is not in the Nigerian environment that such a system can work! Cultural obligations, such as no one in the West perhaps would understand, thwart successful commerce in this kind of manner – most of the time, we simply gave out the books for free! Can you imagine, for instance, taking money from some poor undergraduate who has travelled all the way down to Ibadan from, say, Nsukka, just to find a copy of *Who's Afraid of Solarin*? Or from the lecturer from Ahmadu Bello University in Zaria, who wants to direct *Midnight Hotel*, but has searched in vain for a copy everywhere from Zaria to Kaduna to Abuja, before making the risky and exhausting journey down south to your office in Ibadan? Or from members of the première cast of *Yungba Yungba* who, on hearing that the play has been published, rush excitedly around Lagos and – not finding the book – finally drive down, one desperate weekend, to ask you?

As for earning from production rights on the plays, that was another matter entirely. Of course, in the fluid market of the Nigerian proto-capitalist economy, the issue of copyright is a constantly disputatious arena. This is because, in our troubled transition from an oral ethos – where cultural products are not owned by individuals, or commodified for economic exploitation – to a written tradition, with all its dramatic rites of ownership and proprietary laws, there is still a gaping space where authorship is only loosely recognised. Thus it is very common for plays to be performed in Nigeria without anybody in the production team bothering to inform the playwright about it. And very often I arrive somewhere or other only to meet actors coming to inform me with bubbling excitement of how they have just finished performing my play, or are in the very process of doing so! How do you inform such people that they have in fact committed a serious crime by infringing the law of copyright?

Nevertheless, while one might excuse these occasions of genuine ignorance, it is painful when the playwright finds him- or herself with no choice but to sanction, or even authorise, these acts of piracy. These are the instances when there is an obligation to give permission to actors' groups to reproduce works free of charge. Or what do you do when a group approaches you saying that they want to put on a play of yours, but cannot find copies to buy? Do you insist on your copyright laws, and disallow them from doing the play till the publisher deigns to make copies available? Or do you forgo your rights, so that the production can take place? Of what use is a play, anyway, if it is not performed? How will the ideas that one is trying to share ever be disseminated? Will one not die then, as a playwright?

So the question arose – if publishing in Nigeria does not ensure good quality production, nor promotion, nor distribution, such that the book would be available at least in the important bookstores for readers – why then would one want to continue with it? (One is not saying that the fault is always that of the publishers, though. Sometimes it is the consequence of governmental policy – for instance, the cost of importing paper and printing equipment, and so on; and sometimes it is that of our deleterious economy. Whatever the causes anyway, the author is the ultimate victim.)

For a moment, one thought a viable solution would be provided by the establishment of the African Books Collective (ABC), which a small group of far-sighted and committed African publishers, in partnership with Hans Zell, initiated. At least the ABC would help expand the book market, by providing an overseas outlet for the books published in Africa. This way, it would help boost the income of the local publishers, with much needed foreign exchange. And with these improved earnings, they would presumably be able to improve their machinery, and the quality of their publications – and hence, the income of their authors. I paid a visit some time ago to the offices of the ABC in Oxford, and discovered that, while the ABC has indeed helped some publishers in Africa – and still has the potential to help others develop – I doubt very much if it has helped any of the authors. Certainly it was a surprise to me, to learn how many of my works have been sold in the UK market, because this has never reflected anywhere in the royalties or statements rendered by my publishers! Besides, there was depressing evidence also that one of my publishers routinely ignored requests for copies of books – not only mine – under his imprint, to the extent that the administrators of the ABC were contemplating removing his titles from their list.

Inevitably then, after two decades of this frustration, I sat back and took a second look at my decision of 1973. My reputation at home had been well established – but precariously, because the work was badly remunerated. Particularly at a time when the Structural Adjustment Policy was ravaging the professional class, this issue, for one who was so often published, with so many titles to his name, was upsetting, to put it mildly. Abroad, on the other hand – and as Bernth Lindfors' appropriately named FART (Famous Authors Reputation Test)[2] revealed – my work was only feebly known.

It was time to move on, to other options. And so, as before, I began with my fiction. For years, I had been carrying out an experiment in Nigerian newspapers, of serialising short fiction, which had proved highly popular; and Malthouse Press had eagerly published one of them, *Cordelia*, in book form. But, of course, the usual story followed, with the book not being promoted at all, and being poorly circulated; so that very few people even knew of its existence and royalties from it were correspondingly trite. So now I sent the second of the series, *Ma'ami*, to Heinemann – the one in Oxford, not Ibadan. And after accepting it the publishers offered an advance fee of £250, even before the book came out! No doubt, for one living in England, this would be a pittance. But just imagine how exhilarating I found the offer, after all this previous history of publishing! Following this, my second book with foreign publishers – a collection of plays titled *The Oriki of a Grasshopper and Other Plays* – came out last year with Howard University Press in Washington.

But since then, I have not offered any of my plays to any publisher, although there is now considerable notice abroad. (I have, in the past three years, written and directed new plays for theatre in Atlanta and Minneapolis in the US, in Accra, and in Colombo.)

But it is not without reason that I am hesitating. This year, in spite of my reluctance, two Nigerian publishers have brought out my works, two plays that I wrote mainly for younger readers. The first, *The Engagement*, was by Agbo Areo Publishers. Now, Mr Areo is quite enthusiastic and enterprising, at least with regard to distribution. And his production quality was high. So I am willing to see what will happen to the book. Kolade Mosuro, on the other hand, is a beginner in the area. But no one who has seen him work in other fields can fail to be impressed by his diligence, his concern for high standards and his scrupulous honesty. And indeed, this book of mine that he has brought out, *Making Children Is Fun*, is of the best quality anywhere. Mr Mosuro, having been in book distribution and selling for years, knows about the frustration of authors, and is determined to do something about it. Hence he is not venturing into any ambitiously high print run, he told me – just some two thousand to start with. But first and foremost, even before selling the first copy, Mr Mosuro has calculated the royalties the company will owe on the entire print run – and has paid me fully already, in advance! Not only that: he has begun a vigorous campaign to sell the book in other countries.

So, I hesitate. Is this the advent of a new age then, in Nigerian publishing?

Postscript

It is now almost two years since I wrote the above. I am happy to report that not a single penny in royalty has been received for *The Engagement*. The publisher, a good friend of mine, graciously explains to me, each time I bring up the subject, that he is unable to pay because, even though the book is on the official reading list for schools in Lagos State, his gains have been eroded by pirates. And so, a couple of months ago, I started my own print, the 'Opon Ifa readers'.

Notes

1 The publishers and the books are as follows: Onibonoje Publishers *A Restless Run of Locusts*; New Horn Press *Kolera Kolej, Esu and the Vagabond Minstrels*; Ibadan University Press *The Chattering and the Song*; Scholars' Press *Who's Afraid of Solarin?*; BIO Educational Publishers *Once Upon Four Robbers*; Malthouse Press Ltd *Birthdays Are Not For Dying and other plays, Another Raft, Cordelia*; Longman Publishers *Morountodun other plays, Twingle-twangle A-Twynning Tayle*; Heinemann *Minted Coins, Aringindin and the Nightwatchmen, Yunga Yunga and the Dance Contest*; Evans *Midnight Hotel, Farewell to a Cannibal Rage*; University Press Plc *The Album of the Midnight Blackout*; Kraft Books Ltd *Dreamseeker on Divining Chain*; Agbo Aero Publishers *The Engagement*; Mosuro Publishers *Making Children Is Fun*.

2 Lindfors, Bernth. 'The Famous Authors Reputation Test'. *Tensions Between North and South: Studies in Modern Commonwealth Literature and Culture*. Edith Mettke, ed. Wurzburg: Knogshausen and Neumann, 1990, 222-30. Revised and reprinted as 'The Famous Authors Reputation Test: An Update to 1986'. *Semper Aliquid Novi: Littérature Comparée et littéraire d'Afrique: Melanges offerts à Albert Gérard*. János Riesz and Alain Ricard. Tubingen: Narr, 1990, 131-43. See also: 'Big Shots and Little Shots of the Canon'. Long Drums and Canons. Bernth Lindors ed. Trenton, NJ: Africa World Press 1995, 61-75.

To the Would-be African Female Writer: Husband Yourself First!

Osonye Tess Onwueme

'"Husband *yourself* first." What an outrageous thing to say to an aspiring female writer! Are you crazy, you sinful feminist and corrupter of youths?' I hear the voice of convention lashing out at me. On the one hand for being a woman and daring to write. On the other hand for daring to carve out my own path, or for defying and transgressing against the rules of the game – namely, the assigned role of eternal female dependency on the dominant male hegemony who are the gate-keepers of the critical, writing, performing, publishing 'speakerly' space in today's world! You, the African woman (young and beautiful too!) who choose to write must know that you are entering a *High Voltage Zone where you risk 'dancing with wolves'. For, although you think you bring simply the good of your art to sell, you must arm yourself* with the talent to bargain against many odds, and to ward off other unwritten demands that are expected to be supplied along with your artefacts to appease the voracious hot-tempered gods of the writing market-place.

Know this, my African woman with creative talent … When you go into the book business to bear witness and testify to happenings in the world, you are on trial; at least at the first stage. At this first stage, you are an offering to be eaten, not just by the voracious male critics, but even by other women writers (your peers!) who may either feel threatened or fearful that your entry into the market-place will endanger their own access to the passage. The other enemy that you may encounter on this journey to the writing market-place, is the so-called radical African feminist critic who is still embattled with her own crisis of identity. The so-called radical African feminist critic (sister?) is yet to resolve what she wants to become: the white Western, or the masculine African?

Know this, my African female writer, where you enter, on all counts You Are On Trial! For your fellow women, the radical female sisters are ready to slaughter you with their pens for not being feminist enough, while their male counterparts are ready to slay and assassinate you for being *too* womanocentric. And this ('woman-centricism'), in their reckoning, is a first-degree charge that is punishable by death of your creativity on the following counts: creative incompetence; lack of vision, and, of course, craft!

Thus, my dear writer, you must chart the following course if you are to survive and transcend the vagaries and dangers of the treacherous market-place/crossroads. While paying close attention to the incisive tongues of critics, you should, in the final analysis, learn 'to dance your own dance' and not allow yourself to dance someone else's dance. For verily I say unto you, every one of them (and maybe your audience too!) would rather have you change your step, do it their way, or simply stifle or kill your creativity outright by chipping away at your confidence in your ability. This is because, to begin with, you are a 'woman' who should have stayed confined and contented in pre-assigned place and role. There, in your place, you were expected to be nothing better or beyond. This is one good reason why you must approach the road with extreme caution. In this journey to 'bock Success' you may be flooded with potential 'suitors'. Be wise. Arm yourself with this knowledge: they are suitors alright. But you are (truly) a 'bride without a groom'. And therefore you must learn to jealously hug and husband yourself, and your craft, with love, care and passion by not allowing either the rejection slips (they will come and many too!) or the closed doors by the gate-keepers of the market-place to cripple you. This is absolutely why you must arm yourself with the fervent belief in yourself and in your potential creative ability and vision. This is why it is particularly important to decide in your mind the following: what do you want? What can you give and what can't you give? At the same time studiously school yourself in broadening, deepening and polishing the landscapes of your vision and art. Be firm, confident. Above all, be humble. And most of all, *let your writing sell you and speak for you, and not you your writing or yourself.* To achieve this, you should fall in love with the art if engaging in constant revising, (self-)critical responses, (re)thinking and renegotiating your position, mission and craft.

Thus again, verily I say unto you, neither dramatise the anguish nor let it intimidate you. Now, since I have been asked to speak to you frankly about my experiences in the book market-place, I thought I should do no other but be true to you and myself. My assignment was simply to show you the signposts that experience has revealed to me (personally) on the creative crossroads. And in response, I have chosen the route of the double-voiced. What I say to you is the cumulative experience of nearly two decades of writing, speaking and entering the public stages of drama in Africa, North America, and elsewhere. These experiences have conditioned and empowered me to speak to you multi/double-voiced. If you are impatient with parables, please forgive me for choosing to speak to you in parables. But then what do you expect? I am an African dramatist still tied to the motherlore-motherwit. I cannot seem to be able to help myself, nor sever the ties since it is this idiom that comes to me naturally. Or, rather, the idiom/medium has chosen me for the intricate, private nature of the subject. And, in the course of this narrative, notice too that I have circumscribed the parable mainly at the first stage – knowing that you will not need my counsel once you have crossed this first critical borderline/stage of the crossroads of successful writing.

This said, we can now proceed to the other mundane issues relating to the following: links with publishers; entering for prizes, collecting royalties, payments for personal appearances and book launches. Again, I see a certain continuity and inter-relationship between all these and therefore intend to discuss them as such. To date, I would say that twelve of my plays have been issued by five different publishing companies in this sequence: Heins Nigeria Ltd, Totan Nigeria Publishers Ltd, Heinemann Educational Books (Nigeria); Wayne State University Press, Detroit Michigan, US; and African Legacy Press, Inc., New York. From this roll-call you will have noticed that some of them are much better-known than others, and it is not accidental that my earliest works were published by the smaller, relatively unknown publishers Totan and Heins. These two smaller 'fishes' 'discovered me' – so to speak. And then the bigger (inter)national companies, Heinemann and Wayne State, took over, spread the dragnet and gobbled me up. They began feeding on me and my works.

I note, however, that whether you are dealing with national or international companies, the experiences have been quite similar in the sense that the supply of appetising and engaging creative works available to publishers far exceeds the fiscal and budgetary demands of the business that the publishers can afford. And in this heated territory of the market-place, with numerous competing interests, many potentially viable, but riskier, ventures (like yours and some of mine) get dumped in the waste-basket. This is because they are displaced by the bigger profit margins offered by the better-known names, whose mere 'yawnings' conjure up more sweat-free capital than all your writings and offerings put together, as the publishers in the market-place weigh the risks against their pockets. This excruciating exercise is even more agonising for the economically challenged African publishers, who are currently struggling with the disease. You should also bear in mind that unlike you, who may have gone into writing for pleasure, relief or fame, the publisher is engaged in

'Business' and 'Capital Accumulation' is the primary concern. This is why the writer starting out who may be able to swear by the efficiency of their magical art, may not stand a good chance at all in the initial stage with the larger, well-established (multi)national companies.

So, in this regard, what is my counsel to the would-be writer? Do not succumb and wallow in despair and self-destructive thinking for that is the very antithesis of creativity. Take a deep cleansing breath. Hug yourself and your creative offerings (even when they have been rejected by the bigger companies). What is being called for is perseverance. Keep the faith. While noting negative comments against your work, revise your script (if you can), and take it to smaller relatively unknown publishing companies who may be willing to 'play ball' and to experiment with you. At this first step, take whatever you are given or offered. Be dignified, considerate and compassionate, for these publishers are also fellow travellers on the undulating road to fame and capital. They, too, need to survive, like you and me. That is why I tend to reason that at this first stage, we ought to envisage the relationship as a partnership – for both parties need each other, and may have to sink or swim together in order to succeed. Perhaps on my own part, this consciousness – or what I call the Art of Human Management – has tended to arm me and condition me toward the needs of others as well as myself. At many critical stages in my career, I have tended to fall back on this sensibility to enable me to leap certain hurdles and cross borderlines. For example, on occasions I have had to call upon the Chairman or one of the directors of Heinemann, Heins or Totan to assist me with a vehicle, a driver or a hotel room when I have to pay them a visit in Nigeria.

The same bargaining edge helps when I am called upon for speaking engagements and the people inviting me seem to have a respectable amount of money for an honorarium and, sometimes, even transportation. In this regard, unless one has really 'made it' as they say, it would be advisable to fix the price of one's honorarium/stipend and even royalty, because not every party that wants, or needs, you has the necessary capital to meet your demands. For me, in this kind of situation, I would just be content to engage in the labour in the interim, hoping that, like most good investment products, the seed that one sows and cultivates will grow. The yield will come later. This is why, in some cases, I have even undertaken to speak or lecture for nothing, hoping that some day the idea/seed planted will grow and multiply through those who become affected by it.

Next, always remember whom you are dealing with. Many of our African publishers (especially) are financially handicapped. 'We are financially strapped.' You will hear that chant often, even when they seem to be strong and liquid. With the framing of the (in)famous line, our publishers design these emotive words to resist your penetrating deep into their pockets. Thus, if and when you cross the borderline and enter into that coveted fictional space, with your words standing and staring in the face of the world from every library space – be content (at the initial stage) with the 10 per cent royalties that the publishers are likely to give you. That is, if and when they give. My experience is that even though these publishing 'tenpercenters' promise you that in the contractual agreement, you will be quite lucky if they declare any royalty to you in years – their growing sales, and the fact that your work keeps disappearing from their warehouses, notwithstanding.

When this happens, control is called for. Your Art of Human Management should be invoked to take over! Engage in any verbal or written quarrel with your publisher? No way! That is suicidal! I have not done it, and perhaps never will. And maybe that is why I am still alive and relatively sane and well. With publishers and agents, I have learnt the art of the 'sign-language' competency test that is desperately required for dealing with publishers, book distributors, agents, publicists and their cousins in the book market. Try silence or this sign-language. It works wonders where words fail. Actually sometimes, words fail – and that is why you must learn to hold back and not verbalise everything (especially when you are angry) lest you regret it later.

Whether or not your so-called promoter/publisher grows fat on your intellectual product while endangering your life with a financial diet to kill or shrink, one thing you can at least smile about is that your books are not decaying on the shelf! At least, you are 'speaking' and somebody is listening to you out there. I know this is far from being satisfactory, but wait ... Some day you might begin to write your own ticket! And let any publisher/manager dare come and say anything to you then. When that time comes, I charge you to tear up that contract in their face. And soon, watch them running back to apologise and claim they miss-spoke or were misunderstood – and to prove it, watch them hurriedly commission you to write something for them. That will be your final opportunity to cough into the page and give them the stuff to lap up or sell, while they prostrate and sing 'Thank you. Thank you. Thank you ...'.

Is There an African Writer Out There to Address, Or Is There an African Audience Out There to Write For?

Kole Omotoso

A letter to my daughter

My Dear Yewande,

In 1972, I came to Nigeria after a three-year absence. During that period I finished a doctoral thesis, met your future mother and had two novels published in London. Of all these activities, the least known to my people in Nigeria was the fact that I had published two novels while I was living in the United Kingdom. I was not happy about this, and therefore decided that from that year onwards all my future publications would emanate from Nigeria first and foremost, and thereafter in the metropolis of London, Paris and New York, if possible. I not only kept this promise to myself, I also convinced my friends and close associates to publish their works first in Nigeria and, thereafter, overseas. For me, the culminating episode of this decision is the publication of *Just Before Dawn* in 1988 in Nigeria and its success in the country, and the impossibility of getting an overseas publisher for it. The reason given for this impossibility by the various publishers approached is that the book is too Nigerian! But that, as they say, is another story.

You and your brothers, Akinrinmola and Pelayo, have been trying to write for quite some time. If I was to advise you today as to the way and manner in which to shape your writing career, what would I ask you to do? Would I ask you to publish only in Nigeria? This would be ridiculous advice for the simple reason that you are not living in Nigeria. You are not living in Nigeria because I left Nigeria and brought you to South Africa. Would I then advise you to publish first and foremost in South Africa, and then in the rest of the world? I have published in South Africa, but I have not found an easy access to the international free market promised to those who wish to compete internationally. Which means that for some curious reason or reasons what African writers have to say is still strictly for Africans and we'd better understand that now.

Yet I have no doubts in my mind that there are young people out there, your friends with their email addresses and those on the Internet who would wish to read work from you. How could I ask that you do not address yourself to these outlets?

When I came back to Nigeria in 1972, there was another issue related to creative writing which was also getting a lot of attention: the issue of language. Put simply, it was whether you could write about one culture in the language of another. While I have made it plain to you that the Irish have resolved the issue for me in the positive, (the argument being that there is enough of my life that finds expression in English now to make me feel, in some ways, English – of the African, non-England, version), I still do not know what you feel now that you have learnt to speak Afrikaans and some Xhosa while still retaining your grandmother's tongue as a gift. Yoruba is not your mother tongue as it is mine. Your mother tongue is English of the Bajan variety. What is the implication of this fact for your future writing endeavours? I have a feeling that you and your brother will write in whatever language you feel comfortable to communicate your ideas.

The third issue, doing the rounds at the time I returned to Nigeria in 1972, is that of audience. For whom does the African writer write? There have been two main responses to this question. There are those writers of African origin who say that although they are African, their writing is for all the literate of the world. They are writers first and Africans next. I do not accept this position. The second response is that, first and foremost, the audience for African writing is Africans on the continent; then, people of African descent in the Caribbean, in the United States and in the Arab World. These peoples constitute the communities of African sensibilities and experiences across the continents of the world, and address one another in all the languages of the world. Thus, the African writer who wishes to stick to the languages of his or her people is likely to discover that those languages spread all over the globe. The African writer today must accept the fact of multilingualism.

Let me tell you two very short stories to illustrate what I am saying. Once a mother whose two children were being sent away to distant places to seek their fortunes, baked three cakes. She gave her two children one cake each. She then cut the third cake into two equal halves and gave each one a half. She then advised them to the effect that whichever of them made it good should seek out the other, and rescue him or her from the house of bondage.

The second story concerns a multilingual cat in pursuit of a monolingual rat. The pursuit was hot and long, and finally the rat escaped into a hole and was gone and saved. Or so it thought. At this point the cat sat back and thought what to do to get what he wanted. Then, it began to bark, first quietly as if admonishing a puppy or soothing a lover. Then he barked furiously as if warding off a menace. It was at this point that the rat came out. The cat grabbed him. Before devouring him the cat asked: 'Don't you know anything about multilingualism?'

Keep writing right_ng and good luck!

Kole Omotoso,
fellow writer.

Perhaps I am a Monomaniac?

Taban lo Liyong

When I was young I thought publishers liked publishing stories. There were many short stories in *Oxford English Readers for Africa*. Animals called Ananse, human beings called Lakayana were there. And the address of the publisher was 'Amen House'. We used to wonder at that: Amen House. There was 'Longman, Green and Cox'. To us a man could be 'long'. But how he could be 'green' was something else. If we cannot now remember what points of grammar, or drill exercises we went through, at least we are grateful that snippets of folktales from all over Africa were brought to us. In that primary school in Acholiland, Northern Uganda, we were taught that a man called 'William Shakespeare' was the best writer in the world. A fellow pupil whose brother was in a senior secondary school had *The Tempest* with him. I begged him for it. When I started reading, it had 'Boatswain' and 'Hei hos' and other things in one-word or two-word sentences. It did not read like the Lakayana stories.

Later on, when I was in junior secondary school, I came across books written in African languages about African peoples' histories. There was a novel and a drama. These were now different from the other vernacular books which were *The New Testament*, *Catechism*, and *Prayer Book* which also contained 'Hymns'. One teacher had told us that the composers of hymns lived on the top floors of European houses; that they ate and drank little but drank much tea or wine. We felt sorry for them. But perhaps the frugal menu improved their hymns, especially as they were nearer to God. My junior secondary school was very creative. One old boy had written an historical book in the vernacular, a short morality play, and was later to become my father-in-law. His son, the Headmaster, had written a hunting account for the Margaret Wrong Prize. The other son had translated a health manual from English into the local language.

Writing then, on top of telling more folktales and new tales, as well as composing hymns on topfloors, was usable for writing histories. It was in that school that a lame veteran of the Second World War, living somewhere in the English countryside, sent me (on request) his Christian tract. I translated it into Acholi and took it to the Reverend (later Archbishop) Janani Luwum to improve my translation. He did. I sent it to England, and thousands of my first literary endeavour in Acholi were printed. Apart from knowing that he was lame, I had no knowledge of where he lived: upfloor, or downfloor. But since he wanted to spread peace and goodwill and my elder brother had been wounded in the heel in Burma, I could lend him a hand. When I was still in that school, one of the chiefs who had gone 'home' to visit the 'mother' country came back and wrote his account in the vernacular. I was interested in translating it. Especially where he reports that one of the fellow chiefs, from a cattle-rearing people, finding milk in plenty in England, used to down a whole bottle in the morning. And then drink another before retiring at night. Some kids laughed at his efforts. And so the milk-drinking story, and those of how fast English trains run and of how full of English people the English cities were, never got translated into English.

We then got to the secondary school. Our first novelist in the vernacular was now busy composing songs – but living in a bungalow and drinking water and beer. There was a competition for writing novels in the vernacular. One of my classmates, whom we called 'Lacan Makwo' ('The Poor Man who is Still Alive') after the title of his prize-winning novel, laboured day and night. His efforts were rewarded: the book was published and he now 'professes' Education. The then Provincial Commissioner of our area, a tall (not 'long', now) man called Cotton-Powell, instituted a literary competition in the school. I wrote a very good essay for it. Then spoilt it because it was too, too good. The spoilt version still earned me second place. My reward? *Pickwick Papers*. Thank you Commissioner Cotton-Powell. I liked Samivel and his 'father' Pickwick chasing his hat when the wind took it off his head. But the most hilarious part of the book had to do with the account of a political election.

At secondary school I also read Geoffrey Chaucer's *Canterbury Tales* from the beginning to the end. It was 'tales' as I understood them from Longman, Green and Cox; there, too, I read (now I was up to it) William Shakespeare. And an idiosyncratic dramatist from Ireland called George Bernard Shaw, who wrote longer 'Introductions' to the plays than the plays were long. Shaw wrote a play about the emerging African élite called *Arms and the Man*. We read it for exams. He was pugilistic, long-winded and full of spleen. He would not let a point go unanswered. Back from Cambridge University, the results of the School Certificate. I got the highest grade in the school's three years of attempting the examinations. Had I not spoilt my fine art exam, as I had my Cotton-Powell essay, I would have gone to

Makerere, to the Margaret Trowell School of Fine Arts – as two or three of my colleagues did.

Let us go to the Teacher Training College in the national capital. It had a bigger library. The British Council was busy promoting English Books. The American Information Service had many books against Communism. There was a lame Indian's second-hand bookshop. I spent most of my pocket-money there. Although a colleague and I were already on the way to shedding our Christian belief, it was when we were in Teacher Training College that we studied hard and found intellectual justifications for the break. Those second-hand books of mine, I later left with a friend when I went to the States; the friend left them with another friend, who finally took them to a classroom where everybody helped themselves to them. They were signed 'Taban Pagan'. When I graduated, the Anglican Church engaged me, agnostic as I was, to teach in their school. I went and taught in their missionary school without participating in prayers or in religious services. In my first year at a college in the US South, I belonged to an élite study group. We went through the *Encyclopaedia Britannica*, and *Great Books of the Western World*. I liked Jean-Jacques Rousseau's candidness. He was another Bernard Shaw. When his heroes and a heroine returned to Europe to do agriculture, I thought *The Tempest* had ended again.

Let me then go the national capital of the United States, and get involved in the Honours Program of one of the universities. Although this was now my second year, within my first two years at college, I had scored all the high grades I needed to get a degree. From the third year onwards, I was reading everything that mattered to me. Mostly, as Karl Marx would say, not for understanding the world only, but with a view also to change it. From my third year at college, I started sending out ideas for changing the world, starting from East Africa. When I went to graduate school, the tap was on, fulltime. I returned to East Africa to continue the transformation, through the written word, promoting literacy through popularising the culture of reading, especially in high places. I took a holiday in the South Seas, then returned to the Sudan to continue where I had left off. Went to Japan to gather more ammunition. Rested a bit in Australia. Landed in South Africa where the good old East African days of cosmopolitan acceptance and publishing opportunities are back.

How to change the world is my theme. When I put the arguments in poetic form, they say it is not tight enough. What is not tight? Have you followed the arguments? Am I not performing in the tradition of my ancestors? When clarity is called for are our songs not 'loose'? If I want to be dense, can you defeat my *Another Nigger Dead*? When I input prose, they say I am funny, or hard. What is funny? Am I funnier than Rousseau or Shaw? Talking about hardness: should I compete with Wole Soyinka or Wilson Harris? Why don't they tune in properly? Those who wish to hear Congolese music, or Reggae music, when will they also want to hear *Thus Spake Zarathustra*?

This is the type of 'criticism' I get from my reader. I do not know what type of tales they want told or retold? Perhaps our elder brother Chinua Achebe has established the norm. And any African writer who does not write like Achebe is doomed. Doomed to remain unread. Doomed to remain unbought? Consequently, then doomed to be unpublished? Doomed to be 'unrepublishable'? Especially when the Ministry (not of God, now) of Education does not, or cannot recommend his book for the schools! And 'Thou Shalt Write Textbooks' is now publishing commandment number one.

For now I know for sure, all writers are to become freelance writers of textbooks for the Almighty Ministry of Education. All publishers are enfranchised publishing agents for the Ministry of Education Almighty. And as an agnostic, now in the new dispensation, I cannot be employed by the department since I do not want to go to church and pay even lip service to the new religion. That is why I continue to write. Till publishers come to me. Till James and Jack pester me for an article. Perhaps this Jacobean revolution will turn the tide? For, of the former major, former pioneer, writers of Africa, I can claim to be the most remaindered author in London and Nairobi (and consequently the most 'out-of-print'); as well as the most rejected (consequently storing many returned manuscripts); most persistently foolish (consequently still writing, and paying for typing my kind of books that may never have a publisher).

Perhaps I am a monomaniac? Am I pursuing a mirage, which is obvious to everybody except me with my big blindspot? Perhaps, if it had not been by the happy chance of my earning my living by teaching (or cheating) at the universities, I would have been living on topfloor, or bottom floor, of a European building subsisting on bread and tea. Or fallen by the wayside as some of my colleagues (former) have done. Perhaps I am a coward. Or only believe in Marx, Nietzsche and I!

Random Thoughts on Clocking Sixty-five

Cyprian Ekwensi

Reprinted from *The Essential Ekwensi*, ed. Ernest Emenyonu, Ibadan: Heinemann Educational Books (Nigeria), Ltd, 1987.

I have been most reluctant to set down in writing my thoughts on clocking sixty-five for the simple reason that there must be thousands of fellow Nigerians who would regard it as a childish exercise. Who am I to talk about 'age' which is really the core of the discussion? The age one attains is conferred by various factors including destiny, lucky escapes, acts of God, heredity (my father was ninety-eight years old at the time of his transition in 1976 and my mother is eighty-six plus and is still alive in Nkwelle, Anambra Local Government Area). Under normal circumstance, one would not feel that there is any great achievement or miracle in living to be 100, or eighty, or for that matter, seventy or sixty or fifty in Africa's most populous country. But in a country where letter-bombs, hijacking, kidnapping, coups and counter-coups, even guerrilla warfare against a section of the bureaucracy by an aggrieved robber, are everyday occurrences, circumstances are no longer normal.

The urban Nigerian does not live longer by barricading himself behind burglar 'proofs', or immobilising his car, all in a bid to survive the night only to be stabbed or letter-bombed or shot in the stomach in the middle of the market-place, at noon next day with everyone looking on and nobody doing anything. There is no solace to be found in our younger ones in their new-found escapism via cocaine and heroin which makes them uneasy owners of 50,000 naira Honda Preludes and 190E Mercedes Benz saloons at the age of nineteen or twenty. Can anyone who has attained the age of sixty today paint a convincing and vivid picture to a teenager, of the colonial administration in which he grew up, with its Residents, DOs and Governors, followed by no fewer than eight Nigerian Heads of State in twenty-six years; and between the colonial and independence eras, of that period of SGNN (Self Government for Nigeria Now Campaign), of the NEC

(National Emergency Committee) conjured up by the shooting of the Enugu Coal Miners, the Aba Women's Riots, the first nation-wide strike of railwaymen led by Michael Imoudu?

How can you tell the younger ones that travel was by rail (not by skypower), that when planes started flying between London and Lagos, it took two or three nights to fly Safari from London, touching at routes on the west African coastline? And what has happened to Empire Day (24 May, now Children's Day) and Remembrance Day (11 November, wear a Flanders poppy)? All gone and forgotten. Did two million Nigerians die in the Biafran War, especially the children (at the rate of 1,000 a day from Kwashiokor)?

When in 1970 we heard of 'No Victor No Vanquished', is it true that sixteen years after the war ended, a particular ethnic group still feels underprivileged and discriminated against in major national issues? To have survived all the hazards involved in living in our great country, one is bound to have a lot of memories of crises. In the Nigerian context, crises have always brewed over the question of who controls the centre – in uniform or robes. And since ethnicity has been injected into the Nigerian system of analysing every act and every situation, one cannot help but notice that power at the centre has remained a permanent monopoly of a particular part of Nigeria.

The Colony and Protectorate of Nigeria gave way to a three-region Nigeria dominated by the Big-Three – Zik, Sardauna, and Awolowo – which then transformed itself into, first a twelve-state, and later a nineteen-state Nigeria. The dream of independence remained largely a dream. Each of the eight successive governments continued to promise the people roads, water, electricity, and the promise continues. The economy changed from Cocoa, Palm Oil and Groundnuts to OPEC oil and SFEM. Today the country is in a depressed and confused mood, but still hopeful that a miracle will happen, and the independence dream will materialise into jobs for graduates, food for all, and health for all: water, roads and NEPA (National Electric Power Authority) everywhere. Do we have to work for it? Work was never mentioned when the promises were made.

One Higher College has multiplied into thirteen universities churning out more and more graduates who roam the streets and have been told to be 'self-employed'. But how? Education was one of those independence promises, the golden key to success. Scholarships have disappeared giving way to launchings of five-million-naira education funds and levies (out of no income). Free education at any level remains a worthy aspiration for some aspiring magician of tomorrow. But how do other countries do it?

Why do their telephones work, their mails get delivered on time, their electric power never fails, their prices remain relatively static over years, their police hunt down criminals, their governments never fall to coups, their election results are never rigged, their currency never dives and jumps? How do they do it? Are they superior to us? Of course not. Black is beautiful – and black is also clever.

There was a time when any Nigerian woman who went abroad and returned with the letters SRN, SCM believed she had attained the unattainable and promptly entered the 'Senior Service' with car advance and accommodation. Today's woman is a Senator or a Vice-Chancellor at the University, or a Cabinet Commissioner. Salaries have multiplied from £144 p.a. just pre-independence to 40,000 naira, twenty-six years after, and yet, for the majority, life is not forty times more comfortable than it was then. You could make a good stew with five shillings then. In fact a bank asked you then to open a savings account with five shillings. Now you cannot make a good stew with 20 naira, and the charge on a bank draft is 10 naira, not to speak of opening an account.

Perhaps the difference between one who has attained the age of sixty and above, and one who is in his teens is that the older person stops to ponder the rationale of it all and has the added experience of hindsight (the it-has-'all-happened-before' syndrome). A man in his sixties can look back twenty years when his son was born and see how life has treated him, his family and his son, in all aspects, social, economic and political. From this privileged view, he can absorb the shocks which would jar the inexperienced and forecast that it could happen again.

Suddenly it has become important to have roots. A man lives for forty years in Britain or America and one day decides to go home to Nigeria where he is sure of being arrested and imprisoned, or punished by remaining 'free' to suffer hardship with his uncomplaining countryman. So, home is now best. We are all agreed on this? Any thought I may have on attaining the age of sixty plus, should largely revolve around my writing. What has really happened? Have I been able to attain my goals? The answer is yes and no, mainly no. I have always wanted to be a populist writer, a compulsively-read writer. That I have achieved, but not the output I envisaged. At this moment, I have the outline of 16 novels and novellas I would wish to write and if I had really attained my goals, they would all be down on paper by now, or latest by the end of 1987; and that is why I am busy exploring all means of increasing my productivity, including the use of a word processor.

Full-time writing in Nigeria is still impossible, and it is not only the writers who are responsible. Publishers for the new age need complete orientation, especially the 'older' publishers. The newer ones which have no history of foreign participation and tradition must still learn that publishing is a business of trust and confidence; and when the statement says 4,000 copies have been sold, it should really be 4,000 copies and not 10,000. Writers are the grist that feed the publisher's mill. Royalties must be paid promptly – pirates or no pirates.

Early in my life, I realised that I was cut out for a life in the arts. In primary school, I acted the part of Little Boy Blue in a stage presentation of 'Little Red Riding Hood', produced by an Englishman. The character, Nick Papadopoulous, in *Jagua Nana's Daughter*, was inspired by this man but came as a composite with another Greek resident of Jos at the time, a merchant who had a store on Naraguta Street. We had a yearly concert at Jos Government School (where today stands the Jos Stadium) and our Headmaster who hailed from Cross River State, Mr Okon Edem, played the organ. He supervised our rehearsals during the last quarter of the year, and we performed during yuletide at the African Club at the foot of the hills. The Resident and his wife were Special Guests. Nobody missed our yearly concerts.

Again, in Secondary School, I read everything I could lay my hands on in the school library, concentrating on H Rider Haggard, Charles Dickens, Jane Austen, Walter Scott, and Alexandre Dumas. I contributed articles and stories to the school and house magazines and took part in drama, debates and sports, especially five-a-side football, cricket, athletics and football.

Then came the Higher College days when I registered to study Forestry and soon found myself in Anchau where the government was carrying out an eradication programme against trypanosoma gambiense, tsetse fly that was harassing man and cattle with sleeping sickness. There I met the Fulani people who inspired *Burning Grass*. I did not stick with Forestry but instead went to teach Biology, Chemistry and English at Igbobi College, Yaba, Lagos, where I began to develop a series of novellas. I read out the manuscripts of *Drummer Boy*, *Passport of Mallam Ilia*, and *Trouble in Form Six* to my class, which comprised students who have today distinguished themselves in various aspects in the country's development: Chief Michael Ibru, Ambassador Olisemeka, Emmanuel Omatsola and others. They were then in Form Two and have since become my lifetime friends.

At about this time, I was broadcasting a regular weekly programme called 'The Storyteller' which always on Saturdays succeeded Chief Kofo Abayomi's 'Radio Doctor' which is always introduced with a

Spanish tune *La Golandrima*. The broadcasts originated from Glover Memorial Hall, Marina Lagos where the Radio Nigeria Studios were located. Sapara was still around then, as was Daniel, with Harold Cooper heading the Public Relations Department soon after World War Two. The PRD also had a magazine called *Nigeria Digest* to which I contributed a famous story called 'Big Massa' and another called 'The Gorilla of Umo'. This was about the time I wrote *The Leopard's Claw*.

The series of stories I wrote and broadcast from Glover Hall formed the nucleus of a novel called, at first, *Lajide of Lagos*, and later re-named *People of the City*, written in thirteen nights at sea aboard the *MV Apapa*. I was en route to London where I was going to study pharmacy on a government scholarship. That journey again showed up in another novel written in 1953 but published in 1986, titled *For a Roll of Parchment*. Throughout my literate life, writing has been the only constant factor, through love and hate, failure and success, blessing and disappointment, fame and fortune. I never once stopped writing even when I found myself in a position where I could command others to do the writing for me. I don't believe writing can be delegated. In the long run, you still have to sit down and shape the material to your own thinking and your own style.

The one reason why writing has stubbornly remained with me while other occupations keep changing is that I read an article by a British writer, LAG Strong, who said that anyone seriously contemplating a writing career, must first secure a bread and butter job. In the long days of slogging away at the typewriter and staring at blank sheets of paper, the grocer has to be paid, the landlord has be to appeased, and the body must be covered with clothing. And that means cash in hand. And so, for my bread and butter, I studied pharmacy but kept on writing, even on the eve of the final exams. But pharmacy has never given me bread to say nothing of butter. I can count the number of hundred nairas earned from pharmacy on the fingers of one hand. Not that I have abandoned all hope. There is no retiring age for pharmacists who are self-employed.

Certainly great changes have taken place in the media in Nigeria. One can now make a bread and butter living by working in the press, radio, TV, Information Ministry, and film industry but these are not without hazards – the various sedition and libels laws paled before the Buhari/Idiagbon Decree No. 4 (abrogated in 1985) but revived on 19 October 1986 in the form of the more deadly and lawless letter-bomb whose demolition effects are irreversible. Journalists and producers, writers and historians who come too close to damaging revelations can expect to receive the 'gift' in their homes or in their offices through motor-cycles which become transformed into Peugeot cars after the event.

The satisfaction I have gained from writing can never be quantified. Writing has opened doors for me which would be otherwise closed. Writing has given me honours which no Head of State can match because these honours come from the hearts of my millions of readers most of whom I have never met. Because of the possessive and selfish nature of writing as a calling, a writer needs to build an understanding family, an ideal that requires deep faith and perseverance. A stable home needs more than ordinary patience. To the writer, status symbols and flamboyant living assume secondary positions, if any at all. Once possessed by the creative goddess, nothing else matters, not even food and drink, and this is one secret why so many writers are able to adapt to changing times and hard times. They can isolate themselves into a world of their own creation, like mad men and children.

In these modern days, finding one of your own children who will follow in your footsteps is like looking for the new moon after the Ramadan has passed; but I am lucky. A cousin, Raymond Ekwensi, wrote a novel *Fight, Beloved Continent*, about apartheid. This was in 1974. Raymond lost his life in a swimming accident, but the novel has been published. My own daughter, Njideka Ekwensi, has written her own novel *When Love Whispers Again* (not a successor to Papa's *When Love Whispers*). Njideka is still in Secondary School and is one of the first victims of the 6-3-3-4 system. The love story she wrote is yet to be published.

Sixty-five may sound like a lot of years, but when one can still respond to Jaguas and their daughters, all hope is not lost. At least one can give the younger ones a good run for their so-called youth, if that is all they can boast of. After all, all is fair in love, war and the power game.

Perspectives on
Publishing in Africa

Publishing in Africa: Culture and Development

Walter Bgoya

Introduction

Some years ago in Dar es Salaam, Mrs Shirley Du Bois, wife of WEB Du Bois, the great African American philosopher and architect of the Pan-African movement, told an anecdote that I would like to share with you. After the coup that toppled Dr Kwame Nkrumah of Ghana, a group of soldiers went to her house and demanded to make a thorough search of it. As they were about to enter her late husband's library, she stepped in front of them and challenged any one of the soldiers who was not afraid of the old man's spirit, which resided in his books and papers, to dare touch his things. The soldiers, who had come with much force and determination, looked at the impressive array of books and papers, thought about the matter, discussed it in their mother tongue, and decided it was too risky a business. They excused themselves and left Mrs Du Bois and her books alone. Taking no more chances, she had the library transported to Cairo, where she also went to live soon after. If the metaphor of the book as the house of spirits is extended, the publisher could be the builder of the house of spirits, with the author as its feeder. This metaphor is, of course, not so far-fetched; the concept of the union of the living and the dead is present in all sub-Saharan African cultures. It is what explains the practice of pouring libation before drinking and placing food and drink in specially constructed huts outside the main house for the departed elders, to whom individuals with problems pray for intercession with God.[1]

By its weakness more than its strength, African publishing, which even at its best serves a minority of every African country's population, is cast in a special position of privilege and disadvantage. The privilege lies in its function of producing one of education's most important tools – the book – and the nobleness that function confers on the role of publishing in a country's

cultural development. The disadvantage lies in its lack of a mass
base for reasons of penury in financial, material, and technical
resources on the side of production, and weak purchasing power of
the majority of the population on the consumer side. Situation
analyses of publishing in Africa appear periodically after major
conferences on publishing.[2] In addition, the World Bank has
commissioned book-sector studies, which have provided the Bank
with the basis for its decisions on loans to African countries, with
regard to programmes aimed at 'placing books on the desks of the
children'. The book-sector studies contain much useful information
on the *status quo* in the country under study. However, the
conclusions from those studies have been received with mixed
feelings by African and other Third World publishers, who think
that such studies have tended to emphasise the weaknesses rather
than the strengths of the indigenous publishers, including state and
parastatal ones. Indeed, a significant number of them hold the
opinion that the book-sector studies usually pave the way for British
and other multinational publishers, who follow in the footsteps of
the consultants doing the studies. That opinion is reinforced by the
fact that the authors of these studies, with Mr Anthony Read at the
head, are a British consulting firm with strong links to British
publishing. Of course, the cultural context of those reports may
have more to do with their conclusions than with any inclinations
on the part of the authors in favour of British publishers.[3] To the
best of my knowledge, these studies have not yet been published in
book form and are, therefore, not readily available, although they are
not restricted in circulation either. In the 1970s, UNESCO
sponsored studies on books and reading in a number of African and
other Third World countries that were rich sources of information
on publishing in those countries.[4]

Publishing in Africa – a Brief Overview

Although there are marked differences in publishing output in
different African countries, the situation is generally one of extreme
underdevelopment. Descriptions of the situation invariably refer to the
continent as 'book starved', 'bookless', or as suffering from 'book
famine'. The general crisis that the continent has been undergoing is
nowhere more manifest than in book publishing. An indication of this
is given in UNESCO's yearbook for 1988. The statistics show that the
number of books produced in Africa rose from 1,600 titles in 1955 to
10,000 in 1986, representing a growth from 0.6 per cent to 1.2 per
cent, respectively, of world-wide total book production over thirty-one
years.[5] 'Africans had substantially lower likelihood of having access to

locally published material than citizens of any other region of the world',[6] and the situation has not improved. On the contrary, for most countries it has deteriorated.

There are four models of publishing in Africa: state publishing, where the government owns and runs publishing houses; parastatal publishing, where states own (often majority) shares in publishing companies but do not deal with their day-to-day management; multinational publishing, where foreign publishing companies dominate (Longman, Macmillan, Oxford University Press, Heinemann, Evans Brothers, and Nelsons – for the ex-British colonies; and Hachette – for the ex-French/Belgian colonies); and private indigenous publishing. Of the four models, the really successful one is the multinational. In a few countries – Zimbabwe, Kenya, and Nigeria – a certain level of development has been attained but even in those countries, the ratio of material produced by indigenous publishers to that produced by multinationals or imported is still heavily tilted in favour of the latter. In 1985/86, Longman Zimbabwe and College Press, for example, accounted for 80 to 90 per cent of Zimbabwe's publishing output, and in some countries the percentage dominated by the multinationals is even higher.[7]

Those four models operate in countries at three levels of publishing development. The first group comprises 'adequate capacity' countries that have attained efficient infrastructures of publishing – where private-sector printing, publishing, and distribution operate efficiently and where quality books are available at reasonable prices. This includes Zimbabwe, Kenya, and South Africa.[8] Countries in the second category, and Nigeria is the only example, have basically the same well-developed infrastructure but due mostly to political reasons are unable to meet their book needs. This is defined as 'adequate capacity, raw material constrained'. In countries in the third category, of 'low capacity', only rudimentary infrastructures exist and books are expensive, poor in quality, and erratically produced. Tanzania, Zambia, Ghana, Ethiopia, Sudan, Mozambique, and Angola, among others, fall into this category.[9] These countries happen, incidentally, to have also been the ones that adopted the centralised state and parastatal publishing models soon after independence.

The situation described above refers to the Anglophone countries (whatever 'Anglophone' or its opposite, 'Francophone' may mean in countries in which barely 5 per cent of the people are literate in English or French). In Francophone countries, French publishers dominate the situation, although Nouvelles Editions Africaines (NEA) – which is owned by the governments of Senegal, Côte d'Ivoire, and Togo (60 per cent), and the French metropolitan companies Edicef, Istra-Hachette, Armand Colin, Nathan, Presence Africaine, and Le Seuil – publishes a significant portion of the textbooks.[10] The situation in Lusophone Africa until recently was dominated by the state-owned Istituto national do livros e discos in Mozambique and Angola. Uniao do Escritores Angolano (Union of Angolan Writers) is supported to such an extent by the state that it is hard to think of it in terms other than 'state'.

Textbook Publishing

Textbook publishing is the most lucrative field of publishing in Africa. Schools and/or ministries of education provide the only reliable market for publishers. With profits made from textbook publishing, publishers can invest in producing other books – fiction, higher education, and general trade books. Without textbooks, and in the absence of other sources of finance, publishing cannot take off. In many countries in Africa during the colonial period and after independence, publishing was done either by transnationals or state publishing corporations. In the case of the former, decisions about what to publish, when, how, and at what prices, were made outside the African countries in which these firms operated. In a few countries, transnational publishers have evolved through buyouts into successful indigenous publishing companies,[11] and the value of their presence in Africa, it is often argued, can be demonstrated by how well the successor companies are doing in contrast to the wholly indigenous companies, whose fortunes tend to be uncertain.

That is not, however, the only legacy of transnational publishers in Africa. The debacle of the joint ventures set up after 1965 by Macmillan publishers of the United Kingdom and a number of states – Tanzania, Uganda, Ghana, Northern Nigeria, and Zambia – argues strongly against that model of association between African publishers and transnational corporations. The African partners not only got raw deals in terms of profit sharing; more harmful were the opportunities denied the African partners to develop independent editorial policies and capacities and to decide on what to publish, particularly in the field of fiction, and especially in African languages. For the transnational publishing companies, the only real interest in Africa was and remains textbook publishing. As Per Gedin notes, 'the textbook market for the transnational publishers after the de-colonisation of Africa was in the beginning the most lucrative market in the world. Profits were made not only through insufficient editing and overpricing books but also by dumping books that were obsolete in their own countries.'[12]

In the absence of a 'national' educational philosophy – that is, where there was no difference in form and content between colonial and postcolonial education in a given country, there was obviously no impetus for curricular reform and/or developing new textbooks. In addition, as there were lucrative deals to be made through commissions and kickbacks by the comprador capitalist class, importing books was clearly more profitable than venturing into indigenous publishing.

Although the main thrust of this chapter will be that fiction and journal publishing are the real promoters of literary culture, it would be incorrect to ignore the issue of the quality of general education, which can be facilitated greatly by textbooks that are good and relevant in content (i.e. appropriateness of material for the intended level), depth and organisation, language, and design (including illustrations, layout, and overall presentation). It is no exaggeration to say that textbooks in many African countries (certainly in Tanzania) are generally drab-looking objects that leave a great deal to be desired. The reason for this is the lack of appreciation of the art of book design. Books do not inspire pupils to learn, and even where the subject-matter is adequately covered, very often language and presentation do not receive adequate attention. Illustrations are not attractive and are often even misleading. Problems of curriculum development and insufficiently trained curriculum developers, the tendency in the last twenty years to ignore language training (whether the language is national or foreign), poor working conditions, and, especially, inadequate remuneration (static wages) in conditions of inflation and devaluation all go into making the textbook a less effective educational tool than it ought to be.

One area in which textbooks are especially lacking is gender issues. It has been observed that teaching materials continue to portray men and women in stereotypical roles, and the real contribution of women in such areas as the economy and history are not included in texts.[13] The lower performance of girls compared to that of boys at the end of primary school, in combination with other factors, reduces the chances for girls to pursue secondary and higher education and leads to a dead end as far as employment and a decent future are concerned. The field of gender education is new and there is a need to mobilise educators to grasp its basic elements, particularly as they relate to traditional philosophies of initiation, notions such as the 'future of a woman is marriage', and the fear among educated men of educated women.

Gender biases are perhaps the most easily noticeable, but others with particularly insidious import for race abound in many textbooks

published by transnational publishers. Naturally, those being published today are more sophisticated and less blatant than those
published before independence. But that does not mean that the
problem no longer exists – far from it. On careful examination there
exists, in varying degrees, even in books that are written and published
in Africa by African authors and publishers, evidence of the prejudices
of European colonial and class cultures. This should not cause
surprise: the present generation of textbook writers came up just
before independence and soon after. They were brought up on English,
French, and Portuguese intellectual menus and have not wholly lost
their taste for those diets. Indeed, the important question of relevance
of curricula in use in African schools is given such scant attention that
one would have to be blind and dumb not to see the link between
African education and the colonial models on which it hangs.

The situation has been further complicated in recent years. In
addition to the identification of African intellectuals with Western
intellectual traditions, there are the added attractions and even
'blackmail' in the form of large fees from consultancies offered by
organisations such as the World Bank and the threat of losing them
in the case of 'departures' from conventional ideological prisms. In
conditions of low wages, inflation, and devaluation – products of
Structural Adjustment Programmes – the casualty rate of independent thinkers becomes very high. In her forthcoming book, Birgit
Brock-Utne makes two observations concerning attitudes of some
university professors, whose private opinions of the World Bank
policy study, *Education in Sub-Saharan Africa: Policies for Adjustment, Revitalisation and Expansion*, are very critical but who
publicly support it. As one party official commented, concerning the
public statements of such professors, 'it is our people but the
thoughts are World Bank's'. She concludes that 'it is not easy for an
African intellectual who is unable to live from his regular university
wage to write from an African perspective if this perspective is not
what the donors want'.[14]

Educational publishing is based on curricula, and the syllabus is the
author's and publisher's blueprint for manuscript development and
textbook publishing. Analysing 'the tensions between external standards and internal cultures', Angela Little asks

> if international standards which in many instances means 'external
> standards' produced in the West begin to take precedence over national and
> sub-national standards what are the implications for nationally and
> culturally prescribed curricula? Will an internationalised education assess-
> ment technology begin to drive an internationalised curricula reform? How

much wider will become the gap between the culture of those who control education and who design international tests and curricula, (i.e. the 'supra-national educators') and the culture of the child whose learning is the goal?[15]

It is no wonder that in the end the curricula developers, being themselves products of colonial-type education, need not be externally based to espouse the same values and tastes and to construct the same models of achievement. For publishing houses wishing to publish books different from the run-of-the-mill, it is difficult to find editors who have escaped from the international (Western) cultural mould that locks uncritical intellectuals into an adoration of Western educational and cultural values and a denigration of those that are African.

Liberation History as a Special Publishing Project

If to 'become like the West' is asserted as the modern objective of all development theory, its antecedent and underlying colonial, missionary worldview was that Africa had no history or culture. Since it was in that denial of African history that colonialism and imperialism executed their assault on all other African values, it must be in the reconstruction of that history that the process of rediscovery and validation should be undertaken:

> For several centuries Africa has had to suffer under the conception of the African past formed by Europe. As long as this was so, that European conception was 'true', that is to say, effective. But the present and the future on the other hand will be determined by the conception that African intelligence forms [part] of the African past. Neo-African Culture appears as an unbroken extension, as the legitimate heir of tradition. Only where man feels himself to be heir and successor to the past has he the strength for a new beginning.[16]

Frantz Fanon summed it up well when he stated that 'while politicians situate their action in actual present-day events, men of culture take their stand in the field of history' and that 'the passion with which the native intellectuals defend the existence of their national culture may be a source of amazement, but those who condemn this exaggerated passion are strangely apt to forget that their own psyche and their own selves are conveniently sheltered behind a French or German culture which has given full proof of its existence and which is uncontested'.[17]

Culture is about reliving our past – reworking material from the past while facing the present. In Africa at the present, the major cultural thrust appears to be mostly the reconceptualisation of culture following Western trends. To be valid 'internationally', it is not sufficient that music and literature are African; they must also be 'universal', and if they are not, they are vilified in language that does not hide the deep prejudices of the critics as agents of the colonial legacy or the discomfort of African critics as apologetic victims of the latter. Chinua Achebe's response to Eldred Jones on Wole Soyinka's *The Interpreters* is worth noting. Jones comments:

> This is the confrontation which *The Interpreters* presents. It is not an 'African' problem. Events all over the world have shown in the new generation a similar dissatisfaction ... Thus Soyinka, using a Nigerian setting, has portrayed a universal problem. This is what makes both this novel and the whole corpus of Soyinka's work universally valid.

And Chinua Achebe asks, with piquant sarcasm:

> For supposing 'events all over the world' have not shown 'in the new generation a similar dissatisfaction ...', would it truly be invalid for a Nigerian writer seeing dissatisfaction in his society to write about it? Am I being told, for Christ's sake, that before I write about a problem I must first verify whether they have it too in New York and London and Paris?[18]

And so on ... unless African music is 'reggaefied', unless Tatunane, a Tanzania musical group, wins some prize in Paris and their music is given 'universal' appeal through international instrumentation, arrangement, and synthesis, it is not good enough. It is not good enough that it is African; it must be international – i.e. Western. But the opposite is not the case. To be international, Western music does not have to be Africanised, although I understand the great Moscow Bolshoi Ballet is being pressured to include some 'break dance' routines into its repertory in order to appeal to American tourists and those that are resident in Moscow. No doubt all this can be easily explained as 'exigencies of the market'.

Curricula, Print Runs, and African Unity

One of the contradictions in the drive toward African unity is that the more evident the ways of promoting unity are, the less attention they are given. The dominant definition of Africa and Africans has never been the definition that Africans themselves have shaped, but the one that was shaped for them by colonialism. In that sense, the Organisation of African Unity (OAU) is a continuation of the Berlin Conference. African economies have more in common that is the outcome of the general imposition of Structural Adjustment Programmes (SAP) today than anything Africans have set up before. Highway vendors of cheap imports weaving in and out of cars in bumper-to-bumper traffic jams that I saw in Lagos ten years ago have taken over Dar es Salaam, as it begins to look more and more like Lagos: gold chains and gold rings are on every finger, the kind of ostentation that *Ujamaa* had frowned on. Expensive weddings, christening ceremonies, and prominent newspaper advertisements of funerals and death anniversaries are recent discoveries of a small minority class. These are the values that have accompanied SAP, and are to be seen everywhere one goes in structurally adjusted Africa.

One way that Africa can begin to find its own identity, which I take to be a precondition for development, is first to educate its young in the histories, geographies, and the cultures of its peoples. The answer to the question of who educates the educators must and can be found in new debates about education and development in light of the evident failure of past and present education theories and philosophies. Africa-centred education would demand curricula which ensure that students in every African region learn about other African regions. American universities make the study of Western civilisation a compulsory course for all students including those that are not American. Shouldn't a common African history course be developed for all OAU member states? Shouldn't a set of the best books in history (UNESCO's *General History of Africa*, for example) be adopted for use in such courses?

A few years ago, while investigating the possibility of setting up a SADCC (Southern African Development Co-ordination Conference) University Press, it became clear that as long as the universities in SADCC countries did not have common and compulsory courses based on a SADCC curriculum, there was very little chance of books published in one country finding markets in the other SADCC countries. For example, since students at the University of Dar es Salaam are not obliged to know anything about the geography, history, or other aspects of countries in their region, they can never feel an affinity for these countries. If, on the other hand, universities in the region offered common courses in subjects of common interest, it would be natural for authors, publishers, and book distributors to think more in terms of the region than focusing only on their own countries. Inevitably, as universities and secondary school curricula reflected interests and aspirations of the region, the closer the countries and peoples would become, and the greater the chances would be for regional unity as a precursor to unity or at least to very close co-operation on a continental scale. This is obviously focusing on a limited and narrow area. But it happens to be the most important area because it would root the countries in a common consciousness of their past as well as their future. It would redress the colonial educational legacy of Africans, who were taught everything about the 'greatness' of the colonising power – history, geography, economy, culture, and what have you – but nothing or little (itself distorted) of their own countries. The impact of common curricula for countries in the same region in at least the key subjects of history, literature, and geography (especially its environmental dimension) would not be limited to the ideological benefits. By the same token, early specialisation, with very few general culture courses, limits the breadth and depth of knowledge and the possibility of the broadest participation in politics, science, and culture that is desirable among educated citizens. In the regional context, this limits understanding and identification of each people with others in the region.

Publishing, particularly for university and tertiary levels, would benefit by the large numbers of users. At present, numbers of university students in each country are too small when disaggregated for different disciplines to provide a large enough internal market. That would change if the books were published for a region and not for a country. It is common today to see that even where books would be relevant for a region, the practice is to give them narrow titles to reflect 'nationalistic' sentiments. Multinational publishers encourage and exploit this by packaging books basically to create a multitude of markets for themselves. A book of geography for East Africa will be packaged in three books; one for Kenya, one for Tanzania, and one for Uganda – as if there were different geographies for those countries.

While recognising the limitations that are inherent in the absence of common African languages for this project, one must also recognise the potential even to deal with this question that would be made possible by regional educational integration. African regional languages would have a much better chance to develop and spread than they have in the present situation, where each country grapples with its languages or opts for the easy way out with English and French, or Portuguese and Spanish.

Major Issues of African Publishing

Inter-African Co-operation

There are a number of obstacles facing inter-African co-operation in publishing. In the preceding section, the absence of common curricula was identified as a major obstacle, especially for institutions of higher learning. There are, nevertheless, ways of circumventing the problems. One of them would be to take advantage of the differing levels of publishing in Africa – the fact that some countries (South Africa, Nigeria, Kenya, and Zimbabwe) are ahead of many other countries, both quantitatively and qualitatively. While it is inevitable and understandable that every country should seek some level of autonomy in publishing, there are many advantages to be derived from joint publishing activities. Some benefits entail sharing of print runs, licensing, adaptations, or sharing in origination costs; this is possible thanks to the existence, in some African countries, of developed publishing industries.

There have been some noteworthy achievements in inter-African co-operation in publishing – such as the establishment of the African Books Collective (ABC) in Oxford in 1989, and the African Publishers' Network (APNET) in 1992. ABC, an initiative of African publishers, has received financial support from international donor organisations, and is responsible for marketing and distributing books of member publishers in Europe and North America. It aims to return to the African publishers in hard currency proportionately more than they would obtain from conventional distributors in those countries. ABC is making a major contribution to African book publishing by making African books known to all major public libraries and by exhibiting at important conferences such as those of the African Studies Association, the American Library Association, and at book fairs in London and elsewhere. ABC has also increased African publishers' revenues from export sales to an unprecedented high.

In addition to the financial advantage, there have been other benefits of ABC's trade for member publishers. Introduction and exposure to a wide market will attract African authors, particularly those who in the past could argue that publishing in Africa limited their chances of international recognition. Having one or two sourcing centres for the continent's publishing output will make it easy for librarians and booksellers outside Africa to keep up to date with intellectual trends in Africa, thus facilitating cultural exchange. Another advantage of ABC not foreseen in the beginning is the role it has been playing in facilitating the inter-African book trade. Through such programmes as the Intra-African Book Support Scheme, books from one part of Africa are, almost for the first time, going to other parts of Africa. The irony of books from Nigeria having to go to Oxford first before they can go to Kenya, or even to nearby Ghana, cannot be missed. Still, if that is presently the only way available, there is every reason to support it. But clearly, as books from African publishers circulate in libraries in Africa, there will finally develop a desire to order books directly from publishers in Africa.

APNET was a child of the Bellagio Conference on Publishing and Development in the Third World, which was held in Bellagio, Italy in 1991. Ever since its establishment, APNET has been the focal point for African publishers and their friends to exchange ideas, make plans, and consult. The project and activities report for 1993 and 1994 shows how extensive APNET's international contacts are, along with an impressive list of activities that were accomplished during that year. Significant events to note are development of close working relations with the Association for the Development of African Education (DAE) [now the Association for the Development of Education in Africa (ADEA)] Working Group on Textbooks and Libraries, the Bellagio Group, ABC, UNESCO, the Canadian Organisation for Development through Education, and the World Bank. As a result of contacts with the DAE, a major study on the economics of textbook publishing in Africa will be undertaken involving at least eight countries. APNET receives and distributes information to members on all World Bank education and textbook projects, which will allow members to participate in international competitive bidding for supply of textbooks internationally.

APNET and Publishers Associations as Cultural Institutions
It is gratifying that APNET has been active in promoting not only trade-related activities but also others that are cultural in scope. Publication of the *African Publishing Review* in the three languages of APNET's membership – English, French, and Portuguese – opens up an important venue for publishers to exchange experiences and hopefully to develop a consciousness of themselves and their place in their societies and in Africa in general. Experiences such as the moving lecture given by Kenyan publisher Henry Chakava on 'Publishing Ngugi: The Challenge, the Risk and the Reward', which was reproduced in *African Publishing Review*[19] (reprinted in this Handbook, see p. 111), provides inspiration that is especially needed by young editors and publishers and those who think publishing lacks excitement.

One envisages publishing houses and publishing personalities competing and co-operating: writers, editors, and designers developing through publishing houses; making their debuts and their exits, staying on for years, or changing employment and changing publishers according to fortunes made and lost; or seeking ideological compatibility. One envisages critics gaining fame because their criticism has helped shape literary trends and traditions, resisting censorship and bad taste so that publishing flourishes and literature blooms. National publishers associations, writers unions, booksellers associations, and graphic artists associations are all necessary links in the field of literary culture, and an African umbrella organisation such as APNET can act as a catalyst for publishers' efforts at the national level.

Book Fairs

Closely linked to co-operation in publishing are trade fairs, which provide authors, publishers, book distributors, and librarians the opportunity to meet and establish contact, to see the productions of the antecedent period, and to learn in advance about books planned for the coming period. A number of book fairs are organised on the African continent. So far, the Zimbabwe International Book Fair (ZIBF) has established itself as Africa's premier book fair. There are other fairs, modest but with potential for growth. The annual Pan-African Children's Book Fair in May, in Nairobi, is attracting more and more exhibitors and visitors and could in time become Africa's 'Bologna'. The Cairo International Book Fair is more for the Arab region than it is for the rest of Africa, primarily because of language. Dakar, Senegal, is the venue of another successful book fair mainly for Francophone Africa.

Apart from these four international events, book weeks or book festivals are organised at the country level in Nigeria, Tanzania, Zambia, and South Africa. In the case of South Africa, which has by far the most developed publishing industry, there is no doubt that it is because of the abhorrent policy of apartheid that an international book fair was never contemplated there before. Now that apartheid has been defeated, there are no reasons to stop the organisation of a major book fair. On the other hand, because of the proximity of South Africa to Zimbabwe, and because the ZIBF has already established itself, it could be argued that a South African book fair would be an unnecessary duplication of effort in the region. However, organising book fairs, like book publishing in general, is competitive, and the venue that provides the best cost-benefit advantage will attract more exhibitors. It is in reality a question of participation cost: air fare, hotels, transport, and business potential; whether publishers can sell books through the fair and whether attendance at the fair is large enough to make rights deals possible. That, in turn, would depend on the sophistication of the markets – whether there was a large enough mainstream reading public to make translations of international bestsellers possible and profitable.

The ZIBF serves, first, the African publishers, who are able to see books produced by their counterparts in other countries. It also attracts foreign publishers (from outside Africa) with an interest in African books looking for opportunities to discover new writing.

Clearly, these are publishers that are interested not only in the big names but in the less well known, since for the big names they would not need to come to Africa. They would more likely pick up new titles from the big writers at the Frankfurt Book Fair than from ZIBF.

The role of book fairs cannot be overemphasised. Advocating the widest planning and sharing of the benefits of educational and cultural integration in Africa includes also recognising the necessity of regular venues for encountering, sharing, and reviewing efforts undertaken on a regional and continental scale. Issues already raised in respect to 'educating the educators', new directions in interpretation of historical and cultural events, as well as linking researchers, can be addressed at book fairs as well as at cultural festivals.

Copyright Issues

Most, if not all, African countries are signatories to the Berne Convention. It is evident, however, that the issues involved in copyright are not understood, even generally, by the so-called educated élite of our countries. Neither the benefits of membership in the Berne Convention nor the disadvantages of not signing have ever been seriously addressed let alone debated. Furthermore, whereas protection may be advantageous to some of the intellectual producers, it is not certain that the advantages are obvious to others. The question of an individual creator's benefit as opposed to societal benefits has not been debated enough. One would have thought that this would be of primary importance, considering the fact that in traditional African societies the practice of art was treated as belonging to the social realm rather than to the individual creator, as was also the artist's remuneration. If the issue of copyright remains problematic, it is in part because there is a lack of consensus over it.[20]

Copyright law, as it is understood by most non-specialists, aims to protect the works of authors and to ensure that they are able to enjoy financial and other advantages from the sale of their works. Copyright is presented as a norm of all 'civilised' nations, and its philosophical underpinning is supposed to be self-evident. It seems, however, that what is taken as self-evident is not in fact so self-evident. It is particularly not so when those crusading advocates of today were the bold pirates of yesterday. The United States, in particular, is a case that merits more than casual reference. For more than 100 years, the United States violated – better still, did not recognise – the then existing copyright law for all 'civilised' nations of Europe. Works, mainly from English presses, were pirated as a matter of routine, and it was not unusual for a novel to appear simultaneously in England and America, suggesting that typeset matter was actually stolen before publication. American sources recognise and admit that thanks to this practice, American publishing and printing developed rapidly. Until today, a work is not copyrighted in the United States unless within a specified period of five years it is also printed in the United States. The following quotation from an American authority on copyright says it all:

> In the 19th century, the United States – then a fledgling nation – was the biggest book pirate in the world, freely reprinting European (primarily English) works without either requesting permission or making payment. This activity was clearly piracy in the eyes of the Europeans, but it was completely legal under US copyright laws at that time. The US government chose to enable its citizens to obtain copyrighted works (and the information they contained) at low cost to encourage the growth of domestic printing and publishing industries by enabling them to produce books that were proven sellers in England, or elsewhere in Europe, without payment to copyright holders, thus greatly enhancing their chances of making a profit on their output.

Further on in the essay, this writer states that even after the Berne Convention was passed in 1886, the United States still paid no attention to it to 'avoid suppression of domestic interest that would have been involved in adhering to Berne', and also that, 'actually through a loophole in Berne, the United States was able from 1928 onwards to obtain protection of its authors under the convention without adhering to it, by publishing editions simultaneously in the United States and Canada'. When, based on the foundation that piracy provided, the US publishing industry developed and American books became popular in England, piracy was reversed and American authors and publishers were paid in kind by the victims of their past practices. At that point the United States did acquire a willingness to respect copyright.

The following observations and questions come to mind: first, it is correct that non-observance of copyright harmed US authors. Did it also harm the overall interests of literary culture, and the material interests of the larger segment of creators – publishers, printers, and booksellers? Second, if, as it appears, all countries that have made great strides in promoting reading and publishing – Japan, India, Soviet Union, China, Cuba, Korea, Taiwan, and a number of other Southeast Asian countries – passed through the same stage (some are still not quite out of it), is it wrong to conclude that copyright law is an obstacle to developing publishing and for effecting a general education revolution?

Third, Africa has been the net loser in movements of cultural treasures world-wide. Major museums in Europe and the United States were built from profits that were directly linked to slavery and colonial plunder. These museums and private collections contain more African art treasures (including heads of African chiefs chopped off and taken to Europe during the heyday of colonialism) than there are in Africa. Most of these treasures were acquired freely at best, or they were taken by threat in the violent environment of colonialism. The voices from Africa asking for the return of these objects have fallen on deaf ears. Even worse, the issue is not recognised as a subject of serious discussion prior to negotiations of modalities of total or partial return. Under these circumstances, the question must be posed: is cultural integrity a demand that only Western countries have the right to make?

Fourth, at the present time, when the copyright issue has become something of a crusade in Africa, a process of pirating of plant genetic resources from Africa and other Third World countries is going on at a furious pace. Gene banks in the United States and other countries, set up with the help of peoples of the South, are not freely accessible to the South. In other words, patents and copyrights being established on plant genetic materials that originate in areas far away from the collectors should provide that all materials are the common property of all humankind, with first right of access to the people of countries from which these plants originated.

But this will not be so, and patents, the industrial version of literary copyright, are being established on materials that do not belong exclusively to those who collect them. It was extremely generous of the Chinese, in their recent conflict with the United States over piracy of American goods, not to raise the question of Chinese treasures that were shipped out in enormous quantities to the United States from China throughout the years before liberation in 1949. But are such questions invalid because the United States will not hear them? As if that were not enough, a project in the United States has launched a campaign to

take blood, tissue and hair samples from hundreds of so-called 'endangered' and unique human communities scattered over the globe. The project is supported by the US government's National Institute of Health and linked to the multinational, multi-billion dollar initiative to map the human genetic structure known as HUGO – the Human Genome Organisation – and further ... the material itself may be patentable even without further research. Will profits be made from the genes of poor people whose physical survival is in question? Who will have access to stored genetic material, and where will these collections be located? What benefits, if any, will accrue to the indigenous peoples from whom DNA samples will be taken?[22]

Finally, fifth, with the exception of just a few individuals, African authors are very poorly remunerated, copyright notwithstanding. That is because print runs of their books are low, and prices of books are low, from the point of view of the author's income, and high from that of book buyers. Therefore, when considering support to authors, the focus must be on how to supplement authors' incomes from royalties rather than on reinforcement of copyright alone.

This essay does not suggest doing away with copyright and instituting piracy on a grand scale. It merely wishes to point out that prevailing systems of exchanges of cultural wealth and values are discriminatory when it comes to who gets what and through what means. On paper there are ways by which 'developing' countries can, theoretically, access copyrighted material for a small fee. There are also mechanisms for compulsory licensing of books. But these do not work, in practice, as they are meant to. A plan to allow a twenty- to twenty-five-year moratorium, during which countries in disadvantaged situations would have the right to reprint all the books they needed without hindrance, would be the easiest to implement. Twenty-five years also seems to be the span of time that local publishing industries take to develop their own books. Once governments decide to make education the keystone of development, the demand for books will increase tremendously. Besides, a twenty-five-year moratorium would create a much bigger market for books than ever before, and would in the long run benefit all publishers, local and international. The door would be open permanently, thereafter, for a healthy book trade in which there would be exports to and imports from both sides in a dynamic and fair market.

Admittedly, in the contemporary world copyright is more a matter of software, CD-ROM, and other electronic information storage, retrieval, and transfer technologies; books are a small part of it. This does complicate matters, no doubt, although on the other hand, Northern copyright holders should at least be able to cede rights on the less extensively used of the technologies – the book – without as much loss of income.

Publishing African Literature

In this section of the essay,[23] we discuss prospects of publishing African literature in view of the uncertainties of economics in this field of publishing. This topic will be discussed under the following headings: the general decline of publishing fiction in the decade of

1985-95; the language question; journal publishing; and women in publishing and women and publishing.

The Decline of Fiction Publishing

The UNESCO *Statistical Yearbook* is, unfortunately, unreliable as a source of correct information on subjects such as this one. This is the fault not of UNESCO, but rather of its members, who either do not report, or report incorrectly, or give false reports to justify perceived notions of success and international recognition. According to the last four editions of *African Books in Print* (1975, 1978, 1983 and 1993), the observation of a sharp decline in fiction publishing in Africa (drama and poetry included) over the last six to ten years is correct.

There are, however, regional and country differences. The decline is most acute in West Africa and to some extent in East Africa, with the demise of the East African Literature Bureau in 1977 and of the East African Publishing House in 1988. Neither the Kenya Literature Bureau nor the Eastern Africa Publications that took over activities of the defunct East African Literature Bureau in Nairobi and Arusha (Tanzania) was able to carry on publishing at the level that had been reached by the former company. East African Educational Publishers and Longhorn (ex-Longman) in Nairobi are the two publishers actively publishing fiction. In Uganda, Malawi, Zambia, and Tanzania there is very little fiction publishing. Some works of fiction by writers from some of these countries have appeared under foreign imprints – Malawian Jack Mapanje's poetry and Tiyambe Zeleza's novels, under Heinemann UK; and Tanzanian novelist Abdulrazak Gurnah's *Dottie*, *Pilgrim's Way* (Hamish Hamilton) and *Paradise* (Penguin), which was short-listed for the Booker Prize in 1994.

One country in which output has increased quite dramatically is Zimbabwe, with a number of works winning such international awards as the Commonwealth Writers' Prize, Africa Region, and the Noma Award for Publishing. However, the print runs for works of fiction are quite low, rarely ever above 2,000 copies, with some publishers printing as few as 750 to 1,000 copies.[24] Clearly, such print runs do not offer a chance for the development of national literature, which will remain bleak as long as only a few people have access to these works.

In Francophone West Africa there was a whole broadside of new fiction publishing by Nouvelles Editions Africaines (NEA) in Senegal in the early 1980s. But with the different branches of NEA now going their own separate ways, the output has dropped sharply over the last three to four years. There are also fewer literary titles coming from Céda (Centre de l'édition et diffusion africaine) in Abidjan, and virtually nothing nowadays from Édition CLE in Cameroun. A number of smaller Camerounian publishers have all gone out of business. However, a number of new autonomous publishers have recently emerged in Côte d'Ivoire and Senegal (e.g. Mical-Drehi Lorougnon's Editions du Livre Sud in Abidjan, or Aminata Sow Fall's Editions Khoudia in Dakar, with active, albeit still fairly small fiction lists – interestingly, both are women publishers). Although the publishing output of fiction has probably declined overall in English-speaking West Africa, it certainly has not stopped altogether, and there are several independent new imprints publishing creative writing (for example, Malthouse Press in Lagos or Woeli Publishing Services in Accra). Other publishers with still quite sizeable lists of African writing include Heinemann Nigeria, Spectrum Books, Fourth Dimension, Saros International, and University Press Ltd.

Support for Publishing African Literature

At the 1991 Bellagio Conference on Publishing and Development in the Third World, many recommendations on supporting African publishing were made. They covered a range of macro- and microsubjects, one of which was support for dissemination of minority literature. In the context of present realities, minority literature would rightly include all literature in African languages – because of scant production – in addition to the more conventional understanding of minority literature.

A possible model of support for this field of publishing is the buy-back model – already successfully established and in operation in Tanzania – for children's books. Integrated into library support programmes, this model would ensure that a part of the publisher's print run would be bought (guaranteeing partial or even full coverage of the printing costs) and libraries that are now mostly empty would be stocked with interesting works of fiction, produced in Africa and in African languages. The Norwegian model, where the state purchases copies of every work of fiction published in Norway for the library system, may have to be modified so as to establish selection criteria. Other support should go to publishing of translations of fiction from and into African languages as a part of international cultural exchanges.

The Language Question in African Publishing

The language question[25] in African literature – specifically the debate over whether African writers should write in their mother tongue or in national languages – is not likely to be resolved one way or another. I hope no one advocates that the debate should stop, because it is necessary. It keeps an important issue of African life alive, while accepting as given the fact that writers will continue to write in foreign languages if those are the languages they know best, or if for any other reason they are so inclined. Chinua Achebe makes the following comment on this issue:

> On language we are given equally simplistic prescriptions. Abolish the use of English! But after its abolition we remain seriously divided on what to put in its place. One proffered solution gives up Nigeria with its 200-odd languages as a bad case and travels all the way to East Africa to borrow Swahili; just as in the past a kingdom caught in a succession bind sometimes solved its problem by going to another kingdom to hire an unemployed prince![26]

The question of language is so complex that not everyone can agree on all of the issues it raises. For example, one may not agree that retaining one's own language is a basic human right. However, most people in the world share the perception that it is. Evidence of this is the passions that are evoked when there is a threat of imposition on a people of a language they do not consider their own. A policy, for example, that is unspoken in Tanzania but is there all the same would sacrifice all languages in favour of Swahili. This is an unacceptable policy that cannot be defended, precisely because no argument, no matter how dressed up – national, progressive, or revolutionary – can justify the loss of any language. Language not only serves the communication function, although that may be its most important role. Language carries with it visions of the society that speaks it; language is a corpus of knowledge, of sensibilities and identities, all of which will be lost if the language is not retained.

One crisis facing urban families consists in part of a confusion of identities when, for example, a single family can have three languages – the mother's, the father's, and a third for the whole family, with possibly an 'I only hear' from the children with regard to the languages of the parents. Language is a vehicle for acculturation, and it is safe to assume that in the urban families referred to, the children are in some ways culturally short-changed. Results of a number of studies that were carried out in Tanzania on the use of English as a medium of instruction in secondary schools show incontestably that the majority of the students cannot follow instruction in English. Therefore, they do not pass examinations that are set in English, although when translated into Swahili, they are able to give correct answers.[27] The arguments for using mother tongue/national languages at all levels of education lead one to conclude that resistance can only reflect a deep-seated rejection of the ability of African languages to instruct, in spite of the fact that nearly all production that sustains Africa, all mechanical, electrical, and other engineering occupations are accomplished by people using these languages.

In 1975, the Union of African Writers was formed in Accra. That was the decade when the language debate was at its sharpest. The Writers Union decided that Swahili should be adopted as the all-African language and, furthermore, that its future publications should not only be produced in the three European languages but also and simultaneously in Swahili.[28] Unfortunately, the Writers Union has not been very active. The output of African-language publishing has fared no better either, as *African Books in Print* shows over the last five to six years.[29] More children's books in Swahili have been published in the last five years in Tanzania alone, with more than seventy titles so far published under the Children's Book Project. If productions outside that project in Tanzania and books in Swahili from Kenya are considered, then there is no doubt that there is at least one area of publishing in an African language that is developing steadily. Outside East Africa, no one advocates publishing in Swahili; learning it, yes. In Tanzania, on the other hand, it is the only language that makes publishing possible. Swahili itself seems to be moving all over Southern Africa and winning adherents for itself rather effortlessly. It is interesting that within the ANC (the African National Congress) and PAC (the Pan Africanist Congress) in South Africa, FRELIMO (Frente de Libertação de Moçambique) in Mozambique, and SWAPO (Southwest Africa People's Organisation) in Namibia, we are told that when officials and politicians in high places want to converse in private, they use Swahili. In Malawi, the expansion of Swahili is also reported as being phenomenal.

The question of writing and publishing in African languages will surface every time discussions take place about literature and its role in culture and development. It cannot be avoided as long as the majority of the African people do not speak the foreign languages in which some authors write. Admittedly, for publishers, there is the question of economic and financial feasibility, given that the authorities in power – educationists and cultural policymakers – will do nothing or very little to support local language publishing, and publishers do not have sufficient resources to invest in an area that will take too long to become profitable. Whether the future will continue to favour the foreign languages that have also become 'African' as some people assert (Adewale Maja-Pierce), or whether the present crisis in all areas of African life will lead to a return to sources are matters that remain to be seen. Some people will work for the entrenchment of the foreign languages, and some will work for giving African languages a chance. At some point, Africa will have to decide.

Journal Publishing
One of the main problems for fiction publishing in recent years has been the decline of literary periodicals and 'little magazines'. From the mid-1960s to the late 1970s, there was a plethora of literary magazines, some of the highest quality – *Abbia*, *Asemka*, *Black Orpheus*, *Busara*, *Joliso*, *Kiabara*, *Marang*, *New Culture*, *Okike*, *Oyeame*, *Zuka*, the famous *Transition* (later *Ch'indaba*, which was a political/current affairs magazine), and many more. Although one or two have resurfaced again from time to time (e.g. *Black Orpheus* and *Transition*, the latter now published from New York but bearing little resemblance to the earlier *Transition*), they all ceased publication a long time ago.

New literary or cultural magazines launched recently are either of poor quality, or have generally not survived beyond vol. 1, no. 1. For example, the second edition, published in 1980, of *The African Book World and Press: A Directory* (ABWP), which includes extensive magazine listings, listed thirty-one active literary and cultural magazines (published outside South Africa). Although some of these journals had updated entries in the third or fourth edition of ABWP, many had become dormant, published only sporadically, or had ceased publication altogether. Today, I do not know of a single significant African literary or cultural magazine (sub-Saharan and again, excluding South Africa) that is published regularly, although there are a few recently launched magazines such as *Egerton Journal* (Kenya), *Wasi Writer* (Malawi), *Les Cahiers du CAEC* (Senegal), *Zimbabwe Women Writing*, or the *Zimbabwe Review*; but none of these is a journal of the stature of a *Black Orpheus* or *Okike*.

The demise of literary journals, which has resulted in a dearth of publishing outlets for writers in general and for young and as yet unknown or inexperienced writers in particular, has probably also led to a stifling of creative writing. Much of the early work of the now 'big' names in African literature was first published in a number of then flourishing literary magazines, but today there are fewer and fewer publishing facilities of this sort. This is, of course, a lamentable state of affairs. The demise of the journals that provided the outlets for young talent as well as opportunities for dialogue and debate has its origin in the crises in the African economies that began in the early 1980s. But that is certainly not the only reason. The problem also stems from political causes, intolerance, and the estrangement of African intellectuals from the ruling parties, individual leaders and heads of state, and government. Unfortunately, neither the ruling parties nor the leaders at the highest level, who could provide the protection and patronage, were interested in maintaining the vehicles through which debate and creative writing were carried out.

There are encouraging signs that another period of intellectual renaissance is at hand, thanks in part to the liberation of South Africa – the last part of the continent to be free – and quite honestly because things had fallen so low they can only improve now. New technologies, especially desktop publishing, are making it possible to reduce costs and to do a great deal in-house that was not possible until recently. Nevertheless, it is doubtful that a journal of the calibre of the ones pointed out above could survive in the prevailing economic situation unless it were underwritten by a committed donor or group of donors.

What has been said with respect to literary journals applies to scholarly journals as well. The publication of these journals has suffered the same fate: lack of adequate financial resources, decline of motivation for scholarly work that accompanied political and social instability, the deterioration of infrastructures of printing, and lack of foreign currency to purchase paper and spare parts for repairing the broken-down machinery. In brief, the university environment in Africa in the 1970s and 1980s deteriorated to such an extent that a general destabilisation of scholars and academics occurred and turned them into nomads within and outside the continent, leaving little room for scholarly publishing.

Scholarly journals are an important vehicle for inter-university exchanges and for keeping alive discussion and debate. Ideas are first tested and developed in scholarly journals, and the influence of ideas can be gauged in references to and citation of articles in those journals. The fact that journals take a shorter time to produce and ideally should be less expensive than books makes their influence even greater than that of books. Thanks to the development of new technologies, in particular desktop publishing and sophisticated photocopying machines, it is presently possible to produce journals fairly quickly and of acceptable quality. But those facilities alone are not enough. The most important input will be the ability of the universities to provide the necessary material conditions for academics and scholars that will enable them to pursue knowledge exclusively in an atmosphere of openness and security – something that has been missing for the last twenty years at most university campuses.

Women in Publishing and Women and Publishing

The ABC Research and Dissemination Unit has prepared a provisional listing of women in publishing and book development in Africa that shows how very small their number is relative to the number of men in the industry. Even in Nigeria, where one would have expected more women to be involved in this field, bearing in mind the intellectual muscle of that country in all fields, there are only two women who are in publishing after the regrettable death of Flora Nwapa in 1993. South Africa and Zimbabwe have the largest number of women in publishing, reflecting the relatively privileged position that women in the white section of Zimbabwean society enjoyed in pre-liberation days. In Zimbabwe, the number of black women in editorial positions of responsibility has been growing, and that is also true in other countries. In five to ten years, it is likely that the situation will change greatly in all countries in favour of women in high management positions.

Every oppressed class or gender must take the responsibility for pleading its own causes. It is imperative that women take up publishing books that will develop an ever-increasing awareness of gender issues. At the same time, one can ill afford to subscribe to the idea that a women's press should publish exclusively on gender issues. Although this might be possible where there is a large population of women with considerable purchasing power (as in the case of Kali for Women, in India), it seems unlikely that a commercially viable press that is exclusively for women is possible today in most African countries. It is, however, possible and even advisable in the first instance to specialise in publishing women's journals. This has been tried and shows great potential, although in order to survive and possibly to make a profit, one may have to compromise with those who demand light reading matter and who are not prepared for serious journals.

Conclusion

This essay has attempted to show the necessity of indigenous publishing in Africa for the development effort. In particular, it has sought to show that the colonial legacy in Africa is at the root of the problem of culture and, therefore, of development. For, whereas, 'the simple fact ... that man must eat, drink, have shelter and clothing, before he can pursue politics, science, art, religion, etc.'[30] still remains valid, in ex-colonial societies, where the vestiges of colonial culture are still very much alive, politics, art and religion cannot come after food, drink and shelter. Indeed, politics and culture may be the prerequisite to food, drink, and shelter.

Publishing in Africa has recently been enjoying support from the international donor community, particularly in the field of training. Emphasis has been on textbook publishing, reflecting the preoccupation with education and its problems. Culture and development are naturally not favourite areas of donor aid because, unlike buildings, dams, bridges and, lately, election monitoring, culture is not always visible or tangible. Besides, both in the donor countries and in the recipient countries, cultural activists tend to be marginalised by bureaucrats whose understanding of culture is 'entertainment' and for whom, therefore, culture is not a serious subject.

Systemisation of the balance between work and relaxation, reality and imagination, concreteness and fancifulness are all necessary elements for a healthy mind and body, without which there can be no perfection in any endeavour. It is for this reason that cultural publishing deserves just as much attention as educational publishing. It is also for this reason that publishing in African languages should be given first priority, so that as many people as possible may encounter the adventures of living that are found in fiction, poetry, and drama. The more that people are touched by deeply moving cultural messages, the better placed they will be to draw from those messages the necessary energies for all of life's occupations. Development is the ability to harness the energies within for tasks outside oneself.

Notes

1   Jahn, Janheinz. *Muntu: An Outline of Neo-African Culture.* London: Faber & Faber,

2   Some examples of such events are: Ile Ife, Nigeria 1972 – Publishing in the Seventies; Arusha, Tanzania, 1984 – Dag Hammarskjöld Foundation Seminar on Building Autonomous Publishing Capacities in Africa; and Bellagio, 1991 – Publishing and Development in the Third World.

3   For comments on the book sector concept, see: Amanda Buchan. 'Book Development in the Third World: The British Experience'. In *Publishing and Development in the Third World.* Ed. Philip G Altbach, London: Hans Zell Publishers, 1992, 351.

4   Bgoya, Walter. *Books and Reading in Tanzania,* no. 25. Paris: UNESCO, not dated.

5   1998 *UNESCO Yearbook.* Paris: UNESCO, 1989.

6   Rathgeber, Eva M. African Book Publishing: Lessons From the Eighties'. In Altbach, ed. 1992, 79.

7   Ibid., 87. Longman Zimbabwe is fully British-owned while College Press is 60 per cent locally owned and 40 per cent owned by Macmillan.

8   The South African situation is a special one in that it has both advanced and underdeveloped publishing industries, reflecting the effects of apartheid on publishing. New realities are in the process of emerging, but for the moment the dominant mode of publishing is through British multinationals and a few South African publishing houses.

9   Bgoya, Walter. 'Book Marketing and Distribution in Africa: Towards Creating the Missing Link in the Publishing Chain'. Introductory paper for the Bellagio Network Roundtable on Book Marketing and Distribution in Africa, Dar es Salaam, 28 November 1994.

10 For a fuller treatment of the Francophone book situation, see: Jerry Prillaman 'Books in Francophone Africa'. In Altbach, ed. 1992, 199.

11 Heinemann (Kenya) Ltd was bought out by a Kenyan investor, headed by its managing director, and the company was given a new name – East African Educational Publishers. Longmans was similarly bought out and was renamed Longhorn.

12 Gedin, Per I. 'Cultural Pride: The Necessity of Indigenous Publishing'. In Altbach, ed. 1992, 45. See also: Walter Bgoya. 'The Challenge of Publishing in Tanzania'. In Altbach, ed. 1992, 169.

13 Mbilinyi, Marjorie and Patricia Mbughuni, eds. *Education in Tanzania with a Gender Perspective.* Stockholm: Swedish International Development Authority, 1991, 2.

14 Brock-Utne, Birgit, *Whose Education for All? Recolonising the African mind?* New York: Garland, forthcoming (1999).

15 Little, Angela. 'Education and Development: Macro Relationships and Micro Cultures'. Silver Jubilee, Paper no. 4. IDS, Sussex, 1992.

16 Jahn 1961, 27-28.

17 Fanon, Frantz, *The Wretched of the Earth.* London: Penguin Books, 1978, 168.

18 Achebe, Chinua. 'The Writer and His Community'. In *Hopes and Impediments, Selected Essays.* New York: Doubleday, 1989, 96.

19 Chakava, Henry. 'Publishing Ngugi: The Challenge, the Risk and the Reward'. *African Publishing Review,* Vol. 3 no. 4, July/August 1994.

20 Tanzania, which was not a signatory, finally succumbed and signed in 1994. There was no explanation of why there had been a change of mind. In fact, to date, the change of mind has not been made known to the people. The President of PATA (Publishers Association of Tanzania) learned of the signing of the convention at a meeting overseas to which he was trying to explain the rationale for nonsigning.

21 Gleason, Paul. 'Copyright, Licensing and Piracy'. In *Guide to Book Publishing.* Datus Smith, Jr, ed. Lagos: University of Lagos Press, 1990.

22 RAFI (Rural Advancement Foundation International) Communiqué, Ottawa, May 1993.

23 I wish to gratefully acknowledge the assistance of Hans Zell in researching material in this section and that on journal publishing.

24 Rathgeber, 'African Book Publishing', 89.

25 I wish to acknowledge a stimulating and informative discussion with Professor Wamba dia Wamba, historian, University of Dar es Salaam, on this point.

26 Achebe 1989, 60.

27 Roy-Campbell, Zaline M and Martha AS Qorro. *Language Crisis in Tanzania. The Myth of English Versus Education.* Dar es Salaam: Mkuki na Nyota Publishers, 1997.

28 See: Zell, Hans. 'Interview with Dr Kole Omotoso'. *African Book Publishing Record,* Vol. 2, no. 1, 1976.

29 Communication from Hans Zell, editor, *African Book Publishing Record,* March 1995.

30 Engels, Frederick. 'Speech at Graveside of Karl Marx'. In Karl Marx and Frederick Engels, *Selected Works.* Moscow: Progress Publishers, 1975, 429.

An Autonomous African Publishing House: A Model

Henry Chakava

Introduction

What is an Autonomous Publishing House?

An autonomous institution is one which is responsible to itself, and exercises complete freedom in the control of its policies, finances and management. An autonomous indigenous African publishing house must therefore be one owned and controlled by Africans themselves, either as individuals, or as a group, or working through an independent institution; and must itself be situated in Africa.

The majority of publishing houses in Africa are not autonomous. These include the most dominant category, namely the African branches of transnational publishing corporations controlled from outside the continent, and some state publishing houses which directly or indirectly fall under control of government. At different locations and times, Africans have attempted to set up autonomous publishing houses with varying degrees of success. Many failed to become viable, in a commercial sense, and have collapsed. And a few have survived for some time – without, however, assuming the permanence or commercial resilience of their transnational competitors.

The main purpose of this study is to construct a model of a viable, autonomous, indigenous African publishing house, where viability also is seen to entail longevity and permanence. This model hopefully should assist those publishers already in business and those planning to set up business. But also important – the model visualises authentic and long-term African participation in the future of publishing in Africa. The model itself is not based on any one existing house, but I have obviously drawn on the experiences of several publishing houses over the last ten years, come of which, sadly, are no longer in business.

The Aims and Objectives of a Model Publisher

Our model publishing house should pursue the following aims and objectives:

- satisfy, at all levels, the country's educational needs;
- through its publications help in the popularisation, dissemination and preservation of the cultures and languages of the peoples of the country;
- be active in the production of children's books and adult literacy materials;
- contribute towards the entertainment needs of the country through, for example, works for fiction;
- guard its independence and not succumb to external political, financial and ideological pressures;
- endeavour to reach the widest possible market within the country, in other African countries, and the rest of the world;
- endeavour to be viable and profit-making.

In What Circumstances will the Model Work?

The model will work better in countries where a conducive publishing environment exists or can be established. Below are some of the conditions which must be satisfied, at least in part, before the model can be tested.

- *An entrepreneur:* publishing is a business and, like any other business, it needs an entrepreneur. The entrepreneur could be the publisher him- or herself or somebody who understands publishing and is, above all, committed to it, and is not just using it as a stepping stone to bigger things, such as politics, manufacturing etc. The entrepreneur should not look at publishing as a seasonal or part-time occupation, and above all, must be able to put the money together either through his or her own resources or by means of a bank loan.

- *Finance:* publishing requires considerable funding upfront. In addition to the usual recurrent overhead expenses, our publisher will need money to initiate and develop projects. A title can take up to nine months (in some cases as long as two years) from initiation to finished copies. They must therefore have sufficient funds to see through the initial period when expenditure will exceed income. I recommend a minimum capital of US $250,000 for the entrepreneur wishing to set up a publishing house.

- *Personnel:* our publishing house must be manned by fully trained and experienced personnel, skilled in all aspects of book work, and with qualifications comparable to those employed by foreign-based publishing houses. The publisher should not allow any compromising of standards and professionalism just because the operation is indigenous.

- *Superstructure and infrastructure:* our publisher's work will be easier if an adequate superstructure and infrastructure exist, and in places where these do not exist, every effort must be made to create them. The term superstructure is used here to refer to authors, readers, designers, artists and all those upon whom a publisher draws to get books developed. By infrastructure, I refer to a whole host of auxiliary industries and outlets such as paper manufactures, film and plate-makers, printers, booksellers, etc.

These points recur towards the end of this paper, when I discuss obstacles which hinder the autonomous publisher, and African publishing in general.

The Model Itself

First Principles

- *Offices* choose modest offices in modest surroundings. Remember that in Africa, publishing is still a small business.

- *Staff:* you can open business with a minimum of five staff – yourself, a secretary, an editor, a salesperson and an office helper.

- *Publishing programme:* your publishing programme must be carefully planned. It is important to achieve a balanced mix of short-term, mid-term and long-term projects. I would recommend starting with short-term and long-term projects, by which I mean low-risk books which attract modest investment and are faster to produce. Examples are revision books, students' guides, examination crammers, etc.

- *Recommended subject areas:* in respect to the aims and objectives stated above, you need to identify priority publishing areas which are comparatively less risky. I recommended starting with books at the primary and secondary school level. First produce the supplementary books mentioned above and then, as your publishing expands, you can venture into longer-term investment projects such as textbooks. These require more money upfront, have a longer gestation period and carry greater risks, but they produce attractive profits when you break through.

- *Launching into the market:* launch into the market with at least five titles (preferably ten) so as to make an impact, establish credibility, create a favourable image, and make your sales staff cost-effective.

- *Plan your growth:* do not be over-ambitious by going for every book and every author who comes your way. There may be some virtue in being the largest or the fastest-growing publisher but it also has its shocks, strains and stresses. Once you have a workforce of 30-40 people and are publishing 30-40 titles a year, and have a turnover of around US$2 million, I would advise you to slow down, consolidate your business and increase its profitability to 15 per cent or more, before making plans for further expansion.

- *Distribution:* I would recommend that in the early stages of your business, you distribute your books through an agent or agents, so that you can devote more time to the most important departments in a publishing house: editorial and sales. Only when commission to the distribution agent(s) has fallen to 10 per cent of turnover or below, should you consider setting up your own distribution department or company.

Some Hard and Fast Rules

Readers fees: you will need to develop a corpus of readers in key areas to assess the manuscripts you receive, and to advise you on your various projects. Avoid giving out each and every manuscript you receive to readers, and do not purchase manuscripts outright, however good you may think they are. Keep your readers fees at very modest levels – i.e. pay a token of appreciation rather than a commercial fee. An average of US$30 per manuscript is recommended.

Authors' advance: this should be kept fairly modest, and should be paid only when a larger part of the manuscript is complete. Avoid paying out money on commission, and do not offer an advance for every book or every idea you come across.

Contracts: these should be prepared and signed only when the complete manuscript has been delivered. Negotiate royalty terms of around 10 per cent of published price or 12½ per cent of receipts, or thereabouts. Total advance payable should be in the region of one-third of the anticipated total royalty earnings for the first printing, and should certainly not exceed 50 per cent. High royalty percentages, though attractive on paper, are counter-productive both to the publisher and the author.

Production: you should ensure that books are produced as fast as possible, preferably within twelve months (latest) from delivery of complete manuscript. Shop around for the best printing prices in the market, and strive to obtain at least 60-90 days credit from the printer. You should avoid the temptation of doing your own typesetting or buying your own paper etc., but if you have to do it, wait until much later when you are more established and more profitable.

Print runs: avoid the temptation of printing too many copies in order to get a good unit price. In these days of tight money controls, high interest rates and inflation, I recommend printing only the number of copies you can sell within 12 months.

Pricing: you should price your books in such a way that you achieve a margin of well over 50 per cent; 55 per cent is recommended. Avoid soliciting subsidies to overcome your pricing problems.

Credit terms to booksellers and other retailers: I suggest 25 per cent discount on school books and 35 per cent on general books and a maximum credit period of 60-90 days. If there are not enough bookshops and other distribution outlets in your territory, I personally recommend supplying direct to institutions (for cash) in areas where bookshops do not exist, or through other distribution channels such as grocery stores, etc. I would not recommend sending books out on consignment as this could lead to much loss and wastage. Very strict credit control must be maintained and supplies to those customers who do not pay on time should be stopped at once.

Overheads: make sure that these are contained to within 35 per cent of revenue or less. You should be prepared to take drastic measures, such as cutting down on staff or moving to smaller premises, in order to maintain your overheads at this level.

Cash-flow: in the initial stages your expenditure will exceed revenue, for reasons inherent in the previous points. But you should aim to reverse this trend in the first two to three years. After that you should ensure that your cash-flow is positive, rather than negative, at all times. Take immediate remedial action, such as cutting down on new projects or reducing print runs, in addition to the suggestions given above (see *Overheads* above), if you find yourself in a negative cash-flow situation.

Net profit: aim at a profit before tax upwards of 15 per cent.

Return on capital: aim at a return on capital upwards of 25 per cent.

Success or failure will depend largely on management capability. Careful planning, proper decision-making, a knack for knowing what will sell, judicious employment of funds, close supervision and strict adherence to the controls mentioned above, are essential. Above all, you must remain committed to publishing and determined to make a success of it.

Corporate Image

Publishing is a vital and high-profile industry. You should make it a priority to develop a proper *modus operandi* and a favourable corporate image.

Staff: everything must be done to recruit, train and retain staff of integrity on terms comparable to those offered by foreign publishers and to motivate them so that they are totally committed and reflect a favourable image for the company at all times.

Government: you will need to establish a good working relationship with government. Indeed, you will undoubtedly discover that most people in government know little or nothing about publishing. It will be your duty to educate them about your role as a person of business and an educator. All transactions with government must be at arm's length, and you should steer clear of any corrupt practices. You must seek government protection from unfair competition but should not expect any favours just because you are indigenous.

Public: you will build a good public image for yourself if you publish good books in good time, pay authors' royalties and answer letters promptly, and speed up assessments of manuscripts to within 8-12 weeks of submission. Constant mailings, catalogues and stocklists (which must be updated every year) will keep the reading public continually aware of what you are doing.

Press: as the public are more likely to hear about you and your books in the press than any other way, you need to cement your relationships with newspapers and magazines. It is too expensive to advertise effectively in papers but do maintain a good personal relationship by giving out review copies, press releases, feature articles, etc., and take advantage of whatever features on publishing they themselves set up.

Other publishers: although you are competing for the same market, you would be well advised to maintain a good working relationship with your colleagues in the industry, regardless of whether they work for local or foreign firms. There has been undue emphasis on competition between local and foreign publishers. I believe there is much scope for both kinds of publisher, and room for a mutually beneficial relationship at this stage of development in Africa's publishing industry. Both are involved in developing books and courses in largely unexplored fields and are encountering similar problems, and so can benefit from each other's experiences. Join the Publisher's Association where it exists, and try to set up one if it does not. It will be your mouthpiece in dealing with government and public. Support other book-related industries. Do not import anything you can obtain locally. There are cases of publishers who print abroad when they have a viable printing industry at home, or import paper instead of supporting their own paper mill. Support the booksellers as much as possible while seeking alternative ways of widening the book distribution network in your territory.

International agencies: make yourself known and heard outside your own territory. Pursue joint publication deals with international publishers. Establish links with international agencies such as CREPLA, UNESCO, IPA, etc., and make them aware of your activities. Supply information promptly to such institutions as may be required from time to time. If you can afford it, go to book fairs (Frankfurt, Bologna, Ife, Zimbabwe, etc.) and display your publications there. You may be surprised to discover that international publishers want to buy rights on some of your titles. Also look out for opportunities to buy rights from international publishers for titles which might have potential in your market. Some may approach you to represent them, or distribute their books in your territory. If their list complements your own, you might find them a source of additional revenue, but always remember that you are a publisher in your own right and not somebody else's distributor.

Obstacles

The following obstacles may well occur:

Manpower: there are few people in Africa with the relevant skills in book production. Trained editors, book designers and illustrators are rare and few training facilities exist. The small number of people with the necessary training have been trained by and work for the transnationals.

Finance: publishing is a small, risky and capital-intensive venture. For these reasons, it does not always receive priority from banks and other money lending institutions when it comes to borrowing. The long gestation period before a manuscript becomes a book and before the book can become profitable calls for a long-term loan with a two- or three-year grace period, a prospect which would-be financiers are usually reluctant to accept.

Competition: indigenous publishers find themselves up against competition from the more established transnational publishing firms, some of which operate branches in Africa and have a strong grip in the market. African governments should protect and strengthen African publishing houses and at the same time assist their nationals to gain control of the African branches of the transnationals operating in their territory.

In addition to the above, our African publisher will face certain problems encountered by all other publishers in the continent. These include:

Ignorance: most people, including civil servants and politicians in high positions, do not understand what publishing is about. They are therefore less sympathetic to publishers' problems, and less appreciative of their important role in national development.

Illiteracy: approximately 65 per cent of the continent is illiterate. And 20 per cent have a fairly basic education, with the ever-present danger of lapsing back into illiteracy. The publisher in Africa publishes for only about 20 per cent of the population.

Language: Africa is reported to have well over 1,200 languages in use. Out of these only about 600 have been transcribed. This means that many Africans do not have access to materials written in their own languages. Moreover, speakers of most of the languages already transcribed, including those brought by colonialism, constitute a minority in any one African country. Therefore a decision to publish in any language, be it local or foreign, in most cases cuts out the majority of potential readers in that country.

Reading habits: a reading culture has not yet fully developed in Africa. Few people voluntarily read books and most stop reading at the end of their formal education. The potential market is thus further depressed.

Censorship: some publishers in Africa are victims of state censorship and others censor themselves by not publishing books which ought to be published because of fear of falling foul of the government in power.

Poverty: most people are struggling for the bare necessities of life, and regard books as an unnecessary luxury.

Some Concluding Remarks

In this paper, emphasis has been given to autonomy from foreign control and influence. It must however be recognised that our model publisher will not be free to do whatever he likes; his board, his shareholders and financiers will be there to ensure that his freedom is exercised within limits.

It must also be stressed that the model presented here is not the only way to successfully launch onto the African publishing scene. It is offered not as gospel, but as one possible way of approaching it.

The model was prepared as a working document and can therefore be modified in places or even changed to suit existing situations in the country where it may be tested. Whatever its limitations, it will have achieved its purpose if it stimulates further thoughts and actions towards a strategy for the development of autonomous publishing houses in Africa.

African Publishers – 'Mostly Liars and Cheats'?

Hans M Zell

A few years ago the Nigerian writer Onwuchekwa Jemie, writing in the respected *Guardian* (Lagos) newspaper, lumped all publishers together as 'mostly liars and cheats' (Jemie 1987) and since that time I've frequently come across a variety of other unflattering statements by African writers critical of their publishers, calling them 'incompetent', 'crooks', or the well-worn author pronouncement 'my publisher is hopeless'. African writers generally do not seem to hold their publishers in high esteem; for many their expectations have not been fulfilled, and others feel they have been let down by sometimes unacceptably poor production quality of their books. There has also been a chorus of critical voices telling African publishers what they ought to be doing, and how they should rise to the challenges and the opportunities of the African book industries.

Statements by authors about the failings of their publishers – whether in Africa or elsewhere – must always be taken with a good dose of scepticism. There are publishers in Africa as good as anywhere else – highly professional, committed, innovative, and impeccable in their dealings with authors. But it is unfortunately also the case that there are a good number of African publishers that have a great deal to answer for. Some would appear to be rather short on integrity, transparency, or accountability. Others, whilst not lacking in integrity or honourable intentions, are inefficient or unbusinesslike when it comes to royalty accounting; and when they supply royalty accounts the statements may be bewildering or incomprehensible, making it difficult for authors to decipher exactly how his or her book has been doing, how many copies were printed, how many review and gratis copies have gone out, and how many copies remain in the warehouse.

On the promotion front, some publishers' marketing is perfunctory at best, and there is also the failure of some African publishers to bring their books to the attention of a book-buying public not only at home, but to a world-wide audience. And whilst some of these strictures may apply outside Africa, it has to be recognised that African publishers with these failings are likely to damage the standing of some their colleagues, the good publishers. It probably also contributes to the fact that there are still too many African writers and scholars who continue to publish outside Africa, or place their work with some of the multinationals.

Having said this, it does frequently strike me that although the end product of the publishing process – the book – is generally understood, publishing itself hardly ever is, least of all by writers. We also hear much from authors about publishers who sit on their manuscripts sometimes for years before publication; but how much do we hear from publishers of the other side of the coin: authors who repeatedly fail to meet promised deadlines? Publishers have rights too! So there is an urgent need to bring together African writers and publishers, and start a dialogue to foster a better understanding of the publishing process and how publishers work, and which might then lead to improved author–publisher relationships.

As I see it, the conflict areas – or the potential conflict areas – are roughly these:

1 Many African authors (whether they are novelists, poets or academics) fail to have a proper grasp of the nature of publishing. Some are quite ignorant of the publishing process, and others find it difficult to understand that if their work is turned down the publishers cannot be expected to provide them with detailed suggestions on how to improve or rewrite their manuscript, or, better still, find them another publisher!

2 African authors often accuse their publishers of secrecy, not willing to reveal hard figures, and not being open enough in their relations – though, again, this is a common accusation made by authors all over the world.

3 African writers have complained that publishers are extremely slow in rendering royalty statements, and even slower to part with cash. Moreover, they believe they are getting a raw deal, that publishers are exploitive and that their royalty terms should be much higher; while others suspect that they are being cheated out of their royalties altogether and that publishers deliberately under-declare sales, although 'thousands of copies have been sold'! Another strong bone of contention nowadays is that publishers frequently pay royalties on the basis of net receipts, rather than on the published price of a book, and some authors feel they are up against an unfair and tight-fisted commercial system.

4 On the marketing side statements such as 'my publisher never does anything to sell my book', or 'their promotion is absolutely hopeless' will have a ring of *déjà vu* to many African publishers. Authors often have quite unrealistic expectations of sales, or the publicity and marketing expenditures that can be earmarked for their book.

5 Then there are, finally, the recent fairly dramatic changes in the book industry, perhaps not so acute as yet in Africa, but certainly in the North, where publishing is now heavily dominated by a number of huge publishing conglomerates. Whereas, happily, there are still a number of small independent publishers who continue to put a high premium on fostering good relations with their authors, publishers or imprints which are part of a larger publishing group are now working in an environment which is generally not very author-friendly. Unlike the days when, for example, the Heinemann African Writers Series was developed with a great deal of commitment and enthusiasm by the management and editors of Heinemann at that time – when promising writers were looked after with tender loving care, or were nurtured along and given encouragement even if their first manuscript was turned down – we are now, unfortunately, operating in a rather different publishing climate. Looking back on the development of the series, the late Alan Hill, former Chairman of Heinemann, said in 1990:

> You have to remember that we were not dominated by money-grabbing ideology in those days. Publishing has changed a lot since then, and I don't really care for the accountancy-ridden profit-making of present-day publishing firms which are now in the grip of big corporations who are only interested in the profits which the products make. (Hill 1990)

It is true that we are now certainly working in a much harsher publishing environment, which is largely ruled by corporate accountants and corporate strategists, rather than book people. As anyone who has worked as part of or within a big publishing conglomerate knows, the chief executives of such organisations are interested in product development; they are interested primarily in the mechanics of getting books from point A to B, or from the printer to the warehouse, and process the orders, etc. They show little interest in the human factor of publishing and author relations, and have no grasp of how books and authors have to be nursed and cajoled along until they finally deliver a manuscript. Unfortunately, and whether we like it or not, it must also be said that these 'money-grabbing' publishers are perfectly entitled to dictate their publishing strategies and make changes in policies; and they will rightly claim that if a company is to survive and prosper one must be able to adjust to difficult or changed market conditions.

Frustrated by all this, authors have sometimes set up shop as their own publisher, or groups of intellectuals or writers' associations concluded that they could do rather better by establishing their own publishing company. There have been a number of initiatives of this nature (and not only in Africa), but lacking the right sort of professional skills and sound business and financial management, such co-operative ventures have been generally short-lived, if in fact they took off in the first place.

It is therefore high time for African publishers and authors to come together to start a dialogue, thrash out the issues, and address the situation frankly. Whereas to some extent the issue of protection of authors' rights has already been discussed at the APNET-sponsored first 'African Rights Indaba' held during the 1994 Zimbabwe International Book Fair, there is rather more to it than the rights issue. For example:

- Publishers should be asked to talk about the whole publishing process, and explain that a publisher is not, as some authors would have it merely the person who arranges and pays the printer and then sells the book. Aspects of publishing which should be explained include procedures for evaluating manuscript submissions and the decision to publish; acquisition and commissioning procedures; a publisher's editorial responsibilities; how publishers prepare costings, financial analyses and publishing viability calculations; and there should be discussions on author contracts and fair remuneration. On the promotion and marketing side African publishers might provide practical examples of step-by-step procedures, promotional plans, and marketing budgets setting out the amount of time and resources they are prepared to invest in marketing, and what they hope to get out of it. They, and perhaps some of their publishing colleagues from other parts of the world, could also talk about the publishing realities, how they are coping with difficult market and trading conditions, and might provide examples of sales projections versus actual sales for certain books on their list – their successes and their failures.

- Authors should be asked to explain what they need and expect from a publisher by way of support, and what they feel publishers in general do not understand about the author's legitimate role in the publishing process. They could talk freely about their relationship and past experience with publishers, and about their not unreasonable expectations that their financial relationship with a publisher should be properly, efficiently and honestly handled. And at the same time they could learn a bit more about the finer points in the book publishing business, and that the mathematics of publishing is not always as simple as some authors believe it to be.

It can probably be predicted fairly safely that such a meeting would lead to some rather heated exchanges between authors and publishers! However, it need not be confrontational, and the overall aim of such a conference or workshop should be to facilitate not only a better understanding of the publishing process – and indeed to 'demystify' it – but to establish a spirit of mutual confidence. It would not only be the authors who would come to learn – publishers would learn that protecting authors' interests, and openness with authors, will pay dividends in the long term, and will lead to much improved relationships and author loyalty. Moreover, in order to strengthen author–publisher relationships the meeting might wish to draw up guidelines (perhaps under the umbrella of APNET) for a Code of Practice between African authors and African publishers, draft model contracts and model royalty statements; or initiate other measures that might lead to a more constructive and co-operative relationship between authors and their publishers.

References

Jemie, Onwuchekwa. 'Book Pirates of Nigeria, Awake'. *The Guardian* (Lagos), 25 January 1987, 7.

'Working with Chinua Achebe. The African Writers Series. James Currey, Alan Hill and Keith Sambrook in Conversation with Kirsten Holst Petersen'. *Kunapipi*, Vol. 12, no. 2, 1990, 157.

Before Your Text Goes into a State of Permanence

Dapo Adeniyi

While there have been many changes in African societies during the past decade, the lot of budding and unpublished authors has remained much the same. This is confirmed by many recent experiences in different parts of the continent. In most places I hear the same old complaints, sometimes from myself, as I have added my own voice to claim solidarity with cliques of aspiring writers seeking redress from our 'enemies': the publisher and his or her editors.

Still fresh in the mind is the scene played out in Harare during 1996 on one of the floors of the massive hotel which housed many of those participating in the Zimbabwean Book Fair. One of the very bright ideas of the organisers of the Fair was to bring together editors, publishers, published and unpublished authors at the forum. All fared well until the floor was declared open to the intending authors, when one angry author-in-waiting appropriated the microphone, sacked the moderator and, one by one, called on his fellows to mark guilty publishers in the audience, leaving them with no alternative but to shield themselves with their upheld briefcases!

When the forum broke up, the participants continued the debates begun – there were raucous gatherings in the lobbies and in the bar. As I passed by one of the groups, I heard a fellow journal editor replying to the questions of the writers who had surrounded him. He said: 'What most writers never once stop to see is that it may not be the fault of the publisher at all if he hands out a rejection slip.'

The words did not merely summarise my own response to the vexed question about the snubbing of 'unknown authors' by publishers, they also brought back what I was in a better position than ever before to see: our own insufficient contact with the realities of writer–publisher relations. When we were young and enthusiastic, we writers knew little or nothing about publishing. All over the world writers begin their careers full of fervour and boiling with enthusiasm – and there is nothing wrong with that. Indeed, it requires nothing less to launch a writing career in the face of the hard labour that authorship requires, and of the need to win the confidence of a publisher.

I feel that the confrontation between the suspicious, angst-ridden authors on the one hand, and, on the other, the attitude of the in-house editors charged with dispensing 'racy', often pre-prepared rejection hand-outs, are the products of the difference of perspective. Editors need to be increasingly aware of the sweat and groans behind even the most mediocre of manuscripts, and they should not only give each arriving manuscript a 'fair hearing' but also correspond with the authors in a manner that will preserve their spirit and their self-confidence. Negative attitudes are a major cause of the complaints of many young writers. From their point of view, rejection is a deliberate offence, if not a personal affront! However, those who have been editors will testify that there are factors producing the rejection slip over which the editor/publisher has very little control.

First of all, the average African editor is overworked and, as such, usually has to combine what in other places might have been the labour of two or three expert hands. There are cases where editors are publishers, typists, mail-runners, and sometimes even press super-visors and marketing overseers. They are not helped by the fact that more than three-quarters of scripts arriving will not meet the standard required for publication. Many texts are submitted in longhand, some may be the only copies of novels.

Then the average new writer submitting material to a publisher rarely anticipates that the newly completed work may not reach the standard required for publication. In my experiences as the arts/ reviews editor of a newspaper and as a journal editor, I have found my patience tested by what I considered the unfounded confidence of many a new writer. One such novice, a personal friend, approached me recently with the typescript of his voluminous new novel, his very first effort, and asked me to help him go through it. Of course, he did not intend to take notice of anything I said for he was already – in the same breath – outlining his elaborate plans for launching the book on a national scale. He was, in fact, putting aside money to finance the publication himself should any publisher stand in the way! Faced with his boundless joy and zeal over his creative exploit, I could not bring myself to tell him the brutal truth: his work was unfit for publication, even if he was going to publish himself.

It helps a great deal if new writers understand from the very beginning that the publisher is not in business to publish everything that people submit. Publishers have to make decisions, bearing in mind the judgement of those they have asked to assess the typescript; they have to accept only those scripts they consider suitable and marketable. However, decisions will go in favour of the unknown author if the publisher is convinced that the prospects are good. Often the success of a publishing concern is directly proportional to the number of new writers, unrecognised talents that they are able to identify as virgin talent, for that means a virgin marketing possibility. Thus, while publishers may be anxious to bring out the work of a household name whose career was launched by another company, they are prouder of the new talents that they themselves have discovered and promoted into the bestseller list.

'Rejected authors' can comfort themselves with the knowledge that publishers' readers are not always right. The manuscript that is rejected by one publisher may somehow get to a second review by the next publisher, who may decide to publish with happy results. One out of, I imagine, many cases: William Golding's publisher, Faber & Faber, reports in a study written after Golding's death that the manuscript of his classic *Lord of the Flies* was accepted only after one of the editors peeled off the rejection note already attached to the script and ready for despatch, and gave the text a second glance.

This brings me to the main piece of advice that I have to share with young African writers: every newly produced text needs time to grow so you should not rush it to the press. From experience and personal observation, I think that writers are nearly always in a rush. The newest writer has, understandably enough, publication as an immediate goal. Why do I think literary works should be allowed to grow? First, because of the nature of the printed word: every word committed to the page in print becomes totally irretrievable and permanent. I have observed that in many cases the publisher's rejection, when received in good faith, becomes a real blessing to the work. (We already assume that every writer knows that the rejection slip does not by any means suggest that the manuscript has no future. Even if the accompanying dread note from the editor conveys this meaning, it is definitely not true!)

Many great works in the canon of modern African writing existed in different versions for years before they were eventually published. In some cases, it was the decision of the writers, who were already established authors, to defer publication. This is a trend I strongly recommend to young authors.

The material should be delayed before being moved into a permanent state: it benefits from creative reconsideration and re-examination. It should not be published until the writer achieves a reasonable stylistic stability – by which I mean until there has been a sharpening of the basic facility with language and the development of an individual style in which work can be written with confidence. In the course of undertaking this process, the writer will grow in confidence about the future of the work as an artistic creation. I would stress that in almost all cases good work finds an outlet – this is the area I want to explore before concluding.

I wrote the foregoing in the firm belief that publishing is not, and has no reason to be, the only or immediate avenue open to a young writer anxious for self-expression. And this is where the various artistic groups and writers' associations have important roles to play. A new poem for instance, a short story or an extract from a longer one, may be read to a few literary friends. Usually you will be able to see the impact it has on them even if, as is sometimes the case, they are, like me, somewhat cowardly about expressing honest opinions. More formal readings have become an important part of the monthly programmes of the state wings of the Association of Nigerian Authors, and are noted for a greater degree of honesty and frankness. Then there are the newsletters and bulletins of the same groups, in which young writers may 'post' extracts from an extended work. In a few cases, writers may not feel the need for feedback, but exposure at a meeting or in a newsletter stamps out the frustration of not being able to communicate through publication.

In Nigeria, and in a number of other African countries, newspapers and weekly magazines are committing an increasing number of their pages to culture and the arts; many accept poetry, fiction, even extracts from plays. There is usually an insistence on high standards – and it costs no more than the price of a postage stamp to make an attempt.

All in all, I find most attractive the comments of peers to whom work in progress can be read, especially if the colleagues are constructively critical and have the courage to be frank. An extract from a play in preparation may be tried out with a few from such a close circle of friends and presented as a rehearsed reading at the next literary meeting. You may have observed that many affectionate critics of certain African writers are actually their peers, and were members of artistic groups to which the first versions of early works were read. These critics have watched the metamorphosis of writer and work, taken pride in the achievement of their contemporary, and become critically committed!

The case that I have been trying to put is that the phase marked by problems with publication is a useful weaning period for a young writer. It is – I have to say this – a testing period during which many of those who embark with enthusiasm on a writing career have to reconsider their vocation, and decide whether they can make careers as writers or whether their abilities are best traded elsewhere. If we have been tested, and if we are solidly convinced that we have careers as writers in store for us then nobody will easily put us down.

I would like to share, in conclusion, what for me has been the shocking discovery I have made since the inception of *Glendora Review* – a discovery that ought, strangely, to be a real encouragement to emergent generations of African writers. As I fought and foraged from country to country for reviews and creative writing to include in the journal, I realised that talent does not abound as much as we had thought. And there is invariably a grave tardiness to deliver, even on the part of those – established or emerging – from whom contributions are solicited.

In 'A letter to the Editor' published in *Glendora Review*, Ulli Beier, founding editor of the pioneer African literary journal, *Black Orpheus*, responded to issues arising from an article on publishing African cultural journals featured in an earlier number of *Glendora Review*. He pointed out that queries to editors of journals about their ability to meet specific expectations had to take into account the many constraints governing the production of periodicals, particularly in Africa. For example, the editor of a publication committed to a specific geographical or cultural region may be very conscious of the need to balance representations from the various subregions within the entity. However, if material is not readily obtainable and if solicited articles are not delivered, editors are completely helpless (*Glendora Review* Vol. 1, no. 4).

Worse for *Glendora Review* has been our commitment from the start to new voices, artists, writers and journalists – a policy we have pursued without shutting out the more established voices. We had no way of knowing that we would be coming up against an additional, crippling difficulty which was has contributed to the late appearance of issues so far. This has happened despite commissioning articles well ahead of time, ensuring that writers had more than a reasonable amount of time to do the work. It has turned out that the more time allowed before a piece of work was required, the more likely it was to be forgotten about altogether! In the case of book reviews (which first made their way into the publication and then found space in a companion publication), titles sent to reviewers – after first obtaining a commitment – either made one final retirement onto the book-shelves, never to dismount; or else they embarked on an endless flight between the hands of different borrowers! One of the ways in which we sought to get around this problem was to adapt speeches and unpublished research articles by writers and scholars who had been employed with older and better established journals. These included the *London Review of Books*, with whose editor, Jeremy Harding, I was able to compare notes on a visit to the United Kingdom. *Matatu*, the African literature journal based in Frankfurt, faces the same problems and has the additional disadvantage of being an academic journal. The editor had to obtain responses from editorial board members and referees to articles submitted. It seems that we are all forced to rely on the same small circle of faithful contributors and writers. This, it was comforting to see, is a universal problem – haunting even the *Times Literary Supplement*.

To recognise as universal any single difficulty or experience is always reassuring. It is true of editors and of writers, and we must all find ways to forge ahead nonetheless. If the problems are impossible to dispense with, we must triumph in spite of them. Their existence reinforces my confidence in the conviction that for every original piece of writing doused in genuine sweat, there is an outlet – even if sometimes it takes a while to find. And African publishers are as anxious to publish talented writers as new writers are forever foraging for openings to the list of the favoured which lies on the desks of African editors.

Notes of a Reluctant Publisher

Ken Saro-Wiwa

My introduction to the publishing industry started early, at fourteen, in the Government College, Umuahia in Nigeria. Three of five mornings in the week, I was allowed to stay away from the morning's manual labour and general cleaning in order to devote myself to my assignment as scribe of the Fisher House Magazine, *The Pioneer*.

The five houses of Government College Umuahia at that time each produced a termly magazine – a single copy magazine, handwritten in a big thick-cover exercise book. The magazine had an editorial board complete with editor, sub-editors, artists and a scribe who had to be a boy in Class 2 who wrote a legible or beautiful hand. I was fortunate to be chosen from among the ten boys in my class in Fisher House in September 1955. For one, it was easier to write in the comfort of the House Common Room than to tend flowers or cut grass. For another, I did not really have to get down to work until the editor and sub-editors had chosen and edited all the material that was to be published. This afforded me time to read or study.

Being scribe of *The Pioneer* meant that I had to read all the short stories, essays, jokes and poems which formed the text of the magazine before transcribing them extremely carefully into the magazine proper. Since neatness and accuracy were of utmost importance in my task, I had begun to receive my first lessons in proof-reading. More often, I developed a familiarity with the various literary genres, except the novel.

In the course of my seven years at Umuahia, I became editor of *The Pioneer* and sat on the editorial board of the termly school magazine, *The Umuahian* which was printed. I received further training in publishing when I became editor of the school weekly, *The Umuahia Times*, which was handwritten! Some weeks, there was such a paucity of material turned in by contributors that I had to write everything in the magazine myself!

Copies of *The Pioneer* and *The Umuahia Times* are [not] extant but copies of *The Umuahian* are still available. Looking at them now, I still think we did quite well as editors/publishers.

When I went to the University of Ibadan in 1962, I was thus already versed in the intricacies of magazine publication. I became editor of *The Mellanbite*, the annual magazine of Mellanby Hall, and of *The Horizon*, the magazine of the English Department. I undertook not only editorial but also publishing responsibilities in both magazines.

At Umuahia, money was not a problem. The house magazine did not require much money. What money was needed to buy the notebook, ink, pens and eraser was provided by the Housemaster. The School bore responsibility for *The Umuahian* and *The Umuahia Times* needed only foolscap paper which I provided. But at Ibadan, money had begun to matter. Somehow, I managed to publish both magazines with the help of the Hall Master or of the Head of Department of English.

I did not give any thought to publishing thereafter – for another twenty years. In 1971, I did mastermind, as Commissioner for Information and Home Affairs in Rivers State, the publication of the government newspaper *Nigerian Tide*. But I minded only the policy aspects thereof; I was not a part of the management nor did I feel the pains of publishing it.

The itch to publish began when, in 1984 or thereabouts, I read an extended essay on the poetry of the Nigerian Civil War written by a young academic, Dr Funsho Aiyejina, of the University of Ife. The essay made no mention of the poems I had written on the war which were published in *Black Orpheus* and elsewhere. I decided then that I would have to publish a collection of my poems.

I made contact with Longman in Lagos who had published two of my children's books in 1973. A young editor there told me that the house might not be willing to publish a collection of poetry. Short stories and plays were also not very popular with publishers but novels might receive more welcome attention. I did not bother to leave my poems behind.

Going back to my student publishing experience, I sent off the poems to a critical friend and asked him to assess them for me. When he was done, I contacted another friend, an artist, and suggested a cover. I got an ISBN (International Standard Book Number) from the National Library, and was soon on my way to establishing Saros International Publishers.

I was, at that time, a frequent visitor to the United Kingdom and decided to have my *magnum opus* printed there by a very famous printing firm. I obtained a quotation from them but understood nothing about the quote, beyond the figures. I accepted the figures, sent off the manuscript (or typescript, if you will) and soon had my poetry collection, *Songs in a Time of War*, behind covers. The mistakes I made publishing that title are a trade secret. The mores of the industry stop me from telling about them!

Preparing *Songs in a Time of War* for publication reminded me of the many manuscripts which I had shoved into my cupboard in 1973 when I decided to embark on a business career to help me take care of the problems of day-to-day living. There were the novel, *Sozaboy*, a couple of plays, short stories and a diary of the Civil War. They were at various stages of completion. It seemed right to get them off my chest, so to speak.

I had done all that I cared to do as a trader and the Nigerian economy was headed for disaster. I decided that it was time to return to my first love: writing. So out came all the manuscripts and, before long, *Sozaboy* was on its way to my publishers, Longman. I waited a year but the assessors' reports were yet to arrive at the publishers. And that proved to be still another step to a decision on self-publishing. If I had to wait that long for reports and decisions, many of the manuscripts I had in my drawer might never see the light of day. One way out, I thought, might be to publish them myself.

I was not unaware of the disdain which is normally cast on self-publishing. But I was willing to take the risk. However, in doing so, I decided that I would not adopt any shortcuts whatsoever.

My bafflement over the printer's quotations for *Songs in a Time of War* remained a powerful reminder that I knew little of book publishing. A few phone calls around London pointed me to Book House Trust and the numerous courses the Trust organise annually for all those in the publishing industry. Before long I found myself, and embarrassingly so, the oldest student in a number of short publishing courses. After three or four of such courses, I knew enough to put me on the painful path of book publishing. By the time I did the last courses in 1986, the novel, *Sozaboy* and the collection of short stories *A Forest of Flowers* had been published. Again, the mistakes I made in publishing both books are a trade secret and will remain so in the interest of the industry. But the fact that *Sozaboy* won an Honourable Mention in the Noma Award for Publishing in Africa competition in 1987, and *A Forest of Flowers* was short-listed for the Commonwealth Writers' Prize in the same year, showed that I was not mistaken in deciding to publish the books.

The courses I attended also demonstrated that publishing is largely a marketing operation, which a lover of books and culture with trading skills, money and bravado could undertake. I stuck to my decision to self-publish knowing full well that fiction, which was my only interest, was probably the most unrewarding, financially speaking, of a publishing operation.

One other reason I stuck to my obtuse decision was the lack of interest shown by UK publishers in African fiction. There was enough going on in the UK publishing industry to indicate that if African writing was to survive, Africans would have to publish such writing.

Once I had taken the decision, the problems descended on me by the day. I had begun by printing my books in the United Kingdom. How was I to get them into Nigeria, my primary market? I found that I needed a licence to import them into Nigeria. As a trader, I knew enough of the Nigerian system to convince me that the books might never get to Nigeria. While I waited for the Nigerian licence, I tried to get into the UK market. It is enough to say that every distributor of African books whom I dealt with in five years, went out of business. The losses I made as a result will have to remain another trade secret.

By 1987, it became possible to ship the books to Nigeria without an import licence. But once the books were in the country, the problems of distribution came to the fore. There were four options: the university bookshops; the chain stores such as Leventis, United Trading Company (UTC) and Kingsway; the airport kiosks which specialise in magazine and newspaper sales; and direct marketing by the publisher. I will here summarise the experience of five years.

Direct marketing by a small publisher of six books was out of the question. The cost of vehicles alone prohibited such a venture. The university bookshops, with the exception of the University of Lagos Bookshop, are of no use. The airport kiosks are bad payers, although they offer the books visibility. They are of little use. The trading companies with their chain stores are reliable, but it is hard to convince them to carry the books on a regular basis.

In the end, I had to fall back on the established publishers with experience in the trade. Most were unwilling to do any business with us. As I write, an arrangement has been worked out with Heinemann of Nigeria, but that, I suppose, has only been on the basis of the personal interest of its chief executive. A silver lining in the clouds. Another silver lining has presented itself in the African Books Collective (ABC) based in Oxford – thanks to the effort of Hans Zell and his African colleagues. ABC will now ensure that sales are made to libraries and specialists in Europe and America, and to other African countries.

Apart from distribution, other problems presented themselves. I could not really regard myself as a publisher unless I was publishing other writers. And so I went in search of manuscripts. Nigeria has a host of would-be writers who complain endlessly of the absence of publishing outlets. The charge is well founded. The older houses are not publishing as much fiction as they ought. In some cases, their editorial departments are ill-staffed. But the other side of the coin is that good manuscripts are not pouring in. In my experience, I have only found a handful of publishable work. It is possible that I am not receiving the first attention of writers, but the point has to be made. The two titles by other writers which I have published so far, have won prizes. I continue to search for titles that will fit the imprint.

By 1988 I knew that I could no longer print in the United Kingdom and I began to cast around for Nigerian craftsmen – graphic designers, illustrators (for covers and children's texts), proof-readers and printers. The first two were available, but proof-readers were decidedly nowhere to be found, and printers presented quite a headache.

Nigerian printers labour under a plethora of problems – shortage of spare parts and a lack of able workmen. They are incapable of meeting deadlines. Those who can do so cost an arm and a leg. As of now, we have become a do-it-yourself operation. We typeset in-house, use freelance operators for designs and illustrations, buy paper, film and plates and sit in with the printers and box our way to a final, acceptable book.

And when the book miraculously gets into the market, does it sell? Only if it gets on the examination lists and is compulsory as a text. But then, there will be pirates to contend with. If it does not make the list, and it is not likely to until five years or so, you are not likely to get your money back. For a book comes expensive – an average paperback costing about 5 per cent of a graduate's salary – and in a troubled economy books are not the first item on anyone's list. And novels are not expected to sell in terms of tens of thousands in any event.

Given all of what I have said above, it must seem perverse to continue to publish at all. Possibly. But it will not have been the most foolish thing I have done in my life. In 1991, I published eight titles, seven of them, mine. Which other publisher could have done that for me?

Nor is all lost. Some of the titles are getting on the examination lists at long last. This offers the possibility, in spite of all the odds, that we may soon be getting our money back. But most important of all, the ideas in the books are taking wing. Which is probably the one reason why anyone would want to be a publisher at all.

Self-publishing has also assisted me in my struggles for the rights of the oppressed minorities in Nigeria, and since I became President of the Association of Nigerian Authors in November 1990 I have been able to mediate creditably, I would think, between authors and publishers.

Editors' note: 'Saro-Wiwa and the Syllabus'

In 1991, *Forest of Flowers* by Ken Saro-Wiwa, who was then President of the Association of Nigerian Authors, was placed on the West African Examinations Council (WAEC) syllabus. However, it was subsequently removed when the Ogoni leader became a target of Sani Abacha's wrath. Abacha's fear of Saro-Wiwa, and his determination to expunge all trace of him and his influence, led to execution, removal of the text from the syllabus and also to the elimination 'of Saro-Wiwa's name from ... monuments in Rivers State and other parts of the nation'. After the death of Abacha, there was a change in policy, and by November 1998 there was agitation for the reinstatement of *Forest of Flowers* on the school examination syllabus.

Publishing Ngugi: The Challenge, the Risk, and the Reward

Henry Chakava

The history of Ngugi as a published writer goes back to the late 1950s when he was a student at Alliance High School in Kenya. His story, *Try Witchcraft*, was published in the school magazine when he was in the second form, and another, *Voluntary Service Camp*, appeared in the 1958 issue. Commercial success did not come until he was at Makerere University in Kampala from 1959. While there, he wrote many stories, beginning with *The Fig Tree (Mugomo)*.

His first contact with a commercial publisher appears to have been in 1961, when his story, *The Black Messiah*, won first prize in a competition organised by the East African Literature Bureau. By this time, his potential as a writer of great promise had been recognised, and Heinemann was able to publish his second novel, *Weep Not Child*, in the African Writers Series in 1964, followed almost immediately by *The River Between*, a rewritten version of his earlier story, *The Black Messiah*. His more ambitious work, *A Grain of Wheat*, was published in the same series in 1967.

My own involvement with Ngugi started in the late 1960s when I was a literature student at the University of Nairobi and he was my tutor. Some time after I had secured my degree I joined Heinemann in Nairobi in 1972 as editor-in-training.

During this period, 1972-86, I was responsible for receiving, evaluating, and selecting materials for publication in Heinemann's London-based African Writers Series. In close consultation with my colleagues in London and Ibadan, I was able to introduce new East African voices such as Meja Mwangi, Mwangi Ruheni, Sam Kahiga, Martha Mvungi, Mukontani Rugyendo and Thomas Akare in the series while also publishing the more established writers, such as Okot p'Bitek, Taban lo Liyong, Joe de Graft, Reveka Mkau, and Micere Mugo.

Not only did we publish many more new books by Ngugi over the same period but we also witnessed a transformation in the author–publisher relationship that existed between Ngugi, Heinemann London, and Heinemann Kenya, and finally the transformation of Heinemann Kenya itself into an independent African imprint with the new name, East African Educational Publishers. *Petal of Blood* was the last of Ngugi's novels to be published by Heinemann in London in 1977. Even then, I insisted on a co-publication arrangement and was to fly a few hundred copies into Nairobi so that the title was launched there in July 1977 in the presence of Heinemann representatives from London and Ibadan. I shall return to the author–publisher relationship later as it forms the crux of this paper.

Ngugi, who was then Chairman of the Department of Literature at the University of Nairobi, was constantly reminding me of the need to 'localise' my publishing programme so as to better fulfil the needs of the new curriculum. In response, I commissioned the first ever textbook of oral literature, which became an instant bestseller when it came out in 1982. It remains one of our most successful titles. In addition, I started a series of oral literature studies in Kenya's major languages. Although the running text was in English, the oral texts themselves were rendered in the original language, with English translations alongside. I have, to date, published the oral literatures of the Gikuyu, Maasai and Kalenjin, with those of the Dholuo and Miji-Kenda in process.

A number of supplementary books, useful for the learning and teaching of oral literature, have also been published. Sales of these books were slow at first but they have now established themselves as standard reference books in schools, colleges, and universities. In addition, other publishers have followed our lead, and oral literature is now a popular publishing area.

If we accept that our literatures are to be found from among our own communities, in what language(s) must we express them? How should we share them among ourselves? Although it was agreed that the English language was vital for international communication, it was felt strongly that our writers should write for our own people and that, if the rest of the world saw any merit in what we were producing, they could access that material through translation into their own languages. We felt that it was time to prepare our communities and awaken them to the reality that they were the creators of their own literature. It was during this period (1976) that Ngugi (with his namesake, Ngugi wa Mirii) wrote *Ngaahika Ndeenda* with the full critical participation of the people of Kamiriithu, who were later to stage it at the Kamiriithu Community Centre before large audiences.

But publishing in African languages was quite another proposition. What orthographies would we use, since some communities had none and others were reacting against those prepared for them by missionaries and were busy compiling new ones? Who would buy these books, in view of the fact that the majority of mother-tongue speakers were poor peasants who lived below the breadline, and only a small percentage of whom had achieved literacy beyond the 3Rs? As a publisher, how was I going to promote and distribute these books, in view of the fact that the majority of readers would be people from the rural areas where the roads are nonexistent or impassable for most of the year? In the absence of newspapers, journals, and other promotional outlets in those languages, how was I going to advertise these books?

Ngugi and I agonised over these matters for long hours, him optimistic, me sceptical. In the end we began to realise the power of translation. Who ever remembers that *War and Peace* and *Anna Karenina* were written in Russian? What about other classics like *Dead Souls*, *The Idiot*, *The Cherry Orchard*, *The Caucasian Chalk Circle*, *Hedda Gabler*, *The Plague*, *God's Bits of Wood*, and all those many books that we so much enjoy reading in English? Ngugi regretted that he had enriched the English language and culture with his novels *Weep Not Child*, *The River Between*, *A Grain of Wheat* and *Petals of Blood* without giving anything back to the community, culture, and language that has inspired them. He swore that he would never write any more novels in English, but would henceforth write in the Gikuyu language.

In the years 1977 to 1982 – before and after Ngugi's detention, which was during the whole of 1978 – we spent much time together. The University of Nairobi administration had refused to allow him to resume his teaching duties, so I gave him a desk at my office where he could do his writing. After many discussions together, we were able to rationalise our ideas as follows: every community, every nationality, has its own languages, its own codified body of knowledge, its own literature, music, drama, dance, etc. Every community must accept the duty to preserve its own heritage, and should not rely on anyone else to do this for it. Every community is a concentric circle, complete in itself, and the good from it will flow and get absorbed into a broader national circle, which will in turn flow into a regional or continental circle, with only the best reaching the global circle.

We saw translation as the facilitator of those concentric circles and imagined a world where the Dholuo would be able to access materials written in Gikuyu, and vice versa, and the Luhya and Miji-Kenda would be able to compare their literatures. In our plan, works that transcended the first circle would be translated into Kiswahili and finally into English for dissemination nationally, regionally, and internationally. If people from countries where English is not spoken, such as France, Germany, Russia, Japan, Scandinavia, etc. expressed interest in any of our works, we would grant them rights to translate that work into their own language, sourcing their translation, as far as possible, from original language. In this way, Africa would be exposing only the best of its creative output to the rest of the world.

I decided to start with children's books in mother tongues, and Ngugi himself volunteered to write the first three. I commissioned more children's books from the nation's leading writers – among them David Maillu, Francis Imbuga, Asenath Odaga, and Grace Ogot – and had published six new titles within a couple of years. In all sincerity, and in spite of the enthusiasm displayed by all my writers, I have to admit that these books did not do well and, to date, none of them has been reprinted. I was compelled to skip our second circle – that is, issuing them in Kiswahili translation, and commissioned English translations with some good results. International rights have been sold in only a few, including Ngugi's own.

Publishing Ngugi is a pleasurable and enriching experience. My direct publishing association with him dates back to 1975/76, when we worked together on *Petals of Blood*. Contrary to popular belief among academics and other creative writers who think we automatically accept Ngugi's books for publication, the script of *Petals*, then under the working titles 'Wrestling with God' or 'Wrestlers with God', was sent out for readers' reports in the normal way. I personally gave it an in-depth house report. Although all the reports recommended publication, they raised serious issues about the timing, movement, and content of the story; they noted constant repetition, felt that certain scenes had been contrived to achieve certain desired effects, and decried the predictability or inevitability of the storyline.

Ngugi took all these criticisms seriously and with great humility. He retrieved the script and reworked it for a long time, constantly coming back to seek clarification about some of our readers' criticisms. He listened to, even solicited, every comment, however casual, from my editors and other friends to whom he had given the script at his own initiative. To demonstrate how responsive Ngugi is to criticism and how he uses it constructively, I once made a casual observation to the effect that Wanja's *matatu* journey from Nairobi to Ilmorog, which was then identifiably Limuru, was too long and packed with too many incidents. I made a similar criticism of the delegation of workers and peasants from Ilmorog to Nairobi to meet their 'lost' MP, which I again felt was overstretched and loaded with content that seemed to come out of Ngugi's mouth rather than that of his characters.

He responded to these criticisms by leaving all the incidents intact but 'moving' Ilmorog so that it was now much further away from Nairobi, and its new description had changed from the lush green of

Limuru to a drier place resembling Nyandarua, Kinangop, or Lari, or somewhere deeper into the Rift Valley. As for Wanja and her *matatu* journey, he seems to have edited it out of the novel altogether, later to reuse it in a much more integrated and creative manner in the next work, *Devil on the Cross*, where Wanja becomes Wariinga. Quite frankly, I cannot tell you which edition of *Petals of Blood* is in print, having read several versions of that novel both in manuscript and in proof!

I eventually came to accept Ngugi as being a little fastidious in his writing style, and I now know that, unless you stop him, he can go on rewriting a novel without stopping, responding to his critics, not by following their laid-down recommendations but by adopting a new approach that somehow takes care of their criticisms. The same story applies to proofs, which Ngugi will continue to change beyond his normal allocation, so that the publisher is forced to incur heavy correction costs. But the final product is usually a gem, giving great satisfaction to the editor and, I hope, to Ngugi himself. Ngugi treats his publisher as an equal partner in his creative process, and co-operates fully in carrying out the publisher's assignments and meets his deadlines promptly. I have never seen Ngugi lose his temper during our long publishing association. When we disagreed completely over the introduction to *The Trial of Dedan Kimathi*, which he had co-authored with Micere Mugo, he amicably asked us to rewrite it to what we wanted it to be, and ended the meeting.

My experience with the Gikuyu books was different, although equally enriching. It started with *Ngaahika Ndeenda*, a community-based effort in writing and producing a play. When he handed me the final script, Ngugi informed me that it had undergone a lot of fine-tuning by members of the cast and that he doubted if we needed to do any more work on it.

Beginning with *Ngaahika*, I established a pattern that was to repeat itself in the assessment of all works submitted by Ngugi in Gikuyu. Being a non-Gikuyu speaker myself, I had to find ways of overcoming my linguistic handicap before I could feel confident enough to offer his works for acceptance to our editorial board. The fact that we had no Gikuyu-speaking editor on our staff at that time meant that I could not benefit from an in-house assessment. We devised a strategy that was able to satisfy me as well as Ngugi and all those writers who participated in our 'return of mother tongue' programme.

Firstly, Ngugi would describe the plot in as much detail as possible, inviting comments from me at each stage. I would then give him the go-ahead to proceed with the writing. When the final script was ready, we would go through it together, page by page, with Ngugi explaining the story in meticulous detail. Once satisfied, I would submit the script to one or two Gikuyu readers for reports, and offer it for acceptance if the reports were positive, which they usually were.

Ngugi was determined that the Gikuyu editions of his books should be of the same production quality as their English counterparts, to forestall any thoughts that local-language publications were inferior or second-rate. For this reason, we were compelled to import new fonts for our typesetter, to enable him to do justice to the Gikuyu alphabet. We had to use the best designers and illustrators available, for his books. Once our designer produced a cover for *Caitani Mutharaba-ini*. It depicted a Mau Mau warrior stepping on a dead white soldier and with his AK47 rifle held high up in victory. Ngugi admired this cover for a long time and finally, in his modesty, declared it 'too strong' for *Caitani*. He asked me to keep that cover safely, for he would write a new novel specifically for it. That novel was *Matigari*.

Ngugi is one of the few writers who believe that publishers are honest and decent people. He usually doesn't haggle over the terms that I propose to him. He will accept the percentage royalty proposed and the advance offered and might even agree to forego some benefit in order to 'get the book started'. Unlike other writers I know, he doesn't complain and fret that he has been to so and so bookshop and has not seen copies of his books, although he will from time to time suggest ideas as to how we might promote and distribute our books better. Again, unlike other writers, he does not go behind our back to visit the warehouse to check the bin cards or visit our accounts department to inspect the records to ensure that we are not holding back any royalties. He has absolute faith in people and their good intentions.

A real challenge as Ngugi's publisher was how I was going to distribute his books internationally, in the way that he was used to at Heinemann. I had already had some experience with *Petals of Blood*, published in London, but for which I had asked Heinemann to grant me East African rights in view of the role I had played in 'developing' it with Ngugi. Secondly, when Heinemann declined to co-publish Ngugi and Micere's *The Trial of Dedan Kimathi* with us, arguing that the African Writers Series was not for single collections of plays but for anthologies, I decided to publish the play in Nairobi.

Ngugi and Micere had written this play in anger because they were appalled by the manner in which Kenneth Watene had depicted Kimathi in his play, then just published and entitled *Dedan Kimathi*, and wanted a quick answer from us. Heinemann soon realised their mistake and eventually purchased rights from me to sell the play outside East Africa. I decided that as I did not have the marketing and distribution reach. I was going to sell the rights, including translation rights, as widely as possible.

The African Writers Series was the automatic choice for English-language rights, and in the case of *Matigari*, for example, I was successful in selling French, Dutch, German, Danish, Swedish, American, and Japanese rights with assistance from Heinemann UK. It is my belief and conviction that the books I have published with Ngugi are as well marketed and distributed as were his books when he was published by Heinemann in London.

There have been many threats, direct and indirect, that I or my company has suffered because of the association with Ngugi. Ngugi's books and other textbooks have been removed from official government reading lists; there have been other forms of censorship and harassment and the constant threat of litigation from members of the public who have felt able to pursue their cases in a court of law. It is not for me to tell you how Ngugi himself has suffered, but it has obviously been on a much larger scale; and it is that suffering that still keeps him in exile today.

In spite of the problems I have been through, my association with Ngugi has been very rewarding, both intellectually and commercially. First and foremost, I must admit that my linkage with Heinemann's African Writer Series, and with Ngugi in particular, has played an important part in establishing and enhancing my reputation and that of East African Educational Publishers as the leading fiction publisher in the region, if not in the entire continent. My fiction list consists of drama, poetry, plays, novels, and oral literature works in mother tongue, Kiswahili, and English, not to mention children's books, all numbering 109 titles at present.

Further, there is not a single Ngugi book I have published (except the children's books in Gikuyu) that has not been an instant bestseller. *Ngaahika Ndeenda* and *Caitani Mutharaba-ini* went through three printings within the first year of publication, and their Kiswahili and English translations have performed equally well. I recently released an English translation of *Matigari* and it is performing well and will most likely go to a second printing this year. The original edition of *Matigari* remains in limbo, as we have not yet ascertained if we would be breaking the law by re-issuing it. The essays, *Writers in Politics* and *Decolonising the Mind*, are in great demand, especially in our academic institutions, and are regularly reprinted; and *Moving the Centre*, only recently released, promises to be similarly successful. Rights have been acquired from Heinemann London on the earlier novels, and these, too, are published in Nairobi and continue to do well. Ngugi's long absence from Kenya, and the propaganda campaign that has been waged against him and his writings, has certainly affected the momentum of the sales of his books; but, excepting *Matigari*, all of them are in print and are not officially banned as is sometimes claimed in other circles.

What I have valued most is my intellectual association with Ngugi. He is a lot more committed, more serious, and more idealistic and ideologically inclined than I am, but we share the same philosophical and temperamental worldview. It is Ngugi's advice and the resultant exchange of views that encouraged me to give priority to oral literature in my publishing programmes. It is Ngugi's conviction and my own willingness to experiment with some of his ideas that made me venture into publishing in African languages. Had Ngugi continued to live in Kenya, write more books in this line, and encourage his colleagues to support this venture, the programme would have succeeded. In spite of my present setbacks in publishing in this area, I am waiting for the day when he will return home so that we can continue from where I stopped.

In conclusion, although my association with Heinemann gave me a lot of international exposure, much of this has been sustained by the fact that I am the publisher of one of Africa's greatest and certainly its most controversial avant-garde writer, Ngugi wa Thiong'o. In selling rights of his books, I have had to interact with international publishers from all over the world: Japan, Russia, Germany, France, Scandinavia, and the United States, and some African countries such as Zimbabwe and South Africa. At home, I enjoy quiet respect from serious-minded Kenyans who acknowledge the courageousness of keeping Ngugi's books in print under very difficult circumstances. The strong messages contained in his writings are much appreciated locally, even though this appreciation hardly finds public expression nowadays.

African Books Collective and Creative Writing and Publishing in Africa

Mary Jay

Indigenous publishing is integral to national development, and literature is integral to cultural identity and integrity.

Introduction

Distribution has long been an obstacle for African publishers, and thus for their authors. Whilst the situation varies from country to country within Africa, nonetheless it is broadly true to say that, with the exception of parts of South Africa, networks and systems for national and intra-African distribution of books remains very weak and, in places, non-existent. The major obstacles for publishers are lack of access to capital, poor infrastructure, difficulties of communication, and bureaucratic and exchange problems between countries. Added to this is the lack of purchasing power, and the few – and poorly funded – libraries. The bookshop well stocked with local publications and undertaking promotions and marketing is an uncommon phenomenon.

Writers also want to see their works read and widely disseminated outside Africa. Quite apart from the intrinsic merits, African publishers can gain valuable earnings from overseas sales – income which can be invested in development of the publishing house or, for many, simply helping to keep the company afloat. But it is very difficult for the individual African publisher to compete with well-funded conglomerates in the North. Production of appropriate and attractive catalogues, access to mailing lists, attendance at book exhibits and so on, are obstacles. And now there is Internet marketing. Publishers have too often not received fair returns for the books which reach Northern customers. Most dealers visiting Africa buy books at local prices, often at huge discounts; and the publishers do not receive the benefit of the US dollars and Pound sterling mark-up from the resulting sales in the North. In the light of most exchange rates, the publisher pays a heavy penalty. There have been instances also of dealers going out of business while owing money to African publishers. And until relatively recently, the publishers were denied access to precious hard currency earnings.

There are myriad other difficulties for the African publisher. Publishing is not recognised by governments as a strategic industry, import duties and taxes are still imposed on items such as paper and printing equipment, printing capacity is often poor resulting in low production standards, and – despite so-called 'liberalisation' in textbook markets – few African publishers have a firm foothold in the textbook market. As elsewhere in the world, literary publishing can usually only flourish if it is supported by textbook sales.

Of the many imperatives for a flourishing African publishing industry, one major factor is the need for outlets for literary talent in Africa. With the dearth of literary periodicals and the 'little magazines', new and aspiring writers cannot look to these outlets to get published and hone their craft; they must largely look to publishers as their first resort. And with the strength of the multinationals in Africa, African writers very often preferred in the past to get published as a first option with a Northern publisher, feeling confident of overseas distribution and better returns for their work. The founders of ABC specifically saw the organisation as encouraging African writers to publish with indigenous African publishers, rather than abroad, in the belief that it was both important for African writers and publishers to work together towards the cultural development of the Continent, and it would of itself contribute to the strengthening of African publishing, and thus encourage more publishing outlets for writers. If a writer is assured of effective overseas distribution through an ABC member publisher, then the tide of publishing outside Africa could be turned. There is evidence after ten years of operation that writers are indeed increasingly seeking to publish with an ABC publisher.

As long ago as 1985, these were the background factors which brought together a group of eleven publishers to consider how they, as a group of active, indigenous and autonomous African publishers, could together tackle the practical problems of overseas distribution. What could not be done individually and through conventional commercial channels could perhaps be done collectively.

ABC: Aims and Objectives

Arising from that initial meeting of publishers, African Books Collective (ABC) was founded in 1989 as an initiative of seventeen founding publishers who established, co-own and govern the organisation. ABC works within the context of capacity building and support for the indigenous and autonomous African publishing industry. Its prime purpose is to promote more effectively and disseminate African-published material in the major English-language book markets outside Africa; and in this way to increase export sales earnings of member publishers. Two needs are addressed: the need of African publishers to get their wealth of output on to the shelves of libraries, bookshops and other book buyers in the North, and the need of libraries and others who face often insuperable problems in the acquisition of African publications.

The wider context of increasing overseas sales was to promote African scholarship and writing, cultural identity and autonomy, with important implications for education overseas. African publishers are of course primarily publishing for their own domestic markets. As well as promoting African writing and scholarship, and awareness of African issues, the benefit of the overseas sales is an important contribution to the ability to publish for Africa. The earnings contribute to the publishers' efforts to redress the traditional dominance of the capitalised multinationals, and to make available culturally relevant materials for markets where acute shortages of such books (together with lack of purchasing power) perpetuate low educational attainments, and a paucity of literature for a developing civic society.

Within the overall context, ABC concentrates on two further major areas. We disseminate information and materials about the African publishing industry, and ourselves publish some resource guides primarily for the African book communities. We promote intra-African trade through the Intra-African Book Support Scheme (IABSS), run in partnership with the major UK charity, Book Aid International. Recipient-request led, and donor funded, the scheme supplies African-published books to African libraries – including university, rural, public, schools'– and institutions, and other community organisations.

Structure

ABC is a UK-registered company. The policy-making body is the Council of Management of six member publishers elected by the membership, representing a geographical balance. Each founder member publisher paid an initial one-time membership fee of £1,000 – an astonishing demonstration of commitment in the light of the foreign exchange constraints then prevailing.

The unique nature of ABC is that it is non-profit-making on its own behalf and only aims to cover its operational costs. It seeks to be profit-making for its constituent members, and to increase substan-

tially their export earnings. Thus member publishers enjoy more favourable terms than those available under conventional commercial
distribution agreements, where the distributor must take a discount,
and often pays in local currency. ABC belongs to the publishers themselves. The crucial point about the operation is that the publishers
receive the benefit of their overseas earnings. ABC prices books for the
overseas markets, and remits to publishers on average 60 per cent of the
net sales proceeds in US dollars and Pound sterling. The income ABC
retains is a contribution to the promotion work and overheads.

ABC has small offices in central Oxford, England, with a staff of
three full time and five part time. The publishers established ABC in
the North since the core work is promoting, marketing and distributing books outside Africa. It is common practice world-wide for
publishers to have marketing and distribution organised from within
the territories which they are accessing. Northern markets and
promotion opportunities are very different from those prevailing in
Africa. Full control is retained of the distribution service and credit
and cash collection, so as to safeguard publishers' interests.

Finance

ABC derives its income from two sources: it retains a proportion of net
sales income, before remittances to publishers; and it is donor-
supported. ABC continues to work to build up sufficient sales income
to be self-supporting; but until that time, donor support is sought to
fill the gap between expenditure and income. Organisations recently or
currently supporting ABC are: Danida, Finnida, Hivos, Norad, The
Rockefeller Foundation, and Sida. Other organisations also support
the joint ABC–Book Aid International IABSS.

Membership

Founder member publishers receive $66^2/_3$rds of net sales remittances
and their £1,000 membership fees contributed to start-up costs. It is
open to any other African publisher to apply for membership of ABC,
in two classes: Full Member paying £500 one-time membership fee
and receiving 60 per cent of net sales proceeds returns; or Associate
Member paying no membership fee and receiving 55 per cent of net
sales returns. Occasional single titles have been taken on (no
membership fee, 50 per cent of net sales returns), but generally our
resources are too limited to admit a member with only one title. The
major criteria in considering membership are:

- the publisher must be truly indigenous and autonomous within the
  spirit and ethos of ABC. Branches of foreign-owned multinationals

would not, for example, be considered for membership. The finance, publishing decisions and financial management must be from within Africa;

- the publishing list must be suitable for joint promotion with the lists of existing member publishers, emanating from African culture and perspectives;
- the publishing list is active and dynamic, engaged in publishing about current political, economic, cultural and related issues within Africa; and/or publishing new or established creative writers making a contribution to the literary wealth of Africa; and/or publishing children's books of high content and production quality from within the cultures of Africa;
- the balance of the list between number of new titles published annually, and the backlist, is weighted towards publication of new titles;
- the current publishing programme covers all or some of the subject areas which it is realistic to market outside Africa – this includes African literature and linguistics;
- production standards (particularly for children's books) must be high enough to be marketable outside Africa.

Regard is also paid to regional and gender balance.

Publishers wishing to join who do not meet these criteria are not admitted. But a small number of suitable publishers are added each year – depending on ABC's ability to absorb the extra work and resources needed. Some member publishers whose lists have effectively become dormant have ceased to be members, enabling ABC to take on more active lists. Membership today stands at 42 publishers from 12 African countries; and the stock inventory is some 1,700 titles with between 120 and 150 new titles currently added each year.

Activities

ABC is the exclusive distributor of the English-language titles of its member publishers, with the exception of textbooks. Academic books, literature, children's books, and general books on African culture and heritage are stocked. Promotion and marketing covers the full range of activities open to publishers: joint catalogues – twice-yearly listing new titles, subject catalogues, children's and general trade catalogues; exhibit participation; entry on to international bibliographic databases; advance information; flyers; review copies; display advertising; trade representation and so on. The Internet is being harnessed. Two academic sites have hosted the ABC list for some time, and in 1998 it established its own Web site with full on-line ordering facilities. Titles are also mounted at the Internet Bookshop, a major commercial outlet.

Achievements and Constraints

There has been something of a transformation over the last ten years in awareness and concern about the problems of African publishers, and the integral role of publishing in the economic and socio-development of the continent. ABC was formed in 1989, and the African Publishers' Network (APNET) in 1992. APNET is the pan-African umbrella of National Publishers Associations, and works to promote the African publishing industry through lobbying, training and networking, among other activities. The Bellagio Publishing Network was established in 1991 (and led to the formation of APNET). It acts as a network bringing together donor organisations, African publishers, and other relevant organisations and parties in the support of African publishing. But it would be a mistake to confuse greater awareness and solidarity with actual progress *per se*. Conditions remain very difficult for African publishers, and the central facts of under-capitalisation, insufficient trained staff, and infrastructure problems remain.

ABC has grown since it started trading in May 1990, and now has a turnover of around £300,000 a year, although a major component is the donor-funded IABSS. The rapid rise in sales in the early years reflected the fact that an obvious captive market was waiting to be tapped, despite not especially favourable marketing conditions. But as time has gone on, general market conditions have deteriorated, notably cutbacks in library budgets. ABC has the much harder task of 'mainstreaming' African literature (and other books) and creating markets.

Cultural Pride, and Economics of Publishing

So what does this mean for African literature in the English-speaking countries of Africa? There are two key facts which bear on every aspect of the current state and the 'future' of African literature. First, its importance and place within the culture and development of the continent. 'The lack of a reading culture' is a much bandied-about conventional wisdom, but it is perhaps superficial in some of its assumptions. Lack of purchasing power and poorly stocked libraries are a major factor. The concentration on texts equipping young people for finding employment inevitably works often at the expense of literature for life enhancement. And judgements made about what is available may not take into account local language publishing, of which there is a dearth: there is a multiplicity of languages spoken by small groups and this type of publishing carries the additional burden of a much smaller market than a European/African language which can 'travel'. There is no reason to suppose that African societies would be any less receptive to reading English-language – or any other language – literature if living and employment conditions bore comparison with more economically developed countries. ABC's experience through the Intra-African Book Support Scheme is that there is a huge desire for literature. The scheme is barely scraping the surface of this demand. It hardly needs stressing that the cultural integrity and economic prosperity of a country depends upon an educated citizenry. Indeed, for a healthy country, the two are indivisible. Books are a crucial tool of cultural integrity, as reflected in the words of Niyi Osundare, the Noma laureate and one of Africa's great poets, who has called for 'respect for the book as an indispensable part of the world's cultural and intellectual heritage'.[1] Whilst African literature publishing is primarily for Africa, it is also the means to convey and promote understanding and knowledge outside Africa and the equal standing of African literature with other world cultures.

The second factor is the multiplicity of factors hindering the publication and sale of English-language African literature. Publishing literature is risky anywhere. Walter Bgoya, the Tanzanian publisher, has said: 'If you want to publish a novel you must start with the knowledge that you won't make money on it';[2] and this is seconded by Dafe Otobo, the Nigerian publisher with a prize-winning fiction list: 'You have to assume from the beginning that you're not going to make money on literature.'[3] The underlying problems referred to earlier hinder such publishing: in Africa, publishing is hardly recognised as a strategic industry in cultural and economic development. African publishers – and this is not wholly unique to Africa – are dependent on the lucrative textbook market to subsidise or finance literature publishing. But in many parts of Africa they have been, or still are, at an unfair disadvantage against the activities and methods of the foreign-owned companies who cream off this market. And such publishers rarely retain the profits in Africa, or plough them back into literature publishing or the development of the publishing infrastructure. James Tumusiime, the Ugandan publisher says: 'Unless the publishing of textbooks and educational books takes root on the continent it will be very, very difficult to promote African writing and local-language publishing.'[4] Robert Sulley of Heinemann UK sees here a common interest with African publishers: 'If the textbook market is not open to local publishers, that kills literature too. And that is bad news for Heinemann as the African Writers Series will collapse.'[5]

Negative Images

Selling African literature overseas is, in ABC's experience, an uphill task. Despite having three Nobel laureates (Egypt, Nigeria and South Africa), African literature is not in the mainstream in the same way as the literatures of, say, Latin America, India, and Japan. In the words of Taban lo Liyong, the Sudanese writer, 'We are being represented by our feet rather than our heads. African footballers rather than writers are representing Africa ...'[6] ABC is not merely trying to tap the markets: it is having to stimulate creation of markets. Negative images of Africa in the media do not encourage exploration of the rich written culture, past acquisitions problems have contributed to lack of awareness, and the fact of writers publishing in the North has led to assumptions that there is not much literary publishing in Africa.

The volume of fiction, drama and literary criticism which ABC manages to sell is relatively small, although it comes about fifth in the ranking order of over thirty subject areas in which we sell. Poetry is even harder to sell. But top of the list is 'folklore and oral tradition'. Whilst this is welcome, there is nonetheless a conundrum, summed up in the words of Kole Omotoso, the distinguished writer, essayist and Professor of Literature: 'Are we to promote the notion, "I dance therefore I am?" This is still the image of Africa, at a period when Africa is producing scientists, physicists, people who can measure a thousandth of a second ...'[7]

Conclusion

There was a flowering of autonomous African publishing in the post-independence 1970s and early 1980s. Since then, what statistical evidence there is supports the view that literature publishing overall in English-speaking countries has been on the decline. Of course the picture varies between regions and countries, with Zimbabwe the bright spot in the 1990s. The decline and near extinction of literary periodicals and the 'little magazines', which gave a voice to new and aspiring writers, has been a great loss. Despite all the problems, and however small the output, African literary publishing remains alive. Great novelists, dramatists and poets, holders of part of the key to Africa's 'second liberation', continue the engagement; and some publishers continue the struggle to play their part in the cultural and wider development of the continent. But too many of the great writers are not heard, and too few publishers can sustain this kind of publishing. African publishers have been foresighted in founding ABC, and the task now is for a greater number of creative writers to publish with African publishers, and contribute, to their mutual benefit, to the wide recognition outside Africa of the richness of Africa's literary talent, and indeed to the cultural renaissance of the continent.

Notes

1 Davies, Wendy. 'African Writers–Publishers Seminar. A Seminar Organised by the African Books Collective and the Dag Hammarskjöld Foundation in Arusha, Tanzania, 23-26 February 1998: Seminar Report'. Uppsala: Dag Hammarskjöld Foundation, 1998, 5.
2 *op. cit.*, 11.
3 *op. cit.*, 11.
4 *op. cit.*, 26.
5 *op. cit.*, 11.
6 *op. cit.*, 9.
7 *op. cit.*, 26.

PART TWO

Arusha III and Beyond

A 'New Deal' between African Writers and Publishers

Statement issued by participants at the African Writers–Publishers seminar (Arusha III), Tarangire Sopa Lodge, Arusha, Tanzania, 23-26 February, 1998

Preamble

Twenty African writers and publishers from nine countries and ten resource persons with backgrounds in publishing met at Tarangire Sopa Lodge, Arusha, 23-26 February, 1998, for an 'African Writers–Publishers Seminar' (Arusha III). The seminar was directed by Walter Bgoya (publisher) and Niyi Osundare (writer) and organised by the Dag Hammarskjöld Foundation and the African Books Collective (ABC). The main objective of the Seminar was to respond to the call for a 'New Deal' between writers and publishers in Africa in their struggle to strengthen African literature and culture.[1]

Statement

The starting-point for discussions on a new relationship between African writers and publishers was the following paragraph from the Summary Conclusions of the Seminar on the Future of Indigenous Publishing in Africa (Arusha II), organised by the Dag Hammarskjöld Foundation in Arusha, Tanzania, 25-28 March, 1996:

> Seminar participants were unanimous that the time has come for a 'New Deal' between writers and publishers in Africa. Both groups now understand enough about publishing to be able to place their relationship on ethical and professional grounds where they can fulfil their respective responsibilities and see themselves as inseparable partners in the process of creation of African literature. Towards that end, a conference of African writers and publishers should be organised as soon as practicable with the aim of drawing up a charter to guide relations between the two professions.

It is in this spirit that we now provide some details for this 'New Deal' under the following headings:

- The role of the writer and the publisher's expectations.

- The role of the publisher and the writer's expectations.

- Contractual issues and writer–publisher relations.

- African values and African writing.

We recognise that the context in which both writers and publishers will apply these principles varies considerably from one African country to another.

The Role of the Writer and the Publisher's Expectations

Publishers have a right to expect:

1 a well-produced, original manuscript (i.e. clearly typed, preferably on diskette, but if handwritten it must be legible; the writer must keep a copy of the manuscript)
2 ideas and suggestions for cover design, illustrations and presentation of the book
3 sympathetic acceptance of the process of editing and preparation of the work for publication
4 submission of the manuscript to one publisher at a time with a limited period of response before submission to another publisher
5 the reading and returning of proofs within a specified time and with minimum alterations and additions, unless the writer is prepared to pay the extra costs incurred
6 first option on the writer's subsequent work for sequels only.

Furthermore the writer should inform him- or herself about:

7 details of the publishing process
8 the basic economics of book publishing and book distribution
9 the content of his or her contract, especially covering territorial, translation and publishing rights, and time limits relating to such rights.

The Role of the Publisher and the Writer's Expectations

Writers have a right to expect:

1 written acknowledgement of the receipt of the manuscript
2 communication and transparency about publication schedule and print run/reprints, and provision of regular and accurate royalty statements and payments
3 consultation on details of book production such as cover design, illustrations and the general presentation of the book

4 effective promotion of the publication and the writer him- or herself, and consultation on possible promotional approaches
5 exploration of the possibilities of effective promotion through book launches, readings, book fairs, print media, television, radio and the Internet
6 exploration of the possibilities of 'parallel products' such as cassette recordings and videos
7 a record of reviews on each title and regular communication about these.

Furthermore, the publisher should:

8 assist the writer in gaining a clear understanding of the publishing process
9 seek to nurture and support new writers
10 distinguish between new and established writers in terms of familiarity with the publishing process and not have unrealistic expectations of new writers in this regard.

Contractual Issues and Writer–Publisher Relations

There is a need for a code of conduct as a guide to humane relationships between writers and publishers. Such a code should provide for an adjudication panel to arbitrate in cases of disagreement between the two parties. The panel should be made up of representatives of writers' associations and publishers' associations along with representatives of legal affiliates of the associations, representatives of printers' and booksellers' associations as appropriate in each African country and of copyright tribunals or commissions where these exist.

The publisher, in consultation with the writer, needs to find means of exploiting and harnessing the new technologies, including print-on-demand and the Internet, to the advantage of both parties. The publisher should also seek to inform himself/herself about measures being developed to protect intellectual property against violation due to modern technology.

Publishers and writers need to express a commitment to encouraging and sustaining associations of writers, publishers, printers and booksellers as an element in the creation of an enabling environment for the book industry and a reading culture in African society.

African Values and African Writing

The involvement of writers in discussions on all aspects of book issues in Africa should be encouraged and efforts made to vitalise and support writers' associations. Likewise, we welcome and support the African Publishers Network mission statement, which reads:

'APNET's mission is to strengthen African publishers' associations through networking, training and trade promotion to fully meet Africa's need for quality books relevant to African social, political, economic and cultural reality.'

There is a need to strengthen indigenous textbook production so that it can subsidise creative writing. There is also a need to encourage authors to write in indigenous African languages, to promote positive African values, and for publishers to find the means to publish such works and make them profitable and affordable in Africa.

Strengthening African literature and culture through co-operation between writers and publishers should provide the guiding principle and aspiration for the two professions.

Participants

Walter Bgoya (*Tanzania*); Shimmer Chinodya (*Zimbabwe*); Wendy Davies (*United Kingdom*); Per Gedin (*Sweden*); James Gibbs (*United Kingdom*); Sven Hamrell (*Sweden*); Chukwuemeka Ike (*Nigeria*); Mary Jay (*United Kingdom*); Taban lo Liyong (*Sudan/South Africa*); Flora Lucas (*United Kingdom*); Cont Mhlanga (*Zimbabwe*); Mugyabuso Mulokozi (*Tanzania*); Abel Mwanga (*Tanzania*); Serah Mwangi (*Kenya*); NG Mwitta (*Tanzania*); Olle Nordberg (*Sweden*); Victor Nwankwo (*Nigeria*); Gillian Nyambura (*Kenya/Zimbabwe*); Akoss Ofori-Mensah (*Ghana*); Atukwei Okai (*Ghana*); Kole Omotoso (*Nigeria/South Africa*); Onsonye Tess Onwueme (*Nigeria/US*); Femi Osofisan (*Nigeria*); Niyi Osundare (*Nigeria/US*); Dafe Otobo (*Nigeria*); Katherine Salahi (*United Kingdom*); Irene Staunton (*Zimbabwe*); Robert Sulley (*United Kingdom*); James Tumusiime (*Uganda*); Moyez Vassanji (*Tanzania/Canada*).

Note

1 The document represents the broad consensus of the participants although some of them may not necessarily agree with all the points made in the statement.

Arusha Report

Editors' note: James Gibbs wrote up notes that he had made during the Arusha III seminar and these were published in a Malawian periodical with a particular interest in providing advice for aspiring authors. (See *WASI Writer*, no. 9, 3. 'WASI' stands for Writers and Artists International.) A contribution from *WASI*'s editor, Steve Chimombo, appeared in the same issue as Gibbs' Arusha III report. What follows is a revised version of the initial Report including, in italics, comments made by Chimombo, and responses to them. Readers may want to take in the Report, in which case they should just read the paragraphs in normal script. Or they may wish to savour the debate, in which case they should read the passages in italics as well.

Which Publisher?

In the early 1970s a group of young Nigerians determined, out of a deep sense of conviction, to publish their work with local publishers. One of these writers was Femi Osofisan, who describes his experiences in Part 1. The group of writers challenged the assumption made by some of their elders that multinational publishers were the obvious 'first port of call' for an African author. Significantly, some members of the group have since changed their position.

No one can tell an aspiring writer which publisher to approach – nor, indeed, command him or her to move into the market-place as a self-published author. Any such writer will, from reading books and talking to friends, from visits to libraries and bookshops, have gathered impressions about the advantages and disadvantages of self-publishing, and about what different publishers can offer. Each novel contains not only the story told by the author; in its appearance and from the details inside the front cover, it also tells a publishing story. Writers will have 'read' many of these stories, and will have decided where their work is likely to fit in.

Those who opt to publish their own work set off on a trail that has been taken by many eminent writers. William Blake took independent publishing to an extreme: he made his own ink and persuaded his wife to sew the pages together! In more recent times, authors determined to get their work into print themselves have wrestled with stencils and Gestetner machines, and have navigated routes through desk-top publishing programmes. They have learnt many lessons in the process of printing, advertising, and distributing their texts, and may read what follows with particular insight; but it is only incidentally for them. The writer now addressed is thinking of approaching a publisher.

Since offering a text to a publisher is the beginning of what you hope will be a satisfactory business partnership, intense discussion of the rival claims of publishing houses should precede submission. As with any business arrangement, the 'buyer' – in this case you, the writer – should 'beware'. You should talk to fellow 'customers', investigate the potential partners, find out about their records and reputations, examine their qualifications, their national and international standing.

Chimombo took me to task over matters raised in this paragraph. He claimed that I had inappropriately assumed the existence of a 'publishing culture' in which discussions take place and in which publishers 'open their hearts or their files to the public' or others. But his is negative and defeatist talk. Writers' groups exist, and those interested in authorship share experiences. I think writers have it within their power to improve the situation.

At one extreme stands the 'one-person' publisher. Before embarking on a business venture with such a 'company', you would be well advised to ascertain what arrangements exist beyond the personal. It is appropriate to ask, for example, what would happen to the business were the pivotal individual to die. At the other extreme are huge, distant multinationals, and one of your concerns in working with such conglomerates is the extent to which it is possible to expect the individual consideration, the contact with a particular editor, that remains an important ingredient in publishing. Somewhere between the two will be found well-established companies with a human face, and before signing up with one of them, you will want, in view of the personal element that is part of the business, to know about the turnover of their staff. From all this it will be appreciated that there is much work to be done before a publisher is selected.

Chimombo indicated that his experience had been that multinationals had rejected his work because it would not, in their opinion, have sold in the distant capital where the publisher was based. He continued:

> The multinationals ... do not deem the local writer's customers a big enough audience to publish a book by a Malawian or a Swazi. However good the book is, it will get the rejection slip.

This appropriately draws attention to the publisher's concern with profit. Unless a subsidy is involved or unless strategic considerations encourage the promotion of a 'loss leader' – in this case a title that will lose the company money in the short term but contribute to profit in the long run – acceptance will be based on businesslike expectation that the publication will make a profit. Writers must be aware that publishers are businessmen, and hope to share in successful business ventures.

How to Approach a Publisher

The initial approach to the publisher is likely to be in the form of a letter describing your work and your career, and enclosing a synopsis of the text you want to have published. From the beginning, be meticulous in your paperwork. Keep records of all correspondence and communications. Remember that you are in business, marketing your time and your talent. Expect, indeed demand, high business standards of your publisher. Cultivate them in yourself.

Offer to send a sample of published or unpublished work. Do not expect to send a complete novel in the first instance, and always, always keep a copy of any work submitted. Some may feel that this is obvious and that it is patronising to include the advice here. However, there have been many cases of authors losing the only copies of works, and of publishers misplacing the irreplaceable. So, at the risk of being regarded as patronising, I repeat: always keep a copy of any work submitted.

This topic is so important that it is worth adding: do not trust anybody – not your best friend, not the Minister of Education, not the most famous writer in the world, not the author of this essay – with the only copy of your work. The photocopier is your ally: use it. If you don't have access to one, use other resources. How many times did Leo Tolstoy's wife copy out *War and Peace*? Was it eight or nine?

Chimombo underlined the value of this advice and added that WASI, which offers an advisory service to authors, has sometimes received manuscripts without covering letters, without indication of authorship. On occasions WASI has been informed that that 'this is the only copy'.

Be aware that, in some cases, the market may come to put a value on your original manuscripts, on correspondence, on drafts, even on proofs corrected in your own hand. If you intend to become really famous, keep your working papers in a safe place. Looking ahead to your own inevitable demise, make a will in which you name literary executors. That is to say, list those you want to administer matters connected with royalties, manuscripts and copyright after your death. Put down the names of your heirs.

Chimombo observes that 'the local scene is replete with publishers holding dead authors' royalties'.

Increasingly, publishers ask for work to be submitted on disk with a 'hard copy' (a print out). The preparation of this will make great demands on you. Be aware that when a text is submitted in good shape it saves the publisher time and money. By the same token, when confronted with an error-ridden, hand-written text, a publisher may argue that the editorial input required to turn it into a presentable text will be so considerable that the percentage paid in royalties will have to be reduced! Some publishers routinely cut the royalties to African authors writing in English to 'take into account editorial work'. This is often totally unjustified.

The response to this paragraph in WASI Writer *suggested that it was 'a tall order' for 'most authors in Africa' to submit a 'hard copy'. It seems* WASI *'receives a large number' of submissions as 'hand-written manuscripts' from authors who do not 'have access to a manual typewriter'. This is undoubtedly true (and it would be interesting to know what happens to such manuscripts). It is also true that many have cultivated keyboard skills on the continent, and that, in order to be part of the evolving publishing industry, authors must endeavour to present their work in acceptable form. Standards are rising!*

Ask for confirmation in writing that a text has been received. File this confirmation, meticulously, with the correspondence mentioned above.

Approach only one publisher at a time. Other courses of action – such as simultaneous submissions to several publishers – may involve publishers in unproductive expense that is, quite rightly, resented. Simultaneous submissions undermine the trust that is an important part of the relationship between writer and publisher.

Negotiating a Contract

If you have one, this will be part of an agent's responsibility. But the more common pattern at present is for African writers to enter into direct negotiations with a publisher. This is the relationship assumed in what follows.

If you are offered a contract, read it with great care. If necessary, consider asking a friend to translate the document precisely into a language with which you are very familiar.

Consult widely. Before you put your name to any document, talk it through clause by clause with friends, fellow writers, those familiar with legal language and others with relevant experience. Learn from the plight of talented African footballers who, in their anxiety to join professional overseas clubs, sign contracts that they subsequently find limiting. There are African internationals playing for fourth-rate

European clubs who are bound to them for many years by hastily signed contracts.

Chimombo clearly thought the advice in the previous paragraph wildly unrealistic, and it is worth quoting some of his views:

> Writers cannot 'consult widely'.... Consulting with 'friends and fellow writers' is like a blind man leading another especially on the legalese ... 'Others with relevant experience' are a rare species.

I remain convinced that two, three or four heads are better than one, and networks linking writers exist in many African countries. They certainly exist in Malawi where the Writers' Group based at the University has always brought together students from different departments and schools, including lawyers in training. It will be seen from the Minimum Terms Agreement on page 395 that the reference to 'legalese' as some impenetrable variety of language is inappropriate

Compare the contract you have been offered with the Minimum Terms Agreements recommended by writers' groups in your country and by national copyright commissions. Use such agreements in your negotiations, remembering that they stipulate *Minimum* Terms.

Chimombo suggested that 'this section assumes vast knowledge of contracts and familiarity with information contained in handbooks or yearbooks for writers'. He continued:

> Most small countries do not have writers' groups or associations. If there are any they do not tackle issues like 'contracts' as part of their work.

I challenge the impression of the situation regarding writers' groups (though I realise that the formula 'most small' allows Chimombo to isolate a particular group within the Organisation of African Unity). I would simply insist that where two or three writers are gathered together to discuss their work an 'association' exists, and that such associations should exploit all resources at their disposal to explore, in a systematic way, the business side of authorship.

Give particular attention to clauses concerning rights and options on subsequent writing. Publishers feel they are taking a gamble on a new author, putting time and effort into getting a writing career off the ground. Some publishers maintain that the least they can expect in return for this is 'an option on the next work' (that is to say, the right to publish your second title) should your first prove successful. Authors, on the other hand, want to protect their bargaining position. As a result, you may balk at the prospect of agreeing to give your publisher 'first refusal' on your next or subsequent books. Each case will be different, but, except where sequels are involved, there seems no reason to bind yourself to offering your next book to your first publisher.

Familiarise yourself with the obligations of an author regarding legal matters such as plagiarism and libel. If you have quoted from another author in your text, ensure that this is clearly indicated and that, if appropriate, permission to use the borrowed material has been secured. Be absolutely frank with your publisher about any elements in your work that might give grounds for a case of libel or for other legal action. There have been instances of writers thinly disguising individuals in their texts only to find that those individuals have taken exception to the (mis)representation. Some of the 'originals' have found support in courts of law. If you have, for example, written about a woman called 'Ama Alotey' who is a surveyor working in Bolgatanga make sure that there is no one who, by virtue of a coincidence of name, profession or place of work, might resort to action through the courts. If in doubt, take legal advice.

Chimombo rightly commented that issues of 'copyright, libel and plagiarism' are particularly sensitive for a writer 'if he is just emerging from an "oral culture" where the word is free for re-use'. He is also correct in observing that copyright societies 'seem to concentrate on piracy in music'. I would simply encourage authors to follow the debates, and court cases and settlements, concerning copyright in the music industry. They will learn much that is of relevance to their branch of the arts, and can use it as the foundation for a campaign to raise awareness about copyright and literature.

Insist on being consulted about the cover design of your book and come to an agreement at an early stage as to how you expect the title to be promoted. Be prepared to learn about book design and welcome comments about your ability to give public readings from your work. One fraught area of promotion concerns book launches. The Southern African pattern is for these to be genteel celebrations, but in West Africa some book launches have offered opportunities for vulgar displays of wealth which have offended authors. In the course of such book launches, the virtues of the text have been submerged and writers have felt humiliated.

Chimombo comments astutely that 'Two important areas have been conflated here: book design and book promotion. Each requires more elaboration, especially for a beginning writer.' I hope that readers will refer to other sections of this book for a broad perspective.

New technology means that email provides an alternative to postal and courier services as a means of moving text around the world. As a result of these developments, clauses and addenda may have to be added to existing contracts. Familiarise yourself with the possibilities, costs, and hazards of different means of communication. Be circumspect and, at the same time, grasp the opportunities offered by new technology.

Chimombo regards the technology referred to here as, again, 'far in advance and out of reach for most African writers'. Clearly **many** *have little contact with new technology, but* **many** *are plugged in and on-line. Africans and African institutions are leapfrogging last week's and yesterday afternoon's technologies to benefit from new developments. Whatever the precise pace of change, the new technologies are increasingly being harnessed. There are 'Internet Cafés' springing up in African cities and towns and providing access for those without their own email. Of course, the cost can be high and telephone lines unreliable, but it is a resource to be used not shunned.*

During the Arusha III seminar, Walter Bgoya of Mkuki na Nyota Publishers was able to display a book that had been digitally printed: the text had been emailed from Dar es Salaam and the printing and binding completed, in less than a week, in Oxford. Authors too have responded to this new means of communication. Another of Bgoya's titles was edited by the publisher in Dar es Salaam, Tanzania, and the writer in Kinshasa, Democratic Republic of Congo, entirely by email. (For more details, see 'Internet Resources for African Writers', page 374.)

In the course of negotiating your contract, ask to see the form that your royalty statement will take. Ensure that it is clear and that it contains all the pertinent information. Some publishing houses send out glossaries and explanations to make it easier for their authors to understand their royalty statements. Anticipate the areas of tension on the form that may become battlefields between you and your publisher. These include authentication of print runs, security at the warehouse where stocks are kept, guarantees of accurate sales figures (at home and abroad), and information about the sale of rights. Insist on transparency and accountability.

Chimombo comments that the writer needs more information (i.e. education) on 'minimum requirements'. Some information, including a Minimum Terms Agreement, was included in the forerunner to this volume: A Handbook for African Writers, *edited by James Gibbs (1986). Copies were distributed in Africa, including eight copies to the National Archives in Malawi.*

So that you can argue your case convincingly, acquaint yourself with conditions in the publishing world. For example, find out what the publishing company expects to make out of your book, and how its profit margins will be affected by such factors as the price of paper, the supply of electricity, and the size of library budgets. Interest yourself in such 'political' matters, and remember that laws about Public Lending Rights (PLRs) and Value Added Tax (VAT) will have an impact on the income you can expect from your labour.

Chimombo responded with examples of the reluctance of publishers to divulge information, and he referred to a 'facilitator' at a 'recent marketing training workshop' who 'bluffed: "Pricing ... is a trade secret".' There is certainly no secret about it and writers should have no hesitation in exposing 'bluffers'. Especially if they are posing as facilitators at training workshops! Henry Chakava and Matthew Evans have written with admirably clarity on the issue in Development Dialogue *(Chakava 1994 and Evans 1994). For example Evans breaks down the costs of producing a typical paperback thus:*

Production costs 17.2%
Overheads 21.2%
Stock life 2.6%
Profit 8.5%
Royalty 7.5%
Average discount 43%

(Note booksellers take their 'cut' from the last figure.)

As regards the analysis of production content, Evans produces the following figures:

Typesetting 31.5%
Author's corrections 3%
Text printing 19%
Text paper 13%
Cover production 16.5%
Binding 17%

To see where Chimombo is coming from, it is helpful to quote his final comment on this section of the Report:

A printer could not explain how they calculated the cost of printing WASI so I could understand the exorbitant figure they were charging me.

My first response to this is 'Steve, shop around until you find a printer who can make the situation clear to you.' My second is: 'I see you are "Director and Editor" of WASI *(now subtitled 'Magazine for the Arts') and that you and a Managing Editor make up the Editorial Board. Perhaps you should take on a Business Manager whose responsibilities would include negotiating with printers.'*

Learn all you can about the book trade. Read classics such as Stanley Unwin's *The Truth About Publishing*, articles in the daily press, and specialist publications. Keep abreast of developments in African publishing and bookselling, make enquiries about book fairs, book development councils, copyright boards, writers' groups, writers' workshops, and, indeed, all elements of the African book trade.

Chimombo's comments suggest that this may be possible in the 'well-endowed "developed world"' but is impossible in the 'Third World'. News on publishing is, he says, 'rare, book fairs are scarcely heard of, Book Development Councils are non-existent or suppressed, etc.' Clearly work remains to be done, and there are many distressing silences. But the fax, email and Internet are vital tools for gathering information. Nuggets of information about, say, African literature or African publishing, copyright and censorship can be downloaded provided you gain access to the Internet (perhaps through an institutional library). It gives opportunity to all, whether in Dallas, Oxford, or Bristol, Accra, Harare, or Nairobi.

In your business dealings with your publisher, recognise that the situation may change. You may become famous, even rich. Your book may be adopted as a set text, or it may win a prize making you a highly sought-after author. It may earn you a permanent and pensionable professorial post at a richly endowed foreign university. It may get you on to the international speakers' circuit so that you can command tens of thousands of dollars simply by reading from your book! If it does – and this scenario is very, very unlikely – you will quickly become much richer and much more secure financially than your publisher!

On the other hand, your work may sink without trace. Silence, or a few dismissive reviews, may follow publication. Worse, it may be deemed treasonable and earn you a spell in prison. Your publisher may be left with hundreds of unsold copies of your book. He or she may be compelled to reduce them to pulp and, as a result, go bankrupt.

*Chimombo observed: 'I am glad you are aware that it is highly unlikely for a small-time writer to make the "big time" outside his equally small country.' He added: 'Even winning literary prizes seems like a political event, with some countries destined **not** to win any.' This may be a cry from the heart but it cannot be a cry from Malawi which, through my co-editor and others, has a number of distinguished literary prizes to its credit.*

In your discussions, anticipate all the possible developments and the strains they would put on your relationship with your publisher. Ensure that areas of potential confusion and tension are covered by clauses in the contract and/or by an agreed code of practice/conduct (for examples, see pages 131 and 404). At an early stage in your relationship, identify an individual, or agree on the constitution of a body, to whom you could go for arbitration should either party have a grievance.

Chimombo:

> *In reality some writers are given a 'take it or leave it' options.... If a code of conduct was agreed upon it would be surprising if it was in favour of the writer at all.*

This is an interesting take on the situation and of a piece with Chimombo's view of publishers. I can only say: 'If the code of conduct is not fair and just, then don't sign up to it.'

In your calculations, recognise what the different parties are putting into the business arrangement involved in publishing a book. Note the nature of the investments made by each consenting partner: the writer's lonely nights of toil, the publisher's risk of capital; the writer's emotional involvement, the publisher's professional expertise; and so on. See the book as a joint investment. Be helpful, understanding and supportive towards your publisher. Expect to work together after publication. Inform your publishers about lectures or readings you are giving, and about journeys you are making. Arrange with them when it is appropriate to carry around copies for sale (bought at an author's discount of 30 per cent), and expect to take a full part in promoting your title.

Chimombo detailed his unhappy experience with publishers who had not included him in marketing his titles, and this duplicated the experience of Niyi Osundare with Nigerian publishers chronicled in Part 1 of this Handbook. At Arusha III it became clear that Baobab Books (Zimbabwe) made particularly good use of authors in promoting titles, and Osundare's essay indicates that Kenyan publishers made investments in him that surprised Nigerians. Obviously a variety of attitudes exists.

If, however, you feel dissatisfied with your publisher, and if, having communicated your concerns in writing, you consider that your publisher is consistently failing to promote your work through incompetence or lack of imagination, go to arbitration. Initially, as indicated above, an individual who enjoys the respect of both parties may be a suitable point of reference. If the matter cannot be resolved at that level, a panel made up of national publishers and national writers' associations with legal advisors, or one set up by a copyright council, may be appropriate.

In responding to this Chimombo used the happy expression 'It takes the tenacity of a tick to keep prompting a publisher to let you promote your own publication.' And then he commented as follows on the process outlined above:

> *Putting [promptings to publishers] in writing seems to violate [the relation-ship you have established with your publisher]. Taking it further to legal redress seems almost inhuman in such a situation. In any case most African countries do not have an institution that one can express one's woes to.*

While some will resort to litigation more willingly than Chimombo, I do not share his reluctance to put discontent in writing, to issue 'written warnings' marking significant stages in chronicling dissatisfaction. However, I take his point about the absence of institutions. At Arusha III the possibility of panels (the word 'tribunal' was suggested and overwhelmingly rejected) was welcomed by the publishers present, who, I concede, were a particularly honourable selection of members of their profession. Establishing such a panel might be a wise policy for writers/publishers of Chimombo's status on the Malawian literary scene.

Should you have clear evidence of criminal activity by your publisher, you should take legal advice. Of course, this is likely to be expensive, so involve publishers' associations, writers' groups and support organisations at a very early stage. Writers and publishers need one another. Though some publishers write and some writers publish, the skills they exercise are essentially complementary. Admittedly, there have been some who have managed to make a success of the double task and have become self-publishers. It is perfectly possible for you to get your book designed and printed, and for you to take on the tasks of advertising, distributing and generally selling the copies (see 'What is a Publisher', page 211). But it should be noted that there are comparatively few who have managed to make a long-running success of self-publication on a large scale. There is no reason why an author and a publisher should not work together and should not both do well out of producing a book. For this to happen the relationship should be based on clear understanding and mutual respect. The line 'Good fences make good neighbours' is often quoted. It is also true that 'Clearly-worded contracts make good business partners'.

Getting Started

Language, Adaptations and Translations

Language

When will the Nobel Prize be awarded for work written in an African language? As a transition to the topic of language and the African author, it is appropriate to recognise this question raised by Ali A Mazrui in relation to the Nobel Prize. In 1913, the dominance of European languages was broken by the award of the Prize to Rabindranath Tagore for work written in Bengali, but those writing in African languages are still waiting for recognition.

Of course, prizes are not the real issue in deciding what language to use. Writing is a question of communication and there is always the question of deciding who one wants to communicate with and ascertaining which language(s) those people understand and read – not necessarily the same thing. A biography of Chinua Achebe incorporates an exchange that took the author of *Things Fall Apart* somewhat by surprise and opened up new perspectives. Visiting Australia in 1973, Achebe met AD Hope, a poet of considerable stature, and he recollected that:

> [Hope] said wistfully that the only happy writers today were those writing in small languages like Danish. Why? Because they and their readers understand one another and knew precisely what a word meant when it was used.

It seems that this shook Achebe's assumptions about the desirability of 'the English-speaking Union' and he is quoted as saying:

> There was an important sense in which [Hope] was right – that every litera- ture must seek the things that belong unto its peace [*sic.*, surely 'place' – Ed.], must in other words, speak of a particular place, evolve out of the necessities of its history, past and current, and the aspirations and destiny of its people. (Achebe, quoted by Ezenwa-Ohaeto 1997, 180)

Publishers inevitably weigh up the pros and cons of publication bearing in mind the size of the market for a book in a particular language. Their considerations may not coincide with those of authors or of those campaigning for the right to use a particular language.

Distinctions should be made between African publishers and the transnationals: the latter have a vested interest in ensuring the dominance of English, while having access to technology that will give them a distinct advantage should financial inducements make publishing in African languages profitable. In assessing the present situation for 'Autonomous Publishing in Africa', Walter Bgoya mixed the pragmatic argument with the cultural. He said:

> two conditions ... have to prevail for a book culture to take root: a country must reach a level of literacy capable of supporting a publishing industry; and publishing must be in the language or languages which are read by the greatest number of people. English, French or Portuguese cannot, therefore, be the languages in which African publishing will flourish. This is not only because the number of those who speak and read it are the minority in all African countries, but even more because the literature produced by those who cannot write in the African languages is likely to be incapable of dealing truthfully with the world as experienced by the majority of the population. (Bgoya 1984, 88)

He went on to describe the satisfaction he had taken in publishing *Utenzi wa Ras l'Ghuli* by Mgeni bin Fagihs, and the excellent reception afforded *Bwana Myombekere na Bibi Bugonoka na Ntulanalwo a Bulihwali*, translated from the Kikerebe in which he first wrote it by Aniceti Kitereza (Bgoya 1984, 95).

Ngugi wa Thiong'o's determination to write in Gikuyu, and his emphasis on the obligation of the African creative writer to use African languages, is well known (Ngugi 1993). However, his position on the language issue is worth quoting and his account of his publishing venture is worth scrutinising. He made the following points while being interviewed by Lee Nichols in 1996:

> Literature and the Arts are part and parcel of the struggle for ... human rights which are being abused by the terrorist states in Africa. I am editing a journal in Gikuyu language. It is called *Mutiiri*. 'Mutiiri' is a word with several meanings, but all expressing the idea of the guardianship, the mentor, the prop, the supporter. It is a journal that aims at helping Africa prop itself up. I am trying to create a model to show what is possible in African languages. I believe it is very important that there (should) be fora for the different African languages. And then what is originally written in Gikuyu or in Yoruba or Hausa or Kiswahili can be translated into other African languages and that way we pave for a dialogue between our languages.
>
> *Mutiiri* comes out three times a year. Currently it is based in the Comparative Literature Department of New York University. I believe this is the first time that a journal of modern African literature and culture in

an African language has the base and support of a mainstream department in a major university. So we take the task as being very important, a pioneering kind of task. The journal is aimed at those who can read and write Gikuyu language. The idea is to show that if Gikuyu language, which is not very different from any other African language, can sustain a modern literature and thought, then the same is possible in any other similarly situated language.

After recalling that there was some resistance to reading in Gikuyu from 'some of those educated in English', Ngugi told Lee Nichols:

It is some of the younger people who have shown greater interest in the language. They realise that in a world which is rapidly becoming more and more of a global community, the question of identity, the question of their place in such a world is also becoming more and more important. If we Africans do not take the necessary steps, there will be no Africa in the twenty-first century. If we lose our languages we shall become linguistic appendages of French and English and Portuguese.

Ngugi indicated that at the time of the interview, three issues of the publication, each containing about 160 pages, had been produced. His own contribution to the journal had, he said, been mainly on the editorial side, and he had been able to include both old and new writers. Drawn out by Nichols, he spoke of the problems encountered in trying to reach the target readership, generated by the action of the Kenyan government, a government that was:

very hostile to African languages ... to any national initiatives and this includes creativity in African languages.

Asked, 'Will they let your journal into the country?', Ngugi replied in a way that showed a surprising remoteness from the experience on the ground: 'Well, we hope that they do so.' He subsequently pointed out that 'There are readers outside the country. So even if the regime were to stop it, the journal can still survive.' However, the curious reader wonders what 'survival' means in this context, and may be prompted to ask: 'Is the journal a commercially successful venture? How much does it benefit from its association with a university department? How secure is that academic base?' And to ponder whether the intention of providing reading material that will feed and sustain a popular reader-ship is being met.

While recognising what is currently being achieved in fostering African languages as channels for written communication, the benefits of looking to the past and the future are considerable. At the Conference on Creative Writing in African Languages (London, September 1997), Gitahi Gititi provided a fascinating account of the history of writing in the Gikuyu language, and spoke from the heart about the circumstances in which he found himself with his family. An academic working at the University of Rhode Island, he was watching his children grow up 'Drops of ink in a jug of milk ....') without the support of a Gikuyu-speaking community. Many others are in somewhat similar positions and clearly there is a challenge to be taken up. The exact nature of the challenge has been altered by the examples of writers, such as Ngugi, who are committed to the use of African languages, and by developments in telecommunications. The issues are not new and take off from work done in the first decades of this century.

In an article for *West Africa*, Andrew Amegatcher provided an account of the history of the *Christian Messenger, Kristo Senekafo,* published by Basle missionaries, that showed what had been achieved in the past. The missionary publication contained, *inter alia*, news items, human-interest stories, reports on Chieftaincy affairs, academic discussions, and articles about history and travel. In his conclusion Amegatcher wrote of the news coverage:

> It is obvious that if a person was literate only in Akan and relied on the *Christian Messenger*, he would still be almost as well informed as a person who was literate in English.

He noted:

> However, all this fine work came to an abrupt end in 1917, when the British interned the German missionaries as enemy aliens, expropriating their trading company, the Basle Mission Factory, and confiscating their books in Ghanaian languages.

Ater meditating on how local languages might have developed, and referring to the work of the Bureau of Ghanaian Languages, Crakye Dente and Kofi Asare Opoku, he finished challengingly:

> Is it not ironical that people wax lyrical about local languages being on a par with European languages – talk about the need for a national language – yet have not been able to do what the German missionaries did in the backyard of a boarding school sited away from all the lights of Accra? These missionaries relied on a small and inexpensive machine which was only slightly bigger than the Adana machine. Everything was hand-set, yet mistakes were minimal.
>
> Today, with the computer, fax, cars and electricity, organising something like that needs only sustained determination, not UNESCO or World Bank assistance. (Amegatcher 1997, 61)

The struggle to resist major world languages is being waged with marked success by speakers of, for example, Welsh, Maori and

Hebrew. In his thoughtful contribution to a collection of essays on culture and development in Africa already cited, Mazrui looked both to the past and the future, writing that:

> The Pan-Africanism of linguistic/cultural integration will probably be led by East Africa, which enjoys the good fortune of a regionwide indigenous language. That language – Kiswahili – is able to play a role in binding together Tanzania, Kenya, (to some extent) Uganda, Somalia, and (potentially) Rwanda, Burundi, and Eastern Zaïre. Northern Mozambique and Malawi are also feeling Swahili influences. Swahili is spoken by more people than any other indigenous language of Africa. It will hit its first 100 million people early in the twenty-first century, if not sooner. Kiswahili is expanding more rapidly than any other *lingua franca* in the continent. (Altbach and Hassan 1996, 14-15)

The position of language in Africa continues to evolve and linguistic decisions frequently have political causes. At the 1997 London Conference referred to above, a fascinating range of positions was presented. Although the speakers were involved with major languages (Yoruba, Swahili, Sotho, Xhosa and Gikuyu) the problems facing many African languages quickly became apparent. As did concern about what happened to manuscripts submitted for prizes, texts that had been allowed to go out of print, and contracts abdicating all rights that had been signed with youthful ignorance! It became very clear that there were many elements that made the prospects for writers using African languages particularly uncertain. On three occasions after extracts had been read and translated, Joop Berkhout of Spectrum Books expressed an interest in publishing Nigerian texts, either in English or in Yoruba. It seemed extraordinary that an Ibadan-based publisher travelled to London before he encountered these texts: clearly translators, authors or their agents should be submitting proposals to publishers. Or perhaps publishers should keep their ears closer to the ground.

The impact of locally-made videos on the language issue was also raised. It seems that an increasing number of productions are being marketed with dialogue in Hausa, Igbo and Yoruba. Some time ago, Demola James was quoted by Steve Ayorinde as saying:

> Everybody is in favour of the local language films, if well explored and exploited. Though English producers have started making a serious impact, particularly in terms of quality ... it will take some time before they match the indigenous language productions (Ayorinde 1977, 31)

The impact and influence of Hausa Empires, of Chaka Zulu's military prowess and of Swahili trade routes continue to be felt in discussion about the language of literature in Africa. More recent, political events and cultural upheavals also contribute to the debate. For example, the drive to use Swahili throughout Tanzania has clearly had a dramatic impact on a multitude of languages and the fact that the Soweto Uprising of 1976 was fuelled by rejection of Afrikaans continues to have repercussions. In post-apartheid South Africa, university departments of modern languages have found a marked decline in the number of students taking, for example, Italian, while departments offering tuition in African languages have found they are attracting a larger number of students. The way in which language policies and international politics are intertwined was demonstrated by the steps taken by Nigeria during 1997 to ensure wider teaching of French. The timing of the decision was affected by the unpopularity of Sani Abacha's regime, Commonwealth pressure on the rulers to improve their human rights record, and the position of France and Francophone forces in Africa as Sese Seke Mobutu's position in what was then Zaïre worsened.

APNET sponsored Martins Olusegun Fajemisin to undertake a series of studies on the implications of publishing in African languages, and his reports on Kenya and Zimbabwe were published in *APNET Publishing Review* during 1995 and 1996 (see Bibliography). There are many indications that publishing in various African languages will flourish. The example of Sesotho publishing following the tradition of printing introduced by the Paris Evangelical Missionary Society to Lesotho is only one remarkable example. Stephen Gray (1998) has provided a report, noting, for example, that 'nation-building and printing advanced together', and that a paper first published for Sesotho-speakers in 1863 still appears.

The 1998 Zimbabwe International Book Fair reflected the initiatives being taken in publishing in African languages. Holger Ehling wrote as follows in a report for *The Bookseller*:

> Cambridge University Press (CUP) mounted an impressive exhibit that focused on its African language Library, which provides educational texts in various African languages. CUP, in conjunction with Harare-based publisher Academic and Baobab Books, used the event to launch the Zimbabwean strand of the library, with books in Shona and Ndebele. 'We actively co-operate with publishers in the respective markets', said Tony Seddon of CUP South Africa. 'Editing, marketing and distribution are far easier to facilitate if local resources are used.' (Ehling 1998)

Those present at the Book Fair also had an opportunity to hear Don Long of Learning Media speaking about exciting developments in publishing children's books with colour illustrations in different Pacific Island languages. Briefly, writers are asked to supply their original language text, together with an English version, which is then translated into other languages. Large, relatively inexpensive print runs are possible with advantages in terms of royalties for the authors and in terms of the production values for readers. Long stressed that the texts selected were not 'stilted textbook stories with questions in reading programmes' but 'real' books: 'real children's books written by the best Pacific writers'.

'Correct' Use of Language

The question of 'standardisation' and the elevation of a particular variety of language into the 'correct' form has inhibited many writers. In an extreme form, 'linguistic policing' found expression in Malawi during Banda's period in power, when 'correct Chichewa' was defined by the Head of State and his Chichewa Board as that spoken in and around the Life President's home area of Kasungu. The sudden and malicious methods employed by over-eager servants of the regime to enforce what they believed to be their master's will inhibited some of those anxious to work in Chichewa. The use of other Malawian languages in schools, in newspapers and on the radio was proscribed. Speakers of dialects of Chichewa other than that spoken in the central region naturally felt oppressed, wounded and resentful.

Other languages, including Twi, Ewe and Shona, have escaped dictators only to come under the influence of formidable scholars, of Boards and of Bureaux that have had the effect of establishing – or seeking to establish – certain norms of usage and orthography. In Ghana, the Twi spoken by the refugee community of Akans at Akropong was the variety studied by early linguists and missionaries, whose pioneering work gave it an authority and reputation that continue to this day. Inevitably the processes involved in 'standardisation' are painful to some and give advantages to others.

Some Examples from Igbo

Donatus I Nwoga, a distinguished critic, a much-loved professor and a major figure in the field of Igbo studies, issued the following challenge:

> The responsibility with which we are charged is to standardise for the Igbo people a language which unifies them and gives them an identity, a language in which they can be educated in the tradition which has now established that first-language education is the best, especially in the early years of the educational process. We are charged with the responsibility to forge for our people a language which can bear the burden of giving expression to their experiences and communication to their ideas. The Igbo have always been a people who hanker after new experiences, who latch on to new developments, who travel to new places and acquire new styles.

They have to have language which is adaptable and expansive, a language which does not restrain their efforts to accommodate their experiences, a language receptive to new ideas and technology. The impatience of the Igbo to advance cannot tolerate a language that would tie them to the apron strings of tradition or create tortuous phrases where adapted words would serve the same function of giving names to thoughts, things and situations.

In trying to achieve such a language, we must think of the living. But, most importantly, we must think of generations to come. This means that, in line with our traditions, those of us living today might have to make sacrifices in order that what is not possible in our time may be possible and perhaps bear fruit in the lives of our children and grandchildren.

This carefully phrased appeal gains poignancy from the fact that Nwoga no longer speaks from among the living. It introduces an article in which, drawing partly on PEH Hair's account entitled *The Early Study of the Languages of the Lower Niger and Benue, 1840-1890*, Nwoga traces the history of missionary and other attempts to analyse the grammatical structure of the Igbo language, and come to terms with the variety of dialects of the language. He repeats the stories of the Rev JF Schon of the Church Missionary Society who, having learned one dialect of Igbo in Sierra Leone, discovered that the King of Aboh was 'so bored by pronunciation and intonation which he could not understand that he soon interrupted [Schon's] speech'. The influence of Sierra Leone was also felt by the Rev JC Taylor, who, born of Igbo parents in Freetown, found that the Igbo he spoke was so strange to the people of Onitsha that he had to preach to them through an interpreter. During the second half of the nineteenth century, the Rev Adjai Crowther worked with a team on an Igbo dictionary and an Igbo translation of the Bible using the 'so-called Isuama dialect' (Nwoga 1984, 105). But, it seems, by 1876 Isuama had been discarded, and translations were being undertaken into Onitsha and Bonny dialects. This meant that at a time when Yoruba was being standardised on the basis of Oyo Yoruba, the Igbo language was affected by deep divisions.

The background to Nwoga's appeal quoted above is the failure of successive attempts to achieve consensus on an acceptable form of the language. Various forms have, it seems, been proposed including Union Igbo – a mixture of Onitsha, Owerri and Bonny Igbo that found some advocates between 1904 and 1939, and attracted a number of creative writers including Peter Nwana and DN Achara – and Central Igbo, which combines with Owerri Igbo some elements from northern dialects including Nsukka, Eke, and Udi. Nwoga brought the story of Igbo more or less up to date by writing: 'Since the early 1970s, the Society for Promoting Igbo Language and Culture (SPLIC) has accepted a modified form of this Central Igbo as the basis of the development of the standard Igbo.' He continues:

> This would appear to have sorted out the problem of dialect which had plagued Igbo studies and literature from the nineteenth century. The situation, however, is that vigorous efforts continue to be made to oppose this standard, indicating that the Igbo have not changed their understanding of the possible contribution of the linguistic factor to their unity, identity and development. (Nwoga 1984, 108)

Nwoga moves on to appeal for acceptance of 'the central dialect that has emerged over the years', of the 'Onwu orthography', of borrowing as a means of expanding vocabulary, and of setting up 'a full-scale and full-time Igbo Language Board'. The responsibilities of the Board would be:

> first to promote the standardisation and development of the Igbo language; and, second, to generate the appropriate programmes for increasing the viability of Igbo as a used and growing language. (Nwoga 1994, 114)

Readers of Achebe's fiction have been granted insights into the segmented, dynamic Igbo community which is likely to produce and defend numerous dialects. Deeply engaged by matters of language, Achebe attacked Union Igbo in *ANU Magazine* (1979) and later, in a journal he founded called *Uwa ndi Igbo*, he defended the decision to include poems in a variety of Igbo dialects in an anthology, *Aka Weta*. On that occasion, he expressed his belief that literature should 'give full unfettered play to the creative genius of Igbo speech in all its splendid variety, not to dam it up into the sluggish pond of a sterile pedantry'. He expressed the view that the Igbo language had been:

> saddled one generation after another with egoistic schoolmen who have been concerned not to study the language but to steer it into narrow tracks of their particular pet illusion. That, and not dialects, has been at the heart of our long blackout. (Achebe, quoted by Nwoga 1984, 108. See also Ezenwa-Ohaeto 1997, 234, 237)

Some Examples from English

The history of the English language provides abundant evidence of the extraordinary range of influences on a form of communication, one which has eschewed the dictates of an Academy in the interest of growth, flexibility and freedom, and which currently exists in numerous varieties. Discussion about the state of the language, usage and possible future developments continues with, if anything, increasing vigour. For African writers, the most pertinent issue is sometimes posed in terms of 'What particular qualities should be, firstly, encouraged and/or, secondly, tolerated in the use of English by African authors?'

The story of African literature in English includes the Tale of Amos Tutuola, who asked his publishers at Faber and Faber to correct his grammar and whose later books reveal evidence of a determination to master standard English. The 'story' also includes the example of Chinua Achebe, who asserted at one stage that the English language could carry the burden that he loaded on to it. He also said:

> I do not feel much kinship, basically, with the English tradition although I use the English language. I have no thorough respect or worship for it. It is a very fine instrument, but not an object of ritual. I respect ritual, but it tends to make objects irrelevant to present-day situations when it extends to areas outside religion. (Achebe 1979, quoted in Ezenwa-Ohaeto 1997, 179)

English, it should be appreciated, is a flexible and responsive language. At least Gabriel Okara and Ken Saro-Wiwa appear to have found it to be so, and they are worth listening to on the subject of language. Significantly, they are from small language groups who had to come to terms with the fact that their roles in the vast federation of Nigeria were mostly going to be played in English.

Gabriel Okara

In the early 1960s, Rajat Neogy's magazine *Transition* kept students of African literature – and of politics and culture generally – in touch with developments. Number 11, September 1963, was a typically lively, spiky, provocative, substantial issue. It included a reaction by Obi Wali, partly prompted by the 1962 Makerere Writers Conference. He asserted that 'African literature as now defined and understood, leads nowhere.' And said that the purpose of his article was:

> not to discredit those writers who have achieved much in their individual rights within an extremely difficult and illogical situation. It is to point out that the whole uncritical acceptance of English and French as the inevitable medium for educated African writing is misdirected.

He continued:

> Until these writers and their Western midwives accept the fact that true African literature must be written in African languages, they would be merely pursuing a dead end, which can only lead to sterility, uncreativity and frustration.

Wali's 'Dead End for African Literature' was followed by Gabriel Okara's 'African speech ... English Words', which included the following:

> Trying to express ideas even in one's own language is difficult because what
> is said or written often is not exactly what one had in mind. Between the
> birth of the idea and its translation into words, something is lost. The
> process of expression is even more difficult in the second language of one's
> cultural group. I speak of not merely expressing general idea, but of
> communicating an idea to the reader in the absolute and near absolute
> state in which it was conceived. Here, you see I am already groping for
> words to make you understand what I really mean as an African.

He subsequently observed:

> As a writer who believes in the utilisation of African ideas, African philoso-
> phy and African folk-tale imagery to the fullest extent possible, I am of the
> opinion the only way to use them effectively is to translate them almost
> literally from the African language native to the writer into whatever Euro-
> pean language he is using as his medium of expression. I have endeavoured
> in my words to keep as close as possible to the vernacular expressions. For,
> from a word, a group of words, a sentence and even a name in any African
> language, one can glean the social norms, attitudes and values of the people.
>
> In order to capture the vivid images of African speech, I had to eschew
> the habit of expressing my thoughts first in English. It was difficult at first,
> but I had to learn. I had to study each Ijaw expression I used and to discover
> the probable situation in which it was used in order to bring out the nearest
> meaning in English. I found it a fascinating exercise.

He then illustrated the kind of choices he had to make in order to
convey Ijaw idioms in a way that is understandable in English, and he
justified the resulting innovations as part of the growth of a living
language. He concluded with the challenge, 'Why shouldn't there be a
Nigerian or West African English which we can use to express our own
ideas, thinking and philosophy in our own way?'

The full realisation of Okara's experiment was *The Voice* published
in 1964 by André Deutsch which was greeted with a predictably mixed
response. It remains an uncompromising and radical experiment
which has found few imitators but which has established limits. It
provided inspiration for the writer whose example is considered below:
Ken Saro-Wiwa dramatised *The Voice* in a text that deserves to be
performed and published. Before moving on to Saro-Wiwa, we focus
briefly on the publisher who introduced Okara to the world: André
Deutsch. Following a visit to Nigeria by the founder of the
distinguished, but no longer operating, London-based company,
Okara, JP Clark-Bekederemo (*America, Their America*) and Wole
Soyinka (*The Interpreters*) were all signed up. Deutsch's visit repre-

sented an unusual example of what might be called 'pro-active midwifery' that deserves to be more fully investigated.

Saro-Wiwa, Soyinka, Swahili and Khana

Saro-Wiwa's control of English register was remarkable: he wrote poetry, polemic, standard and 'rotten' English, and he contributed to the language debate in Nigeria and beyond with characteristic wit and versatility. For example, he presented his views on Soyinka's recommendation that Swahili should be adopted as a continental language in a newspaper article entitled 'Bondudekiswahili' (Saro-Wiwa 1991a). The column begins: 'When Baba woke up yesterday, he found his normally affable wife in a strange mood and speaking in tongues.' To Baba's salutations, greetings and enquiries, his wife replies 'Bondudekiswahili', since she has, it seems, decided henceforth to address her husband only in Swahili. The Professor, who diagnoses the situation, ascribes the transformation to the Holy Spirit, asserting that Swahili 'is the language chosen by God to deliver his oppressed children of Africa from the hands of the oppressor'. Baba asks why God could not have chosen other languages. The following exchange takes place between Baba and Professor:

'... Why did he not pick on Yoruba?'
'Yoruba is a language of lies. There are so many Nigerian liars because there are so many Yoruba speakers. That language must die.'
'Will Hausa then live?'
'Hausa is the language of laziness. Nigerians are lazy because they speak Hausa.'
'What of Igbo?'
'Igbo is the language of war! If Nigerians did not speak Igbo, there would be no quarrels, no fights, no wars. National unity would have been achieved.'
'What of Khana?'
'What's that?'
'Some Nigerian language.'
'Never heard of it.'

Saro-Wiwa continues his jesting, his feather-ruffling, his chop-logic. He swipes to left and right, and pulls carpet after carpet from under his opponents' feet. When Baba asks 'And this African pride, will it build bridges, cut the roads, cure the sick, chase mosquitoes, make the people work hard, this Swahili ...?' Professor sweeps in:

'Oh, yes. Don't you see? The Arabs all speak Arabic. They build their own bridges, cut their roads, fight wars bravely, with their own weapons. Whereas those stupid, backward Europeans still speak Dutch, Woloon [sic], Flemish, Gaelic, English, German, French, Russian. Even in a small country like

Switzerland, they are illiterate enough to speak four different languages. It's no wonder they are a nation of wretched hoteliers, watchmakers and bankers. This multiplicity of languages is responsible for the European inability to invent anything.'

From all this it emerges that the article is, on one level, a skirmish in the war for recognition of 'micro-languages', such as Khana, and it comes as no surprise to learn that while in the service of Rivers State, Saro-Wiwa campaigned for the teaching of local languages.

Footnote on Saro-Wiwa and English

Incidentally, Saro-Wiwa's mastery of varieties of English made him acutely sensitive to what he regarded as the misuse of modals, notably the confusion of 'would' and 'will' in standard English. He argued on the matter with outraged energy, and without any sense that here was an instance of a West African variant emerging. Were he alive today, he would encounter numerous examples of the error, confusion, or tolerated deviation.

For information on an organisation that is relevant to this discussion contact Action Group for the Promotion of Publications in African Languages (details on page 209).

Adaptations

There is no reason why a work written in one genre should not be adapted so that it makes an appearance in another form. Throughout this Handbook there has been reference to fiction, poetry and drama – and at times it may have seemed as if these European conventions were being used to account for every literary product from the African continent. This was not the intention: the three terms are used simply as a convenient shorthand. They are rough and ready categories, useful but not limiting. Many authors discover that an idea finds expression in several genres: what begins life as a film-script may come to exist in other forms.

Ousmane Sembene's *Black Girl* exists as both a film and a short story. Wole Soyinka first conceived *The Road* as a film. Nkem Nwankwo's novel *Danda* and Mango Beti's *Houseboy* enjoyed great successes after being moved from the page to the stage. Ken Saro-Wiwa presented *Basi and Co.* on stage, on television, and as a story, having carried out the 'novelisation' himself. Clearly, the examples of 'genre bending', the ducking and diving between forms, are numerous. If you have a good plot, why not use it for a novel, a film, a television drama, a strip-cartoon, a photo-story, a stage play, an animated film, a radio play, a dance drama?

On occasions authors may have to insist upon their rights in an adaptation. Senior Yoruba novelist Oladejo Okediji established an important precedent in Nigerian law by taking a travelling theatre company to court for using his material without permission. However, authors should be aware that it is not always easy to prove plagiarism.

When consciously engaged upon a work of adaptation, authors should obtain permission from the rights holder. Even when the borrowings are barely conscious, credit must be given where it is due. Malian author Yambo Ouologuem suffered greatly after it was pointed out that his novel *Le devoir de violence* was partly a reworking of a European source. On the other hand, it is obvious that there are shared experiences and narrative traditions that are held in common. No one is suggesting that these should not be used.

It is also recognised that each generation of writers feeds off predecessors: for example, there has been no serious suggestion that Osofisan should be penalised for engaging in a dialogue with his elders in *No More the Wasted Breed* and *Another Raft*. In other words, engaging with an idea spawned by another writer is not plagiarism. Precisely where 'engagement', imitation and robbery begin and end is a question for literary critics and historians. The expensive trouble starts when lawyers are invited to become involved with what theorists refer to as inter-textuality.

Translations

> [Writers should] engage themselves actively, from now, on the work of translation. [The challenge is]:
> To translate our English writings into French or Portuguese, and vice versa;
> To translate French, English, Portuguese authors, including foreign classics, into our indigenous languages;
> To translate works from indigenous languages into French, English, Portuguese; and
> To translate works from one indigenous language into another.

Femi Osofisan provoked considerable discussion when, speaking in May 1988 at the Lagos International Symposium on African Literature, he issued this challenge (Osofisan, *et al*. 1991, 49). Many of those who heard him were multilingual and many were engaged in remarkable feats of translation on a daily basis. However, while a large number had been involved in one or two of the undertakings he advocated, very, very few had grappled with the issues raised by all four. An infinitesimal number had taken up the final challenge: to translate works from one indigenous African language into another.

As Osofisan was well aware, translation from European languages has played a huge role in the history of African languages and literatures. For instance, the work of missionaries in translating the Bible, and English classics such as *Pilgrim's Progress,* into African languages has long been recognised as being of importance in establishing conventions for writing in African languages. Cultural, educational, artistic and political initiatives have prompted other ventures, including Thomas Decker's translation of *Julius Caesar* into Sierra Leonean Creole, and Julius Nyerere's more famous Swahili rendition of the same Shakespearean original. In turn, the major works of selected Anglophone and Francophone African writers have, with various degrees of success, been translated into other European and into a number of Asian languages. Thanks to the efforts of Janheinz Jahn, some African works composed in English and French were first published in German translations!

The processes of translation have continued to the advantage of readers of European languages. In other words, it has proved commercially viable to make available the giants of Francophone literature to Anglophone readers, and *vice versa.* There has also been a certain amount of translation into English and French of Portuguese texts.

However, there has been comparatively little translation of African writing into African languages. True, a Yoruba version of *Death and the King's Horseman* prepared by Akinwumi Isola was staged in 1994 and is now available, and *The Trials of Brother Jero* has appeared in a Swahili translation. But the role-call is comparatively short, and when coming to consider books written in one indigenous African language and translated into another we find the situation is very depressing. Osofisan's fourth appeal has rarely been heeded.

African writers cannot be blamed for the dearth of translations. Major authors who have taken on translation projects include JP Clark-Bekederemo, who expended huge efforts on recording and translating the *Ozidi Saga,* and Wole Soyinka, who tackled the complex Yoruba of Fagunwa's *Forest of a Thousand Daemons.* It is to be hoped that appropriate incentives and rewards will be made available to encourage writers to respond to all of Osofisan's challenges. At the London Conference held during September 1997, Isola showed that the issues involved in translating are well understood, and argued that the establishment of university courses to address them is of prime importance.

Isola's translation of Soyinka's work prompted a very important analysis by the brilliant Nigerian scholar Dan Izevbaye. Writing in *Research in African Literatures,* he raises basic questions about translation in Africa, referring to versions of *Pilgrim's Progress* and the fact that Okot p'Bitek first wrote *Song of Lawino* in Acoli. He also examines the status of *Horseman*, and Achebe's *Arrow of God*, and draws attention to factors affecting the emergence of Isola's translations of Soyinka's work. These factors include attending a production of *Horseman* at Ife, discussion with Abiola Irele and Odia Ofeimun, and 'the importunity of Agbo Areo', the author-publisher, who wanted a translation of *Aké* for Yoruba courses in Nigerian schools as well as for the general Yoruba reading public. Izevbaye writes:

> Not much was needed to persuade Isola. What Areo urged on him was to begin with the translation of *Aké* and suspend translation of *Death and the King's Horseman*, which to Isola had primary claims because he felt it would be more immediately available to a Yoruba audience. The translation of *Aké* was duly completed, although its publication [was delayed] ... *Iku Olokun-Esin* (199c) was published first because it was one of the plays chosen to mark Soyinka's sixtieth birthday. (Izevbaye 1997, 156-57)

Izevbaye investigates the translation with authority and objectivity, bearing in mind the performance element and the implications of Isola's choices of vocabulary. He shows how the Yoruba version 'seems to focus more directly on the historicity of the play than the original text does' (158) and writes particularly well on the implications of the usages made familiar by those who translated the Bible into Yoruba, linguists who had what Izevbaye called an 'unecumenical' attitude to traditional religion. A brief extract:

> ... in the Yoruba Bible the Yoruba equivalent of god (*orisa*) is reserved for 'idols' (1 Cor. 8.1[AV]) – more accurately *ere* in Yoruba. This blurs the distinction that is drawn in Yoruba between the inanimate *ere* (idol, image), the live *orisa* (deity), and the supreme Olorun (God). (Izevbaye 1997, 160)

Doubtless this debate will run and run. This translation should provoke passionate discussion. The trouble is that too often the translations have been greeted with near silence. *Forest of a Thousand Daemons* is one of the most under-reviewed of Soyinka's works. Those willing to write about Clark-Bekederemo's dramatisation *Ozidi* have far outnumbered those who have entered into public examination of his translation of the *Ozidi Saga*.

Izevbaye's article draws on research into the history and regional variations of Yoruba; he notes that Isola translated *Horseman* 'into the Oyo dialect', and helpfully points out that at the première Sergeant Amusa was played as an Ekiti man. He highlights the difference 'between the metrical (that is, stress-based) rhythm of English verse and the musical (that is, pitch-based) rhythm of Yoruba chants', and draws attention to the problems raised by having even the character Jane Pilkings, the British District Commissioner's wife, speaking

Yoruba. One of the most difficult lines to translate comes when Jane
Pilkings says Olunde could have been a 'poet munching rose petals in
Bloomsbury'. Izevbaye writes:

> Since a literal translation into Yoruba would be meaningless, Isola seeks a
> cultural equivalent of the general meaning by adopting for his version of an
> *oriki* [Yoruba praise poetry] of a little known community, *Amukuderin*
> [personal communication] from which he draws on the idea of superannu-
> ated hunters subsisting on dried yams ...

Izevbaye adds 'the reference is likely to be obscure, requiring annotation to bring it into the general awareness of the theatre-going
audience' (168-69). One might add that the cultural, social and
historical associations of 'Bloomsbury' are so specific that Isola's
translation does not sound likely to carry much of the weight of
Soyinka's image of effete aestheticism. Perhaps while seeking an
equivalent or substitute, Isola questioned the part of his project that
required translation of the scene between Olunde and Jane Pilkings.
Code switching [moving between languages in a single sentence or
exchange] is a way of life. Isola might have taken the option of
translating only those parts of the play that were, in his words at the
London conference, 'excellent Yoruba written in English'.

It is a pleasure to recommend Izevbaye's work in this context, not
only because it discusses issues concerning translation that will find
echoes in many African countries, but because he provides an account
of the roles played by publishers, writers and an authors' association
(Irele, Ofeimun, Area, the Association of African Languages (ANA)) in
getting a translation into print and on to the stage.

Too often it is forgotten that it takes a 'village' to make a translation
and mount a play.

The debate about publishing in African languages was brightly illu-
minated by Ngugi's decision to embrace the Gikuyu language as the
vehicle for his creative writing. Here was a major author, a man with an
established international reputation, who said that henceforth some of
his work would only be available to a large number of his faithful
readers through the efforts of a translator. There are repercussions here
for author, reader, and – our particular interest here – the translator
seeking to earn a living from his or her special skill. *The Writers' and
Artists' Yearbook* indicates that translators should be able to negotiate
an advance 'on account of royalty of 2.5 per cent and a small share of
the proceeds from secondary uses such as paperback reprint and American rights'. However, presumably partly because Ngugi's international
renown weighed with his publisher, his translator was able to arrange to
be paid 3 per cent.

Those who, following Nyerere, Clark-Bekederemo, Isola and Soyinka, venture into the field of translation should recognise that different kinds of translation involve different skills; and that literary translation is among the most demanding, most satisfying and worst paid. *The Writers and Artists' Yearbook* recommends that those interested in becoming translators should prepare an example of their work – an extended passage of a text they know to be available for translation – and submit this to potential publishers. If it is acceptable, and the publisher purchases the rights to the relevant translation, a commission to translate a novel may be forthcoming. Negotiation of terms can then begin. Rates vary, but, apparently, 'for the commoner languages' (and based on European rates) the advance payment should range from £55 upwards per thousand words and the percentages cited above are useful to bear in mind. Translators, incidentally, should guard their copyright and negotiate with publishers only for specific rights.

Previously published literary translators working in the UK may contact a professional body, The Translators' Association (see Writers' Organisations: A Directory, page 210). The Secretary points out that the Minimum Terms Agreement (page 395) provides a good basis for negotiation for the author of a work in English that is to be translated into another language. For such work the Association supplies its members with a Model Contract, which provides the basis for a working partnership. As more translations appear, so the desirability of translators' associations in Africa increases.

For advice on translation into German see the entry for Peter Ripken and the Society for the Promotion of African, Asian and Latin American Literature (Writers' Organisations: A Directory, page 209).

The discussion initiated by Osofisan's call in Lagos quoted above also produced practical suggestions: it was recognised that 'translation dictionaries' were needed, and that for many African languages there were no 'explaining dictionaries'. The preparation of such volumes was regarded by a number of people as very desirable. In this context, it is encouraging to hear that Nigerian dramatist Ola Rotimi has turned lexicographer and is producing a dictionary for Pidgin English.

The Lagos session concluded with a participant's plea that is all the more moving because it is almost lost in the very activity it advocates, translation:

> Excuse me please. There is one other point I want us to take home and that is as African writers here. I am begging every African country here today at least to make friends and let us exchange our books, our own books to be translated into other country's languages. (Osofisan, *et al.* 1991, 102)

Prizes, Awards, and Contests

'The prize wasn't much, but it made me feel like a poet. I would get up, and, instead of feeling that I was a housewife, I thought "I am a poet".' Testimony reported at the Conference on Organising Literary Competitions, London, September 1997.

Although very few people write in order to win prizes, literary competitions have had an extraordinary impact on the development of authors – and for this reason a discussion of literary prizes provides a convenient point of departure. At the conference on Creative Writing in African Languages held in London during 1997, Oladejo Okediji, doyen of Yoruba novelists, described how his introduction to the world of creative writing came through participation in a literary competition. It does not appear to have been a very well-organised competition since entries seem to have been mislaid! However, again and again published writers at the conference stressed the importance of winning prizes in starting a career in creative writing.

Prizes often involve controversy. Journalists, salivating over the sums of money involved in the largest competitions, delight in exposing the higgling, haggling and horse-trading that goes on when judges are closeted together. This is to be expected since part of the function of a prize is to get literature on to the front pages of newspapers and in among the television news stories. A competition makes people talk about texts. However, the coverage is sometimes somewhat undignified, and tends to bring the competition itself into disrepute. Over and over again, one learns the lesson that literary judgments are highly subjective and that when a handful of articulate and thoughtful, not to say opinionated, people – the sort who are generally asked to judge literary prizes – have to pick a winner, compromise is inevitable.

Journalists often get, or pretend to hold on to, the wrong end of the 'prize stick'. For example, if many books have been submitted for a prize, there is usually, and quite appropriately, a sifting process that eliminates numerous texts before the eminent panel gets to work. However, journalists looking for 'an angle' often come up with a scoop along the lines 'Judge of Literary Prize did not read all texts submitted!' In fact, collecting preliminary assessments and gathering the opinions of assessors is frequently necessary and sometimes inevitable. Losers may feel aggrieved that their work was not read from cover to cover by the chief judge, but they should recognise the kind of venture they have become involved with by entering – or by having their book entered for – a competition.

Some competitions are, unfortunately, poorly organised, and some are sinister in their purpose. Aspiring authors need to be alert and the organisers of *bona fide* competitions should be aware that there is a disreputable underside to their business. There are those who mislead and exploit, whose aim in announcing that there are prizes to be won is to obtain publishable material without entering into proper agreements with authors. There are some who play on the aspirations of authors desperate to get into print. (See variations on this under 'Poetry Prizes – a cautionary word', page 173 and 'Vanity Publishers', page 271.) Writers should be circumspect, aware that the words 'You could win a prize' have proved among the most successful in attracting attention to advertising and promotional campaigns.

At this point, it should be appreciated that establishing literary prizes is neither simple nor cheap. It has been indicated that the sifting of nominations for the Nobel Prize for Literature absorbs as much money as the award itself. Of course, there are those who consider this scandalous and it may be that the members of the Swedish Academy, the academicians charged with selecting the winner, eat inordinately well when they gather to consider nominations.

Some expenses are, however, inevitable. Before a significant prize can be awarded a secretariat has to be set up, the competition has to be advertised, the entries have to be moved around between readers, assessors have to prepare reports and be paid for them, and the judges have to meet – which will certainly involve some eating and may involve travelling expenses and hotel bills. The award ceremony itself has to be organised and some, including some of those among the press corps invited to ensure media coverage, will feel that the importance of the prize is measured by the number of people who sit down to a silver service dinner at the award celebration. There may even be those for whom the vintage of the wine in which the winner is toasted is as important as the quality of the winner's writing.

Since literature is glibly regarded as 'a good thing' and since judging a competition confers power while indicating status, some people will be prepared to help competition organisers without charging for their services. However, payment to 'readers' ensures a professional approach and is to be encouraged. Rates vary but, at the time of writing, £40 for reading a novel and commenting on it is not uncommon in the UK. Indeed it would be hard to offer much less since a specialist is being asked to devote several hours to producing a considered opinion. There are no recognised plumbers or electricians in the UK who would work for the same rate. Expenses incurred by the secretariat mount up so that without firm financial backing any prize is in jeopardy.

Understanding Competitions

The following figures relating to a UK poetry competition run for profit by a small publishing house, a registered charity, are presented in order to indicate the kind of financial implications involved in setting up a modest award. The organisers, as can be seen, benefit from sponsorship, but this is of considerably less significance in the accounts than the income from entry fees. Even a superficial glance will indicate that in this case 'Entry Fees' – which are not common in such events – provide the bulk of the income, and cover both the prizes and administrative costs. The sponsors – their name on the prize – had clearly decided that it was advantageous to be associated with such a venture. The publisher must have felt the event was worth organising – despite all the work involved and the very modest profit.

Income
  Sponsorship (a leading UK supermarket chain) £3,500
  Entry fees £12,729

Expenditure
  Prizes £5,100
  Administrative Assistance £1,000
  Judges' Fees £1,250
  Advertising and Promotion £2,343
  Postage, Packaging and Freight £2,608
  Photocopying and faxes £222
  Travelling, Meeting and Judges' Expenses £750
  Total £13,273

  Net Profit £2,956

Those who enter competitions should ensure that they understand the terms of entry. For example, they should be aware of any implications regarding loss of copyright.

They should – as people concerned about language – be cautious of any competition that is habitually described as 'prestigious' and of any awards lazily dubbed 'coveted'. These adjectives are often used in an attempt to give importance to insignificant prizes or to indicate that the financial benefits are very small.

Selected Representative Competitions

The Commonwealth Writers Prize

The organisation of the Commonwealth Writers Prize is one of the most complex, since it involves both regional competitions (Eurasia, Southeast Asia, Pacific, Canada and the Caribbean and Africa) and an overall winner: the Commonwealth Prize. Those chairing regional judging panels receive about £1,000 and members of each panel are 'paid' about £500. These are small amounts when set against the time spent in reading entries, in arranging and attending meetings. However, in addition to the intangibles mentioned above, there is, since judges are drawn from a variety of countries and meet in a variety of venues, the inducement of foreign travel.

These are some comments from Diana Bailey, project co-ordinator:

> The strengths of the prize are its public relations weaknesses. The rather cumbersome judging process militates against press excitement but the regional juries and the fact that we encourage entries from small publishers around the Commonwealth are at the heart of the prize. We don't want everything to be centred on London because the great richness of the prize is having a group of people looking at books from the cultural perspective of their own region. Year in, year out that has resulted in different decisions being made in the regions from those reached by metropolitan juries.
>
> The whole business of Commonwealth literature is to many people an artificial construct. If you ask the writers who have won the Commonwealth Prize 'What do you understand by Commonwealth literature?' often they will say it doesn't mean anything to them, that they are Australian or Indian writers, or whatever. In academic circles the concept of Commonwealth literature has been overtaken by post-colonial literature. So you have to come back to the notion of the Commonwealth as a political entity, but also as something more than that.
>
> The Commonwealth to outsiders is sometimes seen as an anachronism, as old-fashioned, as imperialist, and many people in this country say 'Why the Commonwealth, what value does it have?' In purely historical terms it shouldn't exist, it doesn't make any sense but it does exist and it is greatly valued by the countries that belong to it: at a political level but also at a people's level. When you look at the things that bind the Commonwealth together they're to do with shared traditions of democracy, law, education, but perhaps the key thing is the shared language – that for educated people in the Commonwealth the shared language is English. Again that's an imperialist hangover, but it's a fact. It's the shared language which is the key to

being able to run the Commonwealth Writers Prize. (Bailey quoted by Moss 1998, 27-28)

And from a judge at the 1998 competition, Kofi Anyidoho:

> ... last month I had the privilege of serving on a panel of judges for the Commonwealth Writers Prize for the Africa Region. About 85 per cent of the entries were ... from South Africa, and of that all but two were by white South African fiction writers. Indeed, the regional prize for the best first-published book went to Pamela Jooste, a white South African woman, for her novel *Dance with a Poor Man's Daughter*. The regional prize for the best first book [also went to a] South African, Ronnie Govender, [for] his collection of short stories, *At the Edge*. And yet, only a few years ago and perhaps even now, many of us would routinely omit white South African writers from all our courses on African literatures! (Anyidoho 1998a, 8)

The (Daily Telegraph) Arvon International Poetry Competition

Established in 1980, this biennial competition was held in 1998 with Fleur Adcock as one of the judges. There are no restrictions on themes, or the number of lines, on the age or nationality of entrants. But the poems must be in English and must each be accompanied by a £5.00 entry fee. Poems that have been published or broadcast are not eligible.

Writing on her experiences of the competition, Adcock drew attention to the significant number of entries from Nigeria among the nearly 7,500 submitted. A simple calculation suggests that Arvon's income from entry fees was approaching £37,500. Arvon did not have to fund the prize from entry fees since the first prize of £5,000 and the £5,000 for five runners-up and for ten whose work was 'highly commended' were contributed by Duncan Lawrie Ltd. However, presumably, they had to provide administrative support and pay the judges. Adcock refreshingly commented, in an article that appeared in the *Daily Telegraph* on 19 September 1998: 'Unlike the competitors, the judges can always be sure of receiving a cheque.' The Foundation, which has an excellent reputation, is active in promoting poetry, and creative writing generally. It organises a number of well-led writing retreats that provide opportunities for amateurs to work with professional writers. Bursaries for those on low incomes, the unemployed, students and pensioners are available.

On judging literary competitions, Adcock wrote:

> I always assure people that a poetry competition is not a lottery, but, in some senses, it is: a bad poem will not win, but an excellent one may well be overlooked.

Personal tastes vary. In a big competition there are too many entries for every judge to read everything; the poems are divided up, so that each judge takes a share, and then reads the other judges' short-list. We never know everything that has been rejected early on.

Clearly the open nature of the competition meant the entries varied vastly in size (there were some book-length poems), in subject (there were a number of responses to contemporary events), and in accomplishment. There were some submissions which Adcock described as 'fumbling attempts at self-expression, which were heart-felt but did not show any evidence that the writers had read any poetry since they left school'. And others which, she said, were 'assured, professional-looking work (that any editor would be happy to publish'.

These observations, and the other comments quoted, should give poets who are thinking of entering a competition cause to pause and think. Have they, for example, been reading poetry – thinking and talking about it? Is their work 'professional-looking'? Adcock is probably kind in referring to 'fumbling attempts at self-expression'. Some work presented for public scrutiny is trite, crass, clumsy, inept. Lots of people write poetry: Malthouse Press (Lagos) receives many texts from poets longing to see their work between covers. But not all of those poets read poetry, think about poetry, criticise poetry, work at poetry. Sifting, rewriting, rejecting, reading aloud, submitting to friends, talking frankly with colleagues – these are some of the processes a poet might expect to go through before spending £5.00 on entering a poetry competition.

The prize-winning poems were among 75 entered for the competition that were included in an anthology of competition entries entitled *The Ring of Words* (London: Sutton and Telegraph Books).

The 'Green' Poetry Competition

The Co-ordination Unit for the Rehabilitation of the Environment (CURE) invited Malawian citizens to take part in a competition to write poems, in English or Chichewa 'on environmental problems in Malawi'. The conditions of entry and an entry form appeared in *WASI Writer*, Vol. 8, no. 2 (1997), and showed that the organisers were well aware of the need to exclude those who might, by virtue of working for the promoters, have undue advantage. The terms of the competition clearly ensured that copyright remained with the authors. The conditions also stipulated that work already offered for publication was not eligible, and indicated that each entrant was limited to submitting three poems of up to 50 lines. The final condition read:

The organisers reserve the right to change the conditions of entry at any time without prior notice. However, failure to observe the above conditions may lead to disqualification.

This provides an escape clause should any undesired and unanticipated developments occur.

The International IMPAC Dublin Literary Award

The largest cash prize offered for a single work of fiction is IR£100,000, and is available for the International IMPAC Literary Award. Established in 1995, the prize money has been guaranteed for ten years by James B Irwin of the US-based consultancy firm that currently gives the award part of its title. He pledged more than £1 million to the cause on the condition 'that Dublin City Council should be responsible for organising the nominations' (Mitchell quoted in Garvey 1998). Two Dublin librarians are seconded to the prize on a permanent basis, but all other expenses, such as public relations, the international judges and the presentation dinner, are met by IMPAC. In an article for *The Bookseller*, Anthony Garvey estimates IMPAC's total commitment at 'about £200,000 a year'.

The prize is unusual in that nominations are invited from library services throughout the world, with each municipal library in major and capital cities entitled to put forward three books either written in or translated into English. Advocates maintain that, because of this link with libraries, the competition keeps its distance from publishers and is assured of an international dimension. Critics argue that librarians are not necessarily 'the people best qualified to assess the quality ...' and maintain that £100,000 is 'too much money going to the wrong people' (quotations from Garvey). There is a feeling that a larger number of smaller amounts likely to find their way to younger writers would be a better way to promote good writing.

For the 1998 Award, an international body of judges sifted the 88 titles suggested by 127 libraries world-wide and produced a short list of ten that included André Brink and, from the Caribbean, Jamaica Kincaid and Earl Lovelace. In June, the winner, Herta Muller, joined the laureates for 1996, David Malouf for *Remembering Babylon*, and 1997, Javier Marias for *A Heart so White*, translated by Margaret Jull Costa. (Marais received IR£75,000 and the translator IR£25,000.)

Writers may wish to alert librarians to obtain details from the Award's Administrative Headquarters, at Cumberland House, Fenian Street, Dublin 2, Republic of Ireland, Tel: +353 1 6619 000, Fax: +353 1 676 16 28.

The Neustadt International Prize for Literature

Established in 1969, the Neustadt Prize is awarded every two years by the University of Oklahoma and *World Literature Today*, an international quarterly that makes energetic efforts to ensure that it reviews major titles published all around the globe. Worth $40,000, the Prize is for 'distinguished and continuing international achievement' and in 1998 went to Nuruddin Farah. Previous winners have included Gabriel Garcia Márquez, Czeslaw Milosz and Octavio Paz. Following the Neustadt system, their cases had been effectively argued by a panel of distinguished jurors, each of whom was asked to nominate and argue the case for an author. *World Literature Today* is recommended reading because it devotes space not only to the critical celebration of winners but also to informed scrutiny of the candidates (see Magazines: A Directory, page 269). Information: Neustadt International Prize for Literature, 110 Monnet Hall, Norman, Oklahoma, OK 73019-0375 US.

The Nobel Prize for Literature

It would serve little purpose to rehearse the detailed issues raised by the award of the 1986 Nobel Prize for Literature to Wole Soyinka. It is enough to draw attention to the fact that, while many rejoiced at the perceived recognition of African creativity and achievement represented by the award, a group considered that the award reflected only Soyinka's undesirable cultivation of a European readership. He was accused of 'seeking' the prize, but it should be noted that authors do not 'enter for the Nobel Prize'. Organisations, such as universities or writers' groups, may write recommending the claims of an author to members of the Swedish Academy.

While the Nobel Prize represents a significant cash bonus, its long-term significance is to be seen in terms of higher earning potential through increased sales, demand for translation rights and movement to a higher level of speaker's fees. Uniquely among literary prizes, the Nobel brings instant international celebrity with all the responsibilities, opportunities and intrusions that accompany such status.

In the heat of the debate about the desirability of Soyinka winning the Nobel Prize, his critics appealed to African businessmen to challenge the influence of Stockholm by establishing a prize for African writing. So far, it seems, no money has been forthcoming. Meanwhile, as an eminently practical gesture and in the wake of the Nobel Award, Soyinka funded the Christopher

Okigbo All-Africa Prize for Poetry which is administered by the Association of Nigerian Authors (see below).

The Noma Award for Publishing in Africa

The Noma Award is well known in Africa, being now in its twentieth year. It is the broadest in scope of the specifically 'African' book prizes, being pan-African, accepting entries in all the languages of Africa, and accepting academic, creative writing and children's books entries. Submissions must be made by publishers, and applications are mailed widely to African publishers. Writers who wish their works to be considered for the Award should therefore consult with their publishers about entering.

The purpose of the Award is to encourage writing and publishing *within* Africa. The first award, in 1979, went to Mariama Bâ for her *Si longue une lettre*. The event attracted a lot of attention: it was an entirely new book award, meant not only for African writers but for works published in Africa, with an African imprint; the first winner was a woman writer, which drew attention to the award; and thirdly, the book had a striking impact – as borne out by its translation into seventeen languages, and subsequent status as a classic of modern African literature. In the words of Professor Abiole Irele, chair of the Managing Committee from 1991 to 1994, 'with the very first selection, the Noma Award found its mission: to promote writing and publishing in Africa and thus give a voice to the continent from within, reversing the trend which made African expression dependent on outside judgement and interests'.

The Award attracts between 100 and 200 entries each year, and all eligible categories have won. Some titles are also awarded Special Commendation or Honourable Mention. Some of the most notable African creative writers have won the Award including Chenjerai Hove, Charles Mungoshi, Njabulo Ndebele, Niyi Osundare, and Mongane Wally Serote, writing in English; Bernard Nanga and Kitia Touré in French; and Marlane van Niekerk in Afrikaans.

The five-person jury comprises African scholars and book experts, and representatives of the international book community. Amongst past members have been Jacob Ade Ajayi, Samir Amin, Abena Busia, and Micere Mugo. The current chair is Walter Bgoya, the Tanzanian publisher, and his predecessors were Professors Abiola Irele and Eldred Jones. Other current jury members are Thandika Mkandawire, Kole Omotoso, Kay Raseroka, and Mary Jay (Secretary to the Award). Given the wide range of categories and languages eligible, the jury is assisted by a panel of some 300 experts who provide assessments on books entered. Assessors must be recognised scholars and experts within their fields, and their names remain wholly confidential. Mary Jay comments that the successful establishment of the Award has been dependent on the high standing and impartiality of the jury (the Managing Committee).

The Award is fortunate in the endowment fund established by the sponsor, and the original spirit continues to imbue its work. There was some concern, following the liberation of South Africa, that South African publishers (all newly eligible to enter) were 'swamping' the Award – some publishers sending up to twenty submissions in a single year. To ensure fairness between publishers in countries within Africa with very different publishing infrastructures, the jury limited submissions to three per publisher; and this has resulted in publishers themselves being more selective. Over recent years the entry conditions have been changed to reflect two further concerns: publishers must be wholly indigenous within the spirit of the Award – not, for example, local branches of multinational publishers; and production quality must reach an acceptable level, within the realities of much of the poor printing infrastructure in Africa which is well understood.

The Okigbo All-Africa Prize for Literature

At the International Symposium on African Literatures held in Lagos during May 1988, Kole Omotoso, speaking in his capacity as an office holder in the Nigerian Association of Authors, said:

> We went into organising this prize along with our other annual prizes, and we had distinguished judges from across the continent who came through to insist that the collection of poems by Tati-Loutard entitled *La Tradition du Songe* deserved to be the first winner of the All-Africa Prize named after Okigbo. (Omotoso in Osofisan *et al.* 1991, 32)

The Okigbo Prize was first awarded in 1992, when the winner was Olu Oguibe (see Aihe 1992). In 1994, it seems that $1,000 was available thanks to an endowment of N30,000.00 provided by Soyinka. Festus Iyayi has subsequently won the prize for *Awaiting Court Martial*, and the range of possible winners has been widened by the success of *Splendid*, a biographical study, as a more recent winner. In 1997, the Okigbo Prize went to Tanure Ojaide.

Authors will find in the Directory below details of other prizes that may be of interest to them or their publishers. They should read the conditions of entry carefully and, to avoid waste of time and effort, assure themselves that their books are eligible before submitting copies.

Poetry Prizes: A Cautionary Word

Many lessons about capitalism were painfully learned after the Berlin Wall came down and the 'Free Market' moved east and south. One was that those emerging from communist domination were often confused by marketing and promotion techniques long viewed with a healthy scepticism in the West. How do you respond to this?

1997 Poetry Guild Official Call for Entries
Your Poem Could Win!
You could be published
You could even win £1,000!

It is with great pride that The Poetry Guild announces its official call for entries for our 1997 National Poetry Competition. Through this prestigious competition, you are invited to submit original poetry for consideration by our distinguished panel of judges. All entries will receive a personal acknowledgement from the committee, and should your poem be selected, you will be honoured with publication in our upcoming, hardbound anthology, *Among the Roses*. A well-deserved showcase for talented poets across the country – and around the world.

(*Guardian Weekend* (London), 12 July 1997)

There is, the advertisement continues, no entry fee, no purchase required, authors retain all rights to their work – a poem of twenty lines or fewer – and everyone who enters receives a free gift, a booklet valued at £2.50 entitled 'How to Get Published'. It would seem to be a 'No lose' situation.

Yet anyone who has survived the flood of promotional offers that flows through the letter-box of the average capitalist door will think 'So, what's the catch?' The 'come on' is predictable and, though it would be fun to spend five minutes dashing off a few lines, and moderately diverting to pass a few weeks in pleasurable anticipation of the arrival of the booklet, it is best to approach the whole venture with caution verging on cynicism. In this case, the absence of an entry fee, the promise that 'no purchase is required', and the poets' retention of rights point to areas in which other operatives have made their killings. The Poetry Guild must be confident that they can persuade enough of the published authors to buy the hardback anthology, *Among the Roses*; perhaps some will buy multiple copies.

The international aspect, summarised by 'and around the world', is an invitation to a globe of poets, to ambitious writers, to those unaware just how empty the words 'Poetry Guild' have become. The very language used in the advertisement is suspect: '... with great *pride* that The Poetry Guild announces its official call for entries for our 1997 National Poetry Competition. Through this *prestigious* competition, you are *invited* to ... our *distinguished panel* of judges .... *selected*, you will *be honoured with publication* in our *upcoming*, hardbound anthology, ... A *well-deserved showcase* for talented poets ...'. This is over-blown, hyped-up, immediately suspect.

At about the same time as the advertisement quoted above appeared, 'Matchet's Diary' in *West Africa* reported that 'Justice and Power' by 'Nigerian Emeka Obiadu' had won the grand prize in the latest poetry competition, organised by 'The International Library of Poetry (TILP)'. The title of the bound anthology (*A Lasting Calm*) in which the best entries submitted by Obiadu and others will appear, and the entry limitations, 'one original poem of 20 lines or less', suggest that the Poetry Guild and TILP are from neighbouring stables.

This sort of competition is all relatively harmless, but one should be aware that organisations such as the Poetry Guild and TILP have no recognised standing. What they are offering, and making their profit from, is the delight felt by those who see their work in print. Their profits come from the 'captive writers' who buy the hardbound anthologies.

Matchet concluded his item in a manner that must have pleased the organisers of the competition by writing with a mixture of naïveté and Eurocentric fervour:

> The ball is now in the courts of all you budding Eliots, Pounds and Wordsworths out there. ('Matchet' in *West Africa*, July 1997, 1077)

Poets who want to see their work in print should take their 'original poem of 20 lines or less' to their local printer and get copies run off. For the price of *A Lasting Calm* or *Among the Roses*, a considerable number could be made.

There is a market for well-printed, single-page publications. Indeed, when, in the late 1960s, Rex Collings left Associated Book Publishers and set up on his own, his first title was a sheet of work Soyinka had been able to smuggle out of Kaduna prison. Entitled 'Poems from Prison', this page initially sold for 12½p. Copies are now worth considerably more than that.

Prizes, Awards, and Contests: A Directory

There are hundreds of literary prizes, awards, and contests, offered by numerous organisations, societies and institutions each year. However, many are limited to recipients who are citizens of or living in the country in which they are presented. The listing below is a selection of prizes and awards which are open to writers from Africa, and which is followed by details of a number of other book prizes offered in several African countries. Prizes for children's books are not included.

For more comprehensive listings of book prizes and contests consult some of the directories listed in 'The Author's Bookshelf', such as the *Writers' and Artists Yearbook*, or its US equivalent *The Writer's Market*.

Note: it is important to make a distinction between competitions which are open to application by writing to the organisers of the Award, and those that are *not* open to application, which are marked by an * asterisk.

All-Africa Okigbo Prize for Literature

Endowed by: Wole Soyinka
Administered by the Association of Nigerian Authors

Contact/Details:
Guardian Newspapers Ltd,
PMB 1217 Oshodi, Lagos, Nigeria
Tel: +234-1-524080/524111
Founded: 1987

Endowed by Wole Soyinka and in honour of Christopher Okigbo, the Nigerian poet who died fighting on the Biafran side during the Nigerian civil war. Aims to give recognition to the best African literature, and to encourage a continent-wide poetic sensibility. It is open to African authors for a book published in any language spoken in Africa. Published works only are eligible for entry, and may be submitted by individual writers or their publishers.
Prize: US$1,500
Closing date: 31 July each year
Note: the Prize has not been awarded every year. Poetry and other forms of literature are eligible.

Arvon Foundation International Poetry Competition

Sponsored by: Arvon Foundation

Contact/Details:
Kilnhurst, Kilnhurst Road
Todmorden, Lancs OL14 6AS, UK
Founded: 1980

This is a bi-annual award for previously unpublished poetry written in English. First prize is £5,000, plus at least £500 in other cash prizes.
Further details from the Arvon Foundation.

**BBC World Service
African Performance
Playwriting Competition**

Sponsored by: BBC World Service

Contact/details:
BBC World Service,
African Performance Playwriting
Competition,
Bush House, PO Box 76,
Strand, London WC2B 4PH
Tel: +44-(0)171-557 2890
Fax: +44-(0)171-379 5683
Email: african.weeklies@bbc.co.uk
Web site: http://www.bbc.co.uk/
worldservice/africanperformance

This performance playwriting competition aims to discover talented new African writers and produce their plays on the radio for listeners of BBC World Service's annual season of African drama. Prizes are offered for the best plays all of which will be produced by the BBC World Service either in Bush House or on location. The contest is open to writers resident in Africa, or African writers resident elsewhere.

Plays must not exceed 30 minutes in length, and there must no more than six characters in the cast; plays can be on any theme of interest to listeners in Africa, but must be either substantially or entirely in English. Entries must never have been performed or published before, and must have been written solely by the entrant. Each page of the script must be numbered and the whole script must be accompanied by a covering sheet setting out clearly the entrant's name, age, occupation, address and phone or fax number where available. Entries can be posted or emailed to the address above. Entries will not be returned. For more details about the competition rules write to the BBC and see pp.178-81.
Prizes: 1st prize: £800, 2nd prize: £500, 3rd prize: £300
Closing date: October, each year.

The Booker Prize for Fiction

Sponsored by: Booker plc

Contact/details:
Sandra Vince, The Book Trust,
Book House, 45 East Hill,
Wandsworth, London SW18 2QZ
Tel: +44-(0)181-516 973
Fax: +44-(0)181-516 978
Email: sandra@booktrust.org.uk
Founded: 1968

The Booker Prize for Fiction is Britain's most prestigious literary award. The prize is given annually for any full-length novel written in English written by a citizen of the Commonwealth. It is designed not only to reward the best novel of the year, but also to raise the stature of the writers in the eyes of the public and increase book sales. Judges are appointed each year from amongst leading literary critics, writers and academics. Any United Kingdom publisher may enter not more than two full-length novels, with scheduled publication dates between 1 October and 30 September. Past winners of the Booker Prize have included Chinua Achebe and Ben Okri.
Prize: £20,000; and each shortlisted author receives £1,000.
Closing date: see above.

Continued on page 182

BBC WORLD SERVICE

GUIDELINES FOR WRITING A PLAY FOR RADIO

AFRICAN PERFORMANCE

Nobody can teach you how to write a good play. Good radio plays result from a mixture of inspiration, talent and craftsmanship. This booklet is about the craft of writing for radio - we leave the talent and the inspiration to you.

THE SECRETS OF RADIO DRAMA

Radio is an extraordinary medium. A radio play can travel through time and space, between centuries and continents. It can take place in an aeroplane, down a goldmine, on a ship; it can also take place within the confines of somebody's mind.

All this can be done for a fraction of what it would cost to do the same in film. But in every case the audience has to be attracted, and its attention held, by the means of sound alone. In addition to speech, the writer needs to think about sound effects, music, and, something rarely appreciated by the inexperienced writer, silence. Silence can convey a variety of things: suspense, anxiety, tranquillity.

Pauses also help listeners take in what they have heard and help prepare for what happens next. Of course, speech is the dominant element in a radio play. Dialogue, or conversation, provides most of the information needed to understand what is going on. Words in a radio play have to carry more meaning than the words written for the stage or television, where there are all sorts of visual clues to help the audience know what is going on. Good dialogue is not simply a matter of stringing together different conversations - every bit of speech must help the plot move in some direction, increasingly involving the listener as it does so.

WRITING A RADIO PLAY – DOS AND DON'TS

THEMES

There is no theme better or worse than another. It is the treatment of the theme that matters. It is, however, important with a half hour play to keep things simple - don't try and cram too much in, either in terms of events or ideas.

STRUCTURE

A radio play has scenes like a stage play, but these can be swift and fragmentary, as well as long and solid. It's useful to think of a scene as a sequence. One sequence, or scene, might consist of one line of dialogue, or it might just consist of a crucial sound effect (known as FX). For example:

```
Scene 3 KWABENA'S OFFICE

(FX: PHONE RINGING)

KWABENA: Hallo......hallo.....hallo!
(FX: DIALLING TONE AS CALLER HANGS
UP.

Scene 4 KWABENA'S SITTING ROOM

KWABENA: She did it again...she's doing it
to drive me crazy, destroy my
family.

KWAME: Take it easy, man...don't let your
imagination run away with you.
```

NUMBER OF CHARACTERS

Do not have more than 6 characters in a half hour play. There's a risk of confusion if you do. Remember also that the listener only knows a character exists if that character speaks, or if another character refers to him/her by name. Please do not cheat by giving lines to anonymous voices (VOICE 1, VOICE 2 etc) on top your allocation of 6 characters.

INFORMATION FOR ACTORS

It is very useful for actors to write into the script adjectives describing the way in which a line should be said (angrily, regretfully, trying to be brave). But there's no point in giving any visual directions - the radio listener cannot see.

The following directions for, example, would be lost on the listener:

```
MOHAMMED: (HIS EYES HALF CLOSED, SHOULDERS
HUNCHED, A CIGARETTE IN HIS LEFT HAND)
I love you
```

✗ NO

Whereas these directions work very well:

```
TUNDE: (HALF WHISPERING, HESITANTLY AND
TENDERLY)
I want you to know....that....that
I love you.

TINU: (CONTEMPTUOUSLY, VOICE RISING TO
CRESCENDO OF HATE)
Love me? You love me? How can you
say that?
That you love me. You do not know
the meaning of the word love.

TUNDE: (CURTLY, ALL TENDERNESS GONE)
OK - if that is how you feel about
me, I shall go now.
```

✓ YES

THINKING IN SOUND

A variety of sounds is essential for holding the listeners' attention and engaging their interest. This variety can be achieved by altering the length of sequences, the number of people speaking, the pace of the dialogue and location of action. The contrast between a noisy sequence with a number of voices and effects, and a quiet passage of interior monologue (the actor thinking to him/herself aloud) is very effective. There's also a good contrast to be achieved between an indoor setting and an outside setting.

SOUND EFFECTS (FX)

These should be used sparingly and effectively. They can be used functionally, e.g. door opening, or to create a mood - dogs barking in the distance on waste-land. If used to excess they become tedious and pointless.
For example:

> A CAR DRAWS UP. ENGINE OFF. DOOR OPENS. FEET WALK TO THE FRONT DOOR, KEY IN THE LOCK. DOOR OPENS. FEET WALK DOWN THE HALL TO THE KITCHEN. ETC

✘ NO

> FX: KNOCKING AT DOOR
>
> IMMACULATE: That must be him now. I must just finish putting these away...
>
> FX: DISHES BEING STACKED ONTO SHELF.
> KNOCKING AT DOOR INCREASING VOLUME
>
> IMMACULATE: (CALLING OUT) I'm coming, I'm coming
> FX: PLATE BEING DROPPED TO FLOOR
>
> IMMACULATE: Now look what I've done....

✔ YES

TRANSMISSION TIMES

Radio plays must run to exact lengths as the programme schedule is always fixed. For example, the plays broadcast in BBC's African Performance run to 28 minutes, excluding the introduction and credits. There is no way of measuring 28 minutes by the number of words or pages. the only reliable method is to read the script aloud against the clock, making allowances for sound effects, music and pauses.

Radio plays can very rarely be produced without some changes to the script sent in - this applies even to very experience writers. If your script is accepted for production, be prepared to work with the producer, making cuts and changes in scenes if necessary.

SPECIMEN SCRIPT

> 1. ABU (LIGHT HEARTED) Oh, come on woman, I was once a soldier. Forget about my leg. A man shoots with the hands, not legs.
>
> FX: BREAKS GUN
>
> (AIRILY) A day or two in practice - that's all, and your very husband will be the best marksman in the world on crutches. (LAUGHS)
>
> 2. EBUN (NO RESPONSE)
>
> 3. ABU When do you leave for work?
>
> FX: POLISHING GUN VIGOROUSLY
>
> 4. EBUN I start evening shift today.
>
> 5. ABU (THOUGHTFULLY) Ebun (SIGHS)
>
> 6. EBUN I am listening.
>
> 7. ABU (BLOWS DOWN BARREL SHARPLY) Working for someone else as a cook in his restaurant is another side of our life I do not wish to last for ever, woman.

SETTING OUT YOUR SCRIPT
(Please also see specimen script)

A clear layout helps us read your script quickly and easily. Here are some points to bear in mind when committing your script to paper

1. Scripts should be typed if possible, using one side of the paper only. If you cannot get hold of a typewriter please write your script neatly.

2. Names of characters should be clearly separated from speech and should be given in full throughout.

3. Sound effects (FX) should contrast clearly with speech.

4. Please attach a synopsis (a brief summary) of the play to the completed script, together with a full cast list and brief notes on the characters.

5. Always keep a copy of your script. We will not return the script you send us, unless you ask us to.

6. Make sure that all pages are numbered consecutively and securely fastened.

DRAMA ON THE BBC WORLD SERVICE

Drama for the World

Twice a week you can hear radio drama from all over the world: specially commissioned plays, new productions of old classics, dramatisation of novels and short stories, and adaptations of new stage plays. Every two years you can try your luck in the World Service Drama Competition open to anyone not resident in the UK.

African Performance

This is the BBC's annual season of six dramatic productions from and about Africa. The season aims to be throught-provoking and entertaining, as well as a unique show-case for new talent on the continent.

Every year the BBC runs a playwriting competition as part of the annual season of African drama. The winning plays are produced in the BBC World Service drama studios in Bush House in London with a cast of professional actors.

If you would like to enter the competition, send your play to the address below, following these guidelines. Copies of the competition rules are also available from the same address.

African Performance
BBC World Service
PO Box 76, Bush House, Strand, London WC2B 4PH, UK.

The Caine Prize for African Writing

Sponsored by:
The Michael Caine Foundation

Details/contact:
(provisional) Jonathan F Taylor,
2 Drayson Mews, Kensington,
London W8 4LE
Fax: +44-(0)171-938 3728
Email: jonathan@jftaylor.com
Founded: 1999

This new prize launched in June 1999 is named in memory of Sir Michael Caine, former Chairman of Booker plc (and Chair of the Booker Prize management committee), and Chair of the 'Africa 95' arts festival held in Britain in 1995. The prize will be awarded to a work by an African writer published in English, whether published in Africa or elsewhere. Unpublished work will not be eligible; works translated into English from other languages will be eligible provided they have been published in translation. The focus will be on the African story-telling tradition, and the prize may be awarded to a short story, a collection of short stories, a novella or a narrative poem. The minimum length requirement is 3,000 words. For the first year, the short-list will be selected from works published in the 24 months preceding the call for submissions. A panel of five judges will be appointed under the chairmanship of Ben Okri, the Nigerian winner of the Booker Prize.
Prize: $15,000 for the winning author, and a travel award for each of the short-listed candidates (winning and short-listed authors will also be invited to participate in writers' workshops in Africa and elsewhere as resources permit.)
Closing date: 1 December 1999.

Cleveland State University Poetry Center Prize

Sponsored by: Cleveland State University Poetry Center

Details/contact:
Cleveland State University Poetry Center, 1983 E. 24 St.,
Cleveland, OH 44115-2440, USA
Tel: +1-216-687 3986
Fax: +1-216-687 6943
Email: poetrycenter@popmail.csu ohio.edu
Web site: http://www.csuohio.edu/poetry/poetrycenter.html
Offered to identify, reward and publish the best unpublished book-length poetry ms. submitted. Charges $15 entry fee.
Prize: $1,000, plus publication of the book under standard contract.
Closing date: submit during December-February *only.* For submission guidelines send self-addressed envelope.

Commonwealth Writers Prize

Sponsored by:
The Commonwealth Foundation

Details/contact:
Jessica Williams/Sandra Vince,
The Book Trust, Book House,
45 East Hill, London SW18 2QZ
Tel: +44-(0)181 516 2974
Fax: +44-(0)181 516 2978
Email: jwilliams@booktrust.org.uk
Founded: 1987

Aims to encourage the upsurge of new Commonwealth fiction and ensure that works of merit reach a wider audience outside the country of original publication The annual prize is for the best work of fiction in English by a citizen of the Commonwealth and published in the year prior to the Award. Publishers must submit three copies to the Regional Chairperson (see below).

Prize: £10,000 for overall best book; £3,000 for overall best first published book; plus, in each of the four regions of the Commonwealth (Africa, Caribbean and Canada, Eurasia, SE Asia and South Pacific) two prizes of £1,000 are awarded each year, one for the best book and one for the best first published book. Professor Kofi Anyidoho is Regional Chairperson for Africa, and his address is:

English Department,
University of Ghana, PO Box LG201, Legon, Accra, Ghana
Tel: +233-21-503043
Fax:+233-21-501392
Email:k-anyi@africaonline.com.gh

'Best Book' winners have included Festus Iyayi, and Africa Region Winners have included Ken Saro-Wiwa, Charles Mungoshi, Tsitsi Dangarembga, Syl Cheney-Coker, Ama Ata Aidoo, Isidore Okpewho, JM Coetzee, and Yvonne Vera.
Closing date: 15 November each year.

Grand Prix Littéraire de l'Afrique Noire

Sponsored by: Association des écrivains de langue française

Details/contact:
Association des écrivains de langue française (ADELF),
14 rue Broussais, 75014 Paris, France
Tel: +33-1-43 21 95 99
Fax: +33-1-43 20 12 22
Founded: 1961

Awarded annually for a work by an African author making an original contribution in the French language. All literary forms are eligible: novels, short stories, tales, history, biography, poetry, etc.

Works submitted must have been published in the year of the Award or the preceding year. Eight copies of each title must be forwarded to the Award's administrators.
Prize: FF2,000
Closing date: 15 June each year.

*The Guardian Fiction Prize

Sponsored by:
Guardian Newspapers Ltd

Contact/details:
The Literary Editor, *Guardian*,
119 Farringdon Road,
London EC1R 3ER
Founded: 1965

Awarded annually for a novel published by a British, Irish or Commonwealth writer. The winner is chosen by the *Guardian*'s literary editor in conjunction with the paper's regular reviewers of fiction.
Prize: £5,000

WH Heinemann Prize

Sponsored by:
Royal Society of Literature under the WH Heinemann bequest.

Contact/details:
Royal Society of Literature,
1 Hyde Park Gardens,
London W2 2LT
Tel: +44-(0)171-723 5104
Fax: +44-(0)171-402 0199
Founded: 1945

Set up to encourage literary works of real worth, and works in any litera-

ture, originally written in English, published during the preceding year, may be submitted by publishers. Although prose fiction is not excluded, preference tends to be given to publications which are unlikely to command substantial sales, i.e. poetry, criticism, biography, history, etc.
Prize: £5,000
Closing date: 31 October each year.

*International IMPAC Dublin Literary Award

Sponsored by: IMPAC

Details/contact:
The International IMPAC Dublin Literary Award Office,
Dublin City Public Libraries,
Administrative Headquarters,
Cumberland House, Fenian Street,
Dublin 2, Ireland
Tel: +353-1-661 9000
Fax: +353-1-676 1628
Email: dublin.city.libs@iol.ie
Web site:
http://www.iol.ie/~dubcilib
Founded: 1995

Sponsored by the US-based productivity improvement firm IMPAC and administered by Dublin City Libraries, this annual award is presented to the author of a work of fiction written and published in the English language, or written in a language other than English and published in English translation, which in the opinion of the judges is of high literary merit and constitutes a lasting contribution to world literature. *Nominations* are accepted from municipal public library systems in major cities worldwide, regardless of national origin of the author or place of publication.

Prize: IR£100,000 (if the winning book is in English translation, the prize is shared with IR£75,000 going to the author and IR£25,000 going to the translator).

Iowa Poetry Prizes

Sponsored by:
University of Iowa Press

Details/contact:
Holly Carver,
University of Iowa Press,
119 W Park Road, Iowa City,
IA 52242, USA
Fax: +1-319-335-2055
Web site:
http://www.uiowa.edu/~uipress

The Iowa Poetry Prizes were initiated to encourage mature poets and their work. The competition is open to writers of English (regardless whether US citizens or not) who have published at least one previous book.
Prizes: two $1,000 prizes are awarded annually.
Closing date: manuscripts should be submitted in May, accompanied by a self-addressed envelope.

*Neustadt International Prize for Literature

Sponsored by:
University of Oklahoma and
World Literature Today

Details/contact:
Neustadt International Prize for Literature, World Literature Today,
University of Oklahoma,
110 Monnett Hall, Norman,
OK 73019-0375
Tel: +1-405-325 4531
Fax: +1-405-325 7495
Founded: 1969

Conferred every two years by the University of Oklahoma and its international literary quarterly *World Literature Today*, the Neustadt Prize is awarded for distinguished and continuing artistic achievement in the fields of poetry, drama or fiction. The prize – which is widely considered to be one of the most prestigious international prizes after the Nobel – may honour a single major work or an entire oeuvre. Selected jurors argue the merits of the author each thinks should be awarded the prize. The writer's work must be available in a representative sample in English or French. A special issue of *World Literature Today* is devoted to the laureate. Prize not open to application.

In 1998 Nuruddin Farah of Somalia became the first African writer to win this prize.
Prize: $40,000

*The Nobel Prize for Literature

Sponsored by: Alfred Nobel (deceased)/The Noble Foundation

Contact/details:
Swedish Academy, Box 2118,
S-10313 Stockholm, Sweden
Tel: +46-8-106524
Fax: +46-8-244225
Email:
sekretariat@svenskaakadmien.se
Web site:
http://svenska.gu.se/academy.html

The world's most prestigious literary award. The Nobel Prize for Literature is given to the person 'who shall have produced in the field of literature the most distinguished work of an idealistic tendency'. It is usually awarded to an author for his or her total oeuvre and not for any single work. No direct application for a prize will be taken into consideration, and there is no competition. Nominations are made by members of the Swedish Academy, and other academies similar to it in membership and aims, solicited nominations from professors of history of literature or of languages, presidents of national writers' organisations, and past Nobel laureates in literature.
Prize: varies from year to year, but usually about SEK7,500,000 (c. £56,000), plus a gold medal.

The Noma Award for Publishing in Africa

Sponsored by:
Shoichi Noma (deceased), and Kodansha Publishers

Details/contact
Mary Jay,
Secretary to the Noma Award,
PO Box 128, Witney,
Oxon OX8 5XU, UK
Tel: +44-(0)1993-775235
Fax: +44-(0)1993-709265
Email: maryljay@aol.com
Founded: 1979

This annual book prize is available to African writers and scholars whose work is published in Africa. It is one of the aims of the Award to encourage the publication of works by African writers and scholars within rather than outside Africa. The Award is given for an outstanding new book in any of three categories: scholarly or academic, children's books, creative writing.

The Noma Award is open to any author who is indigenous to Africa, but entries must be submitted through publishers. Each work must have been published by a publisher domiciled on the African continent or its offshore islands. Only published works qualify.

Any work written in any indigenous or official language of Africa is eligible. Three copies must be submitted to the Award's administrators. Since 1997, a maximum number of three titles per publisher can be entered, in any of the eligible categories.

Winners (in the fiction, drama, poetry categories) have included Mariama Bâ, *Si longue une lettre* (1980); Bernard Nanga, *La trahison de Marianne* (1985); Chenjerai Hove, *Bones* (1989); Niyi Osundare *Waiting Laughters* (1991); and Kitia Touré *Destins parallèles* (1996).

Prize: US$10,000
Closing date: 28 February each year.

The Sandstone Prize in Short Fiction

Sponsored by: Ohio State University Press and the MFA Program in Creative Writing at the Ohio State University

Details/contact:
William Roorbach, Director,
Ohio State University Press,
1070 Carmack Road, Columbus,
 OH 43210-1002, USA
Tel: +1-614-292 6930
Fax: +1-614-292 2065
Email: ohiostatepress@osu.edu

Offered annually to published and unpublished writers. Submissions may include short stories, novellas or a combination of both. Manuscripts must be 250-300 typed pages. Novellas must not exceed 125 pages.
Prize: $1,500, plus publication of the book under a standard contract, and an invitation to Ohio State University to give a public reading and direct a creative writing workshop.
Closing date: Submit in January *only*.

SOME OTHER PRIZES FOR AFRICAN WRITING

PAWA/OAU African Prize for Literature

Pan-African Writers' Association (PAWA), PAWA House,
Roman Ridge, PO Box C546
Cantonments, Accra
Tel: + 233-21-773062
Fax: +233-21-773042
Contact:
Atukwei Okai, Secretary-General

In August 1993, the Resolution on the Institutionalisation of the PAWA/OAU African Prize for Literature was passed by the OAU Conference of Ministers on Culture, Education and Development held in Cotonu, Benin. By the resolution, a decision was taken to establish an African Prize for Literature and, apparently, The General Secretariat (of the OAU) is in consultation with PAWA on (a) the awarding of this Prize; (b) its periodicity; (c) its financing.

African writers will await the results of the consultation with interest. But until financing has been secured, the 'African Prize for Literature' is of academic interest only.

PAWA's aspirations include the establishment of an ambitious array of prizes in various categories.

Fonlon-Nichols Award

In 1994 the Fonlon-Nichols Award for Excellence in Literature, named after a Cameroonian critic, Bernard Fonlon, and an American journalist, Lee Nichols, has been awarded to the late Ken Saro-Wiwa, Nigugi wa Thiong'o, and in 1998 to Niyi Osundare. The bi-annual Award is administered by the African Literature Association which has its headquarters at the African Studies and Research Center, Cornell University, 310 Triphammer Road, Ithaca, New York, 14850-2599.

Nigeria

The Association of Nigerian Author's ANA/Cadbury Poetry Prize

In 1997 the prize was jointly won by Ezenwa-Ohaeto for *The Voice of the Night Masquerade,* and Remi Raji for *A Harvest of Laughters.* Prizes in various categories, including drama prose and children's literature, and prizes linked with commercial sponsors including Cadbury, *Matatu* and Spectrum Books.

More details from: Association of Nigerian Authors (ANA), National Secretariat, 26 Oladipo Labinjo Crescent, Off Bode Thomas, Surulere, Lagos.

British Council Nigerian Book Award

The award is open to all under 45 who are active in book development. Details from: Nigerian Book Foundation, PO Box 1132, Awka, Anambra State, Nigeria.

Zimbabwe

The Zimbabwe Book Publishers' Association organises a variety of prizes sponsored by the Association, Kingston's, Struik, Textbook Sales, and Federation of Masters Printers.

Categories/Winners include:

Best Novel in Shona 1996 – *winner CM Matsikiti;*

Best Novel in Ndebele, 1996 – *no award;*

Best Novel in English, 1996 – *winner S Mpasu;*

Best Play or Volume of Poetry 1996 – *winner Ronald E Mhasvi;*

Best Children's Book
Ages 4-7 years 1996 –
no winner;
8-10 years 1996 –
winner Patricia Farrell;
11-14 years 1996 –
winner Nancy Farmer.
(Also prizes for non-creative writing.)

More details from: Zimbabwe Book Publishers' Association, 78 Kaguvi Street, PO Box C1179, Causeway, Harare, Zimbabwe.

Getting Together

What Conditions Favour Writers?

Niyi Osundare has written:

> ... one thing is sure, the period in which Achebe and Soyinka launched
> themselves on to the literary scene was saner and kinder than the one in
> which their successors are presently trapped. Whereas their works received
> enthusiastic attention from publishers and were distributed all over the
> world, overseas publishers now see African literature as a bad risk, while
> local ones only manage to bring out a few titles over a long period. African
> literature today is thus in a painfully illiterate bind: books published by
> Africans abroad are not available even in their home countries due to
> unfavourable currency exchange rates, while the few published in Africa are
> not available beyond their immediate locality. To make matters worse,
> those journals and magazines which provided vibrant literary outlets in the
> 1960s and 1970s are either now extinct or going through protracted
> dormancy. The bookshops are empty. This is why in a recent article
> frighteningly titled 'When Ugandan Pens Could Write No More', Ayeta
> Anne Wangusa declared: 'Walk into the Makerere University Bookshop –
> it's a joke. One can ride a motor cycle into it and ride out without
> casualties.' (Osundare 1997, 31)

Asked to speak at Cambridge in 1928 about women and fiction,
Virginia Woolf composed what came to be *A Room of One's Own*, a
classic statement on the factors militating against the flourishing of
scholarly and literary endeavour by women. Reflecting on the difficulties faced by women writers, and backing her assertions with carefully
selected illustration, she drew attention to the inequalities in the
treatment of the genders, regarding, for example, access to education
and to academic resources. She maintained that 'material things' were
important, crystallising these into the need for 'a room of one's own
and five hundred pounds'. Clarifying the significance of these 'items',
and drawing attention to the need for a lock on the door, she wrote:

> Even allowing a generous margin for symbolism, that five hundred a year
> stands for the power to contemplate, that a lock on the door means the
> power to think for oneself ... (Woolf 1996, 99)

In some respects the situation has changed, but the question remains: is that still true? How much money is now required to secure 'the power to contemplate'? Will any lockable room do? Does it, for example, have to be a 'room with a view'? Or is it more important to have a room with a regular supply of electricity?

The conditions under which authors work vary considerably. Are some more conducive to creativity than others? In this section the circumstances in which writers work, and work best, are considered. The quotation above from Osundare suggests part of the West African predicament. What was and is the situation like elsewhere?

Ngugi's Experience

Ngugi wa Thiong'o managed to combine creative writing on a substantial scale with university work and journalism. For example, *The River Between*, *Weep Not, Child* and *A Grain of Wheat* were published between 1964 and 1967, during a period when Ngugi, then a student, might have been expected to have had his head in other people's books for so long that he had little time to write his own. In a remarkable way he combined study with creative writing.

There followed something of a hiatus before *Petals of Blood* was completed, a task made possible it seems by a period at a retreat for Soviet writers on the Black Sea. But although 'getting away from it all' seems to have been important for that work, other creative projects were essentially collaborative and came into existence thanks to contact with others. For example, Ngugi's intense involvement with community theatre led to working on large-scale plays – and to imprisonment.

The Kenyan author celebrated his eventual release, and marked the creative processes that he had engaged in during his incarceration, by publishing a play and a novel in the Gikuyu language, and by writing autobiography and commentary: for example, *Detained* and *Writers in Politics*. Ngugi subsequently spent time as a Writer in Residence in a London borough before taking up a Professorship in the United States. There he has been able to promote Gikuyu literature by, for example, the publication of a journal, *Mutiiri* (see pages 147-48).

From this career one might draw the surprising conclusion that imprisonment provides the most fertile environment for a writer, followed by time spent as a student, and, in third place, in a writers' colony.

Magical Years

Starting from another point, Robert Wren poses a different question about literary creativity. He does not ask 'Why does this person write more at this stage of his life than at another?' but 'Why do certain communities at certain times produce so much fine writing?' His book, *Those Magical Years*, subtitled *The Making of Nigerian Literature at Ibadan*, is largely composed of interviews with teachers and students who were at the first university to be established in Nigeria, between 1948 and 1966. Wren felt that an explanation was required for the flourishing of writing by Chinua Achebe, Elechi Amadi, JP Clark [now Clark-Bekederemo], Chukwuemeka Ike, John Munyone, Flora Nwapa, Christopher Okigbo, and Wole Soyinka.

Interview after interview reveals the undoubted importance of the fact that the community of the newly established university brought together an elite group of young people who interacted with talented teachers. To this 'mix' was added the sense of creating a national literary identity and the presence of publications and publishers. I suspect that 'space', 'a room of one's own', and, in some cases, scholarships, also contributed. Sanity and kindness, noted by Osundare at the beginning of this section, were important too.

The Iowa Idyll

The attempt to provide 'near ideal' circumstances in which writers can work has inspired various universities and foundations to create special opportunities for writers. A particularly intriguing way in to the world of international writers' groups is provided by Chukwuemeka Ike's novel *To My Husband from Iowa*, in which the author describes going to America to be with writers and to write. While drawing attention to some aspects of the 'program' offered by the School of Letters at the University of Iowa, the writer comments – through a female persona – on the America encountered. He also conducts interviews with some fellow course members about their experiences as writers. The perspective offered by Ike in his female guise – and of the friendship that develops with an Indian member of the group, Usha – is intriguingly complemented by Lakshmi Kannan (a model for Usha) in 'Sable Shadows at the Witching Time of Night' which is published in *India Gate and Other Stories* (1993). There we read that Ike, 'around six foot five with a physique to match', is a 'seasoned academician' whose 'novels and books were read widely in England, the US and other English-speaking countries'. One might add that he is President of the Nigerian Book Foundation, and that he has written extensively and perspicaciously on publishing and creative writing in West Africa.

Iowa has, by attracting and encouraging distinguished African writers, earned an enviable reputation for its various creative writing programmes. (And it should be noted that Ike and Kannan participated in a programme offered by the *School of Letters*.) However, since the costs involved are vast and sources of financial support severely limited, these courses remain accessible only to the lucky and industrious handful offered Fellowships. It is very much cheaper to stay at home.

Malawi

Attempts to create circumstances in which authors can flourish on the African continent have included the establishment of posts for authors at universities and, in Malawi, there are plans for a Writers' Colony. The following appeared in *This is Malawi* in 1996:

> *Malawi's First Writers' Colony Sprouts*
> If you are a writer who has problems concentrating on writing because of intrusions by nagging spouses, children or colleagues, then Steve Chimombo's WASI Writers' Colony would be the ideal place for you.
> Situated about 30 kilometres north of the old capital of Zomba, the yet-to-be completed WASI Writers' Colony overlooks Malosa mountain. It is about two kilometres north of Malosa Trading Centre and about half a kilometre's drive from the main road.

The article by Bob Chilemba continued by describing the building that is in the middle of the colony: a grocer's shop converted into a library, a research centre which boasts a collection of titles dating back to 1882 and includes publications not available in the University Library or National Archives. The centre will offer seclusion and peace for those writers who start writing when they are 'possessed by the muse', and for whom any form of distraction can be creatively fatal. The slightest disturbance might send them haywire and with no creative potential to complete their writing project.

For those who derive inspiration from a creative community, the colony is significantly 'surrounded by Yao villages with their unique *jando* (circumcision), music and art'. There will also be the possibility of creative interaction with other writers who may be in residence, or with day visitors. Chimombo, described as 'Malawi's foremost connoisseur of writers' colonies having visited seven such institutions', is quoted as saying: 'Writers have to pay for their accommodation and food just like they would normally pay for these at a hotel or any other such place.'

The article concludes with a reference to the importance of the colony as a meeting place for the country's little known and often neglected authors to improve on issues that hinder their progress so that they will be able to contribute effectively towards national development (Chilemba 1996, 16).

Gambia

The Gambia has been the setting for writers' residential workshops
that are largely expatriate in inspiration. London-based tutors Dor-
othea Smartt and Eva Lewin have worked through SAKS Media to set
up one- and two-week writing and drumming workshops. In 1997,
with flights to and from London and full board, the cost was £495.
Contacts have been made with Gambian authors and it is hoped that
they, and writers from other African countries, can be drawn in to
what will become genuinely international writers' workshops. For
details, see Writers' Organisations: A Directory, page 201.

Nigeria

The Writers' Village, Abuja

The Nigerian Government established a meeting place, a writers'
village in the new capital of Abuja, for members of the Association of
Nigerian Authors. In his address at the International Symposium on
African Literatures, held in Lagos, May 1988, Soyinka spoke of the
background to the creation of the centre, the role played 'by the
commitment of a man of war who also happened to be a poet', (a
reference to Mamman J Vatsa) and his personal misgivings about
becoming 'the legal guarantor of a piece of real estate that owed its
existence to the benevolence of a blatantly fascistic regime' (Osofisan
et al. 1991, 27). The contradictions involved in the way the meeting
place was set up prompted Soyinka to sketch a scenario in which his
audience (a hall, filled with writers) was invaded by a protesting crowd
of labour leaders and students shouting 'Down with the bloodsucking
literati and their military godfathers!'

The Essay Foundation, near Abeokuta

Soyinka himself planned a somewhat similar venture, a 'Foundation'
named after his father, a few kilometres from Abeokuta, built to a
design that would provide, *inter alia*, accommodation for writers who
needed to spend time working on scripts. The architectural plans
provided for experimental 'performance spaces' in which 'work in
progress' could be performed, and it was anticipated that writers would
be in residence alongside creative people from other fields. (This is
referred to here and elsewhere as 'The Mbari Ideal'.) Part of the
building was completed and opened on 10 April 1993.

Jahman Anikulapo described his visit to the site in 1993. He
remarked that the invitation referred to 'The Autonomous Domain of

Ijegbaland', and observed that the house was 'sanguined in a vast valley', as part of an estate covering fifty-four plots. Apparently the complex has just four big rooms, with 'many hills and planes, and doors', but there were plans to construct chalets for writers on a nearby hillside. There were also plans to farm in the immediate vicinity and to hunt further away.

Work on the project began after Soyinka resigned from the University of Ife and gathered pace after 'the disaster called the Nobel Prize' (1986). Femi Johnson, an insurance magnate, a veteran of many Orisun Theatre productions and fellow hunter, had lent Soyinka money to get work started, and donations of equipment, including a generator and other electrical items, followed. Soyinka spoke of the complex as being dedicated to the service of 'writers, scholars and loafers alike who still want to give hope to our people' (Anikulapo 1993, 10).

Reports circulating in the late 1990s suggested that, with Soyinka in exile, the buildings were not being put to their intended purpose. Indeed, although the local people were trying to preserve the privacy of the place and provided a measure of protection, the property had been raided, possibly by the security forces who thought that a pro-Democracy, anti-Abacha broadcasting station, Radio Kudirat, might be based there. Electrical goods were taken. On his return to Nigeria, in October 1998, Soyinka was 'sad to see [his] house in such a deteriorating state' (Soyinka quoted by Gyamfi 1998).

Traditions of Story-telling

While many believe that the comfortable myth of the moonlit story-telling session is for foreign consumption only, it remains true that there are some places where traditions of oral narratives have been preserved. The prolific and lamented late Flora Nwapa wrote, and in some cases saw through the presses, a series of novels in which she often draws on her background in Oguta.

The fact that other significant women writers – Buchi Emecheta, Onsonye Tess Onwueme and (the critic) Chikwenyi Ogunyemi are linked with the same area – suggests that some communities have stronger traditions of, in this case, female story-telling than others.

The Writer in Residence and the Writer at Large

A number of African writers have benefited from schemes and employment opportunities designed specifically to support creative writers. For example, Kole Omotoso was a Writer in Residence in a London borough and Jack Mapanje was employed as the first Greater North Writer in Residence to encourage creative writing in British prisons, community centres, schools and libraries throughout the north of England. Ezenwa-Ohaeto, one of those who industriously combines academic research with creative writing, benefited from a Humbolt Prestigious Research Fellowship during 1993.

Somewhat similar opportunities exist on the African continent: Amos Tutuola spent 1979 as a Writer in Residence at the University of Ife, and Chenjerai Hove has occupied a similar position at the University of Zimbabwe. It is to be hoped that opportunities will be increased since it is clear that very few African authors earn more than a pittance from the sale of their books.

In the opening pages of his Booker Prize winning novel *The Famished Road*, Ben Okri included the following:

ACKNOWLEDGEMENTS
To Wole Soyinka and the Arts Council of Great Britain, for 1984;
To Harriet Sergeant and an unknown benefactor, for 1986;
And to David Godwin, for faith.

From reading this a few of the sources of support for a gifted young man can be identified. David Godwin is an agent (a super-agent) with a sharp nose and a quick contract for new writers from 'outposts of Empire' who has a remarkable record of 'agenting' for the winners of the Booker Prize! Readers may be interested to know that in the Acknowledgements to the 1997 Booker Prize winner, *The God of Small Things*, Arundhati Roy included:

David Godwin, flying agent, guide and friend. For taking that impulsive trip to India. For making the waters part.

When approached in connection with this volume, Godwin, through his secretary, thanked them but 'to be honest [did not] think there would be any point in including him'.

Exiles, Self-exiles, and Internal Exiles

It is apparent, then, that experiences differ, and circumstances may not provide the key to creativity. For example, the major debate about the impact of exile on creative writers will run and run. Perhaps the most frequently interviewed of African writers, Wole Soyinka, has drawn attention to the different kinds of exile he has experienced. In 1967 he went into a 'brief' self-exile, having felt cut off from fellow Nigerians at home. When, twenty-eight years later, he crossed the border into Benin to escape the Abacha junta, he spoke of not having really left:

I am on a mission ... I carry my country with me: my interior, my geography, is Nigeria. (Soyinka to Taylor 1995)

When asked about their relationships with their communities, certain authors draw attention to the changes in the circumstances in Africa, and for the middle classes. They feel they live in a state of 'internal exile'. They look back to a time when reasonable remuneration from employment, a democratic system, and an adequate infrastructure made it possible to live comfortably and do some writing. When all this was combined with opportunities for creative people to come together – as in Nigeria's Mbari Clubs or Malawi's Writers Group – and was inflamed with a desire to create a new literary landscape or add a literary tradition to those that already existed, then particularly exciting work was produced.

Much has been written under the broad heading 'Exile and the Twentieth Century Writer'. Articles often begin with the example of James Joyce, itinerant teacher, wandering author, asylum-seeker, father concerned to be near a sick daughter, perpetual exile from the stultifying Ireland described by a character in an early book as 'the old sow that eats her farrow' (Joyce: 1992, 220). The list of exiles continues with, for example, those, such as the Americans Gertrude Stein and James Baldwin, who moved to France; and the Caribbean authors, Sam Sevlon, George Lamming, Andrew Salkey among them, who spent time in London. Recent decades have seen Europe and America benefit from the new African Diaspora. Politics and economics, ruthless, inept rulers and currencies in free fall have driven generations of Africa's ablest beyond the seas.

That it need not and will not always be like this is suggested by the remarkable career of Ezekiel, now E'skia, Mphahlele, one of whose books is actually called *The Wanderers*. Mphahlele left South Africa in 1957 at thirty-seven, worked in Nigeria, France, Kenya, made the Middle Passage and sojourned in the United States with a brief period at the end of the 1960s in Zambia. A paradigmatic figure in African literature, he returned to South Africa after two decades of writing, researching, teaching, editing, organising and travelling. By this time he had published books with a revealing array of publishers. His experience and the list must delay us briefly since they speak so eloquently of the experiences of an itinerant author.

On his return to South Africa the government vetoed his appointment at the University of the North and he became inspector of schools at Lebowa. From that post he moved on to become Senior Research Fellow at the African Studies Institute, University of Witwatersrand. He has also been involved with the Council for Black Education and Research in Soweto, and FUNDA Community College, which began with integrated studies in social, physical and natural sciences and moved on to focus on computer literacy. As circumstances changed in South Africa, he was able to take up an appointment at the University of the North, but from an interview he gave Richard Samin in the mid-1990s, when he was already well into his seventies, Mphahlele also took great satisfaction in running a monthly reading circle. Asked by Samin about his creative writing, he indicated his abiding commitment to literature and his ability to draw on the life around him:

> I started not so long ago to try to compile a book of short stories for young readers. I did two, which were published in journals. I'm certainly bound to that. Another is a novel which has been milling around in my mind for some time now, for the last two years. It has a lot to do with neighbours in the street, typical of this town here, where relations go sour between neighbour and neighbour ... I'm looking for resonances. How can I make this conflict between two families the microcosm of the larger conflict, the human conflict, not necessarily racial because it's a black area, an African area, yet feeling the wash of the tide that racism still is?

The following, incomplete, list drawn from material in *A New Reader's Guide to African Literature* (Zell *et al.* 1983) and *Bibliography of African Literatures* (Limb and Volet 1996), provides its own account of Mphahlele's sources of inspiration and his relationships with publishers. Decades of travelling during rapidly changing times are revealed by the titles and publishers:

Man Must Live, and Other Stories. Cape Town: African Bookman, 1947. Ibadan: Ministry of Education, 1958.

Down Second Avenue. London: Faber, 1959. Berlin: Seven Seas Books, 1962. New York Doubleday, 1971.

The Living and the Dead, and Other Stories. Ibadan: Ministry of Education, 1961.

In Corner B. Nairobi: EAPH, 1967.

The Wanderers. New York: Macmillan, 1971. London: Macmillan, 1972.

Voices in the Whirlwind and Other Essays. London, New York: Macmillan. Hill and Wang. 1972.

Chirundu. Johannesburg: Ravan, 1979. Walton-on-Thames: Nelson, 1980. Westport, Conn.: Lawrence Hill, 1981.

The Unbroken Song. Johannesburg: Ravan, 1981.

Afrika my Music: An Autobiography of Es'kia Mphahlele 1943-1980. Edited by N Chabani Manganyi. Johannesburg: Skotaville, 1984.

Renewal Time. (Short Stories). Columbia LA: Readers International, 1988.

Writers' Organisations: A Directory

The list of writers' groups, associations, and organisations is largely a reprint of the listings which appeared in *A Handbook of African Writers*, and we have been unable to verify whether all of the organisations are still active or whether the addresses we have on file are correct. For many of them we only have a name and address, without other contact details such as telephone/fax numbers and/or email address. Such organisations are encouraged to write to the Editor to ensure fuller listings in the next edition of this Handbook. The list is followed by the names and addresses of organisations which support authors on copyright and reproduction issues; organisations concerned with freedom of expression; and some other useful addresses.

AFRICA

Angola
Uniao dos Escritores Angolanos
CP 2767, Luanda

Botswana
Botswana Writers' Group
Department of English
University of Botswana
Private Bag 0022, Gaborone
Fax: +267-356591

Cameroon
Association des Poètes et Ecrivains Camerounais
BP 2180, Yaoundé

National Association of Cameroon Poets and Writers
PO Box 8250, Yaoundé

The Yaoundé University Poetry Club
c/o Ms Vanessa E Sena
PO Box 5615, Yaoundé

Democratic Republic of Congo
Le Gai Savoir
Agence Internationale de Culture
BP 12924, Kinshasa

Union des Ecrivains Congolese
BP 3001, Kinshasa-Gombe

Congo-Brazzaville
Cercle Littéraire de Brazzaville
BP 2141, Brazzaville

Union des Acteurs et Ecrivains
BP1678, Brazzaville

Ethiopia
Ethiopian Writers' Union
Ya'ityopya 'Andnat
Mahebar, PO Box 5666, Addis Ababa

The Gambia
Ndaan
c/o The Director of Information
Bedford Building,
Ministry of Education, Banjul

Ghana
Ghana Association of Writers
PO Box 2738, Accra

Pan-African Writers' Association
(PAWA)
PAWA House, Roman Ridge
PO Box C546, Cantonments,
Accra
Tel: + 233-21-773062
Fax: +233-21-773042
Contact: Atukwei Okai,
Secretary-General

Guinea Bissau
Casa de Cultura
Conselho Nacional de Cultura,
Bissau

Kenya
University of Nairobi Writers'
Workshop
c/o Kenya Literature Bureau
PO Box 3002, Nairobi

Liberia
Liberian Association of Writers
PMB 2124, Monrovia

Malawi
Writers' Club
Zomba Catholic Secondary School
PO Box 2, Zomba

Writers' Group
Department of English
Chancellor College
PO Box 280, Zomba

Mauritius
Association des Ecrivains Mauric-
iens d'Expression Française
Le Hochet, Terre Rouge
English Writers' Association
Cascadelle, Beau-Bassin

Mozambique
Associacao dos Escritores
Mocambicanos (AEMO)
CP 4187, Maputo
Contact: H Muteia

Namibia
Education and Cultural Association
of Namibia
PO Box 7123, Windhoek

Nigeria
Association of Nigerian Authors
(ANA)
National Secretariat
26 Oladipo Labinjo Crescent
Off Bode Thomas, Surulere, Lagos
President: Abubakar Gimba (Minna)

Sec. Gen: Dr Wale Okediran (Ibadan)
Encourages and promotes Nigerian literatures in all its forms; promotes and aims to protect the interests and rights of authors; and collaborates with other organisations established for the promotion and development of the book industry throughout the country. It operates chapters in several states of Nigeria. The ANA publishes the annual *ANA Review*, holds annual conferences and frequent regional gatherings, and awards annual prizes for published or unpublished drama, prose and poetry. The late Mamman J Vatsa secured a plot of land for the Association in the Federal Capital Territory, Abuja.

Nigerian Book Foundation
4 Ezi-Ajana Lane (Umukwa)
P O Box 1132, Awka
Tel: +234-46-551403
Fax: +234-46-552615
Contact: Chukwuemeka Ike,
Director
A non-governmental, non-profit book development body founded in 1991 as an umbrella organisation bringing together the key participants in the book industry and the book chain. The Foundation has an irrevocable commitment to indigenous book development; 'anchored in the conviction that books build the nation, the NBF has as its mission the development of a vibrant indigenous book industry in Nigeria'. Organises lectures, seminars, workshops, book fairs and an annual conference. The Foundation has published a range of books on publishing and book development, including a *Directory of Nigerian Book Development*, which includes extensive annotated listings of Nigerian published authors, publishers, bookshops, libraries, and printers.

Writers, Artists and Kindred Ensemble
PO Box 4231, Garki, Abuja

Réunion
Association des Ecrivains Réunionnais
Salle des Fetes,
97490 Sainte Clotilde

Rwanda
Comite Consultatif National des Artistes, Auteurs, Compositeurs et Editeurs Rwandais
Université Nationale du Rwanda
Campus de Rhengeri à Butare
BP 56, Butare

Senegal
Association des Ecrivains du Sénégal
127 Avenue Lamine Gueye
Dakar

Gorée Institute
Gorée
Has been involved in planning a 'Poetry Caravan'

Sierra Leone
Sierra Leone Association of Writers and Illustrators
c/o The Sierra Leone Library Board
PO Box 326, Freetown
Contact: Mrs TA Lucan

South Africa
Congress of South African Writers
1 President Street
New Town 2001, PO Box 421007
Fordburg 2033, Johannesburg
Tel: +27-11-833-2530
Fax: +27-11-833-2532
Email cosaw@wn.apc.org
Contact: Kessie Govender
Encourages writers and assists them in getting published. Publishes *Staffrider* magazine. Other activities have included protesting against ill-treatment of writers in Africa, including the late Ken Saro-Wiwa.
Southern African Writers' Council (SAWCO)
PO Box 10024, Johannesburg 2000
Tel: +27-11-836-5853
Email: sawco@sn.apc.org
Contact: Morakabe Raks Seakhoa

Tanzania
Kagere Writers and Publishers Co-operative
PO Box 12222, Bukoba
Contact: Andrew Bagayana

UWAVITA Umoja wa waandishi wa vitabu Tanzania
PO Box 32740, Dar es Salaam
Contact: Professor MM Mulokozi
A Dutch foundation, HIVOS, has provided support for UWAVITA which, under new leadership, has shown renewed vigour in pursuing its wide range of aims. Under an Interim Executive Committee elected in November 1995, an office has been secured, workshops organised, competitions held and a newsletter published. The constitution is being revised to take stock of the current situation.

Uganda
FEMRITE
Uganda Women Writers' Association
Plot 147 Kira Road
PO Box 705, Kampala
Tel: +256-4-543943
Email: femrite@infocom.co.ug
Contacts: Goretti Kyomuhendo, Debora Etoori
Organisation of women writers, established in 1995. One of its main objectives is to unite, promote and inspire creative women writers and assist in the publishing of their manuscripts. Has its own imprint, Femrite Publications Ltd.

Zambia
Writers' Group
Department of Literature and
Languages
University of Zambia
POB 2379, Lusaka

Zambian National Association of
Writers
POB 50054, Lusaka

Zimbabwe
Budding Writers' Association of
Zimbabwe (BWAZ)
78 Kaguvi Street
PO Box 4209, Harare
Tel: +263-4-771621
Fax: +263-4-751202

Zimbabwe Academic and
Non-Fiction Authors Association
c/o Dr Alois Mlambo
Department of Economic History
University of Zimbabwe
PO Box MP167
Mount Pleasant, Harare
Tel: +263-4-303211, ext. 1239
Email: mlambo@ecohist.uz.zw
Contact: Virginia Phiri
Seeks to promote and protect the
rights and interests of Zimbabwean
academic and non-fiction authors.

Zimbabwe African Languages
Writers Association
PO Box UA 196
Union Avenue, Harare
Contact: Ray Choto

Zimbabwe Women Writers
78 Kaguvi Street
PO Box 4209, Harare
Tel: +263-4-774261
Fax: +263-4-751202
Email: zww@telco.co.zw
Contacts: Pushpa Hargovan; Nomsa
Musengezi
Encourages, and seeks to improve
and promote women's writing. Mem-
bership includes women from all
walks of life with the common aim of
writing for the empowerment of
women.

Zimbabwe Writers' Club
PO Box 768, Harare
Contact: Alison Mfiri

Zimbabwe Writers' Union
206 2nd floor Rothbart Building
6th Street
PO Box 6170, Gweru
Tel: +263-54-23284
Fax: +263-54-26147
Contacts: Kenneth Ruchaka
Aims to protect the interests and
rights of Zimbabwean writers and to
promote the use of literature for the
development process. Also seeks to
forge close links with other writers in
Africa and beyond.

OUTSIDE AFRICA

United Kingdom
Gemini News Service
9 White Lion Street, London N1 9PD
Tel: +44-171-278111
Fax: +44-171-2780345
Email: alexw@panoslondon.org.uk
Web site: http:/www.oneworld.org/
panos
Contact: Dipankar De Sarkar, editor
This is an international news service
with subscribers world-wide, rather
than a writers' organisation as such.
However, it accepts story ideas and
articles on culture. Payment is made
for articles that are used.

The Society of Authors
24 Drayton Gardens,
London SW10 9SB
Contact: Mark Le Fanu,
General Secretary
Tel: +44-(0)171-373 6642
Fax: +44-(0)171-373 5768

Email: authorsoc@writers.org.uk
Web site: http://www.writers.org.uk/society
The Society is a non-profit-making organisation founded in 1884 to protect the rights and further the interests of authors. It's current membership stands at over 6,500. Publishes the journal *The Author*.

SAKS Media
42 Chatsworth Road
London E5 0LP
Tel/Fax: +44-(0)181-985 9419
Contact: Kadija (George) Sesay
Arranges programmes for writers who fly out for holidays in the Gambia. Has plans to strengthen links between visiting and local authors.

The Writers Guild of Great Britain
430 Edgware Road, London W2 1EH
Tel: +44-(0)171-723 8074
Fax: +44-(c)171-706 2413
Email: poste@wggb demon.co.uk
Web site:
http://www.writers.org.uk/guild
Established in 1958 the Writers' Guild's mission is to ensure that writers of all media are adequately represented; it seeks to ensure that writers are properly paid and accredited, and get a fair deal in today's increasingly competitive and ruthless market.

COPYRIGHT AND REPRODUCTION RIGHTS ORGANISATIONS

Dramatic, Artistic and Literary Rights Organisation (DALRO)
5th floor SAMRO House
73 Juta Street, PO Box 31627
Braamfontein 2017
Johannesburg, South Africa
Email: dalro@iafrica.com

Contact: Monica Seeber
A reproduction rights organisation and copyright licensing agency. It is affiliated with the International Federation of Reproduction Rights Organisations (IFFRO).

Kopiken
Kenyan Reproduction Rights Organisation
PO Box 31191
Nairobi, Kenya
Tel: +254-2-336771
Fax: +254-2-245146
Contact: Stanley Irura
Reproduction rights organisation which aims to unite copyright holders in Kenya and administer the collection of their dues through collective administration. Affiliated with the International Federation of Reproduction Rights Organisation (IFFRO).

Zimcopy
The Reproduction Rights Organisation of Zimbabwe
712 Gefland House
Speke Avenue / First St
PO Box BE 579, Belvedere
Harare, Zimbabwe
Tel: +263-4-621661/7
Fax: +263-4-621670
Contact: Greenfield K Chilongo
Zimbabwe reproduction rights organisation affiliated with the International Federation of Reproduction Rights Organisation (IFFRO). Although Zimcopy has informal contacts with concerned and involved individuals in a number of African countries, it appears that concerted action on protection of copyright remains a distant hope. Appropriate legislation appears to be the first step.

FREEDOM OF EXPRESSION ORGANISATIONS

Although not necessarily limited to working with writers, the following may be of value to persecuted authors. The following material is reproduced by permission from Index on Censorship.

The growth of free expression organisations outside the West has been one of the more encouraging trends in the past decade. Many are grouped in the International Free Expression Exchange (IFEX) and share information and action alerts via email. Current members are:

Accuracy in Media (AIM)
4455 Connecticut Ave, NW
Suite 330
Washington DC 20005, USA
Tel: +1-202-3644401
Fax: +1-202-3644098

Article 19: International Centre Against Censorship
33 Islington High Street
London N1 9LH, UK
Tel: +44-171-2789292
Fax: +44-171-7131356

Canadian Committee to Protect Journalists (CCPJ)
489 College Street, Suite 403
Toronto, Ontario M6G 1A5, Canada
Tel: +1-416-5159622
Fax: + 1-416-5157879
Email: ccpj@ccpj.ca

Californians Against Censorship Together (ACT)
1800 Market Street, Suite 1000
San Francisco, CA 94103, USA
Tel: +1-510-5483695

Committee on International Freedom to Publish
c/o Association of American Publishers

71 Fifth Avenue,
New York, NY 10003, USA
Tel: +1-212-2550200
Fax: +1-212-2557007

Committee to Protect Journalists
330 Seventh Avenue, 12th Flr
New York, NY 10001, USA
Tel: +1-212-4651004
Fax: +1-212-4659568

Feminists for Free Expression
2525 Times Square Station
New York, NY 10108, USA
Tel: +1-212-7026292
Fax: +1-212-7026277

Freedom of Information Clearinghouse
PO Box 19367
Washington, DC 20036, USA
Tel: +1-202-5887790

Freedom Forum
First Amendment Center
1207, 18th Avenue South
Nashville, TN 37212, USA
Tel: +1-615 321 9588

Egyptian Organization for Human Rights (EOHR)
8/10 Matahaf El-Manial St, 10th Flr
Manial El-Roda, Cairo, Egypt
Tel: +20-2-3636811/36204647
Fax: +20-2-3621613
Email: eohr@link.com.eg

Free Expression Ghana
PO Box 207,
The Human Rights Centre
Ghana International Press Centre
Nkrumah Circle, Accra, Ghana
Tel: +233-21229875
Fax: +233-21237004
Email:
freedom@africaonline.com.gh

Free Media Movement (FMM)
Lucien Rajakarunanayake
73/28 Sri Raranankara Place

Dehiwala, Sri Lanka
Tel/Fax: +941-735152
Email: lucien@eureka.lk

Freedom House
120 Wall Street
New York, NY 10005, USA
Tel: +1-212-5148040
Fax: +1-212-5148050
Email: kguida@freedomhouse.org

Freedom of Expression Institute
(FXI)
PO BOX 30568, Braamfontein 20178
Johannesburg, South Africa
Tel: +27-11-4038403/4
Fax: +27-11-4038309
Email: fxi@wn.apc.org

Hong Kong Journalists Association
(HKJA)
Flat A, 15/F
Henta Commercial Building
348-350 Lockhart Road
Wanchai, Hong Kong
Tel: + 852-25910692
Fax: +852-25727329
Email: hkja@hk.super.net

Human Rights Watch (HRW)
Empire State Building, 34th Flr
New York, NY 10118-3299, USA
Tel: +1-212-2904700
Fax: +1-212-7361300
Email: hrwnyc@hrw.org

Independent Journalism Centre
Tejumola House (1st Floor)
24, Omole Layout, New Isheri Road
PO Box 7808 Ojudu
Ikeja, Lagos, Nigeria
Tel/Fax: +234-1-4924998/4924314
Email: ijc@linkserve.com.ng

Index on Censorship
33 Islington High Street
London N1 9LH, UK
Tel: +44-171-2783213
Fax: +44-171-2781378
Email:
[Name]@indexoncensorship.org

Institute for Studies on the Free Flow of Information (ISAI)
Jalan Utan Kayu 68-H
Jakarta 13120, Indonesia
Tel: + 62-21-8573388
Fax: +62-21-8573387
Email:
harsono@nation.nationgroup.com

Instituto Prensa y Sociedad (IPYS)
Miguel Dasso 153
oficina 7 ÓMÓ
San Isidro, Lima 27, Peru
Tel/Fax: +511-2-211523
Email: postmaster@ipyspe.pe

Inter American Press Association
(IAPA)
Melba Jimenez
2911 NW 39th Street Miami,
Florida 33142, USA
Tel: +1-305-6342465
Fax: +1-305-6352272

International Federation of Journalists (IFJ)
Rue Royale, 266
B-121 Brussels, Belgium
Tel: +322-2232265
Fax: +322-2192976
Email: ifj.safety@pophost.eunet.be

IFJ Affiliates
Federacion Internactional de
Periodistas (FIP)
IFJ Latin American Regional Office
Calle Santos Erminy
Edificio Beatriz, Piso 7, Oficina 74
Sabana Grande, Caracas, Venezuela
Tel: + 582-7631971
Fax: + 582-7633778
Email: fip@eldish.net

IFJ Algerian Centre
Maison de la Presse Tahar Djaout
1 rue Bachir Attar Algiers
Algeria
Tel: +213-2659470,
Tel/Fax: +213-2659479

IFJ Palestinian Media
Monitoring Centre,
Ruba Hussairi, Jerusalem,
Email: ifjruba@trendline.co.il

*IFJ/WAN Co-ordinating Centre
for Balkan Media*
Vosnjakova 8
6100 Ljubljana, Slovenia
Tel/Fax: + 38661-323170
Email: ifj.fiej@k2.net

International Press Institute (IPI)
Spiegelgasse 2
A-1010 Vienna, Austria
Tel: +43-1-5129011
Fax: +43-1-51290 14
Email: ipi.vienna@xpoint.at

Journalist Safety Service (JSS)
Joh. Vermeerstraat 22
1071 DR Amsterdam,
The Netherlands
Tel: +31-20-6766771
Fax: +31-20-6624901
Email: jss@euronet.nl

Media Institute of Southern Africa
(MISA) Private Bag 13386
Windhoek, Namibia
Tel: +264-61-232975
Fax: +264-61-248016
Email: research@ingrid.misa.org.na

*Network for the Defence
of Independent Media in Africa*
(NDIMA)
PO Box 70147, Nairobi, Kenya
Tel: +254-154-41403
Fax: +254-154-51118
Email: ndima@arcc.or.ke

*Norwegian Forum for Freedom
of Expression* (NFFE)
Menneskerettighetshuset Urtegata 50
N-0187 Oslo, Norway
Tel: +47-22-677964
Fax: +47-22-570088
Email: nffe@online.no

*Oficina de Derechos Humanos del
Periodista* (OFIP)
Roberto Mejia, Jr
Huancavelic 320 Of.204, Lima, Peru
Tel: +5114-270687
Fax: +5114-278493
Email: anp@amauta.rcp.net.pe

Pacific Islands News Association
(PINA)
Pina Freedom of Information
Network Mailing Address:
PINA Private Mail Bag
Street Address:
46 Gordon Street, Level II,
Damador Centre, Suva, Fiji Islands
Tel: +679-303623
Fax: +679-303943/302101
Email: pina@is.com.fj or
plomas@ibi.com.fj

Pakistan Press Foundation (PPF)
Press Centre
Shahrah Kamal Ataturk
Karachi, Pakistan
Tel: + 92-21-2633215
Fax: +92-21-2637754
Email: owais.ali@ibm.net

Periodistas
Argentine Association for the Protec-
tion of Independent Journalism
Sarmiento 1334, Buenos Aires
Argentina
Tel/Fax: +54-1-3726201
Email: periodis@mail.netizen.com.ar

Reporters sans frontières (RSF)
5, rue Geoffrey Marie
Paris 75009, France
Tel: +33-144-838484
Fax: +33-145-231151
Email: rsf@calva.net

West African Journalists Association
(WAJA)
Mailing Address: PO Box 4031
Accra, Ghana
Tel: +233-21-234692

Fax: +233-21-234694
Email: waja@africaonline.com.gh

World Association of Community Radio Broadcasters (AMARC)
3575 St Laurent, 611 Montreal
Quebec H2X 2TJ, Canada
Tel: +1-514-94820351
Fax: +1-514-8497129
Email: amarc@web.net

AMARC
Latin American Regional Office
Oficina regional para America Latina
Av. Atahualpa 333 y Ulloa
Casilla 17-08-84, Quito, Ecuador
Tel/Fax: +593-2-501180/5516474
Email: ignacio@pulsar.org.ec

AMARC
European Regional Office
The Media Centre
15 Paternoster Row
Sheffield S1 2BX, UK
Tel: +44-1142-795219
Email: amarc@gn.apc.org

World Association of Newspapers
(WAN)
25, rue d'Astorg, 75008 Paris, France
Tel: +33-14-7428500
Fax: +33-14-7424948
Email: fiej.nemo@nemo.geis.com

World Press Freedom Committee
(WPFC)
11690-C Sunrise Valley Drive
Reston, Virginia 20191, USA
Tel: +1-703-7159811
Fax: +1-703-6206790
Email: freepress@wpfc.org

Writers in Prison Committee
(WiPC)
International PEN
9/10 Charterhouse Buildings
Goswell Road
London EC1M 7AT, UK
Tel: +44-171253 3226

Fax: +44-171-2535711
Email: intpen@gn.apc.org

PEN Canada
24 Ryerson Avenue, Suite 309
Toronto, Ontario M5T 2P3, Canada
Tel: +1-416-7038448
Fax: +1-416-7033870
Email: pencan@web.net

PEN American Center
568 Broadway, Suite 401
New York, NY 10012, USA
Tel: +1-212-3341660
Fax: +1-212-3342181
Email: diana@pen.org

IFEX Clearing House
489 College St, Suite 40
Toronto, Ontario M6G IA5, Canada
Tel: +1-416-5159622
Fax: +1-416-5157879
Email: ifex@ifex.org

Among other organisations regularly supplying *Index* with information on the state of media freedom and attacks on journalists:

Action Committee for Media Freedom
445/1 Prince of Wales Avenue
Colombo 14, Sri Lanka
Tel: +941-3934069
Fax: +941-449593

Alliance of Independent Journalists
RSTA Blok 39 Lt. II No 4
Jl. KH Mas Mansyur 25
Jakarta 10240, Indonesia
Tel/Fax: +62-21-3155918

Asociación de Periodistas de Guatemala
Comisión de Libertad de Prensa
14 Calle 3-29, Zona 1
Ciudad de Guatemala, Guatemala
Tel: +502-232-1813
Email: c/o cerigua@guate.net

Australian Centre for Independent Journalism
PO Box 123
Broadway NSW 2007, Australia

Sierra Leone Association of Journalists
PMB 724 Freetown, Sierra Leone
Tel: +232-22228

Bahrain Freedom Movement
Fax: +0171-2789089
Email:
100542.1623@compuserve.com

B'Tselem
The Israeli Information Center for Human Rights in the Occupied Territories
43 Emek Refaim Street, 2nd Floor
Jerusalem 93141, Israel
Tel: +972-2-617271
Fax: +972-2-610756

Centre Haitien de Défense des Libertés
Boite Postal 2408
Port-au-Prince, Haiti
Tel: +5-5103

CERIGUA news agency
9a, Calle 'A' 3-49
Zona 1, Ciudad, Guatemala
Tel: +502-2324419
Fax: +502-2536670
Email: cerigua@guate.net

Iranian PEN Centre in Exile
c/o The Rationalist Press Association
47 Theobald's Road
London WC1X 8SP, UK
Fax: +44-171-4301271

Frente Nacional de Abogados Democráticos
Nezahualcoyotl 51
Despacho 21
Centro México 06090, DF Mexico
Tel: +761-9457

Glasnost Defense Foundation
119021 Moscow
4 Zubovsky bulv, room 432
Russia
Fax: +7-095-2014947
Directors fax: +7-095-1944848
Email: eoznobki@iphras.irex.ru

Havana Libre
Tel: +53-7-333152
Fax: +53-7-338792

Co-ordinating Centre for Independent Media of the Balkan Region
Cufarjeva 15, 61000
Ljubljana, Slovenia
Tel: +386-61-1317239
Fax: +386-61-1327034
Email:
Balkan_media@Zamir-LJ.ztn.zer.de

Independent Belarus.net site
Tel: +375-17-2390475
Fax: +375-17-2768371
Email: admin@jornal.minsk.by
Web: http://www.belarus.net/

Media Watch
GPO Box 3521, Dhaka, Bangladesh
Tel: +880-2-9567070
Fax: +880-2-9562882
(attn Media Watch)

Free Information Institute
kv. Sv. Troica
bl. 297, Sofia 1309, Bulgaria
Tel/Fax: +59-2-203622
Email: cts.0487@main.infotel.bg

NDIMA
PO Box 70147, Nairobi, Kenya
Tel: +254-154-41403
Fax: +254-154-51118
Email:
ndima@users.africaonline.co.ke

OSCE Mission to Bosnia
Sarajevo Head Office
PO Box CH 4410

Liestal, Switzerland
Email: tanyad@oscebih.org

The Media Institute
Tumaini House
Nairobi, Kenya
Email: GOwor@ken.healthnet.org

Pacific Media Watch
PO Box 273
University Post Office, NCD
Papua New Guinea
Tel/Fax: +675-3267191
Email: niusedita@pactok.net.au
journupng@pactok.peg.apc.org
Web site: http://acij.uts.edu.au/pmw/

CUPAZ
Linea 556, esq D
Vedado 4, Havana, Cuba
Tel: +32-0506
Fax: +32-0490
Email: cupaz@tinored.cu

The following additional organisations to those listed from *Index* above, are also concerned with freedom of expression.

AFRICA

Nigeria
Civil Liberties Organisation
24 Mbonu Ojike Street
off Alhaji Masha Road
Surulere, Lagos, Nigeria
Contact: Osaze Lanre Ehonwa

Zambia
Inter-African Network for Human Rights and Development
1st Floor Church House
Cairo Road
PO Box 31145, Lusaka
Tel: +260-1-226544/ 228913
Fax: +260-1-238911
Email: afronet@zamnet.zm

Zimbabwe
Catholic Commission of Justice and Peace in Zimbabwe
PO Box CY 284, Causeway, Harare
Tel: +263-4-791053

Kunzwana Trust
73 Quorn Avenue
PO Box MP 349
Mount Pleasant, Harare
Tel: +263-4-301519
Fax: +263-14-301519
Email kunzwana@mango.zw
Contact: Keith Goddard
May provide advice to performing artists.

OUTSIDE AFRICA

France
International Parliament of Writers
Parlament International des Ecrivains
10 rue du 22 Novembre, BP 13,
F-67068 Strasbourg Cedex, France
Tel: +33-3-88-520088
Fax: +33-3-88-520107
Email: ipw@wanadoo.fr
The IPW continues to address the issue of censorship while appealing for funds to ensure that the organisation is financially secure.

Salman Rushdie is Honorary President of the International Parliament of Writers. Wole Soyinka President, JM Coetzee a member of the Administrative Council and Ben Okri a member of the General Assembly.

Spain
Observatori de la Libertat de Creació
CCCB- Casa de Caritat
Montalegre 5, E-08001 Barcelona
Tel: +34-33-064115/00
Fax: +34-33-064101/04
Email: vmolina@cccb.es
rmpiug@cccb.es
At a meeting of 60 writers in November 1993 the decision was made 'to set up

an international structure capable of promoting practical forms of solidarity with persecuted artists and writers'. At Strasbourg in 1995 a Charter for Asylum Cities was accepted and by June 1997 a network of 24 cities committed to hosting persecuted writers from around the world had been established in Europe. The Charter shows an acute awareness of the growth of intolerance towards literature both by states and by groups. The signatories of the Charter have responded to these threats by creating 'a true "archipelago" of the imagination'; they have established centres of tolerance and support.

United Kingdom
Index on Censorship
Writers and Scholars
International Ltd
39c Highbury Place, London N5 1QP
Tel: +44-(0)171-278-2313
Fax: +44-(0)171-329-6461
Email: indexocenso@gn.apc.org
Web site:
http://www.indexoncensorship.org/
In the US:
Fund for Free Expression,
36 West 44th Street,
New York NY 10036
Through its monitoring of censorship, *Index* provides an invaluable service for African writers and for those concerned about free expression on the continent. Publishes the journal *Index on Censorship*.

PEN International
9/10 Charterhouse Buildings,
Goswell Road, London EC1M 7AT
Tel: +44-(0)171-253-4308
Fax: +44-(0)171-253-5711
Email: intpen@dircon.co.uk
Web site:
http://oneworld.org/internatpen
Contact: Jane Spender

There are 15 PEN Centres in Africa, and there are plans to twin these with Centres in the North. There is also an African Writers Abroad Centre based in London, and a Somali-speaking Writers' Centre, which, from its London base, is setting up branches in the Horn of Africa. International PEN is the only world-wide association of writers. Its aim is to promote intellectual co-operation and understanding among writers that will both emphasise the central role of literature in the development of world culture and defend it against the many threats to its survival which the modern world poses. Because international cultural co-operation in the field of literature and the development of understanding cannot exist without freedom of expression, PEN acts as a powerful voice in opposing political censorship and speaking for writers harassed, imprisoned, sometimes murdered, for the expression of their views.

PEN is strictly non-political, holding Category A status at UNESCO and consultative status within the UN roster category. Composed of 130 Centres in almost 100 countries, its membership is open to all published writers regardless of nationality, race, colour or religion.

Each Centre acts as an autonomous cultural and intellectual organisation within its own country; individual Centres organise regional conferences and seminars; and all Centres maintain links with each other through PEN's headquarters. International Pen operates four standing committees whose memberships consists of the various Centres of PEN:

The Writers in Prison Committee monitors human rights abuses committed against writers and journalists world-wide and campaigns on their behalf. Such work has in many cases led to the liberation of imprisoned writers or at least an improvement in their situations. In addition member Centres provide individual support, sending prisoners greeting cards, parcels of clothes, medicines and books, and working to sustain their families.

The Translation and Linguistic Rights Committee promotes the translation of works written in minority languages into world languages, to overcome the barrier to understanding raised by difference of language. The survival of a diversity of views, sensibilities and cultures, and in support of such survival the Committee also works to affirm and defend linguistic rights, in particular of stateless languages.

The Writers for Peace Committee, through seminars and programmes, works to find ways for writers to contribute to peace, in particular drawing attention to the misuse of language to disguise national violence and ethnic cleansing.

The Women Writers' Committee focuses on the particular concerns of women writers that have resulted from the traditional positions of women within the social, cultural and religious structures of countries.

United States
Human Rights Watch
485 Fifth Avenue
New York NY 10017-6104
Tel: +1-212-986-1980
Fax: +1-212-972-0905
Email: hrwnyc@hrw.org

OTHER ORGANISATIONS

African Languages Organisations
Group d'Action pour la Promotion de 'Edition en Langues Africaines
Action Group for the Promotion of Publications in African Languages (GRAPELA),
BP 542 Conakry, Guinea
Tel: +224-444538
Fax: +224-412012
Contact: Mamadow Aliou Sow

Promotion of African Creative Writing
Society for the Promotion of African, Asian and Latin American Literature
PO Box 10 01 16
D-60001, Frankfurt
Tel: +49-69-2102-247/250
Fax: +49-69-2102-227
Email: litprom@book-fair.com
Contact: Peter Ripken
A non-commercial literary agency, closely connected with the Frankfurt Book Fair, providing information on all matters of interest to African writers and aiming to promote a better understanding of creative writing from Africa, Asia and Latin America. The society monitors literary trends and selects the best examples of creative writing from Africa, Asia and Latin America for translation into German, promoting them by encouraging contacts between authors and publishers in the 'Third World' and those in the German-speaking region. The Society offers advice and assistance on matters including establishment of first contacts, negotiations, etc. Publishers or authors submit review copies of their books which, according to their knowledge of the European market, might interest a German publisher; the Society's experts review the book; and – through the Society's bulletin – it is presented on the short-list of recom-

mended titles to a wide range of
German language fiction publishers.

In 1997 the Society launched
'Afrikanissimo' – which led to a
greater awareness of African literature
(see also p. 214).

ISBN Agency
The International Standard Book
Numbering Agency
Staatsbibliotheck 24
Preussischer Kulturbesitz
B-10772, Berlin, Germany

Translators' Association
The Translators' Association
84 Drayton Gardens
London SW10 9SB, UK
Tel: +44-(0)171-373-6642
Fax: +44-(0)171-373-5768
Email: authorsoc@writers.org.uk

Indexers and Bibliographers
Association
Association of Southern African
Indexers and Bibliographers
(ASAIB)
PO Box 740, Auckland Park
Johannesburg 2006, South Africa
Tel: +27-11-482-5495
Fax: +27-11-482-6163
Email: jkalley@eisa.org.za
Contact: Dr Jackie Kalley (Chair)

Getting Published

What is a Publisher?

Mary Jay

What is a publisher? The Oxford Dictionary (1998) defines the word as 'a company or person that prepares and issues books, journals, or music for sale'. This is an advance on older versions of the dictionary which described publishers as producers and distributors.

The common misconception, however, that a publisher is a glorified printer, lingers. The publisher is not just a receiver of a manuscript. Printing is simply one of the tasks involved for the publisher.

The publisher commissions a book, or evaluates unsolicited manuscripts; investigates co-publishing possibilities; edits the manuscript; develops a positive and dynamic working relationship with the author in terms of development of the book, contract, promotion and accountability; clears reproduction fees/copyright permissions; prepares an estimate of costs and sales, and sets price; oversees design and layout of the book; commissions illustrations; produces camera-ready copy, or manuscript for typesetting; decides on print run; puts the printing out to tender; oversees and monitors the printing process; undertakes advance promotion; promotes and markets the published book, involving the author in, for example, readings, broadcasts, promotion tours etc.; distributes to booksellers, libraries, Ministries, schools and universities, institutions, and individuals; enters books for relevant prizes; investigates potential for rights and subsidiary rights sales; warehouses the book; fulfils orders; monitors sales; organises reprints/remainders; sends regular royalty statements and payments to the author; keeps the author informed as to sales; monitors overall performance of the publishing house for planning the future publishing programme; administers the company: employment, finance/accounts, premises. The publisher is thus the centre of the book publishing chain: writer, publisher, bookseller, reader.

Not every one of these components is necessarily appropriate for every title: it depends on the nature of the book, whether a textbook, children's book, handbook, general interest – cookery, tourist guides etc., scholarly title, or work of creative writing. It also depends on the publisher's market research as to realistic potential sales and where those sales lie. All the components are cost centres, and big, well-resourced publishers will have separate departments specialising in the different areas, with the publisher co-ordinating the whole. These overhead costs, together with the estimated sales, and a profit margin, set the published price.

It is important for an author to understand something of the publishing process, and particularly to understand the constraints under which many African publishers work. Mutual understanding is beneficial to both parties – and the spirit in which to achieve this is encapsulated in the 'New Deal' statement from Arusha III (see pages 131-34).

Publishers: Good Relations

The whole idea of a 'New Deal' for African writers emerged from the awareness that African authors were often unhappy with their publishers. 'Unhappy' is, incidentally, an understatement: 'deeply dissatisfied' might have been closer to the mark. A collection of *Statements About Writer–Publisher Relations* was prepared for the Arusha III seminar during 1998. This brought together the views, sometimes critical, of African writers on publishers in general and African publishers in particular. This included views and perspectives from generations of African authors, including Achebe, lo Liyong, Ekwensi, Ngugi, Ayi Kwei Armah, Soyinka, Micere Mugo, Tsitsi Dangarembga, Ike, Saro-Wiwa, Cont Mhlanga, Buchi Emetcheta and Barbara Kimenye with observations from such giants of African publishing as Bgoya, Chakava, Lawal Solarin, and Victor Nwankwo. It is clear that the debate has been moving forward, sometimes through the pages of volumes of essays, sometimes in periodicals, sometimes through recorded interviews, and there are several indications that it will continue.

It was also clear that there was a history of exploitative relationships between writers and publishers/printers in some parts of Africa. When Cyprian Ekwensi wrote *When Love Whispers* in the 1940s, he thought that he would have to pay to have his work 'published' by an Onitsha Market producer of pamphlets. A closer examination of the relationships that were the general rule in Onitsha shows that authors usually accepted one-off payments – often very small – for scripts. Publishers then made what alterations and substitutions they wished before employing a printer to set up the text. Sometimes the alterations included changing the name of 'the author'!

The situation has changed dramatically and in order to catch up with some of the important statements by authors, readers are invited to see the collections of interviews with writers transcribed by Lee Nichols and Jane Wilkinson. Individual titles by or about Ngugi and Flora Veit-Wild, provide significant insights on experience with publishers, and the issue is repeatedly raised in regular publications such as the *African Book Publishing Record*, the *African Publishing Review*, *The Bookseller* and *Logos: The Professional Journal of the Book World*. There have been occasional articles of interest in *Okike* and *West Africa*.

In preparing for the Arusha III seminar, the planning group sent writer-participants a questionnaire. An analysis of the ten responses received revealed that the authors had published with twenty-one publishers in Africa, seven in the UK, four in the US and two in Canada. Apparently, seven writers had published with both African publishers and overseas publishing houses; two writers had published only with overseas publishers, and one had only published in Africa. All respondents had published with more than one publisher, some with as many as eleven. Sometimes the move had been made because of the collapse of a publishing house, sometimes because of a commission from another publisher. Often, however, there was dissatisfaction with the performance of the publisher, particularly in terms of promoting and marketing titles.

All those who had published with overseas publishers found them more efficient and more punctual in honouring royalty payments than African competitors. Overseas publishing houses were generally regarded as more professional, though they were sometimes characterised by distant or aloof attitudes. There was clearly deep feeling about the demise of an imprint of a major UK publishing company – could it have been Fontana?

Considerable concern was expressed about lack of transparency in financial relationships and poor response time to correspondence. This applied to publishers both at home and abroad, but was, it seems, more often found at home. Clearly fortunes were not being made: only one author indicated that royalty earnings had contributed 'a significant amount' to his or her livelihood. Two felt able to say that they had earned a 'fair amount' from their books. Authors generally felt the need to be kept better informed, to be told about the number of copies of their books printed and the volume of sales in hard currency markets.

Several felt unable to generalise about the performance of their publishers other than in very few topics – for example, there was widespread dissatisfaction with the marketing patterns followed, and most felt their books were overpriced. Only one writer was able to reply in the affirmative to the question 'Has/have your publisher/s made a conscious effort to explore subsidiary rights sales of your books?', and only one – perhaps the same one – was able to say she or he was 'very satisfied' with a 'current/past publisher'. In identifying ways to improve relations between African authors and African publishers, the qualities that were called for included 'professionalism', 'more openness', and 'humility'.

Some writers felt they would benefit from a better understanding of contracts, contract terms and publishing agreements in general. There was a suggestion that it would be good to visit publishers' offices and learn more about the industry. However, most felt they had a 'good understanding' of the publishing process and some were able to say that they had first-hand experience of the industry.

The small size of the sample – just ten – and the fact that writers who had worked with up to eleven publishers were asked to generalise on their experiences limited the value of the analysis. So did the reluctance to give the names of offending publishing houses. Comparison of the findings with contributions to the first part of this Handbook and with comments made at the conference or in print mean that it is tempting to identify isolated voices.

The preparatory material, reduced to cold print or even chillier statistics, provided background reading for the Arusha III seminar. It did not, however, have as much power to move as the statement made in the course of the opening session by Niyi Osundare. His words brought many of the tensions into the open, as he argued that 'the writer had a right to "a decent life" free from poverty and degradation, and that there should be a "keen interest" on the publishers' part in the personal welfare of their authors' (Davies 1998, 6). With a poet's eloquence, Osundare drew a word picture of a ragged poet left staggering in the dust churned up by a speeding vehicle belonging to his publisher.

The experiences that fuelled Osundare's passion can be found on page 21 where we read, *inter alia*:

> Of my eight publishers, two (one of them UK-based) send me returns on a regular basis, two on a sporadic basis; the remaining four have never said a word about how my books are doing, or paid me a penny. And not one of all my Nigerian publishers has declared how many copies of my books they have been selling outside Nigeria, and how much has accrued from the sales.

Before moving on, it is worth returning to the Seminar Report for a moment to record a measured reaction to Osundare's passion. The Seminar Report reads:

> In response to Niyi Osundare's statement ... Victor Nwankwo said that the expectation of reward for labour, a decent life and freedom from poverty was reasonable only in so far as these could be paid for by the writer's royalties; likewise, the publisher would take a personal interest in the author if they became friends, but there was no obligation to do so. The stereotypes of 'struggling writer and sumptuously-living publisher' also need to be challenged, he suggested; although a small minority is interested only in profiteering, most African publishers are themselves struggling to do a professional job in very difficult circumstances. (Davies 1998)

In looking at the areas of conflict or potential conflict between parties to contracts, it is useful to draw on a wide survey carried out in the UK during 1997 which was analysed by Michael Legat in 'Which Publisher?' in the Autumn 1997 issue of *The Author*, a (British) Society of Authors publication. Over a thousand writers were invited to complete a questionnaire in which they 'marked' their publishers on their performance in six areas (1 very poor, 5 good). The exercise draws attention to a total of twenty-two points which writers should consider:

The Contract
 1 flexibility and willingness to negotiate
 2 overall fairness of the contract
 3 faithful implementation of pre-publication promises
 4 close observations of the terms of the agreement

Editing
 5 promptness in reacting to the manuscript
 6 quality of editorial help
 7 helpfulness about copy editing, proofing, house style, and so on
 8 continuity of editorial staff

Communication
 9 general interest in you, providing information, consulting
10 readiness to answer letters, phone calls, and so on
11 extent of consultation about jacket and blurb
12 extent of consultation before any decision to go out of print or remainder the book

Publication
13 promptness and efficiency of publication
14 adequacy of publicity and marketing
15 efficiency in selling rights
16 extent of provision of information on efforts to sell sub-licences
17 promptness in paying advance
18 efficiency in paying royalties on agreed date

Payment
19 despatch in passing on money from sub-licences
20 clarity and detail in royalty statements

Overall
21 rating of the publisher's performance overall
22 willingness to work with the publisher again

To make sense of this – and of other documents in the writers–publishers 'discourse', the following definitions may be useful:

- **Blurb**. While this word, coined by the American humorist Gelett Burgess (1866-1951) to describe 'a promotional description as found on the back of books', should provide no difficulty, it is worth including it here because West African journalists sometimes render it 'blob'.

- **House style**. Correct or standard English allows for certain variations but publishers often have a preferred form. For example, the following are all correct, but certain publishers employ one rather than another: 15 October 1999; October 15, 1999; 15.10.1999.

- **O/P**. Out of print.

- **Remaindered**. In the knowledge that it costs money to store unsold copies after demand has sunk to a particular point, publishers 'remainder titles': they sell off unsold copies at reduced rates. It can be disconcerting to find one's books remaindered, sometimes on sale in bargain stores at a small fraction of their cover price. Under some contracts publishers are obliged to offer remaindered stock to the author at an advantageous rate.

It is helpful to glance at the results of Legat's analysis of 1,186 reports on 295 publishers (separate forms for separate publishers). Greatest dissatisfaction was encountered in the areas covered by questions 12, 14, 15 and 16. If books are, to use a common analogy, the 'children' of authors, it is understandable that 'parents' will want to be kept informed about the progress of their 'offspring'. Writers should be confident that the 'foster parents' are doing all in their power to ensure success; 'foster parents', in turn, should communicate fully, frankly and clearly.

Significantly, the lowest rating regarding the very sensitive matter of *Contracts* ('The Contract', points 1-4) was scored by 'Harlequin, Mills and Boon'. It seems that in the UK the romantic literature end of the market is particularly hard on writers. This is also the case in Africa and authors working in the genre should take particular care to familiarise themselves with the contractual conditions laid down by the Minimum Terms Agreement (MTA, see page 395). They should find out whether their prospective publishers have accepted this agreement.

There was, as revealed in previous surveys, concern about the presentation of royalty statements (20) and, in many cases, unhappiness at lack of continuity of editorial staff. These are areas of anxiety shared with African authors. As he drew his article to a close, Legat quoted Christopher Priest who wrote in terms that some at Arusha would echo:

The overall relationship between publishers and the trade is carried on
almost covertly, as far as authors are concerned, and the glimpses we get
are usually infuriating and received so late as to allow no intervention.
(Legat 1997)

Among the practices he finds particularly irritating, are 'the discount-
ing of trade books to multiple booksellers' – a complaint that, with the
substitution of 'Ministries of Education' for 'multiple booksellers'
would be endorsed by many African writers.

Of the forty-one publishers that Legat lists those of particular
interest to African writers include Heinemann Educational (8th),
Faber (11th equal), and, significantly, Macmillan – including Pan
(28th).

Good publishers can only profit from transparency and accountability. By and large, the authors surveyed were happy with their
publishers: 80 per cent were willing to work with the same company
again. It would seem that African writers are more unhappy with
African publishers than British writers are with British publishers.
One hopes that, whatever their criticisms, the authors will give credit
where it is due, and will be appreciative when African publishers do
their best. Writers should recognise that publishers are in business in
a volatile area of commerce, part of a neo-colonial economy. Having
said this, writers should not tolerate improper business ethics: if
publishers are not open and honest, they should be exposed by those
badly treated. In the event of an investigation they should be
supported nationally and internationally by writers' groups, and
National Publishers' Associations should assist in invoking the full
rigour of the law against erring members of their profession.

Rewards

Writers are motivated by numerous impulses to seek publication, and
are recompensed in many ways. Some may enjoy the sense of contact
with a community that comes with the appearance of a text in print,
and revel in the status that the title 'writer' confers. Some may write
from a conviction that they are making a contribution to society. In
most, however, the expectation that their bags or pockets will
eventually be weighed down with the reward of their labours is a
significant factor in helping them to keep at their task.

Those who publish in the press may feel aggrieved when they find
that their poems or short stories, though given a high status, do not
bring in the regular salary that is paid to the 'mere' journalists who
turn in reports of football matches and athletics meetings, of political
gatherings or of the latest speech by the head of state. Unfortunately

many publications do not pay their literary contributors; some do not even send them complimentary copies of the publication. Writers who feel inadequately or discourteously treated have several options open to them: for example, they may boycott a publication permanently or temporarily.

For those who have secured a contract the question of remuneration will involve the size of any advance that may be payable, the nature of the author's discount, and, crucially, the percentage of the net sales proceeds paid in royalties. This will vary depending on a variety of factors including anticipated sales, the status of the author and the nature of the text deposited.

It is quite common for an author to start on 10 per cent royalty – and receive that proportion of the net (after discount) price – or the full price, depending on the contract – for the first, say, 1,999 copies. Thereafter the percentage may rise to 12 per cent for another 2,000 books before moving on to 15 per cent.

Sometimes, however, the rate may be less than this even for a volume that appears straightforward, that is to say for a book without illustrations, photographs, or, for example, an explanatory map. Indeed, the Minimum Terms Agreement (MTA, see page 395) contains varying figures – they are minimum figures!

Certain authors, perhaps writing for children in a manner that benefits from extensive illustration, may begin on as little as 4 per cent.

Authors should also be aware whether or not their percentage relates to all sales. For bulk sales, perhaps to a Ministry of Education if the text is on the school syllabus, the books will be offered at a discount. This is excellent in terms of the wide readership; but the writer must be aware that royalty income will be affected by the terms of such (discount) sales, since royalties are customarily calculated on the net sales income.

Co-publishing: A Model

James Currey

Editors' note: There is a dearth of publishing outlets for African creative writers. As expanded in other sections of this book, the economics of publishing realities within Africa mean that a publisher is not likely to make any profit through publishing fiction, and it must be subsidised by profits from other profitable publishing such as textbook sales. Outside Africa, the marginalisation of African literature means that the outlets are sparse other than for the few major established writers. The dearth of literary periodicals and 'little' magazines is another restriction on the newer and aspiring creative writer. 'African Books Collective and Creative Writing and Publishing in Africa' by Mary Jay of African Books Collective (ABC) in Part 1 of this book puts the case for the African writer to publish within Africa; and publishing with an African member publisher of ABC ensures international marketing and distribution through ABC. There is also the potential of co-publication between an African and Northern publisher. This is not developed to any extent for fiction publishing, but has been pioneered by James Currey of James Currey Publishers, UK, for scholarly publishing. The model he has developed with African partners is widely admired as being an equitable relationship for publishers and writers. His article which follows explains the evolution of this method of working. The model could be adapted for publishing fiction and other creative writing, if Northern publishers would take up the challenge. African publishers have long expressed their desire to move in this direction, but the response has not so far been forthcoming.

It is of great concern to authors of books on Africa that their books should be available in Africa. Co-publishing is one of the most cost-effective ways of substantially increasing a book's circulation in Africa. Co-publishing is about building up the print run, thereby spreading the heavy origination costs of a book over as many copies as possible. Academic titles on the social sciences, archaeology, geography and economics are ideal for co-publication. Their origination costs are high. Their print runs are low. School textbooks should be developed for the curricula and teaching needs of individual countries. University books can be used throughout the continent and across the academic world.

James Currey Publishers specialises in the publication of academic paperbacks on Africa. As academic publishers based in Britain using the

English language the firm has built up an informal network of effective co-publishers in English-speaking Africa. We have also built up contacts with most of the academic and university presses in the United States which publish regularly on Africa. We thus plan for publication on three continents by at least three publishers. We aim to sell three times the number of copies that a conventional British hardback academic publisher would expect to sell. The origination costs of academic books are high, whether for a publisher in Africa or ourselves. The author has laboured in a university and in the field to collect exact and meaningful detail and an academic publisher has to spend money on making that information available in accurate, printed form. The books are often over 300 pages and rarely under 200 pages long.

Time and money is spent on assessment by other academics. The book is copy-edited. The cost of typesetting has not risen as fast as other factors but is still heavy because of the number of pages; disks have improved accuracy but have not substantially reduced costs and costly human input. The book has to be read by a proof reader and the corrections collated. The type has to be corrected. The cover has to be designed and originated. All these costs must be spread over as many copies as possible.

Definition of Co-Publishing

Co-publishing is when the originating publishers of a specific book sell a substantial part of the print run to a co-publisher in another country for that firm to sell at their risk under their imprint and at an appropriate price in a defined market. Most books are published for a single country with export as a very secondary concern. The originating company has the apparatus to sell that book effectively in the national market of its own country. Export sales can be made by mailing suitable bookshops and institutions across the world; the publisher may have agents in certain countries to help generate sales. However, the originating publishers may recognise that in certain national markets there will be an exceptional interest in this book and that a co-publisher based in that country can sell far more copies of this particular book than can the originating publisher working from the outside.

The logic of co-publishing is based on two factors:

1 The origination costs of a book are the same whether the book sells a thousand or a million copies.

2 Run-on costs. Once a printing machine has started to run it costs very little to keep it running (though the cost of the paper will remain the same and the cost of binding will only drop a little).

So if the originating publishers can secure, before printing, a substantial extra order then the printing machine can be kept running at very little extra cost. The price paid by the co-publisher will make a contribution to the heavy origination costs, even if the unit cost is kept low to make the book available at an accessible price. An alternative is for the originating publisher to grant offset rights to the co-publisher to reprint the book for a particular market or a certain country or of a defined group of countries. The co-publishers will almost certainly use the original typesetting, will certainly add their own imprint, bar code and price and might produce a different jacket or cover with a blurb which will be more suitable for that market. This sub-license deal is valuable for larger runs where the costs can be spread over a substantial number of copies and the unit cost of the book, using local paper or printing, can be less than the unit run-on costs offered by the originating publisher.

Examples of Co-publishing

Co-publishing is central to the philosophy of James Currey Publishers. It also helps make the finances work. It enables us to issue a paperback edition of a book that other academic publishers would normally think of as a monograph for the hardback library market only. Co-publishing retrieves, with two or three invoices, a great deal of the cash we have spent at our risk. The cash flow is good though the margins can verge on the dangerous in our efforts to keep prices down. Co-publishing and paperbacks are two of the main reasons why authors choose us as publishers. Co-publishing can bring in royalties from three continents. However we do have to ask authors to be patient. Once we have had positive academic reports we have time to be able to agree a substantive deal with a co-publisher in the United States. By the time we have had reports on a promising manuscript we are clear who is likely to welcome taking it on in the United States.

We are more likely to accept manuscripts if they are about a country in which we have a strong co-publishing relationship with an African publisher. However there will be particular interest in a book on Tanzania in Tanzania, in a book on Zimbabwe in Zimbabwe. We published a book in 1995 called *Service Provision under Stress* in East Africa about how the NGOs, foreign and local, are being sub-contracted to take over state functions such as law, education and security. As soon as Semboja and Therkildsen approached us it was clear that this was a natural for co-publishing with Mkuki na Nyota in Tanzania, EAEP in Nairobi and Fountain Publishers in Kampala.

James Currey Publishers took on *Uganda Now* when Museveni had not even reached Kampala. Since then James Tumisiime has built up

Fountain in Kampala to be serious academic and educational publishers. They take 500 to 2,000 of any title on Uganda and substantial numbers of books on regional subjects. It is a sad sign of Uganda being one of the English-speaking centres for aid for the conflicts in the Great Lakes and the Sudan that they co-published *African Guerillas*. We are now engaged with more co-publishing projects in Uganda even than in South Africa.

Money and books are short in Tanzania but Walter Bgoya at Mkuki na Nyota can always sell substantial numbers of Tanzanian titles if they can be subsidised to bring down the price to an accessible amount in Tanzanian shillings. The British-Tanzanian Society got Ford Foundation money for a book on Nyerere called *Mwalimu*. Norad have been particularly helpful to Mkuki. Foreign academics who work in Tanzania show high social conscience and feel strongly that books should be available for the people in Tanzania who have helped them with the research. Thomas Speer, Professor of History at Wisconsin, has found funds for subsidising *Mountain Farmers* and the contributors to *Being Maasai* waived their royalties to make sure that copies are available in Arusha and Moshi as well as Dar.

Henry Chakava of EAEP has made use of Kenyan printing facilities and paper to reprint books at published prices which are often about a quarter of the equivalent price in pounds. Specialist titles on Mau Mau have been taken on because we knew that we had EAEP as co-publisher in Nairobi. However, some of their reprints have been on Africa-wide titles such as Jan Vansina's *Oral Tradition in Africa*, Basil Davidson's *Black Man's Burden* and *Instruments of Economic Policy in Africa*. And we have always worked together on Ngugi's books such as *Decolonising the Mind*.

We are working with Woeli Publishing Services in Ghana on *Economic Reforms in Ghana*; in this case we have edited, Woeli have typeset and Africa World Press in the States are printing. Further co-publishing projects will follow as Ghana's publishing industry continues to revive.

James Currey Publishers has just completed its most ambitious co-publishing project, the eight paperback volumes of the abridged UNESCO *General History of Africa*. This major project was originally planned in 1964. An international team of 300 historians who write in French, Arabic, and Portuguese as well as in English have produced the work under the editorship of scholars such as A Adu Boahen, BA Ogot, JE Ade Ajayi, J Ki-Zerbo and Ali A Mazrui. When the English language rights for the original hardback edition were put out for tender in 1979 there was strong competition from Longman, Macmillan and others. I was told that the reason I secured the Commonwealth rights for Heinemann (for whom I then worked) was that I had brought in University of California Press as North American co-publishers. But the Heinemann companies in Africa said that the hardback price, though subsidised, was still too high in naira or Kenyan shillings. So this great history of Africa was hardly available in Africa.

When UNESCO approached James Currey Publishers in the late 1980s about the publication of the abridged paperback I said that I would only produce it if the books could be available in Africa at affordable prices in national currencies. This was the worst period of what Michael Crowder had named the 'African book famine'. Countries in Africa found it difficult to get foreign exchange even to buy from other African countries; therefore printing in African countries was the only way to make the books available at accessible prices. I persuaded UNESCO to provide sets of the film free to the co-publishers and not to ask for royalties on sales in Africa.

I originally negotiated with publishers in seven African countries. Heinemann Nigeria rushed out volumes in time for a big World Bank funded order for higher education. East African Educational Publishers (EAEP) sales were initially confined to Kenya. Liberalisation has opened access to neighbouring countries and EAEP are now planning to print a regional co-edition of later volumes for Fountain Publishers in Kampala and Tanzania Publishing House. I had hopes that UNZA Press in Lusaka would work on a central African edition with Baobab/Academic in Harare, though that did not materialise. Baobab, like David Philip in Cape Town, pre-ordered copies off the international run in Britain at a low run-on price.

Academic authors can be helpful about making suggestions and connections for co-publication in Africa. Mahmood Mamdani had his book *Citizen and Subject* accepted for a Princeton University Press series. It has substantial sections on Uganda and South Africa so he got Princeton to co-publish with Fountain in Kampala and David Philip in Cape Town as well as with James Currey Publishers in Oxford. It has not occured to this prestigious American university press that they could do anything more than send a few copies to their British agents for library sales. Co-publishing is certainly a factor that academic authors should take into consideration in choosing which publishers to approach in publishing their work.

Publishers: A Directory

Various sources have been used to provide information for this section, and the list of African publishers is taken mainly from the *African Publishers Networking Directory 1999/2000* (Oxford: African Books Collective, 1999). It has been difficult to verify some of the entries, particularly where publishing houses have published literature in the past, but their current list is not known. Most publishers included have literature lists, and where possible their specialist field of literature is noted. A few publishers of critical literary and cultural studies are also included. Many publishers listed also publish in other subject areas (e.g. children's books); but these are not listed for the purposes of this directory.

Abbreviations used in the Directory:
Contact: Contact name
List: nature of publisher's list
Found: year established
BIP: number of books in print
UK/Europe Dist: overseas distributor in the UK/Europe
NA Dist: overseas distributor in North America
ABC: African Books Collective

AFRICA

Benin

Editions du Flamboyant
08 BP 271, Cotonou
Tel: +229-312517/330472
Fax: +229-321119
Contact: Michel Gomez
List: Literature

Cameroon

**Buma Kor Publishing House/
Editions Buma Kor**
Rue Nachtigal, BP 727
Yaoundé
Tel: +237-230768
Fax: +237-230768
Email: cht@iccnet.cm
Contact: BD Kor
List: Literature
Languages: English, French
Found: 1977
BIP: 20

Editions CLE
BP 1501, Yaoundé
Tel: +237-223554/232709
Fax: + 237-207574
Contact: Ngandu Tshimanga
List: Literature
Found: 1963
BIP: 145
UK/Europe dist: L'Harmattan, France
NA dist: Hurtubise, Quebec

Congo-Brazzaville

Editions Heros dans l'Ombre
c/o Mr Touadiss
Ministry of Foreign Affairs
BP 1678, Brazzaville
Tel: +242-822303
Fax: +242-830528
Contact: L Pindy-Manonsono
List: Literature

Found: 1980
BIP: 24
NA dist: African Imprint Library
Services, Falmouth, Massachusetts

Côte d'Ivoire

Editions CEDA
04 BP 544, Abidjan 04
Tel: +225-224242
Fax: +225-217262
Contact: Boare Dramane
List: Literature
Found: 1961
BIP: 300
NA dist: Schoenhof's Foreign Books,
Cambridge, Massachusetts

Editions Livre Sud SA (EDILIS)
10 BP 477, Abidjan 10
Tel: +225-244650/215172
Fax: + 255-244651/225960
Contact: Mical Drehi Lorougnon
List: Literature
Found: 1992
BIP: 23

Nouvelles Editions Ivoiriennes
1, Boulevard de Marseille
01 BP 1818, Abidjan 01
Tel: +225-240766/240825
Fax: +225-242456
Contact: Guy Lambin
List: Literature
Found: 1992
BIP: 230

Egypt

American University in Cairo Press
113 Sharia Kasr el Aini
PO Box 2511, Cairo
Tel: +20-2-3576896/1-3541440
Fax: + 20-2-3557565
Email: ahoteiby@auc-acs.eun.eg
Contact: Atef M. El-Hoteiby
Found: 1960
BIP: 200

UK/Europe dist: Columbia
University Press, New York
NA dist: Columbia University Press,
New York

Eritrea

Africa World Press Inc/ The Red Sea Press Inc
Via Teferi Yazew 19-21
PO Box 488, Asmara
Tel: +291-1-120707
Fax: +291-1-120707
Email: kassahun@awprsp.eol.
punchdown.org
Contact: N Kidan Kassahun
List: Literature
See also Africa World Press, USA

Ghana

Afram Publications (Ghana) Ltd
9 Ring Road East
near UNDP Building
PO Box M18, Accra
Tel: +233-21-774248
Fax: + 233-21-778715
Email: aframpub@ighmail.com
Contact: Eric Ofei
List: Literature
Languages: English, Ewe, Ga, Twi
Found: 1973
BIP: 113
UK/Europe dist: ABC
NA dist: ABC

Africa Christian Press
PO Box AH 30, Achimota
Tel: +233-21-220271/244147
Fax: + 233-21-220271/668115
Email: acpbooks@ncs.com.gh
Contact: Richard Crabbe
List: Literature
Languages: English
Found: 1964
BIP: 130
UK/Europe dist: ABC
NA dist: ABC

Asempa Publishers
Christian Council of Ghana
PO Box 919, Accra
Tel: +233-21-221706/233084
Fax: +233-21-233130
Email: asempa@ncs.com.gh
Contact: EB Bortey
List: Literature
Languages: English, Ghanaian
languages
Found: 1970
BIP: 94

Bureau of Ghana Languages
PO Box 1851, Accra
Tel: +233-21-772151
Contact: JN Nanor
List: Literature in Ghanaian
languages only
Languages: Ghanaian languages
Found: 1951
BIP: 410

Ghana Universities Press
PO Box GP 4219, Accra
Tel: +233-21-76105፡
Fax: +233-21-501930
Email: scs@ug.gn.abc.org
Contact: KM Ganu
List: Critical/cultural, Literature
Languages: English, Ghanaian
languages
Found: 1962
BIP: 202
UK/Europe dist: ABC
NA dist: ABC

Sedco Publishing Ltd
5, Tabon Street North Ridge
PO Box 2051, Accra
Tel: +233-21-221332
Fax: +233-21-220107
Contact: CK Segbawu
List: Literature
Languages: English, Ewe, Ga
Found: 1975
BIP: 129

Sub-Saharan Publishers Ltd
PO Box 358, Legon, Accra
Tel: +233-21-233371
Fax: +233-21-233371
Contact: Akoss Ofori-Mensah
List: Literature
Languages: English
Found: 1993
UK/Europe dist: ABC
NA dist: ABC

Woeli Publishing Services
PO Box NT/601, Accra New Town
Tel: +233-21-229294/227182/228611
Fax: +233-21-229294
Contact: Woeli A Dekutsey
List: Drama, Fiction, Poetry
Found: 1984
BIP: 37
UK/Europe dist: ABC
NA dist: ABC

Kenya

East African Educational Publ. Ltd
Mpaka Road/Woodvale Grove
P.O. Box 45314, Nairobi
Tel: +254-2-444700/445260
Fax: +254-2-448753/532095
Email: eaep@africaonline.co.ke
Contact: Henry Chakava
List: Critical/cultural, Drama, Fiction,
Poetry
Languages: English, Kiswahili
Found: 1965
BIP: 748
UK/Europe dist: ABC
NA dist: ABC

Focus Publications Ltd
PO Box 28176, Nairobi
Tel: +254-2-600737
Fax: +254-2-607489
Email: focus@users.africaonline.co.ke
Contact: Serah TK Mwangi
List: Fiction, Poetry
Found: 1991
BIP: ±10

The Jomo Kenyatta Foundation
Enterprise Road
PO Box 30533, Nairobi
Tel: +254-2-557222
Fax: +254-2-531965
Contact: David Khayo
List: Literature
Languages: English, Kiswahili
Found: 1966
BIP: 300

Kenya Literature Bureau
PO Box 30022, Nairobi
Tel: +254-2-506142/3/8
Fax: +254-2-505903
Contact: SC Lang'at
List: Literature
Languages: English, Kiswahili
Found: 1980
BIP: 800

Lake Publishers and Enterprises
Jomo Kenyatta Highway
PO Box 1743, Kisumu
Tel: +254-35-22291/22707
Fax: +254-35-22291/22707
Email: gadod@arcc.or.ke
Contact: Asenath Bole Odaga
List: Fiction, Poetry
Languages: English, Kiswahili, Luo,
other local languages
Found: 1982
BIP: 90
UK/Europe dist: Hogarth
Representation, London, UK

Longhorn Kenya Ltd
Funzi Road,
Industrial Area
PO Box 18033, Nairobi
Tel: +254-2-532579/532580/532581
Fax: +254-2-540581
Contact: Janet Njoroge
List: Literature
Found: 1965
BIP: 300

Macmillan Kenya Publishers Ltd
Kijabe Street
PO Box 30797, Nairobi
Tel: +254-2-220012
Fax: +254-2-212179
Email: dmuita@macken.co.ke
Contact: David N Muita
List: Literature
Languages: English, French, Kiswahili
Found: 1970
BIP: 50
UK/Europe dist: Macmillan
Publishers, London, UK

Moi University Press
Faculty of Information Science
Moi University
PO Box 3900, Eldoret
Tel: +321-43166/43720
Fax: + 321-43047
Email: mufis@arso.gn.apc.org
Contact: Tom Ouma Ouko
List: Critical/cultural, Literature
Languages: English
Found: 1989
BIP: 15

Nairobi University Press
University of Nairobi
Jomo Kenyatta Memorial Library
PO Box 30197, Nairobi
Tel: +254-2-334244/337293/221382
Fax: +254-2-336885
Email: uonjkml@ken.healthnet.org
Contact: Omari E Gichogo
List: Critical/cultural, Literature
Languages: English, Kiswahili
Found: 1984
BIP: 40
UK/Europe dist: ABC
NA dist: ABC

Phoenix Publishers
Coffee Plaza, 3rd Floor
PO Box 18650, Nairobi
Tel: +254-2-23262/22309
Fax: +254-2-339875
Contact: KE Kasu

List: Fiction
Found: 1987
BIP: 80

Uzima Press Ltd
PO Box 48127, Nairobi
Tel: +254-2-20239/335699
Contact: James Kiraka
List: Literature
Found: 1974

Zapf Chancery Research Consultants and Publishers
10th Floor, KVDA Plaza
PO Box 4938, Eldoret
Tel: +254-321-31413
Fax: +254-321-63043
Email: mufhs@netzoooke.com
Contact: JO Awino
List: Literature
Languages: English, Kiswahili
Found: 1994
BIP: 11
UK/Europe dist: Mallory International Ltd, Devon, UK
NA dist: African Imprint Library Services, ME, USA

Lesotho

Institute of Southern African Studies
The National University of Lesotho
PO Roma 180, Lesotho, 180
Tel: +266-340601/340247
Fax: +266-340000
Email: t.khalanyane@mailcity.com
Web site: http://www.nul.ls/Index.html
Contact: Tankie Khalanyane
List: Drama
Languages: English
Found: 1979
BIP: 59
UK/Europe dist: ABC
NA dist: ABC

Malawi

Dzuka Publishing Co. Ltd
Salmin Amour Road
Private Bag 39, Blantyre
Tel: +265-670880/670855
Fax: +265-671114
Contact: FW Jiyani
List: Literature
Languages: Chichewa, English
Found: 1975
UK/Europe dist: Mallory International

The Kachere Series
PO Box 1037, Zomba
Tel: +265-522705
Fax: +265-522705
Email: kachere@malawi.net
Web site: http://www.tema.liu.se/relvet/unima/
Contact: Klaus Fiedler
List: Literature
Languages: English
Found: 1995
BIP: 22
UK/Europe dist: Church of Scotland, Edinburgh, Scotland, UK
NA dist: International Scholars Press, Bethesda MD, USA

Popular Publications
PO Box 5592
Limbe
Tel: +265-651183/651139
Contact: Joseph-Claude Simwaka
List: Literature, Novels, Short stories
Found: 1974

Sunrise Publications
PO Box 18
Chiwamba, Lilongwe
Contact: Ken Kalonde
List: Literature
Languages: Chichewa, English
Found: 1994
BIP: 3

Mali

Cooperative Culturelle Jamana
BP 2043, Bamako
Tel: +223-226289
Fax: +223-227639
Email: jamana@malinet.ml
Contact: Hamidou Konaté
List: Literature
Languages: Bamanan, English,
French, Peulh
Found: 1988
BIP: 82
UK/Europe dist: France-Menaibuc
International, France
NA dist: Univers Editions, Côte
d'Ivoire

Mauritius

Editions de l'Océan Indien
Stanley, Rose-Hill, Wong
Tel: +230-4646761/4643959
Fax: +230-4643445
Contact: Sadhna Ramlallah
List: Fiction
Found: 180
BIP: 10

Morocco

Editions Eddif Maroc
71 Avenue des F.A.R.
BP 7357, Casablanca, 21000
Tel: +212-2-311526/313073
Fax: +212-2-313565
Contact: Retnani Abdelkader
List: Literature
Languages: Arabic, French
Found: 1980
BIP: 200
NA dist:
Editions Hurtubise
HMH LTEE-1815,
Avenue de Lorimier Montreal
(Quebec) Canada H2K 3W6

Editions Le Fennec
89 B. Bd. d'Anfa
Casablanca, 20000
Tel: +212-2-220519/268008
Fax: +212-2-264941
Email: fennec@techno.net.mo
Contact: Layla B Chaouni
List: Fiction, Literature, Women's
writing
Languages: Arabic, French
Found: 1987
BIP: 135
UK/Europe dist: Dilo-Diffusion, Paris

Mozambique

Associacao dos Escritores Mocambi-canos
Av: 24 de Juhlo 1420
CP 4187, Maputo
Tel: +258-1-420727
Fax: +258-1-304438
aemo@zebra.uem.mz
Contact: Suleiman Cassano
List: Literature
Languages: Portuguese

Namibia

Gamsberg Macmillan Publishers (PTY) Ltd
PO Box 22830, Windhoek
Tel: +264-61-232165
Fax: +264-61-233538
Email: gmp@iafrica.com.na
Contact: Peter Reiner
List: Literature
Languages: Afrikaans, English,
French, German, Iiju'hoan,
Khoekhoegowab,
Oshikwanyema, Oshindonga,
Otsimerero, Portuguese, Rugciriku,
Rukwangali, Setswana, Silozi,
Thimbukushu
Found: 1977
BIP: 750
UK/Europe dist: Macmillan, London,
UK

New Namibia Books (PTY) Ltd
PO Box 21501, Windhoek
Tel: +264-61-221038/221134
Fax: +264-61-235279
Email: nnb@iafrica.com.na
Contact: Jane Katjavivi
List: Literature
UK/Europe dist: ABC
NA dist: ABC

Nigeria

See also the Directory of Nigerian Book Development. Details are listed in the Author's Bookshelf.

Africana Legacy Press
9 James Robertson Street
Surulere, Lagos, Lagos State
and at:
808 Lexington Ave. no.2
Brooklyn, New York
NY 11221 USA
Tel: +1-718-5749452
Fax: +1-718-5749452
Email: sogunedo@aol.com
Contact: Stanley Ogunedo
List: Drama
Languages: English
Found: 1995
BIP:10
UK/Europe dist:ABC
NA dist: ABC

Bookcraft Ltd
29 Moremi Road, New Bodija
PO Box 16279,
Ibadan, Oyo State
Tel: +234-22-8103238
Email: gbenro@infoweb.abs.net
Contact: Gbenro Adegbola
List: Literature
Languages: English
Found: 1989
BIP: 24
UK/Europe dist: ABC
NA dist: ABC

Cogito Publishing Company Ltd
PO Box 4203, Enugu
Contact: Eze che Chiazo
List: Literature

Delta Publications (Nigeria) Ltd
8B Byron Onyeama Close
Newhaven, PO Box 1172
Enugu, Enugu State
Tel: +234-42-253215
Contact: Augustina Igwe
List: Literature

Evans Brothers (Nigeria Publishers) Ltd
Jericho Road, PMB 5164
Ibadan, Oyo State
Tel: +234-22-2413708/2414287
Fax: +234-22-2410757
List: Drama, Fiction, Poetry
Found: 1966
BIP: 1000
UK/Europe dist: Evans Brothers, London

Fountain Publications (Nigeria) Ltd
32 Adenuga Street
PO Box 29263 Secretariat
Ibadan, Oyo State
Tel: +234-2-8100645
Fax: + 234-2-8100245
Contact: BO Aboyade
List: Literature
Found: 1987
BIP: 29

Fourth Dimension Publishing Co Ltd
16 Fifth Avenue, City Layout
PMB 01164, Enugu, Enugu State
Tel: +234-42-459969/453739
Fax: +234-42-456904/453298
Email: nwankwov@nfoweb.abs.net
Contact: Victor Nwankwo
List: Critical/cultural, Drama, Fiction, Poetry
Languages: English, Hausa, Igbo, Yoruba
Found: 1977

BIP: 400
UK/Europe dist: ABC
NA dist: ABC

Heinemann Educational Books (Nigeria) Plc

1 Ighodaro Road Jericho
PMB 5205, Ibadan, Oyo State
Tel:+234-2-2412268/2410943/
2413096
Fax: +234-2-2411089/2413237
Contact: Lawrence O Agge
List: Critical/cultural, Drama,
Fiction,
Poetry, Frontline Series
Languages: English, French, Nigerian
languages
Found: 1962
BIP: 865
UK/Europe dist: ABC
NA dist: ABC

Heritage Books

2/8 Calcutta Crescent Gate 1
PO Box 610, Apapa, Lagos State
Tel: +234-1-871333
Contact: Naiwu Osahon
List: Literature
Languages: English
Found: 1970
BIP: 56

Ibadan University Press

University of Ibadan
PMB 16 UI Post Office
Ibadan, Oyo State
Tel: +234-22-400500/400614
ext. 1042
Email: Ulgislab@infoweb.abs.net
Contact: Festus A Adesanoye
List: Critical/cultural, Literature
Found: 1952
BIP: 170
UK/Europe dist: ABC
NA dist: ABC

Konk Publishers

9 James Robertson Street
Surulere, Lagos, Lagos State
Tel: +234-1-833163
Email: maximuzoatu@yahoo.com
Contact: Uzor Maxim Uzoatu
List: Literature
Found: 1988
BIP: 10

Literamed Publications (Nigeria) Ltd

Plot 45 Alausa
Oregun Industrial Estate
PMB 21068, Ikeja, Lagos State
Tel: +234-1-962512/960450
Fax: +234-1-4972217
Contact: OM Lawal-Solarin
List: Literature
Found: 1969
BIP: 94

Macmillan Nigeria Publishers Ltd

4 Industrial Avenue
Ilupeju Estate, Ilupeju, Lagos State
Tel:+234-1-4962185/4961188
Fax: +234-1-2310066/4932135
Email: macmillan.ng@usa.net
Contact: AI Adelekan
List: Literature
Languages: English, Hausa, Igbo,
French, other Nigerian languages
Found: 1965
BIP: 120

Malthouse Press Ltd

8 Amore Street, Off Toyin Street
Ikeja, Lagos State
Tel: +234-1-820358
Fax: +234-1-2690985
Contact: Dafe Otobo
List: Critical/cultural, Drama
(Modern
Drama Series), Fiction, Poetry
Found: 1985
BIP: 100
UK/Europe dist: ABC
NA dist: ABC

MIJ Professional Publishers Ltd
PO Box 209
Yaba, Lagos, Lagos State
Tel: +234-1-866823
Contact: MI Jegede
List: Literature
Found: 1984
BIP: 3

Obafemi Awolowo
University Press Ltd
PMB 004
OAU Post Office
Ile-Ife, Osun State
Tel: +234-36-230254
Fax: +234-36-233442
Email:seyen@oauife.edu.ng/
jolomo@oauife.edu.ng
Contact: Akin Fatokun
List: Critical/cultural, Literature
Found: 1968
BIP: 200

Pam Unique Publishing
Company Ltd
Ozuoba Publishing House,
PO Box 74
University of Port Harcourt
Port Harcourt, Rivers State
Tel: +234-22-313956
Contact: FOE Igwe
List: Literature
Found: 1986
BIP: 52

Saros International Publishers
24 Aggrey Road
PO Box 193
Port Harcourt, Rivers State
Tel: +234-84-331763/335658
Fax: +234-84-331763
Contact: Olivia Wiwa
List: Drama, Fiction
Found: 1985
UK/Europe dist: ABC
NA dist: ABC

Spectrum Books Ltd
Sunshine House
1 Emmanuel Alayande St.,
Oluyole Est., PMB 5612,
Ibadan, Oyo State
Tel: +234-2-2310058/2511215
Fax: +234-2-2318502/2312705
Email: info@spectrumsafari.com
Contact: Joop Berkhout
List: Literature
Found: 1978
BIP: 218
UK/Europe dist: ABC
NA dist: ABC

University Press Plc
Three Crowns Building
Jericho, PMB 5095
Ibadan, Oyo State
Tel: +234-22-412313/411356
Fax: +234-22-412056
Contact: Law Okonkwo
List: Critical/cultural, Literature
Found: 1978
BIP: 1000
UK/Europe dist: ABC
NA dist: ABC

Vista Books Ltd/
Cross Continent Press Ltd
59 Awolowo Road
SW Ikoyi – PO Box 282
Yaba, Lagos, Lagos State
Tel: +234-1-2692328/7746348
Fax: +234-1-2694161
Contact: TC Nwosu
List: Literature
Languages: English
Found: 1974
BIP: 210
UK/Europe dist: David Hogarth,
London, UK

West African Book Publishers Ltd
Plot D Block 1,
Ilupeju Industrial Estate, PO Box 3445
Lagos, Lagos State
Tel: +234-1-4977700/4970196

Fax: +234-1-616702/824858
Contact: OH Mazi
List: Literature
Found: 1963
BIP: 66
UK/Europe dist: Hambleside
International Ltd, Winchester, UK

Senegal

Editions Khoudia/CAEC
Centre Africain d'Animation et
d'Echanges Culturels
BP 5332 – Poste de Fann, Dakar
Tel: +221-211023
Fax: +221-215109
Contact: Aminata Sow Fall
List: Literature
Languages: French, national
languages
Found: 1988
BIP: 16

Nouvelles Editions Africaines du Sénégal
10 Rue Amadou Assane Ndoye
BP 260, Dakar
Tel: +221-211381
Fax: +221-223604
Email: neas@telecomplus.sn
Contact: Mamadou Kasse
List: Fiction
Languages: French
Found: 1972
BIP: 1000

Per Ankh SARL Publishers
BP 7173, Soumbedioune, Dakar
Tel: +221-205036
Fax: +221-204913
Contact: Ama Gueye
List: Literature

Presses Universitaires de Dakar
Universite Cheikh Anta Diop de
Dakar, BP 5713, Dakar-Fann
Tel: +221-242448
Email: djibagne@refer.sn

Web site:
http://www.ANPLEF_UREF_refer.sn
Contact: Djibril Agne
List: Critical/cultural, Literature
Languages: French
Found: 1988
BIP: 3

South Africa

Jonathan Ball Publishers
PO Box 33977, Jeppestown 2043
Tel: +27-11-6222900
Fax: +27-11-6227610
Contact: Francine Blum
List: Literature
Languages: African languages,
Afrikaans, English
BIP: 196

Educum
PO Box 3068,
Halfway House, 1685
Tel: +27-11-3153647
Fax: +27-11-3152757
Contact: Ernest North
List: Literature, Popular fiction (in
African languages only)
Languages: African languages,
Afrikaans, English
BIP: 900

Heinemann Publishers Southern Africa (Pty) Ltd
Head Office, Old Business Park
PO Box 371, Isando, 1600
Tel: +27-11-4833292
Fax: +27-11-7284665
Web site: c/o Heinemann World web
site
Contact: Nick Evans
List: Literature
Found: 1958
BIP: 809
UK/Europe dist: Heinemann
International, Oxford

Hibbard Publishers
PO Box 40251, Arcadia, 0007
Tel: +27-12-8043990/1
Fax: +27-12-8041240
Contact: Lynette Casey
List: Literature, Popular fiction
Languages: African languages,
Afrikaans, English
BIP: 66

Hodder and Stoughton Educational Southern Africa Pty Ltd
PO Box 39948, Randburg, 2125
Tel: +27-11-8864920
Fax: +27-11-8865326
Email: david@hodder.co.za
Contact: David Lea
List: Literature
Found: 1988
BIP: 200

Human and Rousseau (PTY) Ltd
State House 3-9 Rose Street
PO Box 5050, Cape Town, 8000
Tel: +27-21-251282
Fax: +27-21-4192619
Email:
humanhk@humanrousseau.com
Web site:
http://www.humanrousseau.com
Contact: Tanya White
List: Literature
Languages: Afrikaans, English,
Xhosa, Zulu
Found: 1959
BIP: ±1000
UK/Europe dist: Millbank Books
NA dist: BHB

Juta and Company Ltd
PO Box 14373, Kenwyn
Cape Town, 7790
Tel: +27-21-7975101
Fax: +27-21-7627424
Email: books@juta.co.za
Web site: http://www.juta.co.za
Contact: NS Christian
List: Critical/cultural

Languages: African languages,
Afrikaans, English
Found: 1853
BIP: 2227
UK/Europe dist: BRAD, London, UK
NA dist: ISBS, Portland, Oregon –
Academic titles; William Gaunt,
Florida – Law and Professionals

Kagiso Publishers
PO Box 629
Pretoria, 1
Tel: +27-12-3284620
Fax: +27-12-3284706
Contact: Colin Bower
List: Literature, Popular fiction
Languages: African languages,
Afrikaans, English
BIP: 2500

Knowledge Unlimited (Pty) Ltd
Private Bag 16, Centurion
Gauteng, 0046
Tel: +27-11-6521800
Fax: +27-11-3142984
Contact: HJM Retief
List: Popular fiction
Found: 1992
BIP: 200

Kwela Books
PO Box 6525, Roggebaai
Cape Town, 8012
Tel: +27-21-4062875
Fax: +27-21-4063196
Email: kwela@kwela.com
Web site: http://www.kwela.com
Contact: Annari van der Merwe
List: Literature, Popular fiction
Languages: Afrikaans, English
Found: 1994
BIP: 30
UK/Europe dist: Africa Book Centre,
London, UK
NA dist: Africa Book Centre, London,
UK

**Macmillan Academic,
Southern Africa**
PO Box 31487, Braamfontein
Gauteng, 2017
Tel: +27-11-4840916
Fax: +27-11-4843129
Email: macmillan@iafrica.com
Contact: Cory Voigt
List: Literature, Popular fiction
Languages: English

Maskew Miller Longman (PTY) Ltd
Howard Drive Pinelands
PO Box 396, Cape Town, 8000
Tel: +27-21-5317750
Fax: +27-21-5314049
Contact: F Dada
List: Literature, Popular fiction
Languages: All South African
languages
Found: 1983
BIP: 1500
UK/Europe dist: Longman, Harlow,
UK
NA dist: Addison Wesley, Reading,
Massachusetts, USA

Mayibuye Publications
University of the Western Cape
Private Bag X17, Bellville, 7535
Tel: +27-21-9592529/9593594
Fax: +27-21-9593411
Email: Lavona@intekom.co.za
Contact: Lavona George
List: Critical/cultural, Fiction, Poetry
Found: 1992
BIP: 85

Options Publishing
PO Box 1588
Somerset West, 7129
Tel: +27-24-8524728/7134
Fax: +27-24-512592
Contact: Monica Cromhout
List: Literature, Popular fiction
Found: 1991
BIP: 12

Penguin Books (SA)
Private Bag X14, Parkview, 2122
Contact: Alison Lowry
List: Literature, Popular fiction
Languages: English
BIP: 250

David Philip Publishers (PTY) Ltd
PO Box 23408
Claremont, Western Cape, 7735
Tel: +27-21-644236
Fax: +27-21-643358
Email: dpp@iafrica.com
Web site:
http://www.twisted.co.za/DPP/
Contact: David Philip
List: Literature
Languages: African languages,
Afrikaans, English
Found: 1971
BIP: 300
UK/Europe dist: Africa Book Centre,
London, UK

Queillerie Publishers (Pty) Ltd
PO Box 616
Greenpoint, Cape Town, 8051
Tel: +27-21-4063326
Fax: +27-21-4063111
Email: queiller@queillerie.com
Contact: Frederik de Jager
List: Literature
Found: 1992
BIP: 40

Ravan Press (Pty) Ltd
PO Box 145
Randburg, 2125
Tel: +27-11-7897636
Fax: +27-11-7897653
Contact: Ipuseng Kotokoane
List: Literature
Found: 1972
BIP: 170
UK/Europe dist: Hodder and
Stoughton Educational, London, UK
NA dist: Ohio University Press,
Athens, Ohio, USA

Shuter and Shooter (Pty) Ltd
230 Church Street, PO Box 109
Pietermaritzburg, 3200
Tel: +27-331-946830/948881
Fax: +27-331-943096/427419
Contact: David Ryder
List: Literature, Popular fiction
Languages: African languages,
Afrikaans, English
Found: 1925
BIP: 1027

Snailpress
30 Firfield Road, Plumstead, 7800
Tel: +27-21-217960
Fax: +27-21-4196965
Contact: G Ferguson
List: Poetry
Found: 1990
BIP: 30

Southern Book Publishers (Pty) Ltd
A division of the Struik New
Holland Group
PO Box 3103, Halfway House
Midrand, Gauteng, 1685
Tel: +27-11-3153633/3153637
Fax: +27-11-3153810
Contact: LM Grantham
List: Literature
Languages: Afrikaans, English
Found: 1987
BIP: 200
UK/Europe dist: New Holland
Publishers
NA dist: Menasha Ridge

Tafelberg Publishers Ltd
PO Box 879
Cape Town, 8000
Tel: +27-21-4241320
Fax: +27-21-4242510
Email: RBester@NBH.Naspers.co.za
Web site: http://www.tafelberg.com
Contact: A van Wyk
List: Literature, Popular fiction
Languages: Afrikaans, English, Xhosa,
Zulu and other local languages

Found: 1951
BIP: 1300

University of Cape Town Press
Private Bag, Rondebosch, 7700
Tel: +27-21-244519/244529
Fax: +27-21-232453
Email: uctpress@hiddingh.uct.ac.za
Contact: Rosemary Meny-Gibert
List: Literature
Languages: English
Found: 1992
BIP: 36

Vivlia Publishers and Booksellers (Pty) Ltd
PO Box 1014, Florida Hills, 1716
Contact: S Mota
List: Fiction
Languages: African languages,
Afrikaans, English

Witwatersrand University Press
23 Junction Avenue
Parktown, PO Wits Johannesburg
Gauteng, 2050
Tel: +27-11-4845906/07/10
Fax: +27-11-4845971
Email: wup@iafrica.com
Contact: Pat Tucker
List: Drama, Literature
Languages: African languages, English
Found: 1922
BIP: 159
UK/Europe dist: Africa Book Centre,
UK

Tanzania

DUP (1996) Ltd
PO Box 35182, Dar es Salaam
Tel: +255-51-410137/410500-8
Fax: +255-51-410137
Email: Director@dup.udsm.ac.tz
Contact: NG Mwitta
List: Critical/cultural, Fiction, Poetry
Languages: English, Kiswahili
Found: 1979

BIP: 210
UK/Europe dist: ABC
NA dist: ABC

Mkuki na Nyota Publishers
PO Box 4246, Dar es Salaam
Tel: +255-51-180479
Fax: +255-51-180479
Email: mkuki@ud.co.tz
mkuki@costech.gn.apc.org
Contact: Walter Bgoya
List: Critical/cultural, Fiction
Languages: English, Kiswahili
Found: 1990
BIP: 30
UK/Europe dist: ABC
NA dist: ABC

MPB Enterprises
PO Box 70077, Dar es Salaam
Tel: +255-812-786392
Contact: PB Mayega
List: Literature
Languages: English, Kiswahili
BIP: 14

Tanzania Publishing House
47 Samora Machel Avenue
PO Box 2138, Dar es Salaam
Tel: +255-51-132164/5
Contact: Primus Isidor Karugendo
List: Literature
Languages: English, Kiswahili
Found: 1966
BIP: 200
UK/Europe dist: ABC
NA dist: ABC

TEMA Publishers Co. Ltd
PO Box 63115, Dar es Salaam
Tel: +255-51-113608/110472
Fax: +255-51-75422/37710
Email: ESAURP@ud.co.tz
Contact: Bonnie Mapunda
List: Fiction
Languages: English, Kiswahili
Found: 1994
BIP: 18

Togo

Editions Akpagnon
BP 3531, Lomé
Tel: +228-220244
Fax: +228-220244
Contact: Yves Emmanuel Dogbe
List: Fiction
Languages: English, Ewe, French
Found: 1979
BIP: 46

Editions HaHo
Centre Togolais de Communication
Evangelque Dpt
1 Rue du Commerce, BP 378, Lomé
Tel: +228-214582
Fax: +228-212967
Contact: Marc K Etse
List: Literature
Languages: French
Found: 1990
BIP: 40

Nouvelles Editions Africaines du Togo
239 Bd du 13 Janvier,
BP 4862, Lomé
Tel: +228-216761/216527
Fax: +228-221003
Contact: Dovi Kavegue
List: Literature
Found: 1990
BIP: 88

Tunisia

CERES Editions
6 rue. A. Azzam
BP 56, Tunis, 1002
Tel: +216-1-782033
Fax: +216-1-787516/281646
Email: ceres@planet.tm
Contact: Karim Ben Smail
List: Literature
Languages: Arabic, English, French, German, Italian
Found: 1965

BIP: 500
UK/Europe dist: EDISUD,
Aix-en-Provence, France
Demete, Tunisie

Uganda

Crane Publishers
PO Box 8620, Kampala
Tel: +256-41-272858
Fax: +256-41-251123
Contact: Mustafa Matyaba
List: Literature
Languages: English, Ugandan
languages
Found: 1985
BIP: 80

Femrite Publications Ltd
Plot 147 Kira Road
PO Box 705, Kampala
Tel: +256-41-543943
Email: femrite@infocom.co.ug
Contact: Goretti Kyomuhendo
List: Literature (women's writing
only)
Languages: English
Found: 1997
BIP: 4
UK/Europe dist: ABC
NA dist: ABC

Fountain Publishers Ltd
55 Nkrumah Road
PO Box 488, Kampala
Tel: +256-41-259163/251112
Fax: +256-41-251160
Email: fountain@starcom.co.ug
Web site:
http://www.uganda.co.ug/fountain-
.htm
Contact: James Tumusiime
List: Drama, Fiction, Poetry
Languages: English
Found: 1988
BIP: 170
UK/Europe dist: ABC
NA dist: ABC

Kamenyero Publishing
PO Box 11705, Kampala
Tel: +256-41-266352/266974
Fax: +256-41-250668
Contact: Harriet Namirembe
List: Literature
Found: 1994
BIP: 3

Zambia

Book World Publishers Ltd
PO Box 32581, Lusaka
Tel: +260-1-222688/225282
Fax: +260-1-225195
Email: bookwld@zamtel.zm
Contact: Bharat L Nayee
List: Literature
Languages: English, Zambian
languages
Found: 1996
BIP: 8

Longman Zambia Ltd
PO Box 50496, Ridgeway, Lusaka
Tel: +260-1-292931
Fax: +260-1-294079
Email: longman@zamnet.zm
Contact: Fidelis Katongo
List: Literature
Languages: English, Zambian
languages
Found: 1994
BIP: 56
UK/Europe dist: All Longman
companies
NA dist: All Longman companies .

Multimedia Zambia
Bishops Road Kabulonga
P.O. Box 320199, Woodlands, Lusaka
Tel: +260-1-261193
Fax: +260-1-261193
Email: nmirror@zamnet.com
Contact: Gideon Simwinga
List: Literature
Found: 1971

Zambia Educational Publishing House
PO Box 32708, Lusaka, 10101
Tel: +260-1-229493/222324
Fax: +260-1-225073
Contact: Ray Munamwimbu
List: Literature
Languages: Chitonga, Cibemba, Cinyanja, English, Kiikaonde, Lunda, Luvale, Silozi
Found: 1966
BIP: 500

Zimbabwe

Baobab Books
4 Conald Road, Graniteside
PO Box 567, Harare
Tel: +263-4-755035/755036
Fax: +263-4-759052/781913
Email: academic@africaonline.co.zw
Contact: Chiedza Musingezi
List: Fiction, Poetry, Short stories
Languages: English, Shona
Found: 1988
BIP: 85
UK/Europe dist: ABC
NA dist: ABC

College Press Publishers (Pvt.) Ltd
15 Douglas Road, Workington
PO Box 3041, Harare
Tel: +263-4-757150/757153
Fax: +263-4-754256
Contact: CJ Ngwaru
List: Fiction
Languages: English, Ndebele, Shona
Found: 1968
BIP: 640
UK/Europe dist: Macmillan Publishers, London (and elsewhere)

HarperCollins Publishers Zimbabwe
PO Box UA 201, Union Avenue
Harare
Tel: +263-4-732436/721413
Fax: +263-4-732436

Email: mcmillan@harare.iafrica.com
List: Fiction

Mambo Press
Senga Road, PO Box 779, Gweru
Tel: +263-54-24016/24017
Fax: +263-54-21991
Contact: VB Paradza
List: Fiction
Found: 1958
BIP: 456
UK/Europe dist: Africa Book Centre, London, UK
NA dist: Grailville Art and Bookshop, USA

Mercury Press
22 Kaguvi Street, PO Box 2373
Harare
Tel: +263-4-751874/751515
Fax: +263-4-737640
Contact: DF Sutherland
List: Literature
Languages: English, Shona
Found: 1973
BIP: 25

Mutapha Publishing House
31 Fourth Street
Marondera
Tel: +263-79-24869
Contact: AS Chigwedere
List: Literature

Zimbabwe Publishing House (Pvt.) Ltd
Kamfinsa Centre, Greendale
PO Box BW 350, Harare
Tel: +263-4-497555/497558
Fax: +263-4-497554
Email: apg@id.co.zw
Contact: Monica Mutero
List: Poetry
Found: 1981
BIP: 184
UK/Europe dist: ABC
NA dist: ABC

Zimbabwe Women Writers
78 Kaguvi Street
PO Box 4209, Harare
Tel: +263-4-774261
Fax: +263-4-774261/751202
Email: zww@telco.co.zw
Contact: Pushpa Hargovan
List: Fiction (women's writing only)
Languages· English, Ndebele, Shona
Found: 1991
BIP: 7

OUTSIDE AFRICA

Publishers listed in this section are
the main English-language
publishers of literature or critical
literary and cultural studies. They
do not therefore include such
publishers for Continental Europe.
For a guide to publishers in France
consult *Notre Librarie. Revue du
livre: Afrique, Caraibes, Océan
Indien,* no. 129 Janvier-Mars 1997
(CLEF, 5 rue Rousselet, F-75007,
France); and *Takam Tikou. Le
Bulletin de la Joie par les Livres,*
1999 (Amis de la Jois par les Livres,
Immeuble Atlantic, 361 avenue du
Général de Gaulle, 92140 Clamart,
France). For Germany, the Society
for the Promotion of African Asian
and Latin American Literature can
supply details of publishers in
Germany and Switzerland who
publish literature in German
translation only. The Society acts as
a facilitator promoting contacts
between authors and publishers in
the 'Third World' and those in the
German-speaking region. For more
information see the Society's entry
under 'Writers' Organisations: A
Directory', page 209.

UK

Cambridge University Press
The Edinburgh Building
Cambridge, CB2 2RU
Tel: +44-1223-312393
Fax: +44-1223-315052
Email: jkuper@cup.cam.ac.uk
Contact: Jessica Kuper
List: Critical/cultural

James Currey Publishers
73 Botley Road
Oxford, OX2 0BS
Tel: +44-1865-244111
Fax: +44-1865-246454
Email: jamescurrey@dial.pipex.com
Contact: James Currey
List: Critical/cultural
Found: 1985

Harlem River Press
35 Britannia Row
London, N1 8QH
Tel: +44-171-2263377
Fax: +44-171-3591454
Contact: Glenn Thompson
List: Poetry
Found: 1974
An imprint of Writers and Readers Ltd

Heinemann Educational Publishers
Halley Court, Jordan Hill
Oxford, OX2 8EJ
Tel: +44-1865-311366
Fax: +44-1865-314169
Email: export.repp@bhein.rel.co.uk
Web site: www.heinemann.co.uk
Contact: Natalie Warren-Green
List: Fiction (African Writers Series)
NA dist: Heinemann US

Longman
Edinburgh Gate
Harlow, Essex CM20 2JE
Tel: +44-1279-623623
Fax: +44-1279-623388
Email:
kern.roberts@pearsoned-ema.com

Contact: Kern Roberts
List: Fiction (Longman African Writers)
Found: 1724
BIP:
UK/Europe dist: Longman companies world-wide
NA dist: Longman companies world-wide

Macmillan Press Ltd
Houndmills, Basingstoke, RG21 2XS
Tel: +44-1256-29242
Fax: +44-1256-479985
Contact: TM Farmiloe
List: Critical/cultural, Popular fiction (Pacesetters Series)
BIP: 100

Nia
6 Hoxton Square
London, N1 6NU
Tel: +44-171-7291199
Fax: +44-171-7291771
Contact: Dotun Adebayo
List: Fiction
An imprint of The X Press

Payback Press
14 High Street, Edinburgh, EH1 1TE
Tel: +44-131-5575111
Fax: +44-131-5575211
Email: payback@canongate.co.uk
Contact: Jamie Byng
List: Fiction, Poetry
Payback Press is an imprint of Canongate Books Ltd

The Women's Press
34 Great Sutton Street
London, EC1V 0DX
Tel: +44-171-2513007
Fax: +44-171-6081938
Contact: Kathy Gale
List: Fiction (women's writing only)
Found: 1978

Writers and Readers Ltd
34 Britannia Row, London, N1 8HQ
Tel: +44-171-2263377
Fax: +44-171-3591454
Email: info@writersandreaders.com
Web site:
http://www.writersandreaders.com
Contact: Glenn Thompson
List: Critical/cultural, Fiction
Languages: English
Found: 1974
See also Harlem River Press (an imprint of Writers and Readers Ltd)

The X Press
6 Hoxton Square, London, N1 6NU
Tel: +44-171-7291199
Fax: +44-171-7291771
Email: x@xpress.co.uk
Contact: Dotun Adebayo
List: Fiction
Found: 1992
See also Nia (an imprint of The X Press)

Hans Zell Publishers
An imprint of Bowker-Saur
of Reed Elsevier (UK) Ltd
PO Box 56, Oxford OX1 2SJ
Tel: +44-1865-511428
Fax: +44-1865-311534
Email: hzell@dial.pipex.com
Contact: Hans M Zell
List: Critical/cultural, Reference
Found: 1975
BIP:
NA dist: Bowker-Saur/Reed Reference Publishing
Note: The Hans Zell imprint has been discontinued as from September 1999. Bowker-Saur/Reed Business Information have announced that they will not commission any further titles for the imprint, although they will continue publication of the three 'Hans Zell' journals: *The African Book Publishing Record, International African Bibliography* and *African Studies Abstracts.*

USA

Africa World Press Inc/
The Red Sea Press Inc
11-D Princess Road
Lawrenceville, NJ 08648-2319
Tel: +1-609-8449533
Fax: +1-609-8440198
Email: africawpress@nyo.com
Contact: Kassahun Checole
List: Critical/cultural, Fiction,
Poetry,
(African Writers Library, African
Women Writers)
Found: 1983
BIP: 20
UK dist: Turnaround Publishers
Services Ltd, London
See also entry under Eritrea

Carolina Academic Press
700 Kent Street
Durham, NC 27701
Tel: +1-919-4897486
Fax: +1-919-4935668
Email: cap.press@worldnet.att.net
Contact: Russ Bahorsky
List: Critical/cultural, Fiction,
Poetry
BIP: 6
UK/Europe dist: Basil Blackwell Ltd,
108 Cowley Road, Oxford OX4 1JF

Edwin Mellen Press
POB 450
415 Ridge Street, Lewiston
NY 14902-0450
Tel: +1-716-7542788/2266
Fax: +1-716-7544056
Email: mellen@ag net
Web site www.mellen.com
Contact: John Rupnow
List: Critical/cultural
BIP: 64
UK/Europe dist: The Edwin Mellen
Press Ltd, Lampeter, Dyfed, Wales
SA48 8LT

The Feminist Press at CUNY
Wingate Hall, City College/ CUNY
Convent Avenue at 138th Street
New York, NY 10031
Tel: +1-212-6508890
Fax: +1-212-6508893
Contact: Jean Casella
List: Critical/cultural, Fiction, Short
Stories
BIP: 2

Greenwood Publishing Group Inc
88 Post Road West
POB 5007, Westport, CT 06881
Tel: +1-203-2263571
Fax: +1-203-2221502
Web site: www.greenwood.com
Contact: Cynthia Harris
List: Reference, Critical/cultural
BIP: 500

Heinemann
361 Hanover Street
Portsmouth, NH 03801
Tel: +1-603-4317894
Fax: +1-603-4317840
Email: info@heinemann.com
Web site: www.heinemann.com
Contact: Jean Hay
List: Critical/cultural
BIP: 100
UK/Europe dist: Heinemann UK;
James Currey Publishers

Howard University Press
1240 Randolph Street
Room 106, Washington, DC 20017
Tel: +1-202-6866696
Fax: +1-202-8069029
Contact: Edwin J Gordon
List: Critical/cultural
BIP: 16
UK/Europe dist: Baker and Taylor
International

Indiana University Press
601 North Morton Street
Bloomington, IN 47404-3797

Tel: +1-812-8554203
Fax: +1-812-8558507
Email: iupress@indiana.edu
Web site: www.indiana.edu/~iupress
Contact: Janet Rabinowitch
List: Critical/cultural
BIP: 100
UK/Europe dist: Open University
Press, Celtic Court no. 22,
Ballmoor MK18 1XW

Lynne Rienner Publishers Inc
1800 30th Street
Suite 314, Boulder, CO 80301
Tel: +1-303-4446684
Fax: +1-303-4440824
Contact: Lynne Rienner
List: Critical/cultural
BIP: 80
UK/Europe dist: Eurospan Ltd, 3
Henrietta Street, London WC2E 8LU

Passeggiata Press, Inc
POB 636
Pueblo, CO 80301
Tel: +1-719-5441038
Fax: +1-719-5467889
Email: passeggia@aol.com
Web site:
www.members.aol.com/passeggia/
passeggiata.htm
Contact: Donald E Herdeck
List: Critical/cultural, Fiction, Poetry,
Short Stories
BIP: 11

Riverhead Books
200 Madison Avenue
New York, NY 10016
Tel: +1-212-9518400
Fax: +1-212-2136706
Contact: Susan Petersen
List: Fiction

Scarecrow Press Inc
4720 Boston Way
Lanham, MD 20706
Tel: +1-301-4593366
Fax: +1-301-4592118
Web site: www.scarecrowpress.com
Contact: Shirley Lambert
List: Reference only
BIP: 60
UK/Europe dist: Shelwing Ltd
127 Sandgate Road, Folkestone
CT20 2BL

University of Massachusetts Press
PO Box 429
Amherst, MA 01004-0429
Tel: +1-413-5452217
Fax: +1-413-5451226
Contact: Clark Dougan
List: Critical/cultural
Found: 1964

Treating Writers Right

How should writers expect to be treated? The idea of including this section arose from a discussion about the organisation of a literary festival in an African country to which a London-based African writer was invited. It happened to be the homeland that she had left more than thirty years before, and, since she was a writer of romantic fiction, she had not been invited to other similar gatherings. On her return to London, she said she felt she had been well treated, she had been welcomed at the festival venue and accommodated at an excellent hotel without charge. When asked about her air ticket, she said she had paid for it herself.

There might have been any number of explanations for this situation. The writer might have been planning a journey home and might have been happy to combine a few days of literary festivities with happy interaction with family and old friends. But this wasn't the case: she had gone because of the festival, had been honoured to be asked, and had not thought it unreasonable to pay her way.

There will sometimes be misunderstandings, occasionally exploitation by one side or the other. However, the point from the episode described above is clear: the festival was to honour writers, and writers invited from the UK should have been offered air tickets to get there and back again. In return, of course, they would be expected to participate, to sit on panels, recount experiences, read from work, generally contribute.

Details concerning transport will often raise issues, and not only for writers. For example, if it is agreed that individuals should be flown to a particular venue, what class of air ticket should be offered to whom? Should age, achievement, gender, physical condition, length of flight, and so on affect grading? How flexible should organisers and writers be? Should organisers expect writers to 'rough it' so that the funds available can be stretched further? Should writers bear in mind, perhaps, that if economy-class tickets are purchased, more authors will be able to attend the gathering? Should consideration be given to the source of the funds being used to purchase the tickets – with one option taken if the money comes from, say, an immensely wealthy transnational company, and another option taken if the cash has been scraped together by subscriptions from struggling students? Should writers insist on parity with others? If so, who should they choose to compare themselves with? Scientists? Business people? Civil Servants? Or diplomats? There are no easy answers to these questions, and, even should the day come when writers hold the purse-strings and make the decisions, the debate will still continue far into the night.

Sometimes, after years of fighting for recognition and decent treatment, writers find themselves fêted, honoured by those they considered their enemies. The dangers inherent in this are as great as those suggested by the 'No Air Ticket' scenario. The starkness of one moral dilemma in which he found himself was described by Soyinka in the course of an address given during May 1983. In his talk, he summarised his response to an arrangement whereby a Nigerian Air Force plane had been put at the disposal of writers travelling to an Association of Nigerian Authors gathering in Abuja:

> This plane [he said] would touch down at a number of convenient airports all over the country to pick up delegates converging for the Congress of the Nigerian literati.

Observing that the regime from whom the offer ultimately originated 'was, beyond doubt, a self-vaunting, iron-fisted affirmation of naked power', Soyinka meditated as follows:

> Participating corporately in an activity under its remote sponsorship, accepting even to be airlifted by one of its fleet of dominance, over even the very air that despairing Nigerians breathed, therefore constituted for me a serious problem.

In brief, he 'ended up not going to the Congress, regretful though [he] was, at missing this reunion with [his] long lost comrades' (Osofisan et al. 1991, 27-28).

Magazines and Newspapers

Magazines: Little and Large

From the perspective of the end of the century, the 1950s and 1960s appear to have witnessed a blossoming of literary magazines and journals. Through them African authors were given opportunities to reach large, international audiences, and to debate Pan-African literary issues vigorously (see, for example, the account of the debate on *Language*, pages 146-58). It is tempting to look back at those decades as to a simpler, more innocent and more cultured time. *Transition* prospered in Kampala and *Black Orpheus* emerged regularly from Ibadan, twin pillars of a literary structure; or perhaps, as they manifested themselves, solid foundations on which to build an edifice.

In addition to these giants, there were local publications. Ghana, for example, produced *Okyeame*, and a troop of supporting publications, *The Ghana Review*, *Oba Sima*, *The Legon Observer* and so on, which carried short stories, poems, book and theatre reviews. Such was the importance attached to creative writers finding their voices as part of the independence and post-independence struggles that newspapers devoted space to fiction and humour, sometimes, too, to poetry and criticism. The pattern, which has not been lost entirely, was continued in other countries with variations. (The South African experience in this, as in so much else was significantly different. See below.)

Universities put resources of time and money into publishing literary journals. WH Stevenson has told the story of *The Horn*, what it was and what it did, at Ibadan; and *The Horn* had its rivals and imitators, its siblings and cousins who struggled for survival in other universities. These included: *Celebration, Darlite, Expression, Ijala, Mau, Odi, Ofirima, Opon Ifa, Penpoint, The Students' Eye* ... The list is long, a roll-call of those who struggled, and, all too often, capitulated.

Now, in a world shifted from its course by debt repayment schedules and structural adjustment programmes, old certainties no longer hold. *Transition* and *Black Orpheus* have been through several metamorphoses and, though the former is alive and well, it has become part of the African Diaspora. Now published in New York, its impact in Kampala, or Accra where it sojourned briefly, is negligible. Priced far beyond the reach of impoverished African academics, not even libraries can afford the subscription.

Even though it is not difficult to chant a litany of departed publications – proud names, no longer with us, or appearing so irregularly and with such surprising distribution as to give the impression that they are merely shadows of their former selves; ghosts paying occasional visits to old haunts – all is not lost. In many countries weekly and fortnightly magazines have been published with more or less regularity, variations on *Time* and *Newsweek*. In Nigeria, despite rocketing cover costs, titles such as *Classique, New Breed* and *Tell* have emerged. Ghana supported *Uhuru* for a time, and *The Weekly Review* comes out of Nairobi regularly with at least one page devoted to a book review.

London-based publications, including *New African, Panafrica* (all too briefly); and *West Africa* ('Methuselah was tottering as the writers and publishers converged on Tarangire'), have tried to cover developments on a continental scale with varying degrees of commitment and success. The financial circumstances of each publication vary, which means, in practical and far from satisfactory terms, that some pay, some don't, and that some pay sometimes. *Panafrica*, for example, started off by paying, but quickly became embroiled in financial difficulties, delayed payments and then 'went to the wall'. *West Africa* folded, and its unpaid contributors will have to make their claims to the liquidators. However, in 1999 it was taken over by Graphic Corporation (Ghana), and should return soon.

The study of the life history of Africa's 'little magazines' is aided by reading the passage in Walter Bgoya's paper on 'Publishing in Africa: Culture and Development' (see pages 80-81). For those seeking a fuller account of the various existences of the pioneering giants, Peter Benson's *Black Orpheus, Transition and Modern Cultural Awakening in Africa* (1986) offers a detailed account. The role of the CIA in funding cultural bodies is part of this story, and dramatically illustrates the precarious circumstances in which African journals are often edited. Bernth Lindfors' research among the early works of major African writers and his time as a teacher in Malawi provided some of the background to his informative essay on 'African Little Magazines' published in his *Loaded Vehicles: Studies in African Literary Media* (1996).

The situation, however, must be held constantly under review. Some of the 'little magazines' sell in such small numbers in such limited areas that they are hard to keep in view. For example, Vol. 1 no. 3 of the often overlooked *Kubekrom News*, described as 'a quarterly newsletter published by the Centre for National Culture, Western Region [of Ghana]', came out in December 1994. Its contents included a poetry corner and the third instalment of Charles Odame-Ankrah's play *The Boss is Not Always Right*. The publication is registered (ISSN 085-143X), and it has a distribution system that delivered a copy to the Library of the School of Performing Arts, Legon, but it is not easy to obtain.

Just as it would be wrong to write as if *Kubekrom News* did not exist, it would also be wrong to pen a premature obituary for such irregular publications as *Asemka*, 'a bilingual literary journal officially published annually by the Faculty of Arts, University of Cape Coast, Cape Coast, Ghana'. The reader trying to ascertain how many issues have appeared is invited to consider the possible meanings of 'officially published annually'. Is the emphasis on the official nature of the publication, or is there an admission that, although annual publication is 'official policy', the reality is at odds with this? In 1974 Vol. 1 nos. 1 and 2 appeared; no. 3 followed in 1975. More recently: no. 6 appeared in 1989, no. 7 in 1992, and, as if settling into an 'official' three-year gestation period, no. 8 in 1995!

While at various times it might have seemed justifiable to toll a death knoll for *Asemka*, reports of the journal's demise have clearly been exaggerated. Against considerable odds, in a community shaken by great changes in the funding of higher education and the financial base of publishing, *Asemka* has persevered. Congratulations are due to YS Boafo and the other determined members of the editorial board. African writers will watch developments with interest regarding the publication, as with a wayward friend who pays irregular and sometimes widely-spaced visits: always lively, always welcome, never predictable. In time, too, the importance of the journal's policy of publishing articles in both French and English will be recognised. That policy sets *Asemka* apart from publications that also deserve brief comments: *WASI Writer* and *Glendora*.

WASI Writer and The Lamp

Started as 'The magazine for writers', *WASI Writer* has become simply *WASI: The Magazine for the Arts*. At the time of its launch in January 1990, it was directed at 'the serious, mature and professional writer who wants to bring to his life more effective, efficient and economic ways of conducting his business'. Since then, valuable information about markets, copyright, censorship, local writers' groups and drama companies has been published.

Over the years, reflected in the changing title, there has been a shift from articles containing news and advice to a magazine written largely by the editor on issues not central to writers as such. It is difficult to take seriously, for example, Vol. 8 no. 2 (April 1997) entitled 'Malawi on a platter' – little more than a glorified food and restaurant guide. The initiative in providing a forum for debate about major issues confronting the creative intellectuals in democratic Malawi is passing to *The Lamp*, published in Balaka township.

Glendora Review and *Glendora Book Supplement*

At the time of writing, a determined effort to fill the (huge) space left by the migration of *Transition* and the demise of *Black Orpheus* is being made by *Glendora*, and by its editor Dapo Adeniyi (see pages 99-104 of Part 1 for his contribution). The unlikely name of the publication draws attention to a family business: *Glendora*, 'Nigeria's leading bookstore' supports the venture and ensured an excellent start. There are precedents for that kind of praise being 'the kiss of death' but that should not prevent acknowledgement of the considerable investment and welcome endeavour that the publication represents. *Glendora Review*, an 'African Quarterly on the Arts', regularly makes space available for poetry, fiction and drama – and for criticism of creative writing. It also includes material on such sister arts as architecture and cinema. Indeed, by recognising the many advantages of combining an interest in writing in Africa with concern for the other arts and an awareness of African creativity in the Diaspora, *Glendora* has given new life to the Mbari ideal that flourished during the 1960s. The magazine's stable-mate, *Glendora Books Supplement*, has made a promising start, recapturing ground previously lost to materialism by its commitment to fostering informed discussion of literature.

The African Periodicals Exhibit

It has been a constant refrain that authors should endeavour to become informed about developments in all matters concerning publishing. For magazine publishing the *Catalogue* of the annual African Periodicals Exhibit at the Zimbabwe International Book Fair will be found particularly useful. In addition to listing publications, the 1996 publication contains a valuable essay by Hans Zell entitled 'African Journals in a Changing Environment of Scholarly Communication'. Although the emphasis is on the scholarly rather than creative, Zell's account has much to say that is of relevance to the writer embarking on publication at this time. For example, it would be worthwhile to consider the implications of Zell's observation that 'Electronic publishing, electronic networks, digitising resources for electronic access, and access via the Internet, has grown at a bewilderingly rapid pace ...'

Creative writers are often caught up in the world of scholarly publishing. Some academic journals include fiction or poetry, some carry reviews, others are devoted to the analysis and assessment of authors. There are already journals devoted entirely to the study of Beckett, Conrad and DH Lawrence, and, though the academic industry surrounding African writers has yet to spawn such sharply focused publications, there have been special issues of, for example, *Research in African Literatures* and *The Literary Half-Yearly*, devoted to one or other of Africa's literary giants. Zell's article considers the future of academic journals, the extent to which libraries will be able to afford them and the number of readers who will access them electronically. One of his recommendations is that editors should register their journals with the Copyright Clearance Centre (CCC) in the US 'which operates a centralised authorisation service for publishers, collects the publisher-set royalties on their behalf, and periodically remits them to rights holders'. He adds that 'It would appear that very few African scholarly journals are currently registered with the CCC.' The same can also be said of journals containing creative writing. Authors are concerned about violation of their copyright and the copying of their work. The perpetrators may be villainous pirates or occasional makers of extra photocopies. For more information, a few copyright and reproduction rights organisations are listed in 'Writers' Organisations: A Directory' (page 201).

It would be misleading to end this section without reference to the smallest of the 'little magazines': the school publications which, thanks to the efforts of already overworked teachers, provide young authors with the opportunity to see their work in print. The benefits to be derived from working on and contributing to such ventures are numerous, and generations of writers – Africans such as Achebe, Saro-Wiwa and Soyinka among them – benefited from becoming involved with the publication of school magazines. Advances in word processing have transformed the kind of 'product' that schools can put together and offer for sale. However, high production values are not the same as high literary standards. Sloppy writing and shallow thought will be easily recognised, however majestic the font.

South Africa

Magazines that published short stories contributed greatly to the development of South African literature during the 1950s, a period that saw the emergence of a significant number of writers. For reasons

that have been linked with conditions of the times, many of them
produced short stories rather than novels and indeed there was a
flourishing of the form.

Against the background of the consolidation of apartheid
(introduced in 1948), of repression, forced removals and censorship,
writers found that short fiction guaranteed a good investment of
effort and a reasonable return. Walter Ehmeir's *Publishing South
African Literature in English in the 1960s*, from which quotations
are taken in the account that follows, draws attention to the
possibilities and policies, that, taken together, played an important
part of publishing history. Running through it are the realities that
there were many more publishing opportunities for white writers
than for black, and that exile and banning orders were generally
effective in silencing particular voices.

During the 1950s 'there were essentially three kinds of local
periodicals publishing literary texts ... literary magazines, left-wing
political magazines, and press publications and newspapers with a
mass audience'. *Ophir*, *Standpunte* and *The Purple Renoster* – the
second bilingual (Afrikaans and English), the third only in English but
so sporadic that only three issues appeared in the decade – published
white authors and Mphahlele. He had one story in each, the only black
writer represented.

The left-wing magazines included 'the quarterly *Africa South* and
the monthly *Fighting Talk*'; both included regular literature sections
with one or two stories. *New Age*, a weekly paper, launched several
short-story writing competitions and published the winner.
Mphahlele's work also appeared in these publications, as did
combative narratives by TH Gwala, Alfred Hutchinson, Alex La
Guma, Arthur Maimane, James Matthews and Richard Rive. White
authors included Phyllis Altman, Alan Paton and Alf Wannenburgh.

In order to reach a mass audience, writers submitted work to
newspapers, such as the *Cape Times*, and popular magazines such as
Drum – much the most important – and *Africa*. Mphahlele is reported
as saying that *Drum* stopped promoting literature by the end of the
1950s 'because Jim Bailey (the proprietor) then felt that short fiction
"wasn't selling the magazine"'. This draws attention to the personal
element in many far-reaching decisions – in this case that made by
maverick millionaire-publisher Bailey – at the same time as
appreciating the contribution made during the decade. *Drum*
published a generation of writers including Maimane, Casey Motsisi,
Rive and Dyke Sentso.

During this time significant white writers, including Jack Cope and
Nadine Gordimer, left South Africa and found space in UK

publications, such as *Encounter* and *London Magazine,* and American magazines including *Commentary, Cosmopolitan, Harper's Bazacr, Mademoiselle* and *The New Yorker.* Ehmeir's essay goes on to report that in the 1960s, South African writing occasionally appeared in the *New Statesman, Atlantic, Kenyon Review, Negro Digest* and *Reporter.* At the same time, exile and banning orders drove black South African writers to the new African and Africa-oriented journals, notably *Black Orpheus, Transition* and *Présence Africaine.* There were, however, a number of new developments within the Republic.

Establishing a monthly periodical in South Africa was expensive, frequently requiring a registration fee of £10,000. *Contrast* received support from the Molteno Trust and, like *The Classic,* was funded by the Farfield Foundation, in part through Mphahlele's former employers, the Congress for Cultural Freedom. It was subsequently revealed (see page 315) that this Foundation was used as a channel by the Central Intelligence Agency.

The 1950s saw the continued existence or birth of a number of literary journals: *Contrast, Ophir, The Purple Renoster, New Coin, New South African Writing,* the *Adelphi Literary Review.* These acted as vehicles for white writing while *The Classic* devoted a substantial portion of each issue to black writing and in doing so offered what Gordimer referred to as 'the creation of a common literature' (Gordimer 1967). Those whites who contributed, Gordimer herself and Barney Simon for example, were among those working most energetically to create meeting places for South Africa's diverse population.

The publications came under particular pressure after the passing of the 1963 Publications and Entertainment Act, which authorised the banning of a publication if any part of it was declared undesirable. Ehmeir writes: '... in 1964, the third issue of *The New African* was banned because a story by Can Themba ('The Fugitives') contained the one word "shit-scared"'. According to Randolph Vigne, the printers of *New African* were put under pressure by the Security Police, and on several occasions new printers had to be found (Vigne 1967 quoted in Ehmeir 1995, 123). The more radical publication was not alone in experiencing difficulties: Jack Cope reported that the printer of *Contrast* had refused to complete work on an issue that included a text by Athol Fugard on the grounds that it included 'immoral' words. Cope reported that he made changes in order to save the text and the issue (Cope 1980, in Ehmeir 1995, 122).

While publications risked being banned, the South African Government took the extraordinary step of banning certain writers! Rhodesian-born teacher, law student and activist, Dennis Brutus was one of those affected and eventually, in 1966, he left for England on a Rhodesian passport. While he was under the banning order, *The Purple Renoster* published two of his poems, one anonymously, the other under the pseudonym 'Julius Friends'. Other publications eschewed these kinds of compromise. The operation of censorship in South Africa has produced a considerable number of articles and a few books, including *The Grey Ones: Essays on Censorship* edited by JS Paton. Ehmeir's essay indicates just how special the case of South Africa was, and how, over a couple of decades, writers and editors came to terms with a uniquely oppressive state.

Newspapers

In all probability, the first Ghanaian novel appeared in the pages of a newspaper, and the tradition of providing space for fiction is continued by, for example, the *Daily Graphic* and *Matatu* (Anyidoho, forthcoming). Ghanaian writers far from home have exploited the possibility of reaching mass audiences through the press. For example, while he was in East Africa, Ayi Kwei Armah published some of the work that subsequently emerged under the Heinemann imprint, in newspapers. Similar circumstances exist in other African countries, and other African writers have taken similar steps.

Newspapers often carry short stories and poems. Having work reproduced in a 'Kiddies Corner' or similar 'institution' has provided encouragement for many who have gone on to win literary laurels. In an adult vein, the press was exploited to particular effect by Ken Saro-Wiwa whose two novel-length satires, *Prisoners of Jebs* and *Pita Dumbrok's Prison*, were first encountered by the Nigerian reading public as columns printed in *Punch* and *Vanguard*. Despite an oppressive regime and steeply rising prices, independent expression remained possible – so long as Saro-Wiwa adopted certain conventions.

In the 'Introduction' to *Prisoners of Jebs*, the Ogoni author gave an account of the invitation he received from 'Mr Amuka', the owner of the *Vanguard* newspaper; he describes the emergence of prison as a setting, the use of the weekly column to comment on events, and the impact on it of particular events. Guiding principles included the 'desire to stick to the truth without giving undue offence', and the limitations of space imposed by the newspaper editor. There were inevitably risks – Saro-Wiwa noted: 'My friends expressed grave fears for my personal safety.'

In the 'Introduction' he wrote, without his customary rigour, of his reasons for believing he would not be attacked:

> In the first place, all my stories were taken from fact and opinions already published in various newspapers. Secondly, the main thrust of my story had nothing to do with the government of the day. Besides, I valued the positive

merits of the work over and above any risks to my person. (Saro-Wiwa 1988, 'Introduction')

The circumstances in which the columns were written, the proximity to events, and the sense of contact with an eager readership affected the quality of the writing. This should not surprise us, after all, these are pressures felt, and responded to, by all those (including Charles Dickens) who have set off into uncharted waters and published 'novels in progress' in instalments. It goes without saying that one of the great advantages of publication in this form is that a wider audience can be reached: consumers who are unlikely to be able to afford to buy a book can sometimes scrape together the money needed to buy weekly, fortnightly or monthly instalments.

The example of Saro-Wiwa shows that it is neither possible nor desirable to draw a firm line between those who write political commentary and those who are creative writers; nor to separate those who write for newspapers from those who are published between covers. Very often the two categories merge and the critic-commentator is better employed celebrating quality than trying to pigeonhole versatile individuals.

Anyone concerned about newspapers and magazines in Africa is in debt to Adewale Maja-Pearce who has edited, with a team of helpers, a *Directory of African Media*, which is available from the International Federation of Journalists, Rue Royal 266, 1210 Brussels, Belgium (Maja-Pearce 1996). In addition to details about numerous publications, Maja-Pearce draws on his long involvement in democratic movements and anti-censorship campaigns to provide well-informed introductions to his valuable country-by-country survey. (Such surveys appear in each edition of *Index on Censorship*.) In a review of the *Directory*, the experienced bibliographer Nancy J Schmidt draws attention to a few limitations and makes use of Mette Shayne's compilation *African Newspapers Currently Received by American Libraries* to identify newspapers that Maja-Pearce has not listed.

Many writers will produce work that finds a natural home in the pages of the local press, and many creative writers have given way to impulses to craft succinct feature articles. There are few intermediaries in this field: Gemini News Service provides one example with novelist–journalist Cameron Duodu on its list (see Writers' Organisations: A Directory on page 200).

It should be recognised that newspapers have a variety of important roles to play in fostering a local literary culture. Enlightened editors reserve space for reviews and for contributions by creative writers; they may appoint literary editors and respond positively to publishers who seek to sell serial rights to their latest titles. The impact of a newspaper eager to serve the local literary culture is wonderfully illustrated by the Lagos *Guardian*.

It is a pleasure to recognise the achievements of the *Guardian:* from its first appearance as a serious daily in July 1983 it made it clear that it would, in the words of Yemi Ogunbiyi, 'have to participate in the effort to help "popularise" our vibrant literature' (Ogunbiyi 1988). The result of this determination to participate was a regular – very nearly unfailing – Saturday feature on a literary topic, usually a portrait of a particular writer. Five years after the foundation of the paper, two volumes of these essays were edited by Ogunbiyi under the title *Perspectives on Nigerian literature, 1700 to the Present.* Clearly many at the *Guardian* were involved apart from the editor. These included Alex U Ibru (publisher), Alex Okoh (research assistant), Emmanuel Osajiokweh and Peter Uzorka (typists), and Stanley N Macebuh (managing director). The list of subjects runs what Ola Rotimi might call the 'giddy gamut' of Nigeria's creative writers, and includes Pita Nwana, groundbreaking Igbo novelist whose *Omenuko* (1933) remains 'the most popular novel in Igbo today' (Emenyonu 1988, 13), and Yoruba 'fantasia novelist' DO Fagunwa. The list of contributors, as eminent as their subjects, has included creative writers Harry Garuba, Odia Ofeimun, Femi Osofisan and Wole Soyinka, and critics of the highest calibre have been happy to write for the paper. The names of Romanus Egudu, Abiola Irele, Ezenwa-Ohaeto, Biodun Jeyifo, Chikwenye Okonjo-Ogunyemi and Marie Omaha are to be found on the Contents page of Ogunbiyi's volumes. Appropriately enough, the books are published by the *Guardian* newspaper!

Magazines: A Directory

Abbreviations used in the Directory:

Published by: Publisher
Contact: Contact name
Ed subs: Editorial submissions
Type: Type of magazine (creative writing, criticism)
Frequency: Frequency of issue
ISSN: International Standard Serial Number
1st issue: Year of the first issue

AUSTRIA

Zeitschrift fur Afrikastudien
Published by:
Zeitschrift fur Afrikastudien
Haydngasse 14/8, A-1060, Vienna
Contact: Bernhard Kittel, book
review editor
Type: Criticism
Ed subs: Articles on literature
amongst others
Frequency: Twice yearly
ISSN: 2235-89902
1st issue: 1987
Articles in the social sciences and
humanities. French or German
language.

CANADA

African Literature Association Bulletin
Published by:
Department of Modern Languages
and Comparative Studies,
University of Alberta
Edmonton, Alberta, T6G 2E6
Tel: +1-403-4338510
Email: alab@planet.eon.net

Contact: Stephen H Arnold, editor
Type: Arts criticism
Ed subs: Articles on literature and the
arts in general
Frequency: Quarterly
ISSN: 0146-4965
1st issue: 1975
The bulletin publishes articles on
African literature as well as film and
performing arts, in all languages.

Canadian Journal of African Studies/ Revue Canadienne des Etudes Africaines
Published by:
Canadian Association of African
Studies
Centre for Urban and Community
Studies
University of Toronto
455 Spadina Avenue, Suite 426
Toronto, Ontario M5S 2G8
Tel: +1-416-9787067
Contact: Roger Riendeau, editor;
Richard Maclure, book review editor
Frequency: Three issues yearly
ISSN: 0008-3968
1st issue: 1967
Contributions in French and English.

Wascana Review of Contemporary
Poetry and Short Fiction
Published by:
English Department,
University of Regina
Regina, Sask, S4S 0A2
Tel: +1-306-5854302
Fax: +1-306-5854827
Contact: Kathleen Wall, editor
Type: Poetry, creative writing and
literary criticism
Ed subs: Poetry, short stories and
arts criticism
Frequency: Twice yearly
1st issue: 1966
The editor welcomes unsolicited
MSS: short stories can be up to 6000
words and verse up to 100 lines.

ETHIOPIA

Eastern Africa Social Science
Research Review
Published by:
Organization for Social Scence
Research in Eastern and Southern
Africa (OSSREA)
PO Box 31971, Addis Ababa
Tel: +251-1-119705
Fax: +251-1-551399
Email: OSSREA@padis.gn.apc.org
Contact: Prof Wilfred Mlay, editor
Type: Literary criticism
Ed subs: Book reviews, commentar-
ies etc.
Frequency: Twice yearly
ISSN: 1027-1775
1st issue: 1985
The Review, as its title suggests, con-
tains articles in the social sciences of
special relevance to eastern and
southern Africa.

FRANCE

Jeune Afrique
Published by:
Jeune Afrique
57 bis rue d'Auteuil
F-75016, Paris
Tel: +33-1-47665242
Fax: +33-1-46226638
Contact: Hugo Sada, editor; Marcel
Peju, book review editor
Ed subs: All types
Frequency: Weekly
ISSN: 0021-6089
1st issue: 1960
A popular magazine with a culture
section.

Notre Librarie. Revue du livre:
Afrique, Caraibes, Ocean Indien
Published by:
Club des lecteurs d'expression
francaise (CLEF)
5 rue Rousselet, F-75007, Paris
Tel: +33-1-53693438
Fax: +33-1-4306149
Contact: Marie Clotilde Jacquey
Type: Literary criticism
Ed subs: Articles in French on
French language literature from
Africa, the Caribbean and the Indian
Ocean countries.
Frequency: Quarterly
ISSN: 0755-3854
1st issue: 1969

Peuples Noirs, Peuples Africains
Published by:
Peuples Noirs, Peuples Africains
82 ave de la Porte des Champs
F-76000, Rouen
Tel: +33-2-35893197
Contact: Mongo Beti, editor
Ed subs: Articles on a political or
cultural theme
Frequency: Six issues yearly
ISSN: 0181-4087

1st issue: 1978
Will receive contributions on cultural and political subjects 'concerning Black peoples'.

Politique Africaine
Published by:
Karthala
22-24 boulevard Arago
F-75013, Paris
Tel: +33-1-43311259
Fax: +33-1-56374537
Contact: Dominique Darbon, editor
Ed subs: Articles on political affairs, social and cultural topics
Frequency Quarterly
ISSN: 0244-7837
1st issue: 1981

KENYA

Kanga
Published by:
Gender and Development Centre
PO Box 1588, Kisumu
Contact: Asenath Bole Odaga, editor
Type: Poetry and creative writing
Ed subs: Poetry and short stories
Frequency: Quarterly
1st issue: 1994
The Gender and Development Centre produce this magazine, and aim to provide a forum for women to discuss and learn about important issues, and includes poems and short stories.

MALAWI

Journal of Humanities
Published by:
Chancellor College Publications
PO Box 280, Zomba
Tel: +265-522-222149
Email: inset@unima.wn.apc.org
Contact: Pascal Kishindo, editor

Type: Literary and arts criticism
Frequency: Annual

WASI: Magazine for the Arts
Published by:
Writers and Artists Services International
PO Box 317, Zomba
Tel: +265-522-222/523289
Fax: +265-522-046
Contact: Steve Chimombo, editor
Type: Arts criticism
Ed subs: Features on visual/ graphic arts, performing arts and film
Frequency: Three issues yearly
1st issue: 1990
WASI publishes the work of artists in schools and colleges as well as the wider artistic community.

NAMIBIA

Sister Namibia
Published by:
Sister Collective
PO Box 40092, Windhoek
Contact: Editorial board
Type: Creative writing
Ed subs: Poetry and short stories
Frequency: Six times yearly
ISSN: 1026-9126
1st issue: 1989
The magazine's objectives are to 'raise awareness of gender issues including racism and homophobia', and topics include reproductive health matters, violence against women, child maintenance, poetry and short stories. Four women, assisted by volunteers, run the magazine, and aim to challenge 'structures, myths and stereotypes that are oppressive to women'.

NEW ZEALAND

Takahe
Published by:
Takahe Collective Trust
PO Box 13335, Christchurch, 8001
Tel: +64-3-3598133
Contact: Editor
Type: Creative writing
Ed subs: Short stories and poetry
Frequency: Three to four issues
yearly
1st issue: 1989
The magazine will accept short fiction
and poetry from new and established
writers and poets alike.

NIGERIA

ASE: Calabar Journal of
Contemporary Poetry
Published by:
ASE Journal of Contemporary Poetry
c/o Deparment of Theatre Arts
University of Calabar, Calabar
Contact: Onookome Okome, editor
Type: Poetry
Ed subs: Poetry
Frequency: Twice yearly
1st issue: 1991
The magazine of the University of
Calabar Poetry Club, it seeks to
provide 'an independent forum for the
resuscitation and revitalization of the
discourse of poetics and poetry in
Nigeria'.

Glendora Review
African Quarterly on the Arts
Published by:
Glendora International (Nigeria) Ltd
168 Awolowo Road, PO Box 50914
Ikoyi, Lagos
Tel: +234-1-2692762
Fax: +234-1-2618083
Email: 105271.11@compuserve.com
Contact: Dapo Adeniyi, editor
Type: Literary and arts criticism
Frequency: Quarterly
ISSN: 1118-146X
1st issue: 1995

Okike
An African Journal of New Writing
Published by:
Okike, PO Box 53, Enugu State
Contact: Onuora Ossie Enekwe,
editor
Type: Creative writing and literary
criticism
Ed subs: Creative writing, including
poetry, short fiction and short
drama, as well as critical essays on
various aspects of African literature.
Frequency: Three times yearly
ISSN: 3310566
1st issue: 1971 [dormant from
1991/92 to 1997]
Okike was dormant for several years,
but with funding from the Heinrich
Böll Foundation it has been resur-
rected to serve primarily as an outlet
for creative writing, with critical
essays and book reviews.

REPUBLIC OF IRELAND

IMAGE
Published by:
IMAGE
22 Crofton Road
Dun Laoghaire, Co. Dublin
Tel: +353-1-2808415
Fax: +353-1-2808309
Contact: Jane McDonnell, editor
Type: Creative writing
Ed subs: Short stories
Frequency: Monthly
1st issue: 1975
The magazine takes stories of up to
3,000 words, especially those of inter-
est to women.

SOUTH AFRICA

(Cape Town) Cape Times
Published by:
Cape Times, Newspaper House
122 St George's Street
Cape Town, 8001
Tel: +27-21-4884911
Contact: JC Viviers, editor
Ed subs: Articles suitable for a daily newspaper
Frequency: Daily
1st issue: 1876
Articles to be no more than 800 words long.

(Johannesburg) Sunday Times
Published by:
Johannesburg Sunday Times
PO Box 1742, Saxonwold, 2132
Tel: +27-11-2805102
Fax: +27-11-2805111
Email: suntimes@tml.co.za
Contact: MW Robertson, editor
Ed subs: Short essays, stories and articles of a general – but 'light' – nature
Frequency: Weekly

ADA Magazine
Published by:
JA Sorrell
PO Box 16093
Vlaeberg, Cape Town, 8018
Tel: +27-21-4619937
Fax: +27-21-4612558
Email: ebmilton@aztec.co.za
Contact: Jennifer Sorrell, editor
Type: Arts criticism
Ed subs: Articles on art, architecture, literature, performing arts
Frequency: Twice yearly
ISSN: 1015-5597
1st issue: 1986
ADA Magazine deals with all aspects of South African contemporary culture.

Atio
Published by:
Dye Hard Press
PO Box 32112, Braamfontein, 2017
Contact: Gary Cummiskey, editor
Type: Poetry
Ed subs: Poetry
Frequency: Quarterly
Atio features South African poetry and illustrations.

Barefoot Press
Published by:
Barefoot Press
PO Box 1914, Midrand, 1685
Email: barefootpress@digitec.co.za
Web site: www.pix.za/barefoot.press
Contact: Roy Blumenthal, editor
Type: Poetry
Ed subs: Poetry
Frequency: Approx. every 2 months
Free poetry pamphlets ('footprints') featuring about six poems and a biography of the poet are distributed nationally through bookshops and by readers.

Blêksem
Published by:
Blêksem
PO Box 621, Honeydew, 2040
Contact: Editorial Team
Type: Poetry, creative writing, arts criticism
Ed subs: Poetry, song lyrics, reviews, prose
Frequency: Annual
The editors will accept a wide range of material for their magazine (see type of work) in the interest of promoting poetic and literary awareness (see page 377).

Botsotso
Published by:
Botsotso
PO Box 23910, Joubert Park, 2044
Tel: +27-11-8394036

Contact: Editorial Board
Type: Poetry, creative writing, arts criticism
Ed subs: Poetry, lyrics, short stories, children's literature, reviews
Botsotso encourages submission of unsolicited material ranging from poetry to children's stories to articles concerned with the visual arts.

Carapace
Published by:
Snailpress
PO Box 375, Cape Town, 8000
Contact: Editor
Type: Poetry
Ed subs: Poetry, book reviews
Frequency: Five issues yearly
Published poets are encouraged to send no more than two short poems.

Current Writing
Published by:
University of Natal
Department of English
University of Natal, Durban, 4041
Tel: +27-31-2602340
Fax: +27-31-2601243
Email: english@und.ac.za
Contact: Editorial team
Type: Literary criticism
Ed subs: Articles on recent writing and writing from a southern African perspective
Frequency: Twice yearly
ISSN: 1013-929X
1st issue: 1989
One issue a year has a theme, such as history and historicity; feminism and women's writing; and writing in the 'new' South Africa.

Drum
Published by:
National Magazines
PO Box 7167, Cape Town, 8000
Tel: +27-21-4063510

Fax: +27-21-4062937
Contact: Reg Vermeulen, editor
Type: Creative writing
Ed subs: Short stories
Frequency: Weekly
Drum aims to be a family magazine, and its articles are diverse. Short stories of 1,000-3,000 words tend to treat of life in the townships and rural areas.

Edgars Club Magazine
Published by:
Reaction
PO Box 1984, Parklands, 2121
Tel: +27-11-6424651/4
Fax: +27-11-6423101
Contact: John Metcalf, editor
Type: Creative writing
Ed subs: Short stories
Frequency: Monthly
A light-hearted guide to the entertainment world which also features stories 'with a twist in the tale' of 1,500-2,000 words.

Essentials
Published by:
Flair Media
PO Box 32083, Mobeni, 4060
Tel: +27-31-422041
Fax: +27-31-420191
Contact: Robynne Simpson, editor
Type: Creative writing
Ed subs: Short stories
Frequency: Monthly
Essentials promotes itself as an upmarket women's magazine. Short stories accepted by the editorial team tend to be on a romantic theme, and 1,000-1,500 words long.

Fair Lady
Published by:
National Magazines
PO Box 1802, Cape Town, 8000
Tel: +27-21-4062204

Contact: Roz Wrottesley, editor
Type: Creative writing
Ed subs: Short stories for women, articles on beauty and fashion
Frequency: Fortnightly
Short stories should focus on the entertainment business, travel or romance.

Femina Magazine
Published by:
Associated Magazines
PO Box 3647, Cape Town, 8000
Tel: +27-21-4623070
Contact: Jane Raphaely, editor
Ed subs: Stories with a human interest
Frequency: Monthly
Aimed at young professionals, the magazine is broad ranging in the subjects it tackles.

Gentle Reader
Published by:
Dragon Patterns cc
55 Cecilia Road, Maroelana, 0081
Tel: +27-12-5423939
Fax: +27-12-5423939
Contact: Lynne Jones
Type: Poetry and creative writing
Ed subs: Poetry, short stories
Frequency: Quarterly
Gentle Reader seeks 'to help South African writers get their work published' and to this end welcomes short stories of varied subject matter and poetry, and offers guidelines for writers.

herStoriA
Published by: herStoriA
PO Box 813, Houghton 2041
Contact: Sandra Brayde, editor
Type: Poetry
Ed subs: Poetry
Frequency: Three times yearly
ISSN: 1024-5057

1st issue: 1995
This new venture in feminist publishing is 'for, by and about women', with the objective of fulfilling a need in South Africa for a literary journal dealing with women's issues. Most contributions are factual, but a number of poems are published.

Imprint
Published by:
Nicholas Combrinck
PO Box 5091, Rivonia, 2128
Contact: Marcia Leveson, editor
Type: Poetry and creative writing
Ed subs: Poetry and creative writing
Frequency: Three issues yearly
Imprint postively encourages new writers to submit work to be published alongside that of more seasoned writers.

New Coin
Published by:
Institute for the Study of English in Africa
Rhodes University
PO Box 94, Grahamstown, 6140
Contact: Robert Berold, editor
Type: Poetry and literary criticism
Ed subs: Poetry
Frequency: Two issues yearly
New Coin will accept poetry from new and established poets alike.

New Contrast
Published by:
New Contrast
PO Box 3841, Cape Town, 8000
Contact: Editor
Type: Poetry, creative writing and literary criticism
Ed subs: Poetry, short stories, reviews and literary articles
Frequency: Two issues yearly
New Contrast recommends that budding poets submit four to six poems

for consideration by the magazine's editorial team.

Sidelines
Published by:
SAQ Publications
PO Box 3461, Parklands, 2121
Tel: +27-11-8808854
Fax: +27-11-8808854
Contact: Denis Beckett, editor
Type: Poetry, creative writing
Ed subs: Poetry, short stories, social/political analysis
Frequency: Quarterly
Sidelines' editors 'want, need, welcome and revel in contributions', will consult with writers while editing articles, and will pay according to the quality of the contribution.

Something Quarterly
Published by:
Something Quarterly
PO Box 66384, Broadway, 2020
Contact: Sven Krinkelhaus, editor
Type: Poetry, creative writing and arts criticism
Ed subs: Poetry, prose, illustrations, music/ literary/ art reviews
Frequency: Quarterly
Something Quarterly will accept a broad range of material (see type of work) although it is emphasised that political poetry is unlikely to be published.

Southern African Review of Books
Published by:
SAROB
c/o Department of History,
University of Cape Town
Private Bag, Rondesbosch, 7700
Tel: +27-21-6502965
Fax: +27-21-6504038
Email: robert.turrell@humboldt.uni-ulm.de
Contact: Robert Turrell, editor

Type: Literary criticism
Ed subs: Book reviews, essays touching on major issues of South Africa
Frequency: Six issues yearly
ISSN: 0952-8040
1st issue: 1987
The magazine concerns itself with the cultural politics of Southern Africa.

Tribute
Published by:
Penta Publications
PO Box 781723, Sandton, 2146
Tel: +27-11-8847344/5/6/7/8
Fax: +27-11-8845503
Contact: S'bu Mngadi, editor
Type: Poetry, creative writing and literary criticism
Ed subs: Poetry and short stories
Frequency: Monthly
Tribute features articles on a range of topics, from high politics to polygamy. It also runs poetry and short story competitions, on a monthly and yearly basis.

Writers World
The South African Word Crafter's Journal
Published by: Options Publishing
PO Box 1588, Somerset West 7129
Fax: +27-21-8512592
Email: optpub@iafrica.com
Contact: Monica Cromhout, editor
Type: Creative writing
Ed subs: Poetry and short stories
Frequency: Twice monthly
ISSN: 1019-8326
1st issue: 1991
This lively magazine for writers aims to keep them informed and provide a writers' network. It includes information opportunities and markets for writers, magazine reviews, details of competitions and awards, poems and stories. Primarily aimed at writers in

South Africa, it will also interest writers throughout the continent.

THE NETHERLANDS

Matutu
Journal for African Culture and Society
Published by:
Rodopi, Keizersgracht 302-304
1016 EX Amsterdam
Tel: +31-20-6380948
Fax: +31-20-6380948
Email: orders.queries@rodopi.ni
Contact: Editorial team
Type: Literary criticism and creative writing
Ed subs: Articles, reports, and book reviews in English, German and French; creative writing in all languages of Africa and the Caribbean
Frequency: Twice yearly
ISSN: 0932-9714
The editors actively encourage young scholars, writers and reviewers to submit work.

UNITED KINGDOM

Africa Now
Published by:
Africa Now
7 Rudolf Place, Miles Street
London, SW8 1RP
Tel: +44-171-7358071
Fax: +44-171-735570
Contact: Peter Enahoro, editor; Ken Amankwah, book review editor
Type: Non-fiction and criticism
Ed subs: Human interest stories, articles on travel, tourism, culture
ISSN: 0261-5908
1st issue: 1981
Will also accept 'witty cartoons'!

African Book Publishing Record
Published by:
Hans Zell Publishers
an imprint of Bowker-Saur
PO Box 56, Oxford, OX1 2SJ
Tel: +44-1865-511428
Fax: +44-1865-311534
Email: hzell@dial.pipex.com
Contact: Hans Zell, Cecile Lomer, editors
Type: Extensive reviews of African literature
Frequency: Quarterly
ISSN: 0306-0332
1st issue: 1975
The ABPR covers in full new African publications, and features articles on the African book trade.

African Literature Today
Published by:
James Currey Publishers
73 Botley Road, Oxford, OX2 0BS
Tel: +44-1865-244111
Fax: +44-1865-246454
Contact: Eldred Durosimi Jones and Marjorie Jones, editors
Ed subs: Articles on all aspects of African literature
Frequency: Annual
ISSN: 0852-5555
1st issue: 1968
A volume tends to focus on one particular aspect of African literature – such as poetry, or women's writing – and contributions must tie in with that volume's topic (announced in advance).

Gender and Development
Published by:
Oxfam GB, PO Box 25, Abingdon,
Oxfordshire, OX14 3UE
Tel: +44-1865-311311
Fax: +44-1865-313925
Email: publish@oxfam.org.uk
Contact: Caroline Sweetman, editor
Type: Criticism

Ed subs: Articles on gender and development.
Frequency: Three issues yearly

HQ Poetry Magazine (The Haiku Quarterly)
Published by:
HQ Poetry Magazine
39 Exmouth Street
Swindon, SN1 3PU
Tel: +44-1793-523927
Contact: Kevin Bailey, editor
Type: Poetry and literary criticism
Ed subs: Experimental and traditional poetry
Frequency: Three to four issues yearly
1st issue: 1990
The HQ publishes poetry from many countries, although a substantial part of the magazine is given over to haiku. Also has review section.

Index on Censorship
Published by:
Writers and Scholars International Ltd,
Lancaster House
33 Islington High Street
London, N1 9LH
Tel: +44-171-2782313
Fax: +44-171-2781878
Email: indexoncenso@gn.apc.org
Contact: Ursula Owen
Type: Creative writing
Ed subs: Material previously banned
Frequency: Ten issues yearly
ISSN: 0306-4220
1st issue: 1972
Index on Censorship 'like[s] to publish the banned material of particular artists', including banned fiction.

Journal of African Cultural Studies
Published by:
Carfax Publishing Limited
PO Box 25, Abingdon
Oxfordshire, OX14 3UE
Tel: +44-1235-401000
Fax: +44-1235-401550
Email: enquiries@carfax.co.uk
Contact: Forouk Topan and Michael Mann, editors
Type: Criticism
Ed subs: Articles on literature and the arts
Frequency: Twice yearly
ISSN: 1369-6815
The Journal focuses on literature, particularly African language literatures, performance, art, music, popular culture and cultural issues.

Journal of Commonwealth Literature
Published by:
Bowker-Saur
Maypole House, Maypole Road
East Grinstead, West Sussex,
RH19 1HU
Tel: +44-1342-330100
Fax: +44-1342-330198
Email: custserv@bowker-saur.co.uk
Contact: John Thieme, Shirley Chew, Alan Bower, editors
Type: Literary criticism
Frequency: Three issues yearly
ISSN: 0021-9894
1st issue: 1965
The Journal contains critical reviews and information about all aspects of Commonwealth literature; annual bibliography of Commonwealth writing.

Journal of Contemporary African Studies
Published by:
Carfax Publishing Limited
PO Box 25, Abingdon
Oxfordshire, OX14 3UE
Tel: +44-1235-401000
Fax: +44-1235-401550
Email: enquiries@carfax.co.uk

Contact: Editorial team
Type: Criticism
Ed subs: Writing in the human sciences
Frequency: Twice yearly
A scholarly approach to change and development in Africa.

Journal of Southern African Studies
Published by:
Carfax Publishing Limited
PO Box 25, Abingdon
Oxfordshire, OX14 3UE
Tel: +44-1235-401000
Fax: +44-1235-401550
Email: sales@carfax.co.uk
Contact: Saul Dubow, Jocelyn Alexander, Debby Potts, editors
Type: Literary criticism
Frequency: Quarterly
ISSN: 0305-7070
1st issue: 1974
Contains articles in the social sciences and humanities.

London Magazine:
A Review of the Arts
Published by:
London Magazine
30 Thurloe Place, London, SW7 2HQ
Tel: +44-171-5890618
Contact: Alan Ross, editor
Type: Poetry, creative writing and arts criticism
Ed subs: Poetry, short stories, features on the arts
Frequency: Six issues yearly
1st issue: 1954
The magazine publishes stories of 2,000-2,500 words as well as poems and articles on all aspects of contemporary culture. Must send an sae.

Outposts Poetry Quarterly
Published by:
Outposts Poetry Quarterly
22 Whitewell Road, Frome

Somerset, BA11 4EL
Tel: +44-1373-466653
Contact: Roland John, editor
Type: Poetry and literary criticism
Ed subs: Poetry and critical articles on poets
Frequency: Quarterly
1st issue: 1943
The magazine, as its title suggests, publishes poetry and pieces on poets and their work.

Springboard
Published by:
Springboard
30 Orange Hill Road, Prestwich
Manchester, M25 1LS
Tel: +44-161-7735911
Email: leobrooks@compuserve.com
Contact: Leo Brooks, editor
Type: Poetry, creative writing
Ed subs: Poetry, short stories, articles on writing
Frequency: Quarterly
1st issue: 1990
Springboard runs poetry and short story competitions, and includes helpful articles on writing.

Stand Magazine
Published by: Stand Magazine
179 Wingrove Road
Newcastle upon Tyne, NE4 9DA
Tel: +44-191-2733280
Contact: Lorna Tracy, Rodney Pybus, Peter Bennet, editors
Type: Poetry, creative writing and literary criticism
Ed subs: Poetry and short stories
Frequency: Quarterly
1st issue: 1952
Stand holds a short story competition, for an unpublished short story in English, every two years, and a poetry competition in the interim years.

The Voice
Published by:
The Voice
370 Coldharbour Lane
London, SW9 8PL
Tel: +44-171-7377377
Fax: +44-171-2748994
Email: veeteeay@gn.apc.org
Contact: Annie Stewart, editor
Type: Criticism
Ed subs: General and arts features
Frequency: Weekly
1st issue: 1982
The Voice publishes articles aimed at a black readership.

The Weekly Journal
Published by:
Positive Time and Space Ltd
36 Skylines, London, E14 9TS
Tel: +44-171-5373222
Fax: +44-171-5372288
Contact: Barbara Campbell, editor
Type: Literary criticism
Ed subs: Articles on the arts, society and business
Frequency: Weekly
1st issue: 1992
The journal is published with an African Caribbean readership in mind.

Wasafiri
Published by:
University of London
Queen Mary and Westfield College,
English Department
Mile End Road, London E1 4NS
Tel: +44-171-7753120
Email: wasafiri@qmw.ac.uk
Contact: Susheila Nasta, editor
Type: Poetry, creative writing and literary criticism
Ed subs: Poetry, short stories and reviews
Frequency: Twice yearly
1st issue: 1984

Writers of short stories or essays on literature/ film, and poets, are asked to submit MSS in duplicate, with an sae.

Orbis
Published by:
Orbis
27 Valley View, Primrose, Jarrow
Tyne and Wear, NE32 5QT
Tel: +44-191-4897055
Fax: +44-191-4301297
Email:
mikeshields@compuserve.com
Contact: Mike Shields, editor
Type: Poetry, creative writing and literary criticism
Ed subs: Poetry, short stories, reviews
Frequency: Quarterly
1st issue: 1968
Orbis runs an annual competition for rhymed poetry; will accept short stories of up to 1,000 words, and reviews. Writers are asked to submit work by post only.

USA

Callalloo
Published by:
Department of English
University of Virginia
Charlottesville, VA 22903
Tel: +1-804-9246637
Fax: +1-804-9241478
Email: callalloo@virginia.edu
Contact: Charles H Rowell, editor
Type: Poetry, creative writing and arts criticism
Ed subs: Poetry, short stories and articles on the arts
Frequency: Quarterly
1st issue: 1976
The journal specialises in African American literature, art and culture.

Transition
Published by:
Oxford University Press
2001 Evans Road,
Cary, NC 27513
Tel: +1-919-6770977
Fax: +1-919-6771714
Contact: Kwame Anthony Appiah
and Henry Louis Gates Jr, editors
Type: Arts criticism
Ed subs: Arts reviews
Frequency: Quarterly
ISSN: 0041-1191
1st issue: 1991
Transition's emphasis is on African
and African American concerns.

World Literature Today
Published by:
The University of Oklahoma Press
110 Monnet Hall
University of Oklahoma
Norman, OK 73069
Tel: +1-405-3254531
Fax: +1-405-3257495
Contact: William Riggan, editor
Type: Literary criticism
Ed subs: Literary reviews
Frequency: Quarterly
1st issue: 1927 (then Books Abroad)
The editors welcome 'articles on con-
temporary writers and literary move-
ments in any geographic region or
language area'. Their aim is to
improve international understanding
by the dissemination of world litera-
ture to a broad readership.

ZIMBABWE

African Publishing Review
Published by
African Publishers Network
PO Box 3773, Harare
Tel: +263-4-705105/726405
Fax: +263-4-705106

Email: apnet@internet.co.zw
Contact: Gillian Nyambura
Type: Reviews of African literature
Frequency: Six issues yearly
ISSN: 1019-5823
1st issue: 1992
African Publishing Review is concerned
with the book-publishing industry in
Africa, and seeks to promote intra-
Africa trade and co-operation. Invaluble
for anyone interested in African books.

Horizon
Published by:
Column Width (Pvt.) Ltd
PO Box UA65, Harare
Contact: Andrew Moyse, editor
Ed subs: Short stories, the arts, music,
and political analysis included.
Frequency: Weekly [?]
1st issue: Sept 91

Moto Magazine
Published by:
Moto Magazine
Gweru Diocese, PO Box 890, Gweru
Tel: +263-54-4886
Fax: +263-54-51991
Contact: Donatus Bonde, editor
Type: Arts criticism
Ed subs: Articles on music and sports,
as well as political analysis and factual
reports
Frequency: Monthly
1st issue: 1959
Contributors to Moto Magazine
include both freelance writers and
professional journalists.

Nomdlalo Township Theatre News
Published by:
Amakhosi Theatre Productions
PO Box 7030, Mzilikazi, Bulawayo
Tel: +263-9-79379
Fax: +263-9-76673
Contact: Godfrey Moyo, editor
Type: Arts criticism

Frequency: Quarterly
1st issue: 1991
The magazine treats of the arts in southern Africa. It counts university lecturers amongst its contributors.

Safere
Southern African Feminist Review
Published by:
Southern African Regional Institute for Policy Studies
Box MP 111,
Mount Pleasant, Harare
Contact: Particia McFadden
Type: Feminist issue and poetry
Ed subs: Poetry
Frequency: Twice yearly
1st issue: 1995
This is a bi-annual review produced by the Black Feminist Collective, aiming to reflect 'our ideals as women and particularly as Black women'. Most contributions are factual, but a selection of poems is published.

TsoTso
A Magazine of New Writing in Zimbabwe
Published by:
TsoTso Magazine

Box A53, Avondale, Harare
Contact: Editorial team
Type: Poetry and creative writing
Ed subs: Poetry and short stories in English, Shona and Ndebele
Frequency: Two to three issues a year
1st issue: 1989
The magazine provides a forum for both new and established Zimbabwean writers and poets.

Zimbabwe Women Writing
Published by:
Zimbabwe Women Writers
78 Kaguvi Street, Harare
Tel:+263-4-751202
Fax: +263-4-751202
Contact: Editorial team
Type: Creative writing
Ed subs: Poetry and fiction
Frequency: Quarterly
1st issue: 1993
This is the newsletter of the Zimbabwe Women Writers (ZWW) group, and includes reports on the activities of ZWW. It also aims to provide a platform for the country's aspiring women writers, publishing creative writing.

Vanity Publishers

The *Church Times* (London) regularly carries advertisements from enterprises indicating that they are seeking typescripts from authors who have had difficulty finding publishers. On the same page, the above warning is printed. Presumably the editors have taken action after receiving complaints. Indeed the situation is so serious that the British Standards Authority has investigated the advertisements of various vanity publishers, and have condemned a number of their practices. Authors should acquaint themselves with the way vanity publishers operate and exercise caution; by the same token, *bona fide* publishers should always be honest and open about the sinister, exploitative dimension to their industry. Briefly, vanity publishers encourage writers to send them manuscripts which they offer to publish – on condition that authors bear a substantial proportion of the expense involved. Flattered by the possibility of seeing their work in book form, authors enter into contacts that do not, in fact, offer them a realistic chance of seeing their work promoted adequately. In reality vanity publishers are little more than printers and binders. They are in no position to market books effectively, indeed their name usually ensures that titles are not even considered for review.

The warning on the situation in Nigeria during the early 1980s sounded by Tokunbo Gbadebo should be heeded. He wrote:

There is one group of people whom new authors should beware of. These are the self-styled 'publishers', the 'contractors' of the book world in Nigeria who offer to publish manuscripts for authors themselves. Young authors are not the only victims of these charlatans. I have met one eminent gentleman, a Reader and Acting Head of Department in one of our Universities who has fallen prey to one of these smart young men with a fair knowledge of the printing trade whose offices, for the most part, consist of their shiny brief-cases. Their services, into which the unsuspecting author may well be investing his lifetime's savings, often do not extend to the distribution of their products and many an inexperienced author has lost both his investment and a great deal of self confidence in his dealings with them. (Gbadebo in Bello and Augi 1993, 152)

The key here is 'investing his lifetime's savings' which indicates that a major investment in the costs connected with publication was expected. In the course of preparing material for this Handbook, one of the editors, James Gibbs, was contacted by a Nigerian acquaintance who enclosed a letter she had received from an impressive-sounding 'Press' in London. The Chief Executive of the company wrote in glowing terms of a manuscript he had received: it 'gives a most interesting insight into the organisation of the ... service in Nigeria'. He went on to express agreement that 'this is something people need to know about in order to realise what is wrong'. And to assure the author that her book, if published, would be of extreme benefit. It would, he said help those people 'seeking to improve the system'.

The more unpleasant details come with an ingratiating smile in the second paragraph:

We are happy to publish your book on our standard subsidy and royalties scheme. The subsidy required is £2,400 payable:
1. £600 on signing the contract
2. £600 on approving the editing
3. £600 on approving the typesetting
4. £600 when the work is completed.

After observations on the cover ('semi-stiff laminated'), the Chief Executive spelt out the terms:

Royalties are very generous and so geared as to enable the author to recover the subsidy as rapidly as possible. 30 per cent goes to the author until the entire subsidy is recovered and thereafter 20 per cent which represents the profit element. In addition 50 per cent of all contracts negotiated regarding TV, film, translations, radio etc., rights.

This should be read with extreme scepticism and an awareness that, although 30 per cent looks very attractive the 'standard subsidy and royalty scheme' is entirely in favour of the publisher. Indeed, the whole operation appears totally unscrupulous: no indication is given of the number of books that will be printed for £2,400; the publisher does not risk any of 'his' capital, and the 'catch' is partly that the Vanity Publisher will not incur any expenses in promoting the book. 'He' is acting as a rather expensive printer/binder. The covering letter from my friend concluded: 'I shall appreciate an immediate attention and compliance please. Best regards.'

Far from complying, I recommended my correspondent should consider publishing options in Nigeria.

It is worth pointing out incidentally, that the primary prey of outfits such as the grandly-titled 'Press' are naïve British citizens with a typescript they desperately want to see within hard, or 'semi-stiff laminated', covers. Broadly speaking, authors should not expect to contribute financially to the publication of their books. If they wish to, if having put time and effort into writing a book they want to make some copies of it to give to friends or to sell, that is another matter. The issues involved with that kind of 'self-publishing' are considered below.

In special circumstances authors may want to do more: to approach a publisher with what amounts to a subsidy arrangement. In some cases this entails making use of a publisher (paying him or her) to obtain an International Standard Book Number (ISBN), to provide some editorial input (all texts benefit from checking in draft and proof) and to arrange for printing and binding.

Authors should embark on this project aware that for all the talk of 'ISBNs' and 'Deposit Libraries', it is easy to take on a 'self-publishing venture'. For example, obtaining an ISBN and sending copies to institutions of record can be done without outside expertise. You can ask a publisher in your country whom to contact to request an ISBN. Your National Library or, if it exists, National Book Development Council are often responsible for allocating ISBNs. You should write giving basic details of your book and, if appropriate, you will receive an ISBN by return. Alternatively, you can contact the International Book Numbering Agency Berlin, Staatsbibliotheck 24, Preussischer Kulturbesitz, B1C772, Berlin, Germany for details of the ISBN agency in your country. Other matters, including editorial input and, particularly, distribution, require hard work and considerable expertise. This expertise should be concentrated in publishers' offices, but it can be found outside as well!

Recently the harsh realities of publishing life in Africa have blurred conventional distinctions between 'normal' and 'vanity' publishers. It is not uncommon to hear publishers itemise the support given to them to bring out, say, a well-illustrated history of a West African commercial enterprise; or learn that it had only been possible to publish a certain academic title because there had been a subsidy. In these instances, the parties involved knew exactly what sort of 'deal' they were involved in. Readers and Writers Be Aware.

Windfall Profits

Reports in the European and US press savouring the 'rags to riches' stories of débutante authors can give a totally misleading impression of what authors should routinely expect in terms of income from writing.

Father Christmas and the Missing Reindeers, a mere 5,000 words long, had been accepted by HarperCollins and the firm had made an offer of:

> an undisclosed sum to buy 'the concept' and publishing rights for Sundquist's second project, a series of children's books about a family called *The Giggles* ... Sundquist hopes to give the Walt Disney treatment to both projects ... Nicholas Kennedy, his literary agent, is cautious about disclosing the rewards.

Items such as this occupy space in newspapers, not surprisingly since a vitally important part of the function of the large advance is to make news. Other motives include the desire to add a famous person (model, sportsperson, politician ...) to a publisher's list – even though their contribution to the loudly publicised novel may be minimal – or an urge to add to the prestige of a publishing house by outbidding others for the right to work with a literary luminary. The effect is to create totally unrealistic expectations in less established writers, toiling away at their craft and producing work that is repeatedly rejected.

When offered, advances are usually modest – and are just that: an advance; a down payment against anticipated sales to be paid off from income. The Society of Authors 1997 survey indicated that of the 1,186 authors who responded, 47 received no advance at all; 272 received between £1 and £999; 459 received between £1,000 and £4,999; 144 between £5,000 and £9,999; 128 between £10,000 and £24,999, and 73 over £25,000. Among those at the bottom of the scale were academic authors who were included in the poll (Legat 1997). It seems likely that advances in relation to African publishing are generally very near the bottom end of this scale.

In *A Smattering of Monsters* (Warner Books, 1997), George Green-field, a literary agent who acted for many distinguished writers working in the UK, wrote:

> My guess, based on over 30 years of direct experience ... is that there are perhaps 300 British-born novelists who regularly earn more than £50,000 before tax ... Most authors earn less per hour than an office cleaner.

This provides the very general context for an exchange that was reproduced from Flora Veit-Wild's authoritative book on the life and work of Dambudzo Marechera. It includes a letter from the feisty Zimbabwean writer to the long-suffering James Currey, then Editorial Director at Heinemann, that read in part:

> ...[My fiancée] thinks that I can persuade you to give me another advance on the book. She read in an obscenely scandalous Sunday paper about unknowns who suddenly become instant bestsellers and were paid astounding amounts by unscrupulous USA and Australian publishers. I have not been able to convince her that Mayfair [Heinemann Educational Books] is not exactly that generous to people like me. But there is nothing I can do but ask you for a sizeable amount of money to marry her. ... I think my hangover is loosening now because I can actually see what I am writing. And I don't like it. I suppose long begging letters are an occupational hazard for writers who end up in prison. Anyhow, I have the manuscript now. (This is actually the second time I have lost it.) I will look it over as speedily as possible. I really think there is no reason why you should not pay me another advance. ... I am happy to be out of that Dickensian prison and now that the book will actually be printed and bound and my marriage is itching so much that I can only scratch it with Pound notes I am asking for another advance I do not honestly see, however impossible it may be, any concrete reason why I should not ask you for a further advance ...

To this Currey replied:

... Please rush your manuscript back to me before something else happens to you ... Please disillusion your fiancée ... I repeat that you can only make a living [out] of writing, unless you hit the jackpot, by regular work in reviewing, writing articles, TV scripts, etc. Book publication brings only a small amount of money. I cannot get a further advance for you. (Veit-Wild 1992, 196-99)

Comment is superfluous, but it should be said that the 'Example of Marechera' repays examination in many contexts.

Self-publishing

Those writers contemplating publishing their own works need to advance with care and planning. (Cromhout 1996, 13)

During the Zimbabwe International Book Fair in 1996, a Writers' Workshop addressed the issues of self-publishing and relations with publishers. It was apparent that those involved in publishing their own works were encountering both success and failure, learning as they went along. In her article on the Workshop in the *African Publishing Review*, Monica Cromhout summed up this aspect of the discussion by writing the caveat above. Irritation with publishers and enthusiasm are widespread, but these are no substitutes for 'care and planning'.

There seems to have been a general feeling that the meeting with publishers provided an opportunity to 'reduce the many misunderstandings that develop between these two interdependent groups ...' Cromhout suggested that 'such meetings should be repeated often' thereby reinforcing Walter Bgoya's sentiments quoted in Part 1 of this Handbook and part of the justification for it.

However, bringing writers and publishers together is far from simple. The Ghana International Book Fair in Accra in November 1996 was remarkable for the lack of contact between the representatives of the groups present in the Ghanaian capital. Sadly, while African publishers met at the SSNIT Guest House for a series of discussions, the Pan African Writers Association (PAWA) hosted a lively series of events at their base, PAWA House. Book Fairs would seem to be obvious occasions at which all those involved with books and the book trade can come together, but clearly organisation and goodwill are required to bridge gaps.

How to Publish Your Own Book

Michael Norton

Self-publishing: Is it an Option?

Many people are confused about what a publisher actually does. It's not just printing the book. That's done by a printer. And it's more than just having lunches with authors! The publisher organises the process that links the author (who has something to say) with the reader (who is interested in hearing about it). It may involve coming up with the idea for a book. It often involves working with the author to agree a treatment for the subject and a synopsis of what the book might contain. It involves deciding on the format and length of the book. It involves taking the author's manuscript through to the artwork from which the book will be printed (including the editing, design and illustration processes). It involves agreeing a title and getting a design for the cover. It involves deciding the quality of paper that the book will be printed on. It involves paying for the printing and receiving copies of the book into a warehouse. It involves marketing the book and arranging its distribution. And it involves keeping accounts and ensuring that costs are more than recovered from sales or any subsidy that has been raised towards publication.

There is no magic in any of this, but the experience and technical competence of the publisher will help ensure that the best decisions are made at each stage of the process. The distribution mechanism and the reputation that the publisher has built up will also contribute to the success of the book – ensuring that it is displayed in the right bookshops, sold to libraries, and reviewed in all the best newspapers and journals.

Most authors will want to find a publisher to publish their book. But this is not always possible, and it may not even be the best option. For example:

- There may be times when the publisher cannot market and sell a book successfully. For example, when the market is exceptionally specialist, where the usual marketing methods and bookshop distribution will not reach the intended readership. Or where the publisher only has experience of distributing books in English, and the title is in an indigenous language.

- The publisher may wish to impose unacceptable conditions on the author – regarding length or content, the format or price, or how the book is to be promoted. The author may prefer to have a greater say in how the book is published. Many fiction publishers, for example, try to limit the size of a novel to 128 or 160 or 192 pages for cost reasons, but the author might want to write a longer book. Some publishers are nervous about publishing books that are too critical of a political regime.

- The author may simply find that no publisher is interested in publishing their book – although the author remains convinced that the book is, in fact, worth publishing and people will want to read it.

In these circumstances, the author has two further options for getting the book published:

- To have the book published by a 'Vanity Publisher', who charges the author for undertaking all the publishing functions, and then will charge again to supply copies of the printed book to the author. There is usually no guarantee that the vanity publisher actually will, in reality, sell any copies of the book, and many don't put much effort into doing so. The economics of Vanity Publishing mean that the publisher will make a profit even if no books are sold. But at least the author will have the book in print (albeit at a price), and may find ways of selling or giving away copies.

- To 'Self-Publish' the book. Here the author undertakes all the publishing functions, perhaps finding an editor and designer to help. At the end of the process, the author will have to pay the cost of having the book printed, will own all the stock and will be responsible for selling it. The self-publisher will receive the proceeds of any sales, and if the book can be sold successfully will be able to recover the initial investment and even make a profit.

In this article I hope to show that self-publishing can be a practicable option for any author to consider, and suggest how the author might approach the idea of becoming a self-publisher.

Self-publishing: My Own Experience

There were several points of departure leading to my own involvement in self-publishing. In the mid-1970s, I stumbled across a book called

The Publish-It-Yourself Handbook: Literary Tradition and How To
(1973, Pushcart Press), which was an inspirational introduction to the
idea of self-publishing. It is surprising how many well-known books
and authors have taken the self-publishing route. *Huckleberry Finn* by
Mark Twain, and *The Jungle* by Upton Sinclair were both self-
published. The popular novels of Catherine Cookson, the best-selling
writer in Britain in the 1990s were also self-published. *Common Sense*
by Tom Paine which fuelled both the American and the French
revolutions was also self-published. And a great deal of poetry has been
published privately or through small presses. Then there are Non-
Governmental Organisations (NGOs), societies and institutions who
have something to say, and often a 'captive market' of members or
donors to market their publications to; and many have been extremely
successful in developing publications programmes which by-pass the
use of a traditional publisher.

The *Publish-It-Yourself Handbook* gave me the idea of publishing
my own publications. At the time (in 1975), I was interested in
communication and community action. I published in quick succession through an NGO I had recently launched *The Community
Newspaper Kit, The Slide Tape Kit* and *The Mural Kit.* Each had a
print run of 1,000, paid for out of my own savings. The first of the
three, *The Community Newspaper Kit* was given a quarter-page review
in the *Times Educational Supplement. The Mural Kit* was launched at
a lecture/presentation which was accompanied by a feature in one of
the leading daily newspapers, and this led to coverage on two
television magazine programmes. I also produced a small catalogue
which I sent to some 1,000 NGOs culled from directories. Within two
years, I had sold out and reprinted *The Community Newspaper Kit,*
which eventually went into four editions, and recovered all the costs of
the other two publications.

I went on to publish fundraising advice written up from seminars
and workshops I organised. The first four practical fundraising
handbooks were published simultaneously. Just before publication, I
found to my horror that I did not have enough cash in the bank to
pay the printing bill. So I quickly prepared a leaflet which was
included in the monthly bulletin circulated by the leading network
of NGOs in England (the National Council of Voluntary Organisations). This 'hit the spot'. It generated over 300 sales of each of the
four titles, which was more than sufficient to pay the printer.

The organisation I founded, called 'Directory of Social Change'
(DSC), went on to become the leading provider of information,
training and support to the NGO sector in the UK. The secret of
our success, I think, has been the following:

- Producing information that NGOs need or want, particularly about grants information.

- Developing a range of titles for this readership that can be marketed together by direct mail and through the conferences and events that DSC organises.

- Developing mail-order selling so that DSC became the best mechanism for reaching this specialist market. Our mailing is now 12,000 NGOs

- Sensible pricing. Our publications are not expensive compared with commercially published equivalents, but they are realistically priced to generate an income to pay for the research and development of the publications and all the organisational overheads.

In 1995 I left DSC when it had a publishing turnover of £750,000 per annum, with around 20 new titles per annum. Since then I have gone on to found 'Books for Change' (BfC) in India, using a similar formula. Eighteen months after it was set up, BfC is publishing 24 titles per annum and successfully distributing 1,000 titles on behalf of other NGOs to an NGO audience.

My other experience of self-publishing was at the Zimbabwe International Book Fair in 1996. I had been asked by the Zimbabwe Book Development Trust (ZBDT) to co-organise the workshops that accompany the Fair. We chose as the theme 'Bringing books to people'. Topics included 'Local language publishing', 'Village libraries', 'Publishing for a rural audience' and 'Self-publishing' To draw attention to the underlying themes of the workshop series, we decided to translate and publish in Shona (in an edition of just 100 copies) a documentary cartoon book called *Toni Morrison for Beginners*. ZBDT arranged for the translation, the designer at Writers & Readers, the US publisher that produced the original English edition, replaced the English with the newly translated Shona text; and we produced the 100 copies on a photocopier to sell at a price of Zim$50 per copy. We sold copies to people at the workshop and launched the 'instant book' at a reading at Highfields Township, Harare. This book was one of only a very few Shona publications published that year in Zimbabwe.

I strongly believe that in the African context self-publishing has an important role to play. Publishing in indigenous languages, publishing classroom material for schools that reflects local culture and circumstances, publishing guidebooks for tourists that are less formal and more idiosyncratic than the *Lonely Planet* and *Rough Guides*, publishing material from women writers' workshops, documentation of NGO experience in development (from an African perspective), and many other ideas could all be considered.

With the enthusiasm of the author behind the marketing effort, with 'niche markets' that can be identified and reached relatively easily, with populations hungry for knowledge and information – but few of whom have access to or ever go near a traditional bookshop – I don't see how self-publishing can fail, if the book itself is something that people will want to read.

Self-publishing: In Practice

You should note the following points when considering the self-publishing option:

- Publishing is not always best done by publishers. Your book may have a specialist market which traditional publishing does not reach. You may create your own marketing and distribution opportunities through your work (for example, an environmental campaigner will meet many people interested in reading about environmental issues at conferences, seminars, talks and meetings). Recognising that you could consider publishing your own book is a first important step you need to take.

- In another scenario, you may not be able to find a publisher to take on your book. Publishers receive many more manuscripts than they can actually publish. They have to make difficult choices; and sometimes they make the wrong choices. Just because they turn you down, it doesn't mean that your manuscript is unpublishable. Many people put a great deal of effort into trying to find a publisher, becoming more and more depressed when they fail to do so (either before they have sat down to write the book, or after the manuscript has been completed). If you have boundless energy and enthusiasm, you could direct this same energy towards successful self-publication. Remember that some of the world's best books have been self-published.

On the other hand:

- A publisher brings credibility to your publication. Their reputation and standing, the other books they publish bring credit to bear on your publication. What writer would turn down the opportunity to be published in the Heinemann African Writers Series alongside Chinua Achebe and Wole Soyinka?

- Traditional publishers have developed good access to bookshops, schools, libraries and campus outlets. If you publish the work yourself, you will have to develop these for yourself, unless you are able to tie up a distribution relationship.

What You Need

Any personal computer with a Desk Top Publishing (DTP) programme (such as Pagemaker or Freehand) linked to a reasonable quality laser printer can produce typeset pages ready for publication. This has made it far simpler and cheaper for an author to publish a book. But you will need the following, if you are to succeed:

- Boundless **energy and enthusiasm**. You have to write the book as well as sell it. You also need a measure of **self-confidence**. You will be responsible for the success of the venture, and not just for getting glowing reviews.

- **Money** to pay for the printing and promotion. It is possible to defray costs through advance orders. But the printing bill has to be paid. One self-publisher I know mortgaged his house to pay the printing bill, but ended up making a fortune on his best-selling guidebook to France.

- A **friendly editor**. It is hard for any author to be objective about his or her own book. Asking an experienced outsider to comment on your manuscript and to proof-read the text will be helpful. Someone who works in publishing or a journalist may be prepared to help you, and they will often do this for free.

- A knowledge of **typesetting and book design**. This is important. Your book has to compete with others for attention. It should look good. It should also be produced in an economic format.

- A **name** for your 'publishing house'! The first book you publish may be the first of many.

- A **friendly printer** who will help you produce the type of book you want. Look at the quality of books they are producing for other publishers, and the paper they are using. It is quite a good idea to go into a bookshop and pick up a book you like, which you can use as a model for your book.

- **Storage space** for when the boxes of printed books arrive, glaring at you waiting to be sold.

- A commitment to **promotion and selling**. The book will stay in your entrance hall unless you do something to sell it.

At this stage you will also need to do **a rough budget**, as you need to know the financial commitment that is involved. The biggest costs are the printer's bill including paper and the cost of any freelance editorial or design assistance. There will also be the costs of promotion, which might include printing a small leaflet to publicise the book, mailing and insert costs for getting the leaflet distributed, and possibly the cost of a modest launch party.

You will also need to budget for expected revenue. This is more difficult, as you will have had no experience of selling books. So you will have to guess. But remember:

- Books given away (whether as gifts or review copies) generate no income at all.

- Booksellers require a discount, which covers the cost of their selling it. The level of discount varies from country to country; but allow around a third of the cover price.

- You will not actually receive all the money from the books you have sold. Some cheques you receive may 'bounce'; some booksellers or libraries may 'forget' to pay.

- Unsold copies generate no income. They just stare at you! Think creatively about what to do to get rid of them. You should be able to do better than selling the waste paper for fuel!

As a general rule, you should 'mark up' the cost of producing the book a minimum of three times to allow for the costs of promotion and distribution. This gives you some idea of the level of price you will need to sell the book at. But you also need to work back from the size and type of book and the regular bookshop selling price for such a book. Making money may not be your objective in publishing the book (you may even be prepared to subsidise the costs out of your own savings). But you will usually want to get enough back to cover the outlay, more or less.

An important issue to consider is that the more copies you produce, the cheaper the cost of the book per copy – and so the cheaper you can make the selling price. But on the other hand, the more copies you produce, the bigger the printing bill will be, and the more copies you will have to sell. It is probably best not to be too ambitious; an initial print run of 1,000 is probably about right in most cases.

Writing the Book

The writing process for a self-publisher is very similar to writing for a traditional publisher – except that you are on your own. This means that you need to think through particularly carefully all the issues around the 'concept' of the book. Why is it being published? Who for? And so on. See the *Checklist for Success* (page 288).

You will not enjoy the partnership that develops between editor and writer, and you will probably want to find someone to read through what has been written and comment on it. The tendency of most authors is to be too protective of what they have written or too stubborn to admit that it's not perfect, and an outside viewpoint can be extremely useful. Find a friend who likes books or has some publishing, editorial or journalistic experience to read through and comment on your first draft manuscript. And take good note of their comments.

At this stage, circulate the manuscript to prominent people and literary figures to try to elicit their comments. If they speak positively about what you have written, ask if you can use their comments on the back cover or in your publicity. Their endorsement will help sell your book. You could even think of asking an eminent figure to write a preface or introduction to the book (the appropriateness of doing this depends on the type of book you are publishing).

Going into Print

The self-publisher will be responsible for doing everything from basic page design, cover design, illustrations, to typesetting and finding a printer. You might want to use a freelance designer to help you with this. But if you are familiar with book design and have some DTP experience, you can do all or most of this yourself.

A key issue is cost. If you are publishing yourself, you will certainly want to keep your costs to a minimum. This can be done in two distinct ways:

- **Cost effective design** – everything from format, sensible page layout and type size, use or non-use of colour. The design needs to be cost-effective, but it also has to be effective. It has to highlight the quality of what is written and be read easily. Just because you self-publish, doesn't mean that you can't publish a nice-looking book!

- **Finding a cheap printer**. Paper and printing are going to be the largest items of cost. So you need to find a printer who will do a good job for you at a reasonable price. Prices can vary considerably between printer and printer, so the usual advice is to obtain a number of quotations (at least three normally). You should set out the following in your request for an estimate:

  1 Format.
  2 Print run.
  3 Number of pages (extent of the book), which is usually a multiple of 16.

   4 Whether printed in one or more than one colour. The more
      colours, the greater the expense!
   5 Number of line illustrations and photographs (halftones).
      The printer may charge extra for these.
   6 Paper quality (get samples from the printer). You need
      reasonably good-quality paper where the text printed on the
      back does not 'show through'.
   7 Binding (hardback or softback; stitched or perfect bound).
   8 The cover (how many colours it is to be printed in –
      two-colour will usually be quite sufficient – the quality of
      the card, and whether it is to be laminated, that is coated
      with a film of plastic).
   9 Delivery, destination (this is usually to one address).
 10 When required (much will depend on how busy the
      printer is, the availability of paper stocks, and so on).

The printer will reply to your enquiry with an estimate. Compare
prices, and note differences in quality or terms. You might also want
to try to find a printer who is prepared to give you extended credit for
all or a part of the print price.

Marketing and Distribution

Marketing and distributing the book once it is printed are crucial. As a
self-publisher, you need to do everything you can to make sure that
your book is distributed, and that you get paid for any copies that are
sold. Here are some ideas:

- **Visit bookshops** in person and try to persuade them to take copies
  of your book. Offer them on 'sale or return'. This means that you
  will need to check later on whether the copies have actually been
  sold. Encourage the bookseller to display the book in a good
  position in the bookshop – and in the window. Explain the value of
  the book, the intended readership, and the publicity you hope to
  get. You will need an ISBN if you are to get your book listed in
  bibliographies of books in print. Contact the ISBN agency in your
  country for details (see page 210 for more information).

- Get as much **press and media coverage** as you can. You can send
  out review copies. Is there a story around the publication or
  yourself as author which can be developed into a feature article?
  Try to develop friendly relationships with one or two journalists,
  and encourage them to give you a write-up. Try to ensure that any
  article that is written ends with publication details, including price
  and where it can be obtained.

- Are there **specialist magazines and journals** which would be interested? For example, if it is educational material, there will be teachers' journals which might be interested in reviewing it. Make a list of all possible newspapers, magazines and journals, and then send them a review copy with a press release which highlights the key points about the publication (this makes it easier for them to write something complimentary – you have done it for them!). For smaller publications, you need only send an information sheet and press release with an offer to supply a review copy. Review copies cost money. However, without publicity, nobody will know of your publication.

- Produce **a simple leaflet with an order form**, and circulate this widely to audiences which are your target readership. Getting hold of the right circulation lists is important: these include membership lists of membership organisations, journal subscribers, and so on.

- Go to **conferences, fairs, workshops** which are relevant to the topic of the book, and ask to be given a stall to sell it from. And selling means looking people in the eye, engaging them in conversation, and telling them what a wonderful book you have produced. You really want them to read it!

- Organise **readings** at universities, in community centres, on radio, in the street ... And take along copies of books to sell – then and there – and plenty of publicity leaflets.

- Then there are **your friends**. Some might buy it; some might be given it as a gift.

Reviewing the Experience

The big question for any self-publisher to ask is was it worth it? What did you achieve? Did it make any sort of financial success? Try to set yourself some sensible objectives at the outset:

- Number of copies distributed.

- Number of copies actually sold (which may be different).

- Whether you recouped your financial outlay.

- The publicity obtained (including press coverage and reviews).

- Serialisation or reprinting in other media.

- Unsolicited letters of praise.

And above all did you enjoy it? Would you do it again? Self-publishing can be a lot of fun. It can bring the writer more directly into contact with the reader. It can give the writer a much greater sense of commitment and enthusiasm for the book. It can take you to places you wouldn't normally go. It can give a greater feeling of satisfaction at the end of the day when the print run has sold out.

And some self-publishers have gone on to become successful publishers in their own right.

A Final Story

Some years ago I wrote and co-published an environmental colouring book for children for use in schools. I thought that this might also be of interest to a wider audience and be sold through bookshops, so I decided to see whether any bookshops might be interested in taking copies. I went first to my local bookshop. 'Not our sort of book', they said. 'No, thank you'. I had a similar experience at the next three bookshops I visited. I really was beginning to feel that nobody was interested in selling the book. But I decided to go to one more bookshop before finally giving up. It was just as well that I did. 'That's just the book we've been looking for. We'll take 70 copies for our Christmas table ... And what's the next title in the series, as we'd also be interested in that?' I felt elated. Your self-published book might be the next bestseller!

CHECKLIST FOR SUCCESS

Stage 1: The Idea

At this stage the publisher discusses the idea with the author. With no publisher to talk to, the self-publisher will need to resolve the following points.

Critical Issues
- Who is the book being published for?
- Is it possible to reach these people easily, and will they be interested in a publication?
- Is the printed book the most appropriate medium? Or could you use the Internet, for example?
- Will they want to read what you want to say?
- What is the best language to use?
- What is the proposed scope and tone of the publication?
- What is the proposed format and extent of the publication? And what will this mean regarding selling price? And will the price be appropriate for the market?
- Will there be illustrations? Drawings or photographs?

- Is the content and tone appropriate for the intended readership?

Skills of the Author
- Knowledge of your subject and an interest in it.
- A judgment on what is needed.
- A judgment of the amount of work involved and the time available to do it.

What is Needed?
- A clear statement of the scope and purpose of the proposed work, and the language that it is to be written in.
- An indication of the level, style and tone that should be used, and the length of the book (how many words?).
- A preliminary table of contents.
- Perhaps a sample chapter (to show yourself that you can write, or to show to others for comment).

Key Question
- So what? What would be the difference if you decided not to proceed? Too many books are already being published that really shouldn't be published at all. Perhaps a book is the wrong medium. Or there is either no real reason or no real market for the publication.

Stage 2: Producing the First Draft Manuscript
At this stage, the author produces a first draft manuscript. It is important to get something written down, as it then becomes a simpler task to improve this and bring it up to publishable standard.

Critical Issues and Questions for the Author to Ask
- Can you write clearly and consistently on the specific subject?
- Do you have all the facts, and will what you write be accurate and up to date?
- Can you complete this stage on time?
- Are the photographs (if there are to be any) of publishable quality?
- Have you commissioned an illustrator (if there are to be diagrams or illustrations)?

Skills Required (Author)
- Writing skills.
- Research ability to seek out and find the facts you need.
- Ability to commission and receive contributions from other people in the required form and on time.
- Ability to review what has been written to ensure it meets the criteria that have been set for the publication.

What is Needed?
- A first draft manuscript produced on disk to the specification you have set out (and on time).

Key Problems
- As the author, you do not produce. You make excuses for the delay, and you promise yourself a new completion date – which in turn you do not meet. The discipline of completing the job on schedule is important. And what you write should bear some relation to your original concept for the book.
- The first draft manuscript is far too long. Or far too short. Or it is out of balance, with some sections far too long and others far too short.

Stage 3: Editing and Design

During this stage the book should be read by someone acting as editor. For a technical book, expert opinion might be sought. It may be a good idea to give the book to two 'specialists' whose judgement you trust. Revisions are made to the original manuscript, which is then sent to a designer who will typeset the pages ready for production.

Critical Issues
- Can the first draft manuscript be improved, without the text having to be completely rewritten?
- What is the most appropriate format for the book?
- What is the most appropriate page design?
- How will the book be titled?
- How many colours will be used for (a) the text and (b) the cover?
- How will the book be bound? Hard cover or softcover? Stitched or perfect bound? This is a matter of price, and also dependent on how the book is to be used.

Skills Required (Author)
- Editing skills, which include:
- Editing to produce a good final manuscript, which answers all the questions and concerns thrown up during the editing process.
- Copy-editing, to ensure consistency of language and spelling throughout.
- Sub-editing, to ensure that (a) the final text is letter perfect and (b) no mistakes have crept in during the typesetting and design phase.
- Illustration skills, where strong visuals are an important feature of the book.
- Design skills to produce something that is readable without being

too expensive. The publisher and author should discuss the proposed design to see that it enhances what the book is saying.
- Ability to come up with a catchy title which expresses what the book is about.

What is Needed?
- A properly edited final manuscript on disk.
- An index, which may be prepared by the author or by a specialist indexer.
- A good design brief.
- A competent designer.
- A good cover design (with back cover and spine).
- Camera-ready artwork to send to the printer.

Key Problems
- The manuscript is virtually unpublishable, but the author continues to believe that it can be brought up to a publishable standard. If, in reality, it is just not good enough, a decision should be taken at this point not to proceed.
- The author constantly wants to make changes, and can never decide that the manuscript is the final copy that will be printed.
- The number of pages is not appropriate. Several pages are printed at a time, and most books will be a multiple of 8, 16 or even 32 pages, depending on the size of the printing press to be used. If the book extends to one or two pages more, a whole new section has to be printed, which adds to the cost and creates blank pages at the end. With minor editing or adjustment to the basic design, the book may be easily reduced by the required number of pages.

Stage 4: Printing the Book
At this stage, the printer is sent the complete artwork for the pages and the cover of the book, with instructions as to how it should be printed.

Critical Issues
- How many copies will be printed? This will depend on the expected level of sales, on the 'shelf-life' of the book (before it goes out of date), and on cost factors (a longer print run produces a cheaper book, but involves more risk).
- The quality of the paper to be used. This can have a considerable impact on price. Better paper is required for books containing photographs.
- The quality of the printing – is the printer able to produce to the standard you require?

Skills Required (Publisher)
- Ability to purchase printing and paper cost-effectively from a competent printer. Usually the publisher will work with a selection of printers who can do a good job, and seek competitive quotes for doing the job.

What is Needed?
- Copies of the book produced to specification and on time.

Key Problem
- The quality of printing is too low; or the instructions to the printer have not been obeyed, and the cover is printed in the wrong colour, or illustrations appear on the wrong page or with the wrong caption.

Stage 5: Promoting the Book

This stage should commence in earnest once it is finally decided to proceed with the publication – which is when a firm date for the final manuscript has been set – although ideas for how the book will be promoted should be discussed from the beginning of the publishing process. Promotion is critical to the success of the book: if people don't know about it, they won't buy it.

Critical Issues
- Does the market for the publication really exist, as discussed and planned for at the start?
- Has the market changed in any way during the time the publication has been in preparation? Have any new opportunities emerged?
- How much money is available to promote the book? Usually not very much!

Skills Required (Publisher)
- Ability to work with the author and seek out competent professionals who will be able to advise on any special marketing opportunities (such as professional networks, journals and magazines) relevant to the topic of the book.
- Publishing experience (or advice from someone who has).
- A keen desire to make a success of the book.

What is Needed?
- Creation of demand without spending a fortune.
- Sufficient resources to be able to achieve this, and a creative approach that will generate publicity for little outlay.

Key Problems
- In traditional publishing, the publisher believes that the job has been done as soon as the book is printed – even when piles of the book may be left to rot in a damp stockroom! And the author believes that the job has been done once the final manuscript has been agreed, and fails to put pressure on the publisher to promote the book. For the self-publisher, in the enthusiasm to produce the book, the marketing and distribution may be completely overlooked.
- People like the book, but are not prepared to purchase copies or pay the price being asked: the only solution may be to find ways of giving it away to people who might like to read it.

Stage 6: Distribution and Sales
Once demand has been created, it has to be met through some form of sales mechanism. Possible mechanisms include: retailing through bookshops, mail-order selling, and supply at events such as meetings and conferences.

Critical Issues
- Will the book be distributed only through bookshops? Or will much more be done to increase the availability of the book?
- Where can the book be sold? Music is sold through many different outlets, including through pavement selling. People want to buy music, and it is readily available. Can you think creatively about how your book might be made available?

Skills Required (Publisher)
- Ability to supply copies of the book to meet demand.

Key Problems
- Demand so outstrips supply that the book goes out of stock, and a hasty reprint is needed. This is a 'good problem' to have!
- There is no real demand. If this is the case, then why? And what can be done? It's best to think about this before you start out, and develop a contingency plan.
- Copies requested by mail order are not supplied. You need to be efficient in doing this.
- Copies are returned, as they have been badly printed.
- After the book has been published, it becomes apparent that it is full of errors.

Stage 7: Revising the Book and Preparing for the Next Edition
After the book has been published, the next edition or the next project should be planned, building on the experience of this first publication.

Critical Issues
- Has this first project been successful enough to warrant a new edition or a further publication?
- What are the shortcomings of this first publication? And can they be overcome next time round?
- What is the life-span of the publication? Some information goes out of date quickly.

Agents and Literary Agents

During the months that this volume was in preparation, a letter was received from East Africa enclosing this cutting from *Publishers' Weekly*. An author who had had some success locally was advertising for a Publisher/Agent. It is very unlikely that the enquirer received any response, certainly none commensurate with the substantial investment she or he had made in paying for the advertisement.

Agents are an established part of the literary scene in Europe and America, and they have a foothold in South Africa. This does not mean that all 'Western' authors have agents, or that books will only be noticed by publishers if they arrive from an agent. The perspicacity of the late Rex Collings, a great friend of African publishing, in appreciating the potential of *Watership Down* by Richard Adams is frequently given as an illustration. The author had peddled the typescript of his novel about rabbits on the South Downs around London publishers without success. Only when Collings read the tale was its quality recognised by a man in the profession: once published, it became a bestseller, Adams enjoyed the royalties and Collings was able to negotiate the sale of the rights. Presumably he earned his 10 per cent of whatever he secured for Adams.

Enquiries at Heinemann, in the course of doing research for this book, revealed that texts for consideration in the African Writers Series do not normally arrive through agents. It was claimed that as much attention is given to typescripts sent direct from the author's hand as to those that come with an agent's recommendation. From this and other enquiries it would seem that the best advice is: 'Get an agent if you can, but don't let the absence of an agent prevent you from approaching a publisher.' However, if authors are going to approach publishers directly they should know the proper procedure (see 'How to Approach a Publisher' in 'Arusha Report', page 137), and how to make an initial approach. Furthermore, they should be fully aware of their rights, informed about what it is realistic for them to demand – and cognisant of what it would be foolish for them to sacrifice.

Specialist agents are only just beginning to emerge for African authors looking to Europe, and are still much more open to representing UK-based writers than those actually living in Africa. Ama Ata Aidoo and Nuruddin Farah have both engaged agents, and Farah, like Ben Okri – whose position within the literary galaxy altered radically when he won the Booker Prize – has changed agents on occasions. Presumably, these writers were motivated by the feeling that someone else might do well for them; a specialist might interest a more prestigious publisher, obtain larger advances, obtain a higher percentage on royalties and market rights more imaginatively.

When the history of African writers and their agents comes to be written, the name of Rex Collings, already introduced, will have an important place. He was behind the Oxford University Press (OUP) West African Three Crowns Series in the early 1960s, and then moved on to Associated Book Publishers before setting up his own publishing house towards the end of the decade. Soyinka, whose work he had published with OUP and who had became a close friend, was one of his prominent authors. While OUP continued to publish some of Soyinka's plays, and Methuen retained an interest in his poetry and drama, it was under Collings' own imprint that some of Soyinka's most important work, including actualities and autobiography, first appeared. Collings acted as an agent: for example, he negotiated the sale of rights of Soyinka's collections of verse to Hill and Wang in the US; and he used his influence with Peter Calvocoressi at Penguin to deter him from invoking an escape clause in an agreement when lawyers advised him that material in *The Man Died* was actionable. He also campaigned energetically and courageously for his author's rights when Soyinka was detained.

Soyinka's position was complicated by the fact that he was a playwright, and therefore needed someone to look after the performance rights and royalties. Initially, he delegated to Dennis Duerden of the Transcription Centre responsibility for the rights to his plays in the UK, and employed Ann Elmo to carry out a similar function in the US. However, he granted authority of various kinds to his wife, Laide, and was prepared to be guided in certain matters by his friend, Femi Johnson. It is apparent from the collections of Soyinka's correspondence in the Brotherton Library, Leeds, and in the Harry Ransom Humanities Research Centre, at Austin, Texas, that 'wires occasionally became crossed'. Problems arose particularly when Soyinka was imprisoned during the civil war, when, for months, he was held incommunicado. On the rare occasions when Laide was able to visit him, she emerged with responses to enquiries and with lists of instructions. Twenty years later, Soyinka was represented by Brandt and Brandt (New York) but that arrangement was terminated, and the following response was received to a letter of enquiry to their London branch:

> We don't have African authors on our list ... We take on new authors all the time, on the merits of their writing. Plainly there is an appetite for writing from anywhere in the old Commonwealth, providing it is accessible here.

It is not always easy to locate the agents of even the best-known African authors!

Soyinka's experience – his friendship with a publisher who set up his own company and was familiar with all aspects of the writer–publisher–agent triangle – was rather unusual. Normally writers have to approach agents, and agents have to be convinced that it's worth their while to take on a particular author. They ask themselves: 'Will 10 per cent of this guy's literary earnings be worth the candle?'

The procedure to be followed by an author approaching an agent is carefully laid down (see the list of agents and their requirements, page 304). For example, an initial letter of enquiry may have to be followed by evidence of published or publishable work. At this stage, particular problems may confront the African author since agents often seem unaware that it may be difficult for authors in Africa to provide stamped self-addressed envelopes (SAEs). Asking, as some agents do, for an SAE in order to guarantee a reply may burden the African writer who will ask: 'I'm sending this to such-and-such a country – how can I obtain appropriate stamps?' 'International Reply Coupons' – which some agents require if they are to return typescripts – exist but are not always available, and the costs of postage are often very high. However, the agents' position is clear enough: they work for much of the time on narrow profit margins and cannot foot large postage bills.

There are writers who have read widely in the area and can negotiate from a well-informed position. At the Arusha III seminar, Atukwei Okai described from personal experience the value of meeting publishers having read major texts on the industry. Other writers, despite limited access to discussions about publishing, have the kind of book-keeping skills that are needed to keep track of contacts, agreements and payments. Amos Tutuola had limited formal education and narrow experience of the book trade, yet he kept detailed records of his correspondence with his publishers. His experience provides much enlightenment, and some cause for concern. It should be recognised, for example, that the face of British publishing has changed considerably since Tutuola first made contact with Faber and Faber in the 1950s. The fact that TS Eliot was personally involved in the decision to publish *The Palm-Wine Drinkard* speaks eloquently about the kind of people involved at that time. Furthermore, it seems that, on occasions, Tutuola was, at his request, 'paid' in manufactured items. Members of staff were prepared to arrange for tyres and a fridge to be bought and despatched to Abeokuta. Nowadays, there are few firms that could cope with such requests, but then nowadays publishing is a much less family affair. It would, incidentally, be interesting to know whether Tutuola was always equally well treated by all his publishers. There are suggestions that American publishers took advantage of him, and various Nigerian writers and academics have endeavoured to secure full accounts for trans-Atlantic sales.

Writers who are out of touch with the constantly changing conditions in the international book trade and do not have book-keeping skills may want to engage a specialist to represent their interests. This comes at a price. For the percentages taken by different agents, as well as the way in which each should be approached, see the Directory on page 304. This reveals the uneven spread of literary agents on the African continent, and also points to the diverse roles that representatives in Europe might play, following Collings' example. Peter Ripken in Germany and Jan Kees van de Werk in the Netherlands are, for example, facilitators with wide literary interests and passionate commitment rather than simply agents.

To proceed: if all goes well and the agent is impressed by the writer, contracts can be drawn up and signed. Broadly, writers expect their agents to act on their behalf: negotiate favourable contracts with publishers, be alert to opportunities for commissions and, if appropriate, arrange the sale of rights, including translation and performing rights. Authors should, however, ensure that they remain in control. They should be wary of giving an agent a totally free hand to sell subsidiary rights, and they should not sign away electronic rights or film rights. They must never allow the publisher to claim the copyright – that, to quote one of the agents listed below, 'must always remain the property of the author and must be reflected by the ICC [International Copyright Convention] notice' (see also 'Minimum Terms Agreement', paragraph C.4, page 397).

Agents have undoubtedly fought important battles on behalf of African authors, and are well aware of the particular problems. For example, a good agent would be alert to considering whether a writer's percentage is negatively affected in the recent instance of a British publisher dividing the sub-rights for certain titles. They may be able to assess whether writers are being exploited, or if a just arrangement has been reached. When publishers have made a major contribution to putting together a book, it may be fair for them to retain the lion's share of the profits on sub-rights. The agent should advise accordingly.

It needs to be said that there has to be trust, confidence and professionalism in the contact between author and agent. Only these qualities enable relationships to endure through difficult periods. And, almost inevitably, there are going to be difficult periods. An agent may be frustrated when, after a successful first novel, there is an arid period full of promises but nothing more. Writers may be disappointed when, after a 'runaway success' with a first novel, a second work is greeted with silence or shrugged off as 'more of the same'.

Important Vocabulary

Reading fee Writers should be suspicious of any agent asking for a reading fee. Agents may offer advice, or 'buy in' advisors, but this cost should be met by them.

Rejection slip Authors may receive 'rejection slips' from agents as well as from publishers. These are usually brief and to the point; quite often they follow a familiar formula. Authors often, naturally, feel hurt by these rejections, particularly if the rejection slip is no more than a curt 'thumbs down'. The harsh reality is that providing an assessment of a manuscript, or making helpful criticism, involves time and effort. Since there is no prospect of reward, this doesn't get done.

Opinion
Abdulrazak Gurnah writes:

> Agents make a huge difference if you can get one, principally in the range of publishers they can approach, the speed with which they can get a response out of them, and the kind of advance they can get for the book. I'd advise every writer to get one if they could. Some publishers prefer that writers do not have agents, but I think most of them are happier doing the business professionally. This is not true of the specialist publishers (like the African Writers Series) where the intervention of an agent may mean that they can no longer afford to publish that writer. I think there are too many agents to list the ones who have African writers. Many of them do, and usually any of them are worth a try. (Letter to the editors. Quoted with permission.)

Fact
Agents were used by roughly two-thirds of the creative writers who responded to Michael Legat's UK survey during 1997 and who published with the larger British houses (Legat 1997, 99).

Friends, Mentors and Eggers-on

In the days before agents, writers depended for advice and encouragement on a network of what Valentine Cunningham calls 'friends, mentors and eggers-on' (Cunningham 1998). For example, Mary Anne Evans ('George Eliot') was, apparently, happy to admit that she would never have written fiction without 'patient prodding' from her partner, George Henry Lewes, and she would not have prospered had his tough negotiating skills not been deployed in contacts with her publishers.

Despite possessing finely honed business skills and his own privileged financial circumstances – his grandfather had made a fortune in real estate and his father had an income of $10,000 a year – Henry James (1843-1916), American-born novelist and critic, employed a literary agent. Perhaps he was the first to do so. The move did not ensure complete satisfaction. For what Jonathan Freedman describes as 'complicated reasons', James made practically nothing from the vast popular success of *Daisy Miller* (1897), and he realised only $221 from the sales of the authoritative New York editions of a substantial portion of his output, for which he wrote extended prefaces (1907-10) (Freedman 1998, 15-17).

A Story

How Oonya Kempadoo's unsolicited manuscript became coveted literary property:

British-born with a Tamil Indian father, Oonya Kempadoo wrote a series of character sketches while living in Guyana. After she polished them up for her son and her husband, the latter encouraged her to weave them into a novel. She did so and sent the text, *Buxton Spice*, to the author Earl Lovelace and to the publisher of *Caribbean Beat* magazine, Jeremy Taylor. They encouraged her to find a publisher, and, following advice in writers' handbooks, she sent letters of self-introduction to ten UK publishers and seven literary agents. Minerva rejected the novel as 'Too hot to handle', but Fourth Estate made an offer. She faxed the seven agents and in her words reproduced in *The Bookseller* (10 July 1998, 32): 'David [Godwin] was on the phone at five o'clock in the morning. He was the most forthcoming and easiest to talk to.'

Kempadoo travelled to London where she met four publishers. Phoenix House proved the most attractive.

The Experience of a Leading Literary Agent

Anonymous

Today, if you sent a first novel direct to publishers in New York the chances are that they would tell you that they only accept novels submitted to them by agents – such is the strength and power that literary agents have. It was not always so. Publishers used to be very wary of agents, regarding them as intruders in the cosy relationship between the publisher and author. Now the large publishing houses in New York and London see agents as a source of good books; and whether the publishers like it or not, they have to keep on the right side of agents.

Literary agents exist to represent an author's rights in negotiations with publishers. The first literary agent, AP Watt, started business over 100 years ago. There are now literally hundreds of literary agents, most of them based in London or New York and very few authors who make their living by writing books do so without the help of an agent. Having said that, agents on the whole deal with 'trade' books, both fiction and non-fiction and children's books. There are very few agents who work in the field of academic or school book publishing where the publishers generally control all rights.

For a professional writer it is important to have an agent. Firstly, the agent will find the right publisher for an author's work; secondly, they will negotiate the best possible deal; thirdly, they will sell the rights in other languages and in other media, such as film and television; and finally, they will make sure that the publisher sticks to his or her part of the contract, making payments regularly and accurately and publishing the book professionally. In addition, they will often find work for their clients. Most reputable agents are members of a professional association which lays down a code of conduct and are listed in various reference books such as *The Writer's Handbook* (Macmillan) and *The Writer's and Artist's Yearbook* (A&C Black) (see pages 366-67).

Agents are paid on commission, usually 10-15 per cent of what the author receives. In this way, their interests are immediately related to those of the author. At the end of each contract between an author and publisher there is a clause which specifies that all advances and royalties due to the author will be paid to the author's literary agent;

the agent is responsible for taking his or her commission and passing on what is due to the author.

A literary agent will also have relationships with agents in other countries to sell translation rights – often a major source of income for an author. On sales of translation rights an author will pay 20 per cent, divided between the principle agent and the foreign agent. This may seem a lot, but a publisher controlling those rights might retain anything between 25 and 50 per cent and then sit on the money until required to pay out royalties.

You need no professional qualification to become a literary agent. But most agents come from the field of publishing where they may have been editors, publicists or rights managers. Others climb up the ladder within an established agency. Large agencies, such as William Morris in New York or Curtis Brown in London employ many agents, each of whom looks after the affairs of their individual 'stable' of authors. However, under one roof there will be agents looking after film, television, translation rights as well, in the case of some larger agencies, as actors and presenters.

Agents are by nature entrepreneurial and so it is not surprising that quite often agents will leave the umbrella of a large agency and set up on their own taking their authors with them. This is what large agencies dread. But at least they have the consolation that the authors cannot take their old contracts with them, so the original agency will continue to take its ten per cent on money earned from old contracts. Small agencies have the advantage of flexibility and many authors prefer the more personal style of a one-person band.

Over the last twenty years, the international publishing scene has changed dramatically. Time was when there were many privately owned publishing houses in London and New York which conducted a successful, if not particularly profitable, business. Publishing was very much a 'gentleman's profession' and authors were made to feel part of the family. Now there are very few independent publishers, the majority being imprints of larger conglomerates. For instance, in 1998 the German publisher Bertelsmann, owner of Bantam, Doubleday and Dell bought the US publishers Random House which itself owns many publishers including Knopf, Vintage and Ballantine in New York and Cape, Chatto, Arrow, Heinemann, Hutchinson and Century in England. Huge publishers have given work to lawyers who produce huge and complicated contracts for which, in turn, agents are essential to help in unravelling. In all this change the author's position is less secure and the still point in this turning world is his or her agent.

With the growth of huge publishers, the amount of money available for 'bestselling' authors has increased. Here the agent plays a key role.

Agents often sell their author's work at auction if they feel their intellectual property is sufficiently commercial. An agent will send out the same manuscript or proposal for a book to, say, ten publishers who have expressed interest and will stipulate a day and time some weeks ahead for them to make their first bids, specifying what rights are included. As the amount of money on offer gets larger, auctions may continue by telephone over several days if the bidding gets exciting. Publishers often claim to hate auctions, but at the same time are furious if they are left out.

There is hot competition to be accepted on to the list of a successful agent. Even small agencies receive hundreds of unsolicited manuscripts a year which – since this is a very personal business – may not be at all appropriate for the particular agent. If you are looking for an agent it is best to write or phone in advance with information about your book to see if it is the sort of thing the particular agency might be interested in. The agent will probably ask you to send the first few chapters and an outline plus the return postage. If he (or she) likes what he sees he will ask to see the full manuscript. He may wish you to do a little more work on it before submitting it to publishers. But if he likes it he will agree to take you on as a client; you then sign an agreement in which he becomes your exclusive agent. And into the sunset you walk.

Agents: A Directory

Various sources have been used to provide the details below. The agents listed are interested in literature, and most will either consider literature by African writers, or already represent African authors. It is worth noting that all agents will expect any query letter and/or manuscript submission to be accompanied by a stamped addressed envelope (SAE), or an International Reply Coupon (IRC).

Abbreviations used in the Directory:
Client: authors represented
Contact: contact name
Found: year established
Info: general information
Ms subs: manuscript submissions
Rates: commission rates
Req: requirements from a potential client

AFRICA

Nigeria

Joe-Tolau and Associates (Nigeria) Ltd
Apt 4 Tomoloju Estate
4-6 Yaya Abatam Street
PO Box 7031, Ikeja, Lagos
Tel: +234-1-4922681
Fax: +234-1-4922681
Found: 1983
Ms subs: Fiction and non-fiction; Christian literature.
Req: Send query letter. No reading fee.

South Africa

Frances Bond Literary Services
PO Box 223, Westville 3630, Natal
Tel: +27-31-824532
Fax: +27-31-822620

Contact: Frances Bond, director
Ms subs: A wide spectrum of writing. List includes 'a large number of black writers many of whom originate within South Africa, Nigeria, Zimbabwe' and Zambia.
Req: Charges reading fee because of the shrinking market in RSA and worldwide, and because of working with so many new writers who require help 'through the means of comprehensive reports and where necessary personal consultations'.
Info: Frances Bond organise a School for Creative Writing for gifted children which works through modules on short story writing and articles, novel writing and children's books. A demonstration of the method was well received at the ZIBF Writers' Indaba 1997.
Rates: Reading fee varies according to length of book and amount of work entailed. Frances Bond charge 15 per cent commission on royalties and monies accruing from sale of the book. If the book has to go to an overseas agent, commission is raised to 20 per cent to cover costs.

International Press Agency (Pty) Ltd

PO Box 67, Howard Place

Ms subs: IPA are active in selling South African rights in children's picture books from all countries for translation into African languages and Afrikaans.

Info: See also entry for London office.

Literary Dynamics

PO Box 50971, Musgrove 4062
Tel: +27-11-3092513
Fax: +27-11-3092913
Email: literary@saol.com
Found: 1985

Ms subs: Main interest adult novels. Handles authors resident outside South Africa, including Zimbabwe and the Seychelles.

Info: Services provided include public speaking workshops.

Sandton Literary Agency

PO Box 785799, Sandton 2146
Tel: +27-11-4428624
Found: 1982

Contact: J Victoria Channing, M Sutherland, directors

Req: Write or phone first. Authors outside South Africa are asked to enclose an IRC or South African postage stamps with any submission.

Info: Sandton Literary Agency do not submit work to publishers in the rest of Africa. but do have links with those in the UK, US, Australia and continental Europe.

OUTSIDE AFRICA

France

Shelley Power Literary Agents Ltd

Le Montaud, 24220

Ms subs: General commercial fiction, literary fiction. No film scripts, plays, poetry, short stories or children's books.

Req: Send query letter with a short outline of the project, and enclose sae for reply.

Clients: Lauretta Ngcobo, Njabulo Ndebele

Rates: No reading fee. Commission rates: 12.4 per cent UK; 20 per cent US.

The Netherlands

Jan Kees van de Werk

Zuideroind 73, 1243 KH's-Graveland
Tel: +31-35-6562741
Fax: +31-35-6564610
Contact: Jan Kees van de Werk

Info: Jan Kees is not strictly an agent, but it is convenient to list him here. He is an enabler and encourager, a link between the creative and commercial, an organiser of literary festivals and events.

Spain

Ms Anna Soler-Pont Literary Agency

Santa Theresa 5, Barcelona 08012
Tel: +34-3-4154416
Fax: +34-3-4154416
Email: pontas@lix.intercom.es
Contact: Anna Soler-Pont

Ms subs: Special interest in translation into Spanish. No poetry or drama.

Clients: Veronique Tadjo, Chenjerai Hove.

Switzerland

Mr Gerhard Protscka
c/o Servicebuto fur Fachverlage
PO Box 106, Basel
Tel: +41-61-2730990
Fax: +41-61-2711010
Email: sfgch@access.ch
Contact: Gerhard Protscka
Ms subs: African writers' work. Children's books not a main area of interest. nb only books that have been published in the original language will be considered.
Req: Send query letter, brief synopsis of the work, short CV and a statement indicating why you think your ms would attract a European readership. Copies of unsolicited books will not be returned.
Rates: Commission rates: 10 per cent for first printed rights in Germany; 15 per cent for secondary rights.

UK

BookBlast
21 Chesterton Road,
London W10 5LY
Tel: +44-181-9683089
Fax: +44-181-9324087
Contact: Georgia de Chamberet, director
Ms subs: Literature (no poetry). Authors from the African diaspora.
Req: Send query letter first with biographical information, SAE and list of agents and publishers previously contacted.
Info: No reading fee. Will suggest revisions.

David Bolt Associates
12 Heath Drive, Send, Guildford
Surrey GU23 7EP
Tel: +44-1483-721118
Fax: +44-1483-721118
Found: 1983

Contact: David Bolt
Ms subs: Fiction, African writing (no unsolicited short stories or play scripts).
Req: Send query letter with SAE. No unsolicited mss. Reading fee for unpublished writers.
Clients: Chinua Achebe

Curtis Brown
Haymarket House
28-29 Haymarket,
London SW1Y 4SP
Tel: +44-171-3966600
Fax: +44-171-3960110
Ms subs: Novels.
Req: Send query letter first.

Toby Eady Associates Ltd
Third Floor
9 Orme Court, London W2 4RL
Tel: +44-171-7920092
Fax: +44-171-7920879
Email:
eadyassociates@compuserve.com
Contact: Toby Eady, Alexandra Pringle, Victoria Hobbs
Req: Send query letter. No unsolicited mss.
Rates: UK: 10 per cent; US and Translation: 20 per cent.

Vernon Futerman Associates
17 Deanhill Road
London SW14 7DQ
Tel: +44-181-2864860
Fax: +44-181-2864861
Found: 1984
Contact: Guy Rose (fiction/ biography), Vernon Futerman (academic/ political)
Ms subs: Fiction and non-fiction (no short stories, science fiction, crafts or hobbies).
Req: Send query letter with a brief biography, detailed synopsis and SAE. No unsolicited mss. No reading fee.

David Godwin Associates

55 Monmouth Street
London WC2H 9DG
Tel: +44-171-2405992
Fax: +44-171-2405007
Found: 1996
Contact: David Godwin, Heather Godwin, directors
Ms subs: Literary fiction and general non-fiction.
Req: Send SAE for return of mss. No reading fee.

International Press Agency Ltd

19 Avenue South, Surbiton
Surrey KT5 8PJ
Tel: +44-181-3904414
Contact: Ursula A Barnett
Ms subs: South African children's books.
Req: Send query letter describing work. No unsolicited mss.
Clients: Lesley Beake
Rates: No reading fee. Charges 10 per cent on any money due to author.

Labour and Management Ltd – Tricia Sumner Literary Agency

Milton House, Milton Street
Enfield EN9 1EZ
Tel: +44-1992-711511
Email: triciasumner@classic.msn.com
Found: 1995
Contact: Tricia Sumner, director
Ms subs: Fiction and non-fiction; multicultural literature a special interest.
Req: Send letter, synopsis, sample chapters and a SAE.

New Authors Showcase

Rivendell, Kingsgate Close
Torquay TQ2 8QA
Tel: +44-1803-326617
Fax: +44-1803-326617
Email: newauthors@compuserve.com
Web site: http://ourworld.compuserve.com/homepage/newauthors
Contact: Barrie E James
Ms subs: All literary work.
Req: Send query letter and synopsis first.
Info: An Internet site where new unpublished writers can display their work to publishers, and published authors can advertise their work.
Rates: No reading fee.

Felix De Wolfe

Manfield House, 1 Southampton Street
London WC2R 0LR
Tel: +44-171-3795767
Fax: +44-171-8360337
Found: 1983
Ms subs: Fiction only.
Req: No unsolicited mss. No reading fee.

USA

The Connor Literary Agency

2911 West 71st Street, Richfield
MN 55423
Tel: +1-612-8661486
Fax: +1-612-8694074
Found: 1985
Contact: Marlene Connor, John Lynch
Ms subs: Contemporary women's fiction, popular fiction.
Req: Send query letter first. No unsolicited mss.

Ralph M Vicinanza Ltd

111 8th Avenue, Suite 1501
New York, NY 10011
Tel: +1-212-9247090
Contact: Ralph Vicinanza, Christopher Lotts, Sharon Friedman, Christopher Schelling
Ms subs: Literary, women's, multicultural, popular and children's fiction; non-fiction.
Req: No unsolicited mss.

Confessions of a Publisher's Reader and a Reviewer

James Gibbs

When publishers receive interesting scripts – texts that interest them and that they feel may have a life between covers – they sometimes back their own hunches and take the responsibility for acceptance or rejection themselves. However, sometimes they employ a Reader to give them an opinion. Readers are not often identified publicly: their task is to assess a manuscript and, in a letter to the publisher, recommend either publication or rejection. Publishers may pass on comments to authors, but they rarely – and I hope never in the case of rejection – pass on the names of Readers to authors whose work is rejected.

Readers are paid for their services (I seem to remember that in the 1970s the rate was about £30 per novel) and have no commercial interest in the publication that may depend on their opinions. The Reader's task is to be as objective as possible; they should be quick to recognise 'old fashioned literary virtues', and ready to appreciate the value of the experimental, new or strange. They should be prepared to recognise the appeal and validity of, say, 'Fantasia Novels' or 'Spiritual Realism'.

In the past, London-based publishers often relied on UK-resident, British readers. As people 'established themselves' by virtue of teaching in African universities and writing on African literature, so they moved on to the lists of publishers' readers. Readers made mistakes, or publishers, desperate for a title they thought they could get on to a syllabus – relaxed their standards. For this reason, Heinemann's African Writers Series, for example, includes titles that were fortunate to get into print: it is uneven. But if some got through because a reader was lax, there were undoubtedly others that were rejected because a reader failed to respond to genuine qualities. Sometimes, these may have been qualities that reflected the African character of the text, qualities that a Eurocentric, inflexible mind had failed to respond to.

The disadvantages of using, say, British Readers for African writing are obvious to all But a number of African writers have nevertheless preferred to take their chances with international publishers rather than going to local publishing houses. This is because they fear choosing a publisher who might not preserve their anonymity and might submit their work for assessment by a colleague, or at least a fellow countryman, who has a vested interest in obstructing a burgeoning literary career. It is necessary to acknowledge the existence of certain individuals in positions of influence who may be more determined to sabotage the progress of their colleague's career than to promote it; or, at least, to see justice done.

The relationship between the Publisher's Reader and the author is infinitely complex. The two examples already cited – an objective but ill-informed expatriate Reader on the one hand, and a knowledgeable but subjective African Reader on the other – are among many possible arrangements. However, the intricacies are almost always impossible to follow because of the confidential nature of the correspondence between the publisher and the Reader. It is more important to move on to consider relationships between authors and reviewers, because these raise many important issues, and they are aired in public. The topic is a vast one: every so often, as one surveys a volume of reviews, one is struck by the way writers and critics, reviewers and editors handle one another's work. On occasions old scores are settled, favours returned or 'grudge matches' continued in reviews sections. For example, there is a history of disagreement – not to say vituperative exchange – between Soyinka and Chinweizua, and no one aware of this would expect the latter's review of Art, Dialogue and Outrage in a serious London publication to be a straightforward response to the text.

It is possible to go back further to see how reviews generated debates. The Palm-Wine Drinkard was famously welcomed with a torrent of Welsh enthusiasm by Dylan Thomas, whom, I suspect, was enlisting supporters from the fringes as part of his attack on London's literary dominance. He began his piece for the Observer: 'This is the brief, thronged, grisly and bewitching story, or series of stories, written in young English by a West African ...' and he concluded:

> The writing is nearly always terse and direct, strong, wry, flat and savoury the big, and often comic, terrors are as near and understandable as the numerous small details of price, size, and number; and nothing is too prodigious or too trivial to put down in this tall, devilish story. (Thomas quoted in Lindfors 1975, 7-8)

Some Nigerian critics interpreted this as stemming from a patronising attitude

Amos Tutuola's work touches on a particularly sensitive area: it
may be instructive to reproduce an extract from Soyinka's essay 'From
a Common Backcloth' written in the early 1960s and, as is clearly
apparent, from a contemporary perspective, engaged in a series of
controversies.

> There are ... two kinds of offerings directed at the moment to the European
> palate. One is for acceptance in the Western creative idiom. I have
> mentioned the example of *The Radiance of the King*. There is William Con
> ton's proper resolution in *The African* of a Durham-to-Jungle adventure by
> an outrageously imposed Christian forgiveness; and there are the new poets
> in Nigeria who regroup images of Ezra Pound around the oilbean and nude
> spear. The prophets of negritude at least dared these and scorned them,
> substituting a forthright although strident reaffirmation of truly 'African'
> values, but breeding only the second offering, the burnt offering, image of
> the charred skin on a defiant platter. It is futile now to knock negritude; it
> is far more useful to view it as a historical phenomenon and to preserve the
> few truly creative pieces that somehow emerged in spite of its philosophical
> straitjacket.
>
> But it is not so easy to ignore the facile exploiters of the fallacy since
> they, even more than the muscular emblem-bearers of negritude, have been
> welcomed most readily into the bosom of the foreign critic. In a special
> issue of *The Times Literary Supplement*, a critic, reviewing a novel by a
> Nigerian writer, Nzekwu, says: '... but he cannot help presenting the
> traditional Ibo religion and culture in the more attractive light. It is this
> that will be the main attraction to the European reader: the masquerades,
> the prayers, the charms and the tribal social structure are described from
> within and with luminous comprehension. He is also old-fashioned enough
> to tell a straight story with a moral. This is the kind of story his people
> like.' Obviously, a book that has something both for the European and for
> the African reader cannot help but be successful! Even the fumbling first
> novel of this writer is described as 'very successful', and with two other
> Nigerian novelists the writer makes, 'an unbeatable Treble Choice'.
>
> A very long time ago the discerning African rejected the anthropological
> novel. Perhaps during the next 20 years his foreign counterpart will do the
> same. Since even now African writers work against a similar back cloth, it
> is on the level of interpretation that the individual artist, as in any other
> culture, must be judged ... (Soyinka 1963, 389-90)

A somewhat similar case was made against Edward Blishen, whose
enthusiasm for African writing led to him being dubbed 'Blushless' in
the pages of *Transition*. Blishen, an energetic biographer, has described
the painful impact of this attack and defended himself against it by
drawing attention to the fact that his positive and enthusiastic attitude

was not confined to African literature but was characteristic of his approach to literature as a whole.

A Reader's Report and some Reviewers' Reactions

James Joyce's *Portrait of the Artist as a Young Man* was serialised in *The Egoist* between February 1914 and September 1915. It was, however, rejected by London publishers and when Joyce's patron, Harriet Shaw Weaver, tried to have it published as a book, the printers refused to print it! An example of the rejection letters that the text elicited is provided by the following, based on the comments made by Edward Garnett to publishers Duckworth and Company. Duckworth sent the letter to Joyce's agent, James J Pinker. It is reproduced here to show the limitations of a Reader's response to what has become recognised as a profoundly innovative piece of writing:

> James Joyce's 'Portrait of the Artist as a Young Man' wants going through carefully from start to finish. There are many 'longueurs'. Passages which, though the publisher's Reader may find them entertaining, will be tedious to the ordinary man among the reading public. That public will call the book, as it stands at present, realistic, unprepossessing, unattractive. We call it ably written. But the author must revise it and let us see it again. It is too discursive, formless, unrestrained, and ugly things, ugly words, are too prominent; indeed at times they seem to be shoved in one's face, on purpose, unnecessarily. The point of view will be voted 'a little sordid'. The picture of life is good; the period well brought to the reader's eye, and the types and characters are well drawn, but it is too 'unconventional'. This would stand against it in normal times. At the present time, though the old conventions are in the background, we can only see a chance for it if it is pulled into shape and made more definite.
>
> In the earlier portion of the MS, as submitted to us, a good deal of pruning can be done. Unless the author will use restraint and proportion he will not gain readers. His pen and his thoughts seem to have run away with him sometimes.
>
> And at the end of the book there is a complete falling to bits; the pieces of writing and the thoughts are all in pieces and they fall like damp, ineffective rockets.
>
> The author shows us he has art, strength and originality, but this MS. wants time and trouble spent on it, to make it a more finished piece of work, to shape it more carefully as the product of the craftsmanship and imagination of an artist. (Garnett quoted in Anderson's edition of Joyce 1961)

The first edition eventually appeared in New York, published by BW Huebsch and Company, in December 1916. *The Egoist* then imported printed sheets from the US and, presumably by-passing protesting printers, issued the first English edition (750 copies) in February 1917.

Soon afterwards, Joyce and Harriet Shaw Weaver paid for a selection of extracts from reviews to appear in the April 1917 issue of *The Egoist*. The selection was generally favourable, though the following comment which had appeared in *Everyman* was included:

> Garbage ... We feel that Mr Joyce would be at his best in a treatise on drains.

For advertising purposes, Joyce had a thousand copies of the page of extracts printed, and the editors of *The Egoist* – presumably anxious to clarify that Joyce's selection had been an advert and therefore did not reflect their own views– followed it with a compilation of their own. They used 'headwords' to organise responses and, for example, included:

> CLEANMINDEDNESS: This pseudo-autobiography of Stephen Dedalus, a weakling and a dreamer, makes fascinating reading. ... No cleanminded person could possibly allow it to remain within reach of his wife, his sons, or daughters. – *Irish Book Lover*

As these reviews indicate, Joyce's adventures in the book trade make fascinating and instructive reading. They could be amplified to provide a coherent account of his struggle to find conditions under which he could write, publishers who would accept his work, and printers who would set it up! His wanderings and experiences show, for example, the importance of patronage, persistence, publicity, and periodicals, and the conflict with the attitudes reflected in the comments above. The conditions of the time were also significant. For example, as mentioned above, the manuscript of *Portrait* was submitted to Duckworth during the First World War when publishers were in straitened circumstances, and was first published serially in *The Egoist* in 1914-15. In Easter 1916, the situation of publishers and other businesses in Ireland was made more insecure when Irish nationalists rose against British occupying forces and laid siege to the Post Office in Dublin. This event, incidentally, was of profound significance for the Anti-Colonial struggle in the twentieth century.

The text was subsequently sent, with the above letter containing Garnett's opinion, to Herbert J Cape. In 1924, as 'Jonathan Cape', he published the first English edition. This 'pseudo-autobiography' has since come to occupy, with Joyce's other fiction, a prominent place in the canon of great literature. That is to say, his position in twentieth-century Letters is assured and he is widely read. For African authors his position has been of great significance: as an Irish writer emerging at a time of cultural nationalism, as a colonial subject confronted by British imperialism, as an author seeking to write in English without being English, as a theorist determined to raise issues about aesthetics, and as an artist in exile.

In 1972 Rex Collings and Eyre Methuen published Soyinka's *A Shuttle in the Crypt* which included 'Ulysses', a poem that is partly concerned with withstanding 'the rain of nails/ That drill within to the archetypal heart/ Of all lone wanderers'. The poem that bears the name of the long-term exile, the warrior wanderer, is sub-titled: 'Notes from here to my Joyce Class'. Ten years after it appeared, Chinua Achebe travelled to Dublin, a guest of the Irish government, to participate in the events arranged to mark the centenary of Joyce's birth. He was impressed by the modest manner in which Irish leaders comported themselves on that occasion and by the interest they took in the literary symposium. The episode illustrates how Irish experiences provided the Nigerian writer, as they had provided a generation of others in the anti-colonial movement, with part of their literary and political education (Achebe 1983, 34-35). An awareness of Joyce's experiences as a writer is helpful to African authors at the end of the twentieth century.

Getting on with the State

Writers and Politics

'If you want to know what is happening in an age or a nation, find out what is happening to the writers, the town-criers, for they are the seismographers that calibrate impending earthquakes in the spirit of the times.' (Ben Okri, radio interview)

Ben Okri is among those who have suggested the importance of writers for those trying to understand what is going on at the heart of a community. There have been many who have made claims for the rights and duties of authors, some by the titles of their works, others by their membership of a political party, or by their commitment to an ideological position. JP Clark-Bekederemo significantly entitled his first collection of poems *A Reed in the Tide*, drawing attention to an image from nature that provides a neat overlap with Okri's technological comparison. Other writers have been involved in 'party politics'. Determined to contribute to debates within Nigerian politics, Chinua Achebe held a senior position within the People's Redemption Party. And Ngugi's political opinions smoulder in all that he writes. Whether as 'sensitive soul', or as an articulate and responsible citizen, African authors have often fulfilled political roles. Not surprisingly, they have also been wooed by rival factions, both within and outside their homelands, and it is helpful to survey briefly the ways in which larger 'blocs' have sought to embrace writers in the past, and also valuable to glance at the current situation.

Between 1958 and 1988, the Afro-Asian Peoples' Solidarity Association, through its Permanent Bureau of Afro-Asian Writers, organised a series of conferences. Important gatherings were held in Tashkent, Cairo, Beirut, New Delhi, Kaszakstan, and Tunis at which the social role of literature was a constant item on the agenda. After the Cairo conference of the late 1960s, *Lotus, a Journal of Afro-Asian Writing*, appeared in Arabic, English and French, carrying the work of major African writers together with material by their Asian colleagues. During the early 1970s, anthologies of poetry and short stories were also produced in Cairo, evidence of a drive to embody a vision of Afro-Asian solidarity and of a desire to lodge a claim for artistic leadership.

Following the Camp David Accord and the isolation of Egypt by the Arab states, the editorial offices of *Lotus* were moved from Cairo to Beirut, and then to Tunis, where the journal fell on lean times. By 1989, it had reached no. 68, but it had begun to appear only in Arabic and its demise was imminent. In the words of David Dorsey, in his fascinating paper 'Literary Studies in Cairo': '... with the collapse of the Soviet Union, *Lotus* ceased to exist' (Dorsey 1996). The decline of the East exposed the foundations of the non-aligned movement. Many must have reconsidered the ideological implications of the emphasis on 'the social role of the writer'; some may have linked the leftist view of the writer's function with the challenge to the rights of the individual by its emphasis on 'The greatest good for the greatest number'.

The *de facto* Eastern orientation of the Permanent Bureau, and indeed of the whole movement, meant that conferences and publications often included acute analyses of United States' involvement in apparently neutral publications. This was not without justification: while at least part of the Soviet subsidy and of the anti-colonial support was being channelled through the Afro-Asian People's Solidarity Association, Washington – and particularly the Central Intelligence Agency (CIA) at Langley – was establishing an elaborate system through which it could disperse funds and, perhaps, exert influence. It was eventually revealed that the CIA was using the grandly titled 'Congress for Cultural Freedom' in Paris to channel money to agencies it considered worth supporting. These agencies included the London-based Transcription Centre, which prepared radio programmes and tapes for African broadcasting stations as well as educational institutions, and the Chemchemi Cultural Centre in Nairobi. Exactly what the CIA hoped to gain from its funding is not spelt out: in part it seems to have been a reaction to the cultural challenge thrown down by the East, and an Anglophone response to perceived Francophone radicalism. The point is that, particularly during the 1960s, East and West financed organisations and publications that involved African writers.

Precisely how much those being used by the CIA knew about the sources of funding is also not entirely clear. However, research among the Duerden Papers in the Harry Ransom Humanities Research Center, Austin, Texas, reveals evidence which suggests that both those who worked for the Transcription Centre, and some of those who came into contact with it, were aware of its links with entrenched capitalist interests. For example, in September 1961, Duerden travelled widely in Africa assessing the situation in which the Centre might operate. His report to the Congress for Cultural Freedom, entitled 'Broadcasting in Africa', included notes on contacts made in Ghana with AA Opoku, back from a training course in the USSR, and with Efua Sutherland, already established as a leading light in the national theatre movement. Opoku said he would assist the BBC but not the Congress, and Sutherland 'immediately pronounced the Congress to be an anti-Marxist organisation and not one to be talked of too much if [Duerden] wanted a favourable reception in Ghana'.

Since Ghana, at the request of the left-leaning Casablanca Group, had been commissioned to circulate scripts of relevant radio programmes to other African states, this degree of political sophistication about the Transcription Centre is not surprising. But many of those who came on to the scene later are ignorant of the Centre's source of funding. The most frequently encountered relics of the Centre's work are the Heinemann volumes on *African Writers Talking* (Duerden and Pieterse 1972) and *African Writers on African Writing* (Killam 1973), versions of material prepared for broadcast or distribution by the Centre. These volumes, together with the files in Texas, reveal how deeply the CIA was, through the Transcription Centre, entwined within the guts of the new body of African writing.

The American Society for African Culture (AMSAC) was also extensively funded by the CIA, perhaps in an effort to distract some African Americans from the Civil Rights Movement by interesting them in their African heritage. Inevitably AMSAC – which had promoted visits to West Africa by such artists as Odetta, Saunders Redding and Langston Hughes – suffered when the links with a sinister arm of the United States Government were revealed. Indeed, the chill wind of exposure was felt by many beneficiaries of Uncle Sam's largesse including the literary-political publications *Black Orpheus* and *Transition*, and AMSAC's more academic *African Forum*. A number of titles from among the many books written about the workings of the CIA are listed in the Bibliography (page 411) for the benefit of those interested in pursuing this episode in the history of African literature.

The extent to which individual writers were compromised by links to East or West will continue to be discussed. From these discussions, it will become clear that, during the Cold War, rival powers and ideologies sought to manipulate African writers, editors, conference organisers and publishers. Following this experience, no one can ever be innocent again. Authors may be 'reeds in the tide' or 'seismographers calibrating impending earthquakes', but they can be sure that interest groups will try to manipulate them, to point them in wrong directions and give inaccurate readings.

It should be noted that, following the exposure of the workings of the CIA and the advent of the 'New World Order', the United States' assistance programmes have been reorganised so that the 'aid scene' is currently very different from that described above. Its current working can be observed through the support given to African drama groups wishing to put on plays. The British Council has long been involved in this kind of sponsorship, and its work has been complemented by that of the Alliance Française and the Goethe Institute. There are now other agencies in the field. To take a single example: Bode Sowande wrote a play to mark the French Revolution; he prepared a text, partly inspired by Pinocchio, for an Italian Theatre Festival; and took a production of a Tutuola text to London for the Africa '95 festivities. Working writers should be aware of the influence of aid agency rivalries which are particularly strong in relation to language issues. Having analysed the situation, writers should resist exploitation, and be ready to take advantage of every changing wind.

Governments and Book Foundations

More and more people are becoming illiterate; books, as a matter of policy, are not being produced and made available. So there is a politico-economic dimension to the question of book production and distribution, and until this matter is faced, I believe that we will not understand the dynamics that fuel the problem that we are dealing with.

Today we are aware that on the African continent for example, over thirty countries are implementing the so-called Structural Adjustment Programme, a policy imposed on them by the International Monetary Fund. In Nigeria, the effects of SAP are such that there is a systematic campaign by the government for illiteracy. (Festus Iyayi)

These arresting statements were made by Festus Iyayi at the Lagos Symposium in May 1988. While he drew attention to underlying causes and accused governments of waging a 'systematic campaign' for illiteracy, others argued that governments should take on a wide range of responsibilities and sign a variety of treaties.

There will, of course and inevitably, always be differences of perception and approach. There will be those who believe they should expose, confront and denounce – Iyayi is clearly one of those. There will be others who, no less perceptive, assess the situation differently and speak of it in more moderate, albeit world-weary, tones. Lawal-Solarin, Chairman of the Nigerian Publishers' Association, is one of these. He wrote, in the course of an article for the *African Publishing Review*:

Government simply believes that publishing is a commercial venture that is profit-oriented and that any entreatment to Government to moderate tariffs or slash postage on books is seen as an attempt by publishers to increase their profits, especially when some publishers are so eager to bribe their way into getting their books adopted as textbooks by Ministries of Education. (Lawal-Solarin 1997, 10)

Governments often pay lip service to enterprising publishing projects and occasionally praise the literary endeavours of groups or individuals; but few encourage publishers and many are frightened of authors. Books are not valued, reading is not encouraged, and writers are not safe from persecution. In this situation, it is rarely worth making rhetorical appeals, and some people advocate quiet and persistent pressure. The situation will inevitably vary from country to country.

It is difficult to know how productive it is to have a leadership that is concerned about literature, and legitimate to ask:

- Did the Senegalese benefit because the state was ruled by a 'poet-president'? Was Leopold Senghor's interest enlightened and encouraging, or was it partisan, narrow, constricting, too concerned about Negritude? Was it, as the reaction to Ousmane Sembene's film *Ceddo* seemed to indicate, fearful and petty?

- In what ways did Ghanaian writers benefit from the fact that Kwame Nkrumah and Kofi Busia were themselves authors?

- What benefits have Nigerian authors derived from rule by a succession of leaders faithful to a creed, Islam, that accords high status to poets?

- If the heads of state have been ineffectual, have there been committed individuals who have been able to use positions of influence to secure benefits for writers?

- Can the influence of Efua Sutherland or Mohammed Ben Abdallah in Ghana, or of Mamman J Vatsa in Nigeria, be regarded as vital in improving the lot of writers by, for example, extracting state funding for publications, or for a theatre building, or for a base for a national writers' association?

- Have writers, working through local or national groups, brought benefits to their profession or to the literary culture in their country?

In attempting to assess the situation, the example of the Nigerian Book Foundation (NBF) provides an example that may be helpful, not least because it shows what a determined individual, Professor Chukwuemeka Ike, has been able to accomplish. The fact that Ike and his colleagues established the Foundation, in a vast and fissiparous state during a period when an oppressive regime waged a campaign against writers and freedom of expression, is all the more remarkable. The forerunner of the NBF, the Nigerian Book Development Forum, was founded on 24 May 1990 at a meeting of writers, publishers and representatives of various professional groups. Ike was elected convenor and was supported by a representative Task Force that met nine times between June 1990 and June 1991. During that time it addressed the Presidential Advisory Committee four times. Reflecting a general trend in organisational structure, the Task Force opted to become a non-governmental non-profit Foundation rather than a government parastatal, and, in time, to give way to the NBF. The

Nigerian Book Foundation held its first meeting in Lagos on 15 April 1993, and by October of the same year had established its secretariat at Awka in Anambra State.

Defining its mission, the NBF circulated the following in a pamphlet about itself:

> With an irrevocable commitment to indigenous book development, an-chored in the conviction that books build the nation, the NBF has as its mission the development of a vibrant indigenous book industry in Nigeria. As an umbrella organisation bringing together the key participants in the book industry, the NBF adopts a holistic approach to national book development, to ensure that all components in the book chain – the author, the publisher, the printer, the bookseller, the librarian, the producer/importer of raw materials for book production, et cetera – function maximally, and that the State provides a conducive environment for the book to flourish.

Among the objects of the Foundation can be found 'the encourage-ment and promotion of authorship', and:

> To co-operate with Government agencies and any other organisations, companies, or bodies engaged in the production of paper and other materials required for book development, with a view to keeping such paper and other materials readily available and at minimal costs.

The organisation has a Board of Trustees and a National Advisory Council. The former's terms of reference include 'The general superintendence of the policies, finances, and physical assets of the Foundation', while the latter 'enables the NBF to respond with one voice on behalf of the Nigerian book community as and when necessary'. This is clearly of great importance if the intention is to shape government policy! The Nigerian Book Foundation provides a model for imitation and many will find inspiration in the work of Professor Ike and his colleagues.

One of NBF's remarkable achievements is the publication, with Fourth Dimension Publishing Company, of the *Directory of Nigerian Book Development*, a 228-page volume containing information about: Published Nigerian Authors (749 entries), Book Publishing Houses (66 entries), Book Printing Presses (66 entries), Bookshops and Book Distribution Organisations (70 entries), and Libraries in Nigeria. The lists of libraries shows a certain unevenness. For example, libraries in Adamawa/Taraba States include those in Primary and Junior Second-ary, Secondary and Vocational Schools giving a total of 180; whereas Ogun State, for example, is far more selective and only lists 15 libraries. There are also problems with other lists: for example, Harry

Garuba is not among the authors and Malthouse is absent from the list of publishing houses. The distinction is not always made between an individual's role as editor and as sole author: Ime Ikiddeh edited *Drum Beats* and wrote not *Blind Cyclos* but *Blind Cyclops*. Sub-titles occasionally usurp titles, as in the entry for Ola Rotimi that includes *A Tragedy of the Ruled* but omits the main title *If*. However, the volume represents a remarkable compendium of information, gathered against considerable odds and despite a low level of response to questionnaires. The address for the Nigerian Book Foundation secretariat can be found in Writers' Organisations: A Directory (page 198, and see also page 364).

The debate about relations between writers and governments is on-going, as is right and proper. For example, an *Indaba on National Book Policy: The Key to Long Term Book Development* was held at the Zimbabwe International Book Fair, 1995. The Proceedings have been edited by Murray McCartney and published by the Zimbabwe International Book Fair Trust.

Censorship – and Self-censorship

There will always be two major types of censorship: including that imposed from outside, and that from within. The creative writer is often the victim of unendurable pressure that may come from the state or from groups within the state; this may affect opportunities to have material published and may lead to the isolation of – sometimes the imprisonment or even death of – a writer. This sort of censorship, broadly 'Political Censorship', will be examined first.

During the 1970s, censorship in Malawi was insistent and oppressive. Rubber-stamped by a Parliament dominated by Malawi Congress Party members, a Censorship Board was established with far-reaching powers to control everything that was published, screened, presented on stage or offered for sale in the country (1968). If they hoped to reach readers, authors had to write in a manner that would not give offence to those charged by the Censorship Board with assessing material.

A similar need for circumspection affected those writing for and working in the theatre. Their hope of seeing their work staged was affected by the fact that producers were obliged to ensure that each venue had a theatre licence and that a permit had been obtained for each performance of each play. Bookshop managers were required to ensure that they did not stock or display titles that had been banned by the Censorship Board.

Objection was made to a wide range of publications, including biographies of the Head of State and novels. Particular exception was taken to fictional accounts of life in Malawi, in other African countries under corrupt civilian regimes, or in states affected by coups. In Sonnet 66, Shakespeare wrote of 'art made tongue-tied by authority' and Malawian writers were undoubtedly affected in this way. Some of them became praise singers for the Banda regime, some lapsed into silence, some were content to censor themselves into producing bland effusions to which no one could take objection, some went into exile, some were detained – and some managed to speak to fellow Malawians over the heads and under the very noses of members of the Censorship Board. It goes without saying that writers need to acquaint themselves with any relevant censorship regulations: how they react thereafter will be a matter of choice.

Many African countries have experienced similar periods of repression, and authors have responded in a variety of ways. For example, in the course of Soyinka's opposition to a series of Nigerian regimes, he has used guerrilla theatre techniques, satirical revues, radio and television drama, press conferences, recordings of various sorts, and newspaper articles to reach audiences that have not been able to get to mainstream theatres. On occasions, he has found his attempts to get texts into newspapers thwarted and he has sometimes been unable to put on plays where and when he wanted to. Famously, a production of *Opera Wonyosi* was prevented from being seen in Lagos during an International Theatre Institute gathering. Extreme though this was, there have been other examples of censorship of Soyinka's work: in 1996, a group producing a 35-year-old text, *The Trials of Brother Jero*, was harried by nervous officials, aware that the author was an opposition leader and determined that he should not be given any sort of platform.

These examples indicate blatant forms of censorship: those in which a government assumes far-reaching powers and attempts to shield itself from criticism or ridicule. In certain instances the issues may be clear-cut, particularly in cases where critics are responsible and accurate. Repressive regimes have, inevitably, been quick to pick up on this issue of 'responsibility', using it to silence legitimate criticism. As a result, observers need to remain constantly alert, ready to strip away the accusations in order to expose the underlying motives for action.

In addition to government interference, the courts may be used to prevent communication in a fundamentally similar way. Soyinka's *The Man Died*, published by Rex Collings even though he knew there were threats of criminal and civil legal action, was the subject of a banning order because Femi Okunu objected to the way he had been presented in the book. In this way, the courts hindered the sale and inhibited the circulation of a major writer's comments on recent history.

Wole Soyinka has said that he is 'against censorship of every kind' yet there are many, including many African writers, who would stop short of this blanket statement. At the Zimbabwe Book Fair in 1995 there was a confrontation over the presence of a stand displaying Gay and Lesbian literature, and, under intense pressure from local public opinion, the festival organisers withdrew permission for the stand. The debate which followed raised every issue surrounding the freedom of the writer and in 1997, the matter was handled more discreetly. The issue will not, however, be removed from the agenda: Gay Rights remain a crucial issue; a point at which principles and deeply held attitudes come into conflict, a flash-point for writers, artists, religious leaders, politicians, indeed societies.

Writers are under pressure from many sides, as was demonstrated during the final session at the Arusha III seminar, when the statement entitled 'A "New Deal" between African Writers and Publishers' (see pages 131-34), was being hammered out. The final section of the document includes the following paragraph:

> There is need to strengthen indigenous textbook production so that it can subsidise creative writing. There is also a need to encourage authors to write in indigenous African languages, to promote positive African values, and for publishers to find the means to publish such works and make them profitable and affordable in Africa.

Initially, Taban lo Liyong proposed that the second sentence included the words 'to promote African values'. Kole Omotoso, from the Chair and in line with his characteristically progressive stance, took exception to Taban's formulation. Those listening to the discussion wondered exactly what African values were? Were we, for example, talking about female genital mutilation? Was the group being bound to support that? In the event – and significantly – the insertion of the word 'positive' was felt to render the formula acceptable to all. The ideological gulf between Taban's position and Omotoso's was huge, and if all the ideas represented in the room had been canvassed a wide variety of opinions would have found expression. The Statement was not binding – it is described as representing 'the broad consensus of the participants'. Many present did not feel it necessary to express an opinion.

As this episode shows, the question of how Africa should be presented by her authors, and by writers from other parts of the world, continues to be widely discussed. The determination of African authors to have their say about their continent, and, if possible, to do so without editorial interference from non-African publishers, has fuelled much of the best work produced in the last forty years. The Empire, and what used to be part of one empire or another, has, in Salman Rushdie's words, been writing back.

But not all voices have been equally welcome. This may be seen in the controversies that have surrounded the writing of VS Naipaul. Peggy Nightingale summarises them thus:

> ... many critics and reviewers bitterly condemn [Naipaul's] comments on various post-colonial societies, which he has invariably characterised as impoverished by their history as colonies and unlikely to break free of the past to establish a strong independent presence in the world. (Nightingale 1991)

In his play, *A Map of the World*, which is centred around a Naipaul-figure (Mehta), British dramatist David Hare examines some of the issues raised by the writer as critic, particularly those, like Naipaul whose presentation of 'the children of Empire' has generally been considered negative. A crisis is provoked within the drama when the Mozambican delegate to a UNESCO conference on poverty demands that Mehta prefaces his remarks to a plenary session by a statement that devalues his writings. The statement, which represents a kind of censorship, reads:

> Fiction, by its very nature, must always be different from fact, so in a way a man who stands before you as a writer of fiction is already half-way towards admitting that a great deal of what he makes up and invents is as much with an eye to entertainment as it is to presenting literal historical truth –

At this point Mehta has had enough and 'explodes':

> No, no, no, no! It is not to be endured. ... It is Nazi.

Subsequent attempts to negotiate a compromise crumble in the face of a 'personality clash' (Hare 1997, 142). The writer insists on the right to consider his fiction more faithful to historical truth than a mere recitation of facts.

Self-censorship

Precisely how a writer presents his or her experiences in his or her work will be affected by many considerations, some of them external: quite understandably, he or she may, for example, not wish to court imprisonment.

There will also be self-imposed restrictions. Normally these are taken for granted: an unwritten code as to what is acceptable and what is not. Only when this is breached, or pushed back, is there public debate. For example. When Hanif Kureishi's *Intimacies* (Faber 1998) appeared there were readers who felt that – for a transparently biographical and autobiographical work of fiction – the volume was deeply embarrassing, and that it would profoundly shame the author's children and ex-wife Secrets of the family and the conjugal bedroom were exposed to public gaze in a way many people considered ill-advised; the privacy of those he loved, or had once loved, had been invaded and the usual justification for such invasion – 'the public interest' – seemed to these critics an inadmissible excuse.

The issue of self-censorship is raised most often in autobiographical writing, and, since the concern in this book is with creative literature, to a large extent falls outside our remit. However, it is useful to note Anthony Appiah's account of the way in which different ideas about the arrangements for his father's funeral divided his relatives Some of them felt that the public analysis of

events presented in *In My Father's House* was inappropriate,
revealing the failure of the Western-educated author to appreciate
adequately the sense of decorum of his relatives. There are, many
would argue, some matters that are only for the ears of a family
circle. We do not always, as Jaguna puts it at the end of *The Strong
Breed*, 'have to speak with a full mouth'.

In his own autobiographical writing, Soyinka has walked a narrow
path between revelation and concealment, and he too has been
accused of being too ready to reveal 'intimacies'. For many years, he
ruled out the possibility of continuing his autobiography beyond *Aké*,
and beyond the 'age of innocence'. It was, therefore, a surprise to many
when he published his account of 'The Penkelemes Years' in *Ibadan*
which took him deep into the 'age of experience' (Soyinka 1994b).
Although presented as 'faction', and written in the third person, the
volume incorporates material which is based firmly on his recollection
of his own life and involves, for example, his second wife and the
mother of one of his children. Soyinka has continued to tantalise
readers by scurrying back and forth between the invented and the
historical, deliberately blurring boundaries that are, in any case, rarely
absolute.

The extent to which an author should be unrestrained in presenting
intimate relationships will long be a matter for discussion.

Censorship: Nothing Has Changed

Regina Jere-Malanda

The travails of African writers and the media in general have been well-documented. But the 1990s have been remarkable. The decade brought new hopes both in terms of political democracy and media and literary activity. Dictatorships were crumbling and hopes for real freedom of expression 'coming home' were high. But the stark reality today is that censorship, whether self- or state-inflicted, remains a big problem and is as entrenched as ever.

The harsh, overt censorship practised by cruder dictators, such as Malawi's late Kamuzu Banda and Nigeria's General Sani Abacha (who also died, last June), may seem to be less common today: yet opposing censorship on the continent is still as dangerous as it has always been. The catalogue of current events and victims of censorship are innumerable and stretch from killings of journalists in Sierra Leone and Algeria, to torture and being forced into exile in Nigeria and Ethiopia. Only a little can be covered here. Detentions and imprisonment of writers and journalists are almost natural throughout the continent. The late dictator Mobutu Sese Seko was bad, but Kabila 'The Liberator' is worse. The trend of censorship in all countries is similar: harass, intimidate, suppress and eventually silence. Yet despite all this, there is still hope; most of the victims and their publications still survive. The censors have, in most cases, failed to silence opponents and this gives cause for some celebration in the African writer and journalistic circles. It encourages upcoming writers.

The price of opposing censorship is high. The current civil war wrecking Sierra Leone provides sad examples of what can happen to journalists who refuse to be cowed by either of the warring factions. Rebels have recently been on a wanton and ruthless killing spree targeting journalists whom they feel are biased against them. At least five were killed in the first few months of 1999 alone. Many others are missing. One of them, Paul Kamara, was killed together with his wife and two small children. On the other hand, the Government last year sentenced five journalists to death on unproved charges that they encouraged support for the rebels in their reporting – charges they strongly deny.

African writers both old and new know the history of intimidation which literary giants like Wole Soyinka, Ngugi wa Thiong'o and others of their time went through at the hands of agents of repressive regimes. It was, therefore, with cautious optimism that many writers and journalists welcomed the changing political scene of the 1990s. It brought hopes that what Soyinka and others went through could be a thing of the past. Alas, this is not the case: censorship in most countries today is almost endemic. A writer can be praised as a hero one day and damned as a traitor the next. For example, Zambia's *Post* newspaper managing editor, Fred Mmembe, used to be one the darlings of the current ruling MMD Government of Frederick Chiluba. The paper's muckraking reporting before the 1991 elections played a huge role in bringing to an end former President Kenneth Kaunda's 27-year rule. Mmembe was hopeful that the new leaders would uphold their democracy pledges. Today he spends more of his time in the courtroom fighting Government suits than in his newsroom. His reporters are perpetually harassed. Only two weeks before this was written, six of them were arrested and charged with espionage for reporting that Zambia would stand no chance in a war with Angola because of its inferior military power. The threat of war between Angola and Zambia is an issue that has been reported on internationally since Angola began accusing Zambia of aiding rebel UNITA militarily in exchange for diamonds last year.

Good journalists and writers in a badly run African country know that writing a good story can mean putting oneself in line for questioning by police and a spell in jail. At worst, it may mean torture and death. Nigerian journalist and publisher Christine Anyanwu spent months in a cell with rats, which she says 'could not only hop but walk on two feet'. Like many others writers in her country, she had been given a fifteen-year sentence for writing a story based on an interview she had with a relative of a suspect in an alleged coup plot. She has, following Abacha's death, since been released. 'Guerrilla journalism' was a term coined at the height of the Abacha tyranny, meaning that editors, reporters and publishers were constantly on the run, operating underground. Despite these difficulties, their publications – for example, *Tell* and *The News* magazines, managed to reach the newstands. At times, frustrated military authorities arrested or threatened to punish family members, such as a wife or mother, in the place of the scribes – just to force them out of hiding. Up to the day of Abacha's death, the Nigerian media remained unrepentant.

Today, however, there has been a sea-change in Nigeria. Abacha's successor, General Abdulsalam Abubakar, is trying to open a new chapter of hope; one that seeks to cut-off forever the censor's hand of harassment, arbitrary arrests, torture and killings. As a start, he has quickly released most imprisoned journalists and writers, including Anyanwu and the poet Ogaga Ifowodo, as well as political prisoners.

In May. Abubakar handed over power to a civilian government led by former General Olesugun Obasanjo. In his grave, Abacha must be cursing at the unfolding events in a country he reduced to his own fiefdom. Abubakar's gesture has, however, been received with mixed feelings: scepticism and a wait-and-see attitude. Will Obasanjo continue in Abubakar's way? Cracks are already showing. While some journalists have been released, others are being arrested or intimidated.

Information Minister John Nwondo has hinted at making libel a criminal offence; and has said that the Press Council Law would be amended 'to give it more teeth'. Criminalisation of freedom of expression is one of the vicious censorship tools used by most African governments, who, on the whole, have failed or refuse to repeal draconian media laws left by their predecessors.

A recent report by the Uganda Journalists' Safety Committee said that intimidation and attacks on journalists by both government and rebel factions was becoming common. President Yoweri Museveni was quoted as saying:

> [The press] think that when we move on them the international community will cut off aid. This may hold for now but there will be a time when we shall not need foreign aid. Then we will turn on them.

In January 1998, Malawi soldiers stormed the offices of an independent daily paper threatening to kill journalists, particularly the author of a story which claimed that the rate of HIV/AIDS was higher in the army than in general society. They damaged the paper's computers and cameras, warning the journalist not to 'play games with the army'. The Government, which triumphed in Malawi's first democratic election on the platform of enhancing freedom of expression and the press, offered no protection; neither did the police. The system of censorship introduced by Banda remains intact.

Repression like that in Malawi continues in other countries. Offices of Ethiopia's *Tobiya* newspaper were burnt down, destroying its computer database and archive material. Its staff were later arrested by the police officers who had earlier refused to come to the scene of the fire claiming work overload. Ethiopia has many authors and journalists who have been in prison for years without trial; many others have fled into exile.

In Cameroon, Pius Njawe, editor of the outspoken *Le Messager* newspaper, has for the past nine years been at the receiving end of the country's censor. Following a pardon from President Paul Biya last month, he was released from a one-year prison term for publishing an article written by another journalist, that raised questions about Biya's health. Njawe spent days in a cell with a hundred convicted murderers and dangerous armed robbers. His bunkmate was the leader of a gang that raided his own neighbour's house. But even in his prison cell, the ugly head of censorship followed him. He was prevented from writing for his newspaper, about his stay in prison, by the prison governor who told him that while in his 'care', he 'shouldn't lift his pen'. Njawe told this story in a speech which was smuggled out of prison, to thank the organisers of the 1998 UNESCO/Guillermo Cario Press Freedom Award for honouring him.

His message to his fellow writers, both old and new, was challenging, and included the following:

> I am paying for having refused to plunge into the trough. I am paying because every choice must be paid for. But I am proud of my choice. My only regret is that we still have colleagues who think compromising with the powers that be is the only way out.

In many countries new leaders are hounding media people and other writers even more than their predecessors did. The majority of the new democracies still hang on to the control of the main media, putting direct restraint on journalists, who – for fear of losing their source of income – are left with no choice but to dance to the tune of their employers. They censor themselves to save their jobs. In Zambia, during June 1998, journalist Joy Chula nearly lost her job for admitting in a national television debate how journalists in the state-owned media practised self-censorship. They were acting on the apt adage, 'You do not bite the hand that feeds you.'

While journalists seem to bear the brunt of censorship, other areas of the media have not been completely spared. In September 1998, Hamdy Al-Batran, author of the *Diary of a Police Officer in the Countryside*, was suspended from the police for publishing his novel without permission from the Interior Ministry. Earlier on, police raided the Sina publishing house in Cairo and took copies of two books by Khal Abdel Karim: *The Yathrib Society* and *The Raaba Songs on the Companions of Prophet Muhammed*. This confiscation was carried out because the Islamic Research Academy said the books were blasphemous. The American University in Cairo, in May 1998, was forced to remove from its library shelves and database, the book *Muhammad* by Maxine Rodison, because a newspaper columnist said it 'denigrated the Islamic faith'. This action went well beyond the Higher Education Ministry's request that the University remove the book from a teaching course.

Current events in many parts of Africa bring little hope to its writers and journalists. The disappointment is made worse when coming to terms with the reality that the new democracies, now slowly disintegrating in their turn, only brought with them new censors. The culture of intolerance and desire to stay in power at all costs which they inherited remains unchanged.

Writing Against Repression

An Interview with Niyi Osundare

After almost five years in the grip of Abacha's dictatorship, Nigeria is currently going through another 'transition to democracy' under yet another military ruler. This is a period of anxiety, scepticism and guarded optimism. Poet and playwright Niyi Osundare talks to Omowunmi Segun about the past, present and future of human rights in Nigeria.

Segun: Between June 1993 and June 1998, many Nigerian journalists and writers were tortured and jailed. Others like Wole Soyinka had to go into exile in fear for their lives. Did this affect your writing?

Osundare: It affected it in two ways – negatively and positively. There were times when I held my head in my hands. A certain kind of empathetic anxiety descended on me – a sense that this could happen to anyone. Take the newspaper editor Kunle Ajibade for instance. He did not take part in any coup. Nigeria became a big prison: those who were jailed left us behind in the bigger prison. This didn't break the spirit of Nigerian journalists. Many of them went underground and fought. It was so effective that Abacha had to employ an image-maker. I committed myself to writing. I did a long poem for Kunle Ajibade. A copy of it was smuggled to him in prison. I was happy when Kunle said he had seen it. One tried to react that way. Nothing scares a despot more than the names of those he is trying to destroy. Everywhere I went, I kept mentioning their names. I thought I was doing it for my own sanity as well.

Some people are of the opinion that writers should not get involved in politics. Do you share this view?

Writers cannot close their eyes to what is happening around them. Our experience in history has also shown that writers are not only the conscience of their society, but that they are at risk wherever they are. Writers are distinguished by the fact that they feel intensely and intelligently. Writers feel, and because of that they are able to put issues in historical perspective. They are able to intrude upon events, to anticipate, to warn. It is that ability to sit down and brood and think about what has been and look at what might be. The vision of the despot controls and subjugates other human beings and mortgages the rights of others. There is always a conflict and a clash between these two visions. One is evil and pathogenic and other one is essentially humanistic and healthy. Tyrants have always seen visionaries as the enemy. It's not possible for a conscientious writer not to be engaged.

Amnesty International and *Index on Censorship* should be thanked for the little we've been able to achieve in Nigeria in the last decade. Two basic phenomena are necessary in a dictatorial regime: violence and the lie. In real human society, dictatorship should not exist. A dictatorship is trying to disrupt the normal flow of human rationality. Every despotic regime is always frightened. To keep existing, it must keep lying. Nigerian human rights groups put their lives on the line. They were not just opposing Abacha, they were creating a certain atmosphere, they were creating the soil for democracy.

General Abdulsalam Abubakar seems determined to improve Nigeria's human rights record. How do you view the fortuitous turn of events in Nigeria since June this year?

General Abubakar has become Head of State by accident. He did not prepare for leadership. I can't claim to know Abubakar, I can only guess from what is said about him and what I have read. He seems to be well-meaning. In a situation like Nigeria, even an ordinary smile is seen as a grandiose gesture. It doesn't matter how he came to power. What he does is important. We have to let him know that there are problems on the ground. The structure of democracy is very shaky. The Nigeria that Abubakar inherited is like a country that has been through a gruesome war or a hurricane and has been terribly devastated. Where do you start? You have to know what democracy means and pay more than lip service to it. By nature, soldiers are not supposed to be democratic people. They cannot tolerate dissent. Nigeria as a policy has made futile attempts at democracy because we've been building in a structure that is shaky. We don't have a nation, but a collection of tribes. *Dance of A Forest* [by Wole Soyinka] describes Nigeria as a gathering of tribes. At no time has this definition been truer. I don't believe Nigeria should disintegrate; there are men and women there who can build the country. It's a pity that they haven't been able to assume power. We have learned some lessons. About fifteen years ago, human rights NGOs weren't so prominent in Nigeria. Now everyone knows about Amnesty International and other human rights groups in Nigeria. They've prepared the ground for democracy. But again, vigilance: we cannot take any soldier by his word any more in Nigeria.

December 1998 marked the fiftieth anniversary of the UDHR [Universal Declaration of Human Rights]. What part do writers have to play in promoting the message of the UDHR?

Writers owe a duty to our world. The human rights struggle is a challenge to every writer, even those who write theories. There's a lot of complacency in our current discourse. Theorists on postmodernism see chaos and futility everywhere, and they feel writers should reflect that angst. For my part, I think the writer should join humanity in finding a cure to restore our world to sanity. In a world where you have so much, writers should have a role. Writers are getting more conscientious. They have teamed together to give support to Salman Rushdie. Wole Soyinka has played a vital role in opposing the Abacha regime and brought other Nobel Laureates to a deeper awareness about what is happening. Writers have a duty of making the world aware of itself. Literature is an important weapon. When I read Tolstoy, something of the Russian spirit comes to me. When you have read a great work by a writer, you can't forget the country she or he is from.

How do you think governments all over the world, and particularly in Africa, can be made to live up to their obligations to promote and protect the fundamental human rights of all?

The price of freedom is eternal vigilance. We must be part of that vigilance. We must expose all those things that dictators are always trying to hide. We must value our rights. We must see the world as one place. Dictators thrive because some parts of the world shut their eyes to other parts. It's common knowledge by now that Mobutu, Barre, Bokassa and Doe seized power and lasted so long because of the support they received from powerful nations who practise democracy at home, but foster tyranny in other places. This double standard has to stop.

Amnesty International is currently doing a campaign in the UDHR. Individuals are being asked to make a personal commitment and pledge to reinforce the message of the UDHR. Have you already made a pledge?

No.

Would you like to make a pledge?

Yes. Human beings without human rights are like animals. I stand for human rights. I would like to see human beings live their lives to the fullest – free, fulfilled and self-respecting.

Omowunmi Segun's first novel *The Third Dimple* won the prose fiction prize of the Association of Nigerian Authors. She is a member of Al Nigeria.

Getting on with the Law

Performance and Publication

When Adam told stories and Eve sang songs who was then the publisher?

In this Handbook, the term 'published' is generally considered in terms of material that has been written down and reproduced in print, with copyright protection, to be sold for profit. In many contexts – particularly in the past, but in certain instances in the present also – this is an inadequate account of the situation. Some kinds of creative work, including songs and films, hardly exist in print and yet they should be protected – as they need to be, since they are particularly vulnerable to pirating. That is to say the general public very often has access to tape recorders, video recorder or video cameras that enable them to make copies very easily – albeit of varying quality. Bootlegged versions of newly released films sometimes appear on the market after a criminally inclined member of an audience has smuggled a video camera into a cinema at a première and made a recording of what passed on the screen. Cash-rich companies have employed lawyers and, in some cases, specialised copyright bodies, to prosecute these pirates.

In some countries new laws have been set in place to try to provide protection against those who make use of new technology to steal creative or intellectual property. However, the extent to which victims of piracy can expect support from the state varies. In some countries, the law-makers have failed to move with the times and the statute books are ill-equipped to deal with hi-tech crime. In others, the laws may exist, but they may be flouted with impunity by criminals who buy off, or frighten off, enforcement agencies suffering from rock-bottom wages, poor back-up or low morale. In some cases the amount of money lost to the company may not justify an elaborate court case.

Creative members of society should know that proof of publication does not depend in every case on appearance in print. Indeed, some playwrights regard a production as more significant than the printing of the text: the presentation is the real 'out-dooring'. Mohammed Ben-Abdallah is one of them. Asked why there was such a long delay between the première of his plays and their appearance in print, Abdallah said he regarded performance as publication.

The same is true of some poets. In this connection, it is valuable to listen to Kofi Anyidoho writing on 'Poetry as Dramatic Performance: The Ghana Experience:'

> We need to revise our understanding of the concept of 'Publication' to include the act of public poetry performance. Otherwise, how do we account for the fact that even poets whose works are already in print nevertheless insist on publishing their poetry through continued public performance ... a whole generation of Ghanaian poets who enjoy national recognition include many who have never published a single poem. (Anyidoho 1991, 45)

It is easy to see how this situation has come about, given the relationship that has almost always existed between poetry and its recitation/performance. After all, for centuries poets such as Homer and bards that followed him recited the *Iliad* from memory, while *griots* performed historical sagas and poems about the heroes of the Mandinka for a similar period.

Anyidoho himself has been lucky enough to find publishers, notably a local publisher, Woeli Publishing Services. And it is astonishing to discover that the proprietor of that venture, Woeli Dekutsey, was prepared to take on not only poetry but also drama – he brought out Ben-Abdallah's collections. Such vision and enterprise are rare, and not always found – even on the Ghanaian publishing scene since poetry and drama do not usually provide a profit.

A major problem with publishing through performance concerns the question of ownership. Anything that is performed can be copied. Take the case of comedians: comedians have jokes – 'stand-up comedy routines' – and they earn money by performing before audiences. They live in the knowledge that their material may be 'stolen'. Sometimes this will be simply a case of a member of the audience repeating an exchange for the amusement of friends over a drink. More seriously, ambitious, but uncreative, would-be comedians may appropriate whole chunks of an act and pass them off as their own. They may earn money by reproducing the stolen material for paying audiences. Clearly, repeating a joke in a bar is unlikely to cause offence. Equally clearly, making a living from repeating someone else's comedy routine is a serious offence, and the law may be called in to sort out the theft. However, predictably, each case is not always crystal clear and the law may become entangled in issues of influence, and led into 'grey areas'.

Ownership of the material is at the heart of the issue and some cases may be fairly easily proved. A comedian may be able to call upon members of an audience that saw him perform his original material before it was stolen, imitated – 'bootlegged'. But what about the case of somebody who is drawing on folk material? In a sense, possession of a body of folklore belongs to the community that produced it, and can be inherited by any member of that community. The story-teller owns the tale by retelling it, by stamping individuality upon it and by sharing it with an audience.

The issue is sometimes discussed in relation to the story of the young woman who scorned suggested suitors and married a beautiful stranger who turned out to be a monster. This is a familiar tale in West Africa. It is famously retold in the written tradition by Amos Tutuola as part of *The Palm-Wine Drinkard*, and it lies behind Efua Sutherland's *Foriwa*, where, significantly, the 'stranger' is 'a north-erner' who is enlightened, an admirable partner for the play's progressive princess.

Some of those who were taken aback at Tutuola's success with British readers played down his originality, pointing out that his stories were a familiar part of a body of folklore. This missed a point that is apparent whenever Tutuola's version is read aloud, recited or performed to an audience: namely, that his inventiveness is striking, his eloquence immediately recognised. Experience of performances shows that his narratives are wonderfully comple-mented by his comparisons, his details, his dexterity and his daring. To dismiss Tutuola because he raided the community's memory bank for plots is to misunderstand the nature of creativity, and push to the centre a narrowly romantic image of the artist. From Shakespeare to Bertolt Brecht, to Tutuola and Soyinka, the artist has ransacked the common store, put old plots to new uses, infused the familiar with the original.

What happens, to take another angle, when someone invents a story? A number of legal cases have been brought against authors for stealing plots. One of them concerns *Six Degrees of Separation*, a play that has at its centre an episode in which a young man passes himself off to a wealthy couple as a friend of their children and as a son of Sidney Poitier. The author acknowledged that he had been inspired by an anecdote – or *donnée* – about a hoax that was reported in the New York papers. After the production of the play, the young man who perpetrated the hoax claimed that he had made an original contribution to the play. In a sense he had: his was an original idea, which explored the desires and failures of New York families, to which the playwright added his labour, insight, and eloquence. It should not be beyond human wit to come up with a formula for sharing rewards to the satisfaction of both sides.

Another example, this time with a Nigerian link, features a short story by Jeffrey Archer. This revolved around an African leader who appears to be concerned to investigate the Swiss bank accounts of one of his fellow countrymen. He visits the bank and demands that a bank official break the conventional code of confidentiality and divulge secrets about a bank account. When the banker hesitates the demands are followed by threats and a gun is produced. However, despite the possibility of being shot, the banker refuses to divulge details. At this point, the visitor switches tack: it seems that he was just testing the system and, having found it secure, puts away his gun and says he wishes to make a deposit himself. It has been suggested that Archer appropriated this story and his informant has claimed a share of his earnings from it.

Many of the cases in which creative people have been accused of theft of material have concerned music. This is not surprising in view of the amount of money involved in the music business and the ease with which tapes and records can be copied. In various ways, copyright control of printed material has followed in the wake of attempts to control criminal activity in the music industry. In Ghana, GAW has followed MUGS: that is to say the Musicians Union of Ghana has led the way and the Ghana Association of Writers has followed. A pertinent case that demonstrates the complexities at stake concerns Paul Simon's use of the *Yaa Amponsah* theme in the album 'Gracelands'. Aware that he was making use of the motif, thinking it was a 'traditional Ghanaian melody', and anxious to do the right thing, Simon came to a financial settlement with MUGS, as a representative of the national musical tradition. At this point claims were made by the descendants of an individual composer. They claimed that *Yaa Amponsah* was not the work of an anonymous, 'traditional', contributor to 'traditional Ghanaian music'; but that it was actually composed by an identifiable individual who was, in fact, their relative and whose musical estate they had inherited.

Libel: The Case of *The Man Died*

The Man Died is the despair of critics with a rigid attitude to genres. Quite simply, it doesn't fit neatly into a familiar category, and yet, quite obviously, it is in part a work of creative literature – and the work of a creative author that 'should' be placed in one genre or another. These considerations, and the clarity with which the book raises legal issues, justify its close examination to highlight issues of libel.

In June 1975 Peter Calvocoressi of Penguin Books spoke on the phone to Rex Collings, Soyinka's publisher-friend, about *The Man Died* – a title that Penguin had undertaken to publish. Collings noted the gist of the conversation on a piece of paper that is on file with other papers in the Brotherton Library at the University of Leeds. It is a fascinating document: here were two men of principle – Calvocoressi and Collings – confronting a terribly difficult decision about a text by an author whom they both admired. Calvocoressi was a very distinguished lawyer who had edited the proceedings of the Nuremberg Trials at which Nazi war criminals were sentenced. He was, moreover, an immensely influential figure in a publishing company with a distinguished history, links around the globe, and many employees. Collings headed a tiny publishing enterprise which he piloted with passion and principle. The author whose book they were considering was an idealist and a man of action, an author who had quite fearlessly – or recklessly – decided to 'name names' in a prison diary that cast discretion to the winds. In *The Man Died*, he made assertions about fellow Nigerians that were by turn brilliantly accurate and vulnerable to legal examination.

Collings recorded that pressure was being put on Calvocoressi: his company was 'threatened with action for libel and for seditious libel' if plans for a Penguin edition of *The Man Died* went ahead. The action would, Calvocoressi feared, 'be taken against Longman's organisation in Nigeria'. He did not specify the source of pressure, but he regarded its application as raising two issues. The first was the personal safety of staff: people working for the Penguin affiliate, Longman, in Nigeria were particularly at risk. The second was financial: Calvocoressi was acutely aware that 'huge damages (might) be claimed', especially if a libel case were to be tried in Nigeria. The controversy had come at a particularly difficult time for Penguin, since Penguin/Longman had incurred bad publicity following the decision – seen by some as craven

– not to publish Philip Short's biography of Hastings Banda. Calvocoressi was considering whether he should go to Nigeria to assess the situation, and asked Collings what course he would follow. Collings answered only partly that he needed to talk to Soyinka about it. He preferred not to put the matter in writing in a letter that would have to be sent by post to Nigeria.

A few days later, on 24 June, Collings raised the matter again. He wrote to Calvocoressi 'Thinking about Friday's question: what would you do?' Collings went on to give his own answer that he would publish, putting his trust in the independence of the Nigerian judiciary. Collings continued that he thought if Penguin published the book it would be banned; and Longman might face action even extending to expropriation of property. As a compromise, he suggested selling the Nigerian rights to a Nigerian company. Regarding Soyinka's position, he wrote: 'Please see him when he is in London ... He is a very close personal friend, one of the people nearest to me, and I would hate to feel that I was hiding something from him.'

Just under a month later, on 21 July 1975, Calvocoressi wrote to communicate Penguin's decision to drop plans to publish *The Man Died* because 'action is indeed probable'. Calvocoressi was convinced, or had been advised, that the book contained libellous matter, and that the company might face legal proceedings if it was published. He assured Collings that Penguin would pay the remainder of the contracted advance, and observed that the episode was painful because this 'is a fine book'.

Some of what happened following this arrangement is in the public domain. Collings published the diary in hardback and Femi Okunnu took legal action against it. In Nigeria, a few copies were circulated surreptitiously, but the book was withdrawn from sale. Whether this was because of enforceable legal requirements or a conditioned reflex of bookshop managers who anticipated the visits of the security forces is not clear. The case eventually came to court and Okunnu received derisory damages. Penguin eventually brought out a paperback edition that differs in some respects from the Collings hardback. The episode illustrates the way in which a book that 'names names' might be handled. Authors must know what they are doing with names. They may want to assess the legal risks and pillory individuals. That is their – and their publishers' lawyers' – decision.

Authors should be open with their publishers about any issues of libel raised by their texts. Care should be taken that they do not, through choice of a name, or profession, or place of work, appear to libel an individual.

Rights and Territorial Rights

Increasingly, African authors making agreements with multinational publishers reserve the rights to publish in their home country, and then ensure that a local edition is produced for their 'home' market. The Fountain Publications (Ibadan) edition of *Isara* (set by Wemilore Press), for example, is sold beside the Methuen (London) edition (printed in Bury St Edmunds) and other 'outside Nigeria' editions.

The legend 'Not for sale in the USA' is frequently found inside editions of books, an indication that another publisher holds some of the rights. The warning allows a glimpse into the way 'Publishing Empires' operate. Perhaps surprisingly – or perhaps not – as far as the rights to books are concerned the world is divided broadly between publishers based in the UK (usually London) and the United States (often New York). The areas of influence in the case of the former predictably cover Europe and the Commonwealth, that of the latter cover Latin America and the Philippines. The old walls, however, are crumbling and writers should be aware of this. New Zealand has abolished territorial rights and South Africa has witnessed a clash that deserves further discussion. Meanwhile, the Internet and the growth of Internet sales between areas of influence – over the wall, as it were – has meant that UK customers are ordering books from the US. This has many implications for Africa.

In South Africa, the clash came between UK-based Random House and the South African book chain Fact and Fiction (F&F). As indicated, South Africa is usually included in UK territorial rights, but F&F purchased discount-priced copies of John Grisham's *The Street Lawyer*. This title had been published in the US by Doubleday, a subsidiary of Bertelsmann, which *The Bookseller* reported had been bought by Random House (McHardy 1998). The conflicting parties squared up to one another: Random House threatened to take action if the sales of the book became 'statistically significant'; while F&F's marketing director refused to give way, saying that the company had taken legal advice which suggested that 'The legitimacy of territorial rights arrangements are unlikely to hold up in a South African court.'

The tension increased when Random House air-freighted stock for early sale while suspending trade with F&F, demanding the cancellation of the advertising campaign for the Doubleday edition and the removal of copies from the shelves. According to Françoise McHardy, the chief counsel to the International Publishers Copyright Council, Charles Clark, 'said territorial rights were clearly laid out in international copyright conventions, to which South Africa was party' (McHardy 1998).

Getting on with the Book Trade

Book Launches and Publicity

> I prayed the ground to open and swallow me as 'launchers' of a new book
> walked to the podium and extracted bundles of currency notes from
> unwilling pockets (I am almost tempted to add socks); as students chanted
> 'Sap' to 'donors' whose names were called out but failed to turn up. I did
> wonder then what were the limits of vulgarity. (Saro-Wiwa 1991c)

These words, dated 12 October 1989, can be found in the 'Open Letter
to Wole Soyinka' that Ken Saro-Wiwa was prompted to write in the
wake of the combined launch of one of Soyinka's books and of the
'Essay Foundation' at the Institute of International Affairs on 5
October 1989. Saro-Wiwa directed his concern partly at the Essay
Foundation and partly at the tradition of fundraising that had become
a feature of book launches in Nigeria. His words recalled a launch at
one of the Annual University of Calabar International Conferences of
African Literature and the English Language where these embarrassing
events above occurred.

Saro-Wiwa's letter formed part of a continuing expression of concern
about the direction in which Nigerian literary culture was heading and
concluded with a 'threat': the formal launching of the Essay Foundation
was to take place on 5 January 1990; if Soyinka called:

> upon some money bags to publicly launch the Foundation with donations,
> announced or not, I will not hesitate to request you to return your precious
> Nobel Prize and your recent French honour and make your way back to
> Otta where you will find, on Temperance Farm, your compatriot (General
> Obasanjo) who, having received a whopping 60,000 naira (or was it more)
> from a 'launcher' of one of his books, proceed to write as follows in his next
> book: 'Meanwhile the obscene rich élites continue a flagrant and unre-
> strained assault on moral values through their macabre taste. The
> consequence of such ribaldry [sic] assault on social norms, on the entire
> society is the odious and noxious debt bomb that is now asphyxiating our
> development efforts' – I think I must stop there before I get asphyxiated.
> (Saro-Wiwa 1991c: 87)

In fact the confrontation was part of a long-running exchange, since
Soyinka is a fierce critic of what he has called 'Launching Culture'.

One of his observations on launches is embedded in the answer to a question about the apparent lack of new Nigerian writing during the last decade. As will be apparent, the interview, given during 1994, raises issues that reverberate through this volume:

> The publishing situation in Nigeria is very, very parlous. The culture of publishing has become detrimental to healthy literary output, but I assure you that I have seen quite a lot of manuscripts and, you know, the Association of Nigerian Authors has a policy of trying to publish at least two works a year. I have sent manuscripts to some publishers and all they can think of is 'Will we be able to recover our money at the launching?' Launching culture has replaced publishing culture. We have thought of a number of solutions, setting up co-operative publishing houses and so on and so forth. (Soyinka 1994b, 1270-71)

One of the functions at which both writer and publisher might expect to be present is at the launching of a new title. In London, such an occasion might be marked by a certain amount of eating and drinking, of literary gossip and speech-making. In West Africa, launches have become major social and commercial events, sometimes incorporating the dramatisation of episodes from publications, and almost certainly involving fundraising by the auctioning of numbered copies of the new title. Publishers have come to hope, as Soyinka makes clear in his comments, that, through 'Vanity Buying' or 'High Profile Purchasing' they will be able to recoup a significant portion of their investment in a book. These occasions at times combine 'harvesting' with conviviality, dignity and appropriate emotion, but the balance is difficult to strike and the vulgar display of wealth is sometimes apparent. Deep embarrassment can be caused, both to author and members of the audience, unless only those who have previously agreed to buy copies or make donations are called upon. At Soyinka's book launch, which prompted the Open Letter, the sums handed over were not disclosed and this preserved an important element of decorum.

Writers and publishers are now well aware that the opportunities for self-advertisement afforded by book launches may be combined with duplicity. The experience of Aig Higo and those attending the International Symposium of African Literatures (Lagos 1988) provides a salutary lesson on the evils of 'Big Man-ism'. According to Higo:

> I recall that two governments ago, in Nigeria, we launched a poetry volume in one of the halls (at the National Theatre in Lagos). The then Minister who came to perform the launching of the book said: 'I am buying 5,000 copies of this book on behalf of the Federal Government.' We all clapped.

Till today, officials of his Ministry say to me 'He only said that as a joke'. (Osofisan *et al.* 1991, 110)

This worrying narrative is embedded in an argument about the desirability of following what Higo calls 'the Norwegian example', whereby the government purchases – direct from the publishers – 1,000 copies of each new title for distribution to public libraries. Clearly, bulk purchases are an appropriate way of using money and supporting literature; and, equally clearly, launches are a suitable occasion at which to announce them. They are not, however, an appropriate place for attention-seeking comedians or jokers of the kind at the heart of Higo's anecdotes.

In all probability, writers will be prepared to attend book launches, and their presence will add immeasurably to the occasion. Book signings, interviews with the media, promotional tours and public readings are just some of the ways in which a determined publisher can, in co-operation and consultation with an author, publicise a new title. The question of how much time and effort writers should devote to assisting their publishers in promoting titles should be talked through gently. On a visit to England at the time of the release of *Changes* by Woman's Press, Ama Ata Aidoo, suffering from restricted mobility, found the number of promotional interviews arranged for her to give very exhausting. However, presumably, she was paid for the interviews given to the BBC and other organisations, and presumably the publicity led to increased sales – and an increase in royalty payments. Contracts sometimes spell out what is expected of an author in terms of book promotion. Where there are areas of uncertainty it is advisable to return to the terms of the contract and both sides should ensure that 'the handshake does not go beyond the elbow'. There is no reason why mature and distinguished novelists should be exhausted by a programme drawn up by a youthful, ambitious and inconsiderate publicity officer.

Differences between the situations of publishers concerned with 'marketing' Ama Ata Aidoo in Europe and Africa were revealed at the launching of *The Girl Who Can and Other Stories*. At this very pleasant occasion, held in the Toyota Pavilion at the Trade Fair Site in Accra to coincide with the November 1996 Book Fair, it was suggested to her publisher that Ms Aidoo might give an interview on the radio. The reaction was 'How much will it cost to buy time on the radio?' Expectations and experiences vary considerably. Radio stations are funded differently from one county to another, and producers have varying attitudes to 'cultural products' and 'intellectual property'. On BBC 'chat shows' and on Oprah Winfrey-style programmes guests are permitted – indeed, on occasions, encouraged – to mention, promote or 'plug' a recently published book. In other words, regulations and conventions controlling advertising are, quite rightly, not always applied to literature.

A final comment from a publisher who links launches with issues of distribution:

> Millions of Naira are collected at the launching, especially if the book is written by or about a serving or recently retired general whose favour is being curried by contractors or beneficiaries of government largesse. It has always been difficult to find these books anywhere after the launching, even from publishers. (Lawal-Solarin 1997, 11)

Book Fairs: A Directory

Note and Acknowledgement: The listings below – and excerpts from descriptive information – have been extracted, with permission, from *Book Marketing and Promotion: A Handbook of Good Practice* by Hans M Zell; London: International Network for the Availability of Scientific Publications (INASP), 1999.

SOME MAJOR INTERNATIONAL BOOK FAIRS

Note: This is a small selection of some of the major international book fairs in the countries of the North. For more extensive listings (and details), consult *Book Marketing and Promotion: A Handbook of Good Practice* mentioned above. The Fair dates indicated, which are usually the same each year, are those for 1999 and, if known at this time, also the dates for the year 2000 and beyond.

Europe

Frankfurt Book Fair
Reineckstrasse 3
60313 Frankfurt am Main, Germany
Tel: +49-69-21020
Fax: +49-69-2102227 or 2102277
Email: services@book-fair.com
(Exhibitor services)
marketing@book-fair.com
(Marketing)
or international@book-fair.com
(International division)
Web site:
http://www.frankfurt-book-fair.com
Venue: Messegelände (Trade fair complex)
Contacts: Franz Fenke (Technical Director, for exhibitors); Wolfgang von Schumann (Marketing, for trade visitors)
Fair dates: 1999: 13-18 October
2000: 11-16 October
2001: 10-15 October

This is the biggie among the book fairs, and Frankfurt remains the key event in the international book fair calendar each year. It is the largest and oldest event of its kind in the world, and is so large, varied and diffuse that it is almost impossible to summarise. It has an exhibitor area of some 184,000 square metres, and some 300,000 books and electronic products are on show in six halls broadly divided by category: electronic products/multimedia, graphic arts, international publishers (halls 3 and 4), children and juvenile books, art books, maps and travel guides, school books, religious books, STM (science, technical medicine), fiction and non-fiction (i.e. general trade books), and remainder books. Some 9,600 exhibitors (publishers, multimedia producers, distributors, software suppliers, literary agents, etc.) from over 100 countries attend annually, and Frankfurt attracts close to 300,000 visitors each year:

publishers, booksellers, librarians, writers, agents, and a vast number of journalists. It is open exclusively to trade visitors for the first four days and to the general public for the remaining two days (usually a Saturday and Sunday).

London International Book Fair (LIBF)

Oriel House, 26 The Quadrant
Richmond, Surrey TW9 1DL, UK
Tel: +44-(0)181-910 7899
Fax: +44-(0)181-910 7930
Email: libf@reedexpo.co.uk
Web site: http://www.libf.co.uk
Venue: London Olympia, Kensington
Contacts: Helen McLachlan (Exhibition Manager); Patrick McLaughlin (Sales Manager)
Fair dates: 1999: 28-30 March
2000: 19-21 March

Established in 1971 the London International Book Fair is now a significant event in the international book trade calendar. It is held in the spring of each year, attracting primarily UK publishers, library suppliers, printers and service companies, but also with a substantial number of exhibitors from Europe, Commonwealth countries, North America and the Far East, and including booksellers, distributors, wholesalers, and literary agents. In 1999 the fair attracted nearly 13,000 visitors from 100 countries, and in terms of exhibitors 45 countries were represented at almost 1,500 publishers' stands. There is also an International Rights Centre to enable rights directors and literary agents to conduct business negotiations during the Fair, and to serve as a venue for meetings with contacts. Each year there are also seminars – organised by the Southern

African Book Development Trust (SABDET) – involving the African book professions, and which are usually linked to the theme of the Zimbabwe International Book Fair (ZIBF; see below), and which are intended to support the educational and cultural programmes and events associated with ZIBF each year.

Fiera del Libro per Ragazzi/ Bologna Children's Book Fair

Piazza Costituzione 6
40128 Bologna, Italy
Tel: +39-51-282 111/282 361
Fax: +39-51-282 333
Email: dir.com@bolognafiere.it
Web site: http://www.bolognafiere.it/BookFair/welcome.html
Venue: Bologna Fiere
(Bologna trade fair complex)
Contacts: as above
Fair dates: 1999: 8-11 April

Bologna has been the leading showcase for children's book publishing for many years now (for books and other media) but it is now also increasingly attracting educational and school book publishers. It draws 1,400 exhibitors from 70 countries, and some 70,000 visiting professionals, including those specialising in co-production of books and software and multimedia products for children and young adults, comics, educational software, electronic publishing, as well as authors, illustrators, literary agents, book packagers, distributors, booksellers and librarians. Each year the Bologna Book Fair honours a different 'guest country' and its illustrators through special exhibits and events. In 1999 it was the turn of Africa, which coincided with an impressive exhibition of the work of African illustrators.

Gothenburg International
Book Fair
Bok and Bibliotek i Norden AB,
PO Box 5222
40224 Gothenburg, Sweden
Tel: +46-31-708 84 00
Fax: +46-31-20 91 03
Email: anna.falck@bok-bibliotek.se
Web site: http://www.bok-bibliotek.
se/Engelsk/01engelsk.htm
Venue: The Swedish Exhibition
Centre, Gothenburg
Contacts: Bertil Falck (Managing
Director); Anna Falck (Exhibitors);
Gunilla Sandin (Conference)
Fair dates: 1999: 16-19 September

The Gothenburg International Book
Fair, the largest in the Nordic countries, is not only a book fair but also a
major cultural event each year, with
an extensive programme of lectures,
readings, talks, debates, and seminars, and which has included many
prominent writers and scholars from
Africa, Asia and Latin America.
Unlike the Frankfurt and London
book fairs, it is not principally for
trade visitors and exhibitors, but very
much involves the general public. In
1998 it recorded more than 100,000
visitors, and this includes a substantial contingent of teachers and librarians. About 60% are trade visitors.

International Book Fair of Radical
Black and Third World Books
76 Stroud Green Road
Finsbury Park, London N4 3EN
Tel: +44-(0 171-281 4662
Fax: +44-(0)171-281 4662
Fair dates: not know at this time

This book fair – which has attracted
several African, Asian and Caribbean
publishers during the twelve years
the fair was held – is currently
dormant. No fairs were held since the

last one in 1996. According to a statement issued by the Organising Committee of the Fair in February 1997, it
was decided not to continue with the
book fair in London 'in its present
form', and the statement went on to say
that 'the Committee has already begun,
and is continuing with extensive discussions about the restructuring and
reorganising that we ourselves need to
carry out in order to continue the Book
Fair tradition and spirit in new conditions in the contemporary world'.

United States

BookExpo America
383 Main Avenue
Norwalk CT 06851
Tel: +1-203-840 5614
Fax: +1-203-840 9614
Email: bookexpo@reedexpo.com
Web site:
http://bookexpo.reedexpo.com
Venue: Varies each year
1999: Los Angeles (Convention
Center); 2000: Chicago 2001: Chicago
Contacts: Courtney Muller
(Vice President and Show Manager)
Fair dates: 1999: 30 April-2 May

Previously know as the ABA [American
Booksellers Association] Convention
and Trade Exhibit, this is a huge and
glitzy show and is usually scheduled for
four days over the (US) Memorial Day
weekend. Some 1,500 publishers
exhibit each year, and there are usually
around 25,000 visitors in total. In addition to publishers it attracts mainly
bookstore buyers and managers, wholesalers, distributors, as well as authors,
literary agents, celebrities, and a strong
media attendance. International participation is relatively modest, and
many international publishers are represented through exhibits organised by
national book trade associations. There

are some 900 booths and there is also a small press section. Most of the exhibitors are trade publishers, but some scholarly presses are also in attendance. In addition to books and multimedia and electronic products, various other merchandise is on show e.g. magazines, art, collectibles, gift items, etc. A number of panel meetings and 'educational sessions' run concurrently with the show—and have included Feng Shui basics for shaping a better bookstore!

MAJOR AFRICAN BOOK FAIRS

Zimbabwe International Book Fair (ZIBF)

PO Box CY 1179, Harare Gardens
Julius Nyerere Way
Harare, Zimbabwe
Tel: +263-4-702104/8
Fax: +263-4-702129
Email: zibf@samara.co.zw
Web site: http://www.zibf.org
Venue: Harare Gardens,
Julius Nyerere Way
Contact: Trish Mbanga
(Fair Director)
Fair dates: 1999: 31 July-7 August
2000: 30 July-6 August

The Zimbabwe International Book Fair was first held in 1983, and at that time it was jointly organised by the Zimbabwe Publishing House and the Zimbabwe Ministry of Information, Posts, and Telecommunications. In 1991 it was formed into an independent trust, representing publishers, booksellers, writers and ministry officials, and is now held annually in the attractive surroundings of the Harare sculpture gardens. It has been going from strength to strength and is nowadays widely recognised as Africa's pre-

mier book trade gathering each year. It has also become an important trading crossroads for the African book industries – especially as a venue for right negotiations, co-edition or licensing deals – and has provided a point of access to a wider African market for exhibitors and other participants. It has also managed to attract wider and wider international participation, although much of this has come from international organisations, NGOs, various not-for-profit organisations, foreign publishers represented in national collective stands, or other co-operative exhibits.

It has always been the policy of the ZIBF organisers to combine the function of a commercially viable trade fair with a public celebration of books and reading, and as such each year's fair coincides with a diverse programme of cultural and literary events, writers' workshops, as well as a programme of conferences, workshops, seminars, and public events linking up with the fair's theme each year. (e.g. in 1997 it was 'Libraries', in 1998 'Books and Children', in 1999 'Women', and in the year 2000 it will be 'Celebrating African Books'). Other events include a major 'Indaba' conference, as well as training workshops for the book professions, including a regular book marketing workshop. The recently formed African Pan African Booksellers' Association (PAPA) has held two conventions during the Fair, and the African Publishers' Network (APNET) also organises meetings and forums during the Fair. And an African Periodicals Exhibit, now organised by the Nairobi-based African Journals Support and Development Centre at the African Academy of Sciences, is another regular annual feature.

The Fair is open for 'Traders only' on the first three days of the Book Fair week (though 'traders' embraces not only the book trade, but also librarians, teachers and authors/writers), and for the last two days it is open to the general public, at a modest admission charge.

Cairo International Book Fair (CIBF)

General Egyptian Book Organisation
Corniche El Nil, Boulac
PO Box 1660, Cairo. Egypt
Tel: +202-775371
Fax: +202-5754213/765058
Email: ssarhan@idesc.gov.eg
Venue: Exhibition grounds, Medinet Nasr (Naser City)
Contact: as above
Fair dates: 1999: 5-20 February

This well-established fair, currently in its 31st year, attracts primarily publishers from the Arab world, including a vast contingent from Egypt itself. The emphasis of the fair is very much on public involvement, and huge crowds of people converge on the Fairgrounds each year. Cairo does however also attract foreign exhibitors, a number with separate exhibits, but most represented by collective exhibits. An area of some 120,00 square metres is grouped into 27 separate pavilions, each of them bringing together specific groups of publishers by subject, by language, or publishers from Arab nations, international organisations etc. In 1998 it attracted over 2,400 publishers, representing 78 countries, exhibiting some 3.7 million books. A range of public seminars is held throughout the fair, bringing together scholars, academics, and distinguished intellectuals, and there is usually extensive media coverage.

Pan African Children's Book Fair (PACBF)

Foundation for the Promotion of Children's Science Publications in Africa (CHISCI)
PO Box 61301, Nairobi, Kenya
Venue: Kenyatta International Conference Centre
Contacts: Mary Bugembe (Fair Director), Alex Chamwada Ayego (Marketing Executive)
Fair dates: 1999: 2-6 June

This Fair, first held in 1992 – and started by the Foundation for the Promotion of Children's Science Publications in Africa (CHISCI) – focuses on the book and reading needs of children. Each year the Fair coincides with a range of seminars and workshops on writing for children, illustrating children's books, selling children's books, and other topics. In addition to the now well-established Children's Reading Tent – a concept pioneered by the Pan African Children's Book Fair – associated events also include a 'Booksellers and Distributors Bazaar', a 'Writers and Illustrators Bazaar' and there are also exhibits of educational toys. In 1993 it launched a 'Children's Home Library Campaign' and inaugurated 'The Alchemist', a children's discount bookstore and book club.

Foire Internationale du Livre et du Matériel Didactique de Dakar/ FILDAK
(Dakar International Book Fair)

Centre International du Commerce Exterieur du Sénégal (CICES)
Route de l'Aéroport, BP 3329
8166 Dakar-Yoff, Senegal
Tel: +221-231011/201375/231070
Fax: +221-350712/204605
Venue: Dakar International Congress Centre

Contact: as above
Fair dates: [last held 4-11 November 1997] 1999: November (dates not known at press time)

First held in 1985, and now staged as biennial event, the Dakar Book Fair is organised under the aegis of the Ministry of Culture of the government of Senegal, and with the support of the Agence de Coopération Culturelle et Technique (ACCT). Past fairs have attracted sizeable contingents of publishers, and suppliers and manufacturers of educational materials from francophone Africa and the Maghreb countries, and there has always been a strong presence of major publishers from France, Canada, and some other countries. Although the Fair is held at the International Congress Centre some 10km outside Dakar, the fairs have been well attended not only by trade visitors but also by the general public. Throughout the Fair there is usually a lively programme of talks and lectures on various aspects of publishing and book development, together with authors reading from their books, special exhibitions, and events for children.

Ghana International Book Fair

Ghana Trade Fair Company Ltd
PO Box 111
Trade Fair Centre
Accra, Ghana
Tel: +233-21-776611/772376
Fax: +233-21-772012
Email: GTFA@ighmail.com
Web site:
http://www.internetghan.com/gtfa
Venue: Ghana International Trade Fair Centre, Accra
Contact: as above
Fair date: 1998: 4-10 November
2000: to be announced

This new West African book fair attracted considerable attention when it was first held in 1996, especially as until then there had not been a major international West African book fair since the demise of the Ife (Nigeria) Book Fair some years ago. The intention is that the new Ghana International Book Fair should be held every second year, and that the existing Dakar Book Fair (see details above) should be held in the intervening years. In this way there would be one major book fair in West Africa every year, alternating between the francophone and anglophone countries, and encouraging interchange between the two. The Fair is organised under the umbrella of the Ghana Book Publishers Association, and the first two days of the Fair are reserved for trade and corporate visitors, with the public admitted for the remaining five days. It aims to be 'the largest book, stationery and printing fair in West Africa'. The first Fair had just over 100 exhibitors, largely from West Africa, plus a small number from other parts of the continent, and there was a sprinkling of overseas exhibitors.

Events organised around the Fair include seminars sponsored by the African Publishers' Network (APNET), workshops organised by the Ghana Book Publishers Association, and there have also been a range of cultural and literary events, and meetings involving writers sponsored by the Accra-based Pan-African Writers Association.

Nairobi International Book Fair

Kenya Publishers' Association
PO Box 42767, Nairobi, Kenya
Tel: 254-2-573259
Fax: 254-2-339875

Email: info@saritcentre.com
Venue: The Sarit Centre, Nairobi
Contacts: Peter Moll (Public Affairs
Co-ordinator)
Fair dates: 1999: 15-19 September

The Nairobi Book Fair has been held
intermittently for some time now
(though 'International' has now been
added to its name). Formerly organised, at various venues, by the private
firm African Bookman Consultants
Ltd, it is now taking place under the
umbrella of the Kenya Publishers
Association, with show management
entrusted to a specialist exhibitions
contractor. As from 1998 it is now
held at the refurbished Sarit Centre, a
busy shopping mall in central
Nairobi. The Fair dates are set to
coincide with the start of the new
school year for international schools
and the start of the last term in
Kenyan schools which follows the
8–4–4 curriculum. In 1998, the fair
only managed to attract very modest
international participation.

SOME OTHER AFRICAN BOOK FAIRS AND BOOK PROMOTIONAL EVENTS

Note: Fair dates given in parentheses
are those for 1999 unless otherwise
indicated.

Book Festival
(26-28 September) [1998]
Book Publishers Association of
Malawi
c/o Dzuka Publishing Co. Ltd.
Private Bag 59, Blantyre, Malawi
Tel: +265-670880/750855
Fax: +265-671114

International Children's Book Fair
[December 1999, dates not known at
press time]

BP 3035, Lomé, Togo
Tel/Fax: +228-224965

Lesotho National Book Fair
(27-28 February) [1998]
Lesotho Publishers Association
c/o Institute of Southern African
Studies
National University of Lesotho
PO Box Roma 180, Lesotho
Tel: +266-340601
Fax: +266-340000
Email: mmc@doc.isas.nul.ls

Mbapira Festival
Association of Namibian Publishers
(14-18 March) [1998]
c/o NEPRU
59 Bahnhof Street, PO Box 40219
Windhoek, Namibia
Tel: +264-61-228284
Fax: +264-61-231496
Email: nepro@lianam.lia.net

NPA Book Fair
(21-24 October) [1998]
Nigerian Publishers Association
14 Awosika Avenue,
off Oshuntokun Avenue, Old Bodija
PO Box 2541, Ibadan, Nigeria
Tel: +234-22-412313
Fax: +234-22-412056
[c/o University Press plc]

Salon International du Livre d'Abidjan
(12-18 April)
ASSEDI
09 BP 682, Abidjan 09, Côte d'Ivoire
Tel: +225-3954479/395801
Fax: +225-212112
Email: univers@africaonline.co.ci

Tanzania National Book Week Festival
(28 September-4 October)
Publishers Association of Tanzania

PO Box 1408, Dar es Salaam
Tanzania
Tel: +255-51-180474
Fax: +255-51-183462/181624
Email: pata@cctz.com

Uganda National Book Week
(30 August-4 September)
Uganda Publishers Association
PO Box 7732, Kampala, Uganda
Tel: +256-41-270370/251353
Fax: +256-41-251352

Zambia Book Fair
(26-30 May)
Booksellers and Publishers
Association of Zambia
Lusaka Room G 081
CDC Building, PO Box 31838
Lusaka, Zambia
Tel: +260-1-225422

Adventures in the Book Trade

The references to the hotels and to the guides suggest that this advertisement is pitched at tourists, and assumes it is worth trying to interest them in historic documents, such as maps, and in books old and new The advertising copy reminds the reader that the book trade has a long tail: publish a book today; and in twenty years it becomes 'old [and] out-of-print' – apparently, these are positive qualities to the people staying at the Mount Soche, and those pausing at Ryall's hotel, some of whom may be fascinated by or wish to invest in books as art objects.

This Handbook focuses on the aspiring writer who is anxious to gather information about the contemporary publishing situation. At the same time, it contains references to matters which suggest a longer-term interest in the book as a commodity that passes from hand to hand, perhaps acquiring added value over the years. References to book signings imply a special value (sentimental or commercial) is conferred on a book signed by the person it is written by. There have also been references to literary executors, to last wills and testaments – all of which look towards the future, suggesting that the passage of time may give certain items a particular value. These anticipate a sector in the book trade that is likely to grow in importance in the next few decades: the sector suggested by the advertisement for Antiquarian Books above.

Certain items of African literature are already valued as commodities: rare items to be collected and catalogued, to be bought (perhaps as 'investments') and sold (preferably 'at the top of the market'). A couple of Soyinka's publications have already been listed in catalogues at prices much higher than the layman might expect. For example, the single-sheet publication entitled *Poems from Prison*, brought out by Rex Collings in the late 1960s while Soyinka was still in Gowon's detention, originally sold for 12½p. It was a curious production in several ways, not least because it carried an obvious misreading of the manuscript. Yes, dear reader who is also a writer, despite all that has been said about the need for authors to submit type-written texts, it appears that the poems arrived in London in hand-written form; and Collings did not only read them, he also misread them. He read the characteristically Soyinkan 'core' – as in 'Earth's sated core' – as the nonsensical and totally unSoyinkan 'cove' – 'Earth's sated cove'! He even insisted on his reading (printing), arguing, when challenged by John Ferguson, that 'It is quite clearly "cove".' (Correspondence of 21 July 1969 and 25 July 1969: Collings File, Brotherton Library, University of Leeds.) It was left to Soyinka, on his release, to instate the word he had originally selected.

To tell the story this far is to draw on a number of sources that show how the interest in Soyinka's texts has developed – and, perhaps, how narratives and mistakes (curiosities) may increase the value of a document. Some of Soyinka's letters (those sent to Dennis Duerden) have been bought for the Harry Ransome Humanities Research Center, Austin, Texas. Others, including letters to his friend and publisher Collings, along with corrected proofs, are in the Brotherton Library at Leeds. Apart from these two significant collections of Soyinka material there is a major, specialised archive established by Henry Louis Gates Jr in the United States. This contains material from Soyinka's own files. It may be remembered that Ibrahim Babangida wanted to prevent these files from being taken out of the country, although he did not put up any money to buy them.

To return to our example, copies of the *Poems from Prison*, with their curious misreading – especially if in good condition – now sell for considerably more than they originally cost. Another text by Soyinka has appeared in catalogues of second-hand African books ('Africana') at surprisingly high prices: the Orisun Theatre Edition of revue sketches entitled *Before the Blackout*. This was brought to press by Bola Ige towards the end of Soyinka's time in detention, and it has the distinction of being undated. A box of copies was sent to Collings to be sold on the London market but went missing in about 1969: turn up these books in pristine condition, subsequently release on to the market slowly, and someone might make a killing. (On the other hand, news of the find might leak out and the bottom might fall out of the market for *Before the Blackout*, so perhaps anyone who comes across a box of copies should burn all except for half a dozen, so as to keep the price high.)

Many people have little time for the cult of the book as art object; they see it as manipulated by people who are – like the notional book burner just cited – clearly 'fundamentally anti-book'. However, writers should be aware that such people exist in the world they are entering when they move towards publication. Authors asked to sign copies, for example, may find this flattering or gratifying. Their signature might make the book of greater sentimental value to its owner, particularly if accompanied by a personal inscription, and it may increase the commercial value of the book. This is not, however, always the case; and this is illustrated by a story that the poet Dannie Abse tells:

> One day, in a second-hand bookshop in Hay on Wye – a small town on the border of England and Wales famous for its second-hand bookshops, Abse found a copy of an edition of one of his own books that he no longer had on his shelves. He decided to buy it and took it along to the counter. The assistant serving him did not recognise the poet and looked inside the cover to ascertain the price. He then noticed that the book had been signed – by Abse of course – and he remarked, 'Oh, I see, it's been signed but I won't charge you extra because, well, Abse signs easily.' Preserving his anonymity, Abse handed over his money and left the shop with the book, a smile playing about his lips as he wondered just what it meant to be an easy signer.

The reference to 'edition' in the story draws attention to an important dimension of this part of the book trade. First editions are, generally, the most highly prized. In part this is because when a book by a new author, such as *Things Fall Apart*, is first printed, the publisher has little idea what the demand will be and opts for a small print run. In the case of a novel this may be 2,000 in paperback and much fewer – perhaps 500 – in hardback. It is unlikely that a paperback that came from, say, the twenty-fifth reprinting of Chinua Achebe's first novel will increase in value, but a first edition in good condition has done so considerably.

For this section of the market much will depend on the condition of the book. In most cases, hardbacks are particularly collectable, and the presence of the dust-cover – or wrapper – adds a surprising amount to the value. The appearance of the book – whether it has been affected by damp or termites, for example – is also of importance to collectors. Remember they probably do not intend to read it; they just want to put it on a shelf or in a glass case.

What are the implications of all this for the writer? Maybe very little; this is a side of the book business that so far, despite the advertisement from Central Africana Limited, has made only a limited impact on the continent. However, it is clear even from the brief references to Tutuola's experiences in this volume that manuscripts are important. And one might ask: 'If people are willing to pay over the odds for *Poems from Prison*, what would they give for the original, the hand-written document smuggled out of prison?' And add: 'If research centres and libraries are buying up the papers of those who, like Duerden and Collings, worked with a generation of African authors, how much more will they pay for the collected papers of the authors themselves?' It seems, incidentally, that many of Achebe's papers and early editions/ translations were destroyed along with his house during the Nigerian Civil War. It may be that early materials by Achebe, such as letters, will become particularly highly valued because of their scarcity.

The point may already have been carried too far and perhaps young authors already dream of taking early retirement and living on the proceeds of selling drafts of stories to well-endowed academic bodies. Every writer should certainly look after examples of his or her own work, and be aware of the kind of market-place that Central Africana represents. They should not allow relatives to use their drafts to wrap groundnuts in. However, they should keep their feet firmly on the ground and await developments in this sector of the African book trade with equanimity. In order to do this they may care to ponder the following: On 14 October 1922, AE Housman, poet and translator, wrote as follows to his publisher Grant Richards who had informed him that there were some misprints in the first published edition of his *Last Poems* and Richards wondered whether to insert an errata slip. Housman was firm:

> No, don't put in an errata slip. The blunder will probably enhance the value of the first edition in the eyes of bibliophiles, an idiotic class.
> Yrs
> A. E. Housman.

(Quoted Pryor, ed. 1988, 262)

Coda: The Death of the Author

In some volumes of literary criticism and cultural analysis, the title of this section would indicate that a theoretical debate was about to take place. Here the matters are far more practical and follow the question 'What happens when a writer dies?'

Inadequate means of communication have meant that brother and sister writers have not always heard of the passing of a fellow writer in good time. It was, for example, only quite by chance that a message reached Nigerian writers about the funeral arrangements for Joe de Graft. It is to be hoped that fax and email links between national and international writers' groups will improve the position.

It is entirely appropriate that writers' groups should prepare for the passing of a fellow author, and be ready to mark the event properly. A reluctance to file obituaries in advance should not prevent the collection of material with which obituaries can be written. A shrinking from anticipating a death should not stop family, friends and fellow writers from ascertaining any wishes about funeral arrangements.

Under the pressure that follows death, writers and artists have shown they can come together and mark the passing of a co-worker in the arts with flair and appropriate ceremony. The funeral of Efua Sutherland in January 1996 was an imaginatively planned occasion at which many of those she had inspired, and many of those she had worked with, were able to participate. The booklet of tributes published was a moving document, beautifully produced and containing contributions from around the world. It showed what could be done when urged on by the desire to produce a volume worthy of a woman who had been involved in the cultural development of Ghana in myriad ways. On the other side of the continent, UWAVITA, the Tanzanian Writers Association, has been able to report that it has 'organised memorial services for deceased members, and collected monetary contributions to help the bereaved'.

When Amos Tutuola passed away on 7 June 1997, the Nigerian press reported that he had died a pauper and left a large family of dependents, including four wives and eleven children. Editors, journalists and creative writers indulged in a prolonged period of breast-beating, mourning the death of a man who had rarely been honoured by his fellow countrymen in life. The interment was postponed until 4 October 1997 and, while the writer's body was in the mortuary, members of the family sought funds to cover the expenses of the funeral. A bank account was opened for international contributions in the name of 'Tutuola, A Oluyinka' and appeals were sent out. The possibility of state support was raised.

In the midst of all this the fate of Tutuola's manuscripts was raised. The story is a long one and deserves close scrutiny. It seems to include Nigerian academics who had borrowed copies of texts years before – but who had failed to return them. It also included cultural nationalists who had blocked the export of certain documents on the grounds that they should be housed in a carefully supervised archive in what was then the University of Ile Ife. In the event this archive was never established. Some of the lessons of this series of events are clear, and the first one is:

- Look after your manuscripts – including correspondence – they may keep you in your old age, or help to meet the expenses incurred in your funeral, or pay the school fees of your orphaned children. Be very careful about entrusting your manuscripts to others. It may be flattering to find that academics are interested in your papers but that is no reason to let them leave your files. National Archives are all very well but there is no reason why writers should be forced into poverty in order to endow them with documents.

Complete gentlemen and women emerge from universities as well as the forest, and they have a persuasive line in rhetoric and flattery – but there is no reason why writers should be impressed by them. Authors have family responsibilities and should be aware that their manuscripts have commercial value. Tutuola died intestate and his son, Yinka, was quoted as saying :

He was too African to write a will. He was the type that likes to keep what you are able to give them while you are alive. If he gives you this pen for instance, he believes you should be able to keep it and use it for your own good. If you show otherwise he won't give you any. If he was asked to write a will, Papa would have written something like this: 'Give to a man what he can keep.' In any case Papa doesn't have much to will. The greatest thing he never had he willed to us while alive. And of course his name which is known throughout the world. The best legacy he willed to us is his name and education. Apart from these, Papa really didn't have much to will. He has only one house in Ibadan and a car, a Ford Cortina which he bought in 1976 and which he rode till he died. Outside these he has nothing anywhere. (Oshunkeye 1997)

From this moving but confused expression of filial piety, it is clear that Yinka Tutuola was unaware of the rights and duties owed to his father's heirs from his literary estate. Writers should appoint executors, whom they should keep well-informed about their business affairs, and to whom they should leave clear instructions. Only if this happens can the appropriate measures be taken after death to ensure that heirs inherit all that is due to them. Royalties on an author's work continue to be payable after death for fifty years, in some cases, and seventy-five years in others. Legal advice should be taken on this matter.

At the funeral of Amos Tutuola, Segun Olusola announced that plans had been made for an annual Amos Tutuola Odegbami Festival to be held each year on 7 June. Reference was also made to the establishment of an Amos Tutuola Foundation. The Nigerian literary and academic communities have already united to unveil a plaque marking Christopher Okigbo's links with Cambridge House, Ibadan; and in June 1996 the first annual lecture in memory of Zulu Sofola was delivered.

The Author's Bookshelf

Hans M Zell

There are hundreds of books, manuals and guides on the topic of writing, authorship, how to prepare and submit a manuscript, how to get published, how to publish on your own, how to write for profit – or books on specific forms of writing, including romantic fiction, crime fiction, writing for children or teenagers. This section provides details of only a small number of books – most of them recently published, and most relatively inexpensive – which are recommended for African writers, and would-be self-publishers. A number of them are published in Africa, and will therefore be particularly relevant, but others are published elsewhere and I have concentrated, for the most part, on books and reference resources published in the UK rather than in North America.

The full addresses of all the publishers whose titles are listed here can be found at the end of this section.

Dictionaries, thesauri, or books about words and language, are basic and essential tools for writers anywhere. They are not included here, but a word about dictionaries.

Many good dictionaries are available, large and small, e.g. the *Oxford Dictionary for Writers and Editors* (Oxford University Press, £8.95), the *Oxford Concise Dictionary* (Oxford University Press, £13.99), the *Collins English Dictionary* (HarperCollins, £25.00), or *The Cambridge International Dictionary of English* (Cambridge University Press, £16.80). It is worth getting yourself a decent size and recently-published dictionary. This is especially important as new and 'hot' words and phrases are constantly coming into vogue. The latest editions of the major dictionaries now present vastly improved and exciting formats, and there have been fresh approaches to dictionary making. If you can afford it, get yourself *The New Oxford Dictionary of English* (Oxford University Press, 1998, 2,152 pp. £29.99 cased ISBN 019861263X) which breaks new ground. It has a revolutionary new entry style and is probably the biggest single-volume dictionary currently available: 350,000 words, phrases and definitions with over 70,000 examples, together with over 2,000 words and senses new to the language, as well as 52,000 scientific and technical words, 12,000 encyclopaedic entries, and a large number of especially highlighted usage notes. It is a truly wonderful dictionary.

REFERENCE and ADDRESS SOURCES

Africa-specific or African published

African Books Collective Ltd
The African Publishers Networking Directory 1999/2000 3rd edn
Oxford: African Books Collective Ltd, 1999.
72 pp. £18.00/$30.00 pap. ISBN 0952126931

This is an updated and expanded version of a popular reference guide and networking tool for all those interested in the book industries and book development in Africa. It is also a very useful reference resource for African writers and academic authors. The directory provides detailed information on some 300 major and/or most active publishers operating in Africa today, giving very full information for each entry, including name and address, telephone/fax numbers, email addresses, Web sites (where available), names of chief executives, number of titles in print, average number of new books published each year, and the nature of each publisher's list and areas of specialisation. Other listings include details of book trade organisations, book trade journals, and reference resources.

Book Aid International
Publishing Information and Training Resources
Books, Periodicals, Training Materials, 1999-2000
London: Book Aid International, 1999. 56 pp. gratis

This is the third edition of a handy annotated catalogue which provides access to a wide range of titles relevant to the particular needs of publishers in Africa. It is also a useful source for authors who want to find out more about the business of publishing, and/or who are thinking of publishing on their own. Divided into chapters covering broad subject areas such as editorial functions and procedures, design and production, electronic publishing/DTP, marketing, sales and distribution, it lists reference material and books on all aspects of publishing for both experienced professionals and those new to publishing There is also a section on multimedia to reflect the growing use of email and the Internet.

Robert Frances
A Writer's Guide to South African Magazines
Somerset West, South Africa: Options Publishing, 1996.
117 pp. R54.00 pap. 1875086080

A useful reference resource providing practical guidelines for freelance writers who wish to tap into the opportunities for publishing outlets offered by a variety of South African magazines. Each listing contains an analysis of a sample copy of the various magazines (type of features and material accepted for publication, regular columns, payment offered, guidelines for contributors, etc.) together with full name and address, telephone and fax numbers (and email addresses for some), name of editor, frequency, format, average page extent per issue, and advertising content.

Note: Mick and Monica Cromhout's Options Publishing publish and distribute (in South Africa) a large number of books, how-to guides, manuals, and reference sources for writers and self-publishers, including several of those listed here. It also publishes a bi-monthly magazine called *Writers World. The South African Word Crafter's Journal*, plus two newsletters, *Publish!* and *Just Write*, with listings devoted to news, events, markets, competitions, contacts, and tips for writers on how to get published. For more information, or a free copy of their 'Writer's Bookshelf' catalogue, write to Options Publishing, PO Box 1588, Somerset West, 7129 South Africa; fax +27-21-851-2592; email: optpub@iafrica.com, or visit their Web site at <http://users.iafrica.com/o/op/optpub>.

Chukwuemeka Ike (ed.)
Directory of Nigerian Book Development (Maiden Edition 1998)
Awka, Nigeria: Nigerian Book Foundation, and
Enugu: Fourth Dimension Publishing Co., 1998.
228 pp. £35.00/$63.00 cased ISBN 9783347349 £25.00/$45.00 pap. ISBN 9783347330 (distributed by African Books Collective Ltd, Oxford; reduced prices apply within Nigeria)

This is a remarkable and pioneering publication and is probably the first reference work published anywhere in Africa which provides a wide range of information about the entire book community in a single country, and in a single source. Published jointly by the Nigerian Book Foundation (NBF) and Fourth Dimension Publishing Company, the project forms part of the NBF's mission to establish a comprehensive database on all aspects of book development in Nigeria. It brings together a massive amount of information, which is grouped under five distinct parts, each preceded by a short introductory essay. Of particular interest to writers and academic authors will be Part 1, a Directory of Published Nigerian Authors, a total of 749 entries covering both creative writers and academic authors. Entries include full name and address, telephone number, date of birth, details of published books, awards and honours received, and other information; and Part 2, which is a Directory of Book Publishing Houses, 74 entries giving a wide array of specifics on each publisher, e.g. date founded, number of books in print, number of new titles published annually, types of books published and primary markets, in addition to financial information, number of employees, name of chief executive, and full name and address, telephone/fax numbers. The remaining three parts cover listings of book printing presses, the retail trade and bookshops, and a directory of libraries throughout Nigeria.

Laurice Taitz (ed.)
Directory of Book Publishing in South Africa, 1995
Parktown, South Africa: Publishers' Association of South Africa, and Braamfontein, The British Council, 1995.
158 pp. R40.00 pap. ISBN 0620193034

Provides fully annotated listings of individuals and organisations in the South African book world, including publishers and publisher's agents, freelance editors and proof-readers, designers, illustrators, etc. and also includes a directory of book training institutions, as well as a listing of book-related and writers' organisations. Now somewhat dated, but still useful for authors looking for publishers to whom they can submit their work.

Publishers' Association of South Africa
The PASA Directory 1997/98
St James. South Africa: Publishers' Association of South Africa, 1997. (New edn in preparation)
[unpaged] R80.00 ISBN 0620216263 [also available on CD-ROM, and also accessible at the PASA web site at
<http://www.icon.co.za~pasa>]

Contains very full information on some 130 PASA member publishers, each entry giving name and address, telephone/fax numbers, and details of email addresses and Web sites where available, together with information on executive and senior personnel (and their positions, e.g. editorial directors), number of employees, number of titles published annually, nature of list and areas of specialisation. Most entries also include a short but informative company profile.

Other

The Writers' and Artists' Yearbook – 1999 92nd edn
London: A&C Black, 1999.
694 pp. £11.99 pap. ISBN 0713649313

This marvellous reference book deservedly enjoys a reputation as being
something of a 'bible' for writers, and those aspiring to get published.
Sub-titled 'A directory for writers, artists, playwrights, writers for film,
radio and television, designers, illustrators and photographers' it was
first published in 1907. It is absolutely cram-packed with information
and each year it is thoroughly revised and updated, and with many new
entries and articles. There are extensively annotated listings (all with
full address details, telephone/fax numbers, email addresses, Web sites
where available, editorial contacts, profiles, etc.) of book publishers in
the UK and overseas, newspapers and magazines, TV and radio stations, and literary agents in the UK and elsewhere, including descriptions of the type of books they handle, commissions and reading fees
charged, clients, etc. Other listings include societies, editorial, literary
and production services, prizes and awards, literature festivals, and
picture agencies. There is also much sound advice about preparing for
publication, getting published, copyright and libel, together with chapters on current publishing practice and publishing agreements, word
processing and desktop publishing, and resources for writers. For
African writers looking for publishing outlets in the UK or the US this is
an absolutely indispensable handbook.

Note: The publishers of the *Writers' and Artists' Yearbook*, A&C Black also
publish a wide range of 'how-to' handbooks for writers, all priced between
£7.99 and £11.99, including *Freelance Writing for Newspapers, Writing for
Children, Writing Crime Fiction, Writing Erotic Fiction, Writing Fantasy
Fiction, Writing Historical Fiction, Writing for Magazines, Writing for Radio,
Writing for Television, Writing a Thriller, Rewriting, Sports Writing, Research
for Writers*, and other titles. For more details about these books write to A&C
Black, 35 Bedford Row, London WC1R 4JH.

Kirsten Holm (ed.)
The Writer's Market 1999 edition.
Cincinnati, OH: Writer's Digest Books, F&W Publications, 1999.
1,120 pp. $27.99 pap. ISBN 0898798507

This is roughly the US equivalent of the *Writers' and Artists' Yearbook*
(see entry above), except that it is almost twice as long! This massive

tome contains annotated listings (all with phone/fax numbers, email addresses, and Web sites where available) of 1,170 North American publishers, 1,534 consumer magazines, 446 trade magazines, 250 script buyers, plus literary agents, book producers, syndicates, and even greeting card publishers! The latest edition uses a system of icons for faster information access. The listings will also tell you who to contact, what to send, how to send it, your chances of acceptance, and how much you are likely to get paid. There are also lots of writing and 'inside tips', and articles about approaching publishers, how to submit book proposals, together with a range of author profiles and author interviews. If you hope to place work with magazines in the US or Canada, this is probably your best bet, and it is an excellent resource for any writer who needs information on publishers in North America.

Note: Writer's Digest Books is the US's premier publisher of how-to books and reference resources for writers, and for a complete list of their catalogue write to: Writer's Digest Books, F&W Publications, 1507 Dana Avenue, Cincinnati, OH 45207, USA; fax: +1-888-590 4082; email: datac@fwpubs.com – or visit the Writer's Digest Web site and on-line book store at <http://www.writersdigest.com>.

Barry Turner
The Writer's Handbook 1999 12th edn
London: Macmillan, 1998.
760 pp. £12.99 pap. ISBN 0333719255

This is another well-established and popular handbook containing a wealth of information. There are over 5,000 entries covering publishers and small presses (separate sections for UK, Continental European and US), magazines, newspapers, news agencies, film, TV and Video production companies, theatre producers, book clubs, literary agents (separate sections for UK and US), professional and literary societies, editorial and research services, press cutting agencies, bursaries, fellowships and grants, and more, together with advice on taxation and the role of agents. It does not list as many outlets as in the *Artists' and Writers' Yearbook* (see above), but it provides more extensive details for each entry: for publishers, for example, it gives slightly more contact details, turnover figures for some, founding dates, and the publisher profiles are a bit longer. For literary agents it provides roughly the same information as that contained in the *Writers' and Artists' Yearbook*.

368 HANS M ZELL

GUIDES FOR AUTHORS

African published

Chukwuemeka Ike
How to Become a Published Writer
Ibadan: Heinemann Educational Books (Nigeria) plc, 1991.
230 pp. £13.95/$25.00 ISBN 9782652 [distributed by African Books Collective Ltd, Oxford; reduced price applies within Nigeria]

Written by one of Nigeria's most distinguished and most widely published novelists (and now Director of the Nigerian Book Foundation), Chukwuemeka Ike here shares his wide experience as a writer of both fiction and non-fiction, using an informal and conversational style. The book is designed to lend a helping hand to aspiring writers and to assist them to become published. Part 1 of the book is devoted to writing fiction (creating characters, plots, organising a story, style, etc.), and part 2 deals with non-fiction (articles, essays, book reviews, biography, textbooks, etc.). The final part provides advice on how to find a publisher and how to safeguard the author's interests, and also looks at the prospects for authors considering the self-publishing route.

Basil van Rooyen
How to Get Published in South Africa 2nd edn
A Guide for Authors
Halfway House, South Africa: Southern Book Publishers Pty Ltd, 1996.
254 pp. R60.00 ISBN 1868126617

A very useful hands-on type of guide for authors, containing many helpful tips and a great deal of practical advice, that also examines the business of publishing from the publisher's point of view. Part 1 consists of a range of overview articles on the book publishing industry in South Africa and the different areas of publishing, including a chapter on publishing in African languages. Part 2 provides advice on how to find the right publisher and describes how a publisher decides what to publish. Part 3 sets out how publishing works (including an excellent chapter on publishing contracts and royalty agreements discussing a standard publisher's contract on a clause-by-clause basis). Part 4 gives helpful advice on how to prepare a manuscript, and how to structure a book, read proofs, and prepare an index (where required); and part 5 is a fully annotated directory of South African publishers giving details of each publisher's list, and pointing authors directly to the publishing house most suitable for his or her type of book. Although intended primarily for authors and writers in South Africa, this guide provides a valuable companion for authors in other parts of the continent.

Other

Blackwell Guide for Authors
Oxford: Blackwell, 1991.
76 pp. £5.99 pap. ISBN 0631164618

This is a good, concise, and inexpensive guide offering helpful advice to aspiring authors, both those writing fiction and non-fiction. It tells you what to look out for when trying to find and when assessing a publisher, how to make the initial approach, and how to prepare a typescript efficiently and see it through its copy-editing and proofing stages until it emerges as a book. It also discusses questions of style, choice between reference systems (for academic titles), methods of indexing, and provides hints on how to prepare disks on your computer for use in typesetting.

Michael Legat
An Author's Guide to Publishing 3rd edn
London: Robert Hale, 1998.
254 pp. £9.99 ISBN 0709062273

Although based primarily on UK practice, this is one of the very best guides to the profession of authorship, and is invaluable for any author seeking to break into print and dealing with publishers. There are useful accounts on the publishing processes and the structure of publishing, together with chapters providing advice on how to submit work to publishers, dealing with contracts, common questions and complaints, author–publisher relations, and legal matters. A chapter on the 'Rewards of Writing' provides a realistic view of what authors can expect in terms of royalty earnings (and royalty advances), and forewarns that the average author's earnings are likely to be pitifully small, and that very few authors can make writing a full-time career unless they have other means of some kind. The book also contains a glossary, reproductions of British Standard symbols used in correcting proofs, and a model royalty statement with explanatory notes.

Michael Legat
The Writer's Rights
London: A&C Black, 1995.
128 pp. £8.99 pap. ISBN 0713640189

Written in a clear and accessible style, this book describes what rights
an author has, and how to protect these rights. Topics covered include
copyright and using copyright material/permissions, agents' contracts,
the publisher's rights, the author's rights under a publisher's contract,
plagiarism, electronic rights, agreements for publishing in magazines
and newspapers, and authors' rights and terms for dramatic scripts for
use on radio or TV.

Michael Legat
Writing for Pleasure and Profit 2nd edn
London: Robert Hale, 1993.
176 pp. £6.99 pap. ISBN 0709052618

Another excellent book by Michael Legat, a practical guide to the craft
and business of writing with much useful advice, and tips how to
avoid the common pitfalls. It is particularly strong on aspects of
writing a novel – general principles, characterisation, dialogue, backgrounds and research – and there are also chapters on writing poetry,
plays, radio and television scripts, writing for children, as well as
articles and non-fiction. All this is combined with down-to-earth,
sensible advice about how to prepare a typescript, where and how to
submit it, and 'Selling your Work'. This is an invaluable guide, of
interest both to the experienced writer as well as the novice.

Chris McCallum
Writing for Publication 4th edn
How to Sell Your Work and Succeed as a Writer
Oxford: How to Books, 1997.
192 pp. £9.99 pap. ISBN 1857032268

This is a good beginner's guide to the business of writing and getting
published, with many useful hints and a great deal of practical advice,
and it also includes detailed constructive advice on criticising, revising
and editing your own work. Individual chapters setting out basic
considerations for getting started, and preparing and submitting work,
are followed by chapters on writing for different types of outlets and
genres (fiction, non-fiction, writing for magazines and newspapers,
writing for children, etc.), writing competitions, and self-financed
publishing.

Note: In addition to the book listed above and a further title below, How to Books publish a whole range of other books on successful writing, most priced at £9.99, including *Copyright and Law for Writers, Creative Writing, Writing c Textbook, How to Write for Television, Writing Romantic Fiction, Writing and Publishing Poetry, Writing Science Fiction, Fantasy and Horror, Writing Short Stories and Articles, Making Money from Writing, Writing Humour,* and many more. For a complete list write to: How to Books, Plymbridge House, Estover Road, Plymouth PL6 7PZ, UK.

Barry Turner
The Writer's Companion
The Essential Guide to being Published
London: Macmillan Reference, 1996.
303 pp. £12.99 pap. ISBN 0333621336

The publisher's blurb on the back cover describes this book as 'a route map through the media jungle, an indispensable guide for established writers and newcomers alike who seek to make the best commercial use of their talents'. And there is indeed a wealth of practical advice in here, from a beginner's guide on the 'Nuts and Bolts of Authorship' to writing a potential bestseller, writing romantic fiction, writing for children and teenagers through writing for theatre, film and TV, and how to get poetry published. Additional chapters are devoted to how to find an agent, how to deal with publishers, how to avoid contractual pitfalls, issues of copyright and libel, and more.

The Society of Authors
Quick Guides
London: The Society of Authors, var. pp. [var. publication dates]

The Society of Authors' 'Quick Guides' series are intended to give an outline of topics relating to various areas of writing and publishing, such as authors' agents, authors' rights, libel, etc. Each pamphlet is 4-8 pages long providing good basic advice. The guides are updated and reissued periodically. They are free to members; others may purchase them at £1.00 each (post-free). The following guides are currently available:

Authors' Agents
Bringing a Claim in the County Court
Copyright and Moral Rights
Copyright in Artistic Works (inc. Photographs)
Electronic Publishing Contracts
email
Film Agreements
Ghost Writing/Collaboration Contracts

SELF-PUBLISHING / HOW TO DO IT YOURSELF

Dan Poynter
The Self-Publishing Manual 9th rev. edn
How to Write, Print and Sell Your Own Book
Santa Barbara, CA: Para Publishing , 1996.
458 pp. $19.95 pap. ISBN 1568860186

Dan Poynter's book is something of a classic in the field which has reportedly sold more than 100,000 copies since it was first published in 1979. The author prudently starts off with a 'Warning/Disclaimer' in which he states that 'self-publishing is not a get-rich-quick scheme. Anyone who decides to write and publish a book must expect to invest in a lot of time and effort.' The purpose of the manual, he says, is to 'educate and entertain', and in that he succeeds admirably. The book contains a massive amount of practical, hard-nosed advice for the would-be publisher, who is taken through the entire publishing process on a step-by-step basis. It must be added immediately of course that much of this advice is geared towards prospective self-publishers in North America, and some of the sections will be of little relevance in an African situation, for example the chapters on promotion and marketing, review outlets, and distribution through US bookstores and wholesalers. However, other sections contain a wealth of information for the uninitiated anywhere, and for writers who are considering the self-publishing option. Perhaps one day someone will write a how-to manual for self-publishing in Africa (and see also Michael Norton's contribution in this Handbook). Meantime this is probably one of the best nuts-and-bolts books on the market for writers who are keen to break into print.

Robert Spicer
How to Publish a Book:
A Practical Step-by-Step Guide to Independent Publishing 2nd edn
Plymouth: How to Books, 1996.
158 pp. £9.99 pap. ISBN 1057030710

Largely targeted at the do-it-yourself publisher, this is a guide to all the processes of the publishing, promotion and marketing of a book, including essential practicalities such as orders processing, distribution and storage, and maintaining basic business accounts. Using the example of two fictitious would-be publishers – one a success story, the other a dismal failure – the book provides numerous helpful tips and shows how to avoid the pitfalls, rightly emphasising the need for good house-keeping throughout. It is liberally illustrated with charts, records and forms, specimen letters, sample estimates from printers, sample invoices, sample contracts with distributors, and more. Although the book is intended mainly for the 'amateur publisher' primarily in the UK, this is a very useful handbook, full of practical advice.

Addresses of Publishers Listed in this Section

African Books Collective Ltd, The Jam Factory, 27 Park End Street, Oxford OX1 1HU, UK
A&C Black 35, Bedford Row, London WC1R 4JH
Blackwell Publishers Ltd, 108 Cowley Road, Oxford OX4 1JF, UK
Book Aid International, 39/41 Coldharbour Lane, Camberwell, London SE5 9NR
The British Council, 76 Juta Street, Braamfontein 2001, South Africa
Fourth Dimension Publishing Co., 10 Fifth Avenue, City Layout, PMB 01164, Enugu
    Nigeria
Robert Hale Ltd, Clerkenwell House, Clerkenwell Green, London EC1R 0HT
Heinemann Educational Books (Nigeria) plc, PMB 5205, Ibadan, Nigeria
How to Books, 3 Newtec Place, Magdalen Road, Oxford OX4 1RE (Orders to
    Plymbridge House, Estover Road, Plymouth, PL6 7PZ)
Macmillan, 25 Eccleston Place, London SW1W 9NF
Nigerian Book Foundation, 4 Ezi-Ajana Lane, Umukwa, PO Box 1132, Awka, Anambra
    State, Nigeria
Options Publishing, PO Box 1588, Somerset West, 7129 South Africa
Para Publishing, PO Box 8206, Santa Barbara, CA 93118-8206, USA
Publishers Association of South Africa, PO Box 116, St James, Western Cape, 7946
    South Africa
The Society of Authors, 84 Drayton Gardens, London SW10 9SB
Southern Book Publishers Pty Ltd, PO Box 3103, Halfway House, 1685 South Africa
Writer's Digest Books, F&W Publications, 1507 Dana Avenue, Cincinnati, OH 45207,
    USA

Internet Resources for African Writers

Hans M Zell

Although computer-based communication and the use of electronic mail (email) is now increasingly aiding writers, scholars and the book professions in Africa, there are unfortunately still many who, for a variety of reasons and constraints, are not yet 'wired up', and are therefore unable to take advantage of the exciting new opportunities now offered by the Internet. For many African institutions lack of funds hinder efforts to provide full Internet access on any significant scale; and the reliability of telephone lines remains a major hurdle. For individual writers the cost of Internet 'surfing' may still be prohibitive; and even if access is possible connection speeds may be agonisingly slow.

There is no doubt, however, that the Internet is one of the most significant innovations for communicating, sharing, exchanging, and seeking educational, professional, and cultural resources. In addition to acting like a huge on-line encyclopaedia providing access to almost unfathomable amounts of information on any conceivable subject, the Internet is a particularly rich information source for writers. The information that is now accessible on the Net is truly awesome. For the writer there are many useful sites which offer market information, tips on writing, literary awards and competitions, writing tools, practical advice about finding a publisher and how to break into print, Web sites devoted to self-publishing, address sources for publishers, and more, together with a large number of literary and cultural journals and magazines, as well as many on-line African newspapers. Every day more and more information and resources on Africa are appearing on the Internet. Additionally, the Web can also provide free access to many references works such as dictionaries, thesauri, encyclopaedias, place-oriented reference tools, sites for searching facts and statistics, and a wide variety of on-line literary reference resources.

If you do not already have access to the Internet, the five groups of Web site selections that follow are intended to whet your appetite!

They are extracted from *The Electronic African Bookworm: A Web Navigator*, which can be found at

<http://www.hanszell.co.uk/navtitle.htm>.

This is a gateway Web site and resource that combines links relating to Africa, African studies, and African publishing with more general book-related links. Developed by Hans Zell Publishing Consultants in Oxford as part of their Web site, it has been designed specifically for use by the book professions in Africa, and by African writers and scholars, particularly those who may be new to the Web. It currently (April 1999) offers almost 1,200 links, and is a quick-access guide and pick-list to some of the best Internet sites on Africa, African and development studies, and on African publishing and the book trade. It also provides links to the home pages of African and Africanist journals, African newspapers, to Web sites of libraries in Africa and to some of the major Africana libraries in the countries of the North, as well as annotated listings of the major publishers (outside Africa) with African studies lists. Additional links cover a variety of resources for writers, African literary and cultural journals, and a number of African literature sites. There is also a section on ICT and the Internet in Africa and electronic networks for development, with many useful Web sites featuring discussions and resource material on Internet infrastructure and connectivity in Africa.

In addition to Africa- and African studies-related Internet sites, *The Electronic African Bookworm* offers a substantial number of links to Web sites (not Africa-specific) relating to book and journal publishing and the retail book trade, book professional associations and societies, publishing services, libraries and library associations, library journals, library and information science resources on the Internet, and links to a number of major international organisations, donor agencies, foundations, networks, and NGOs. There are also links to some of the best general reference sources, Web guides and directories, and to some of the major Internet tools, to search engines, search aids, and Internet learning materials.

A *print version* of the *Electronic African Bookworm* is available from African Books Collective Ltd, and is supplied free of charge to the African book communities, and to writers and scholars in Africa. The present print version is current as at September 1998, but ABC hopes to produce an updated edition in due course, and which will include all the new links added since September.

The print version also includes these introductory sections not available on the on-line version: 'Getting wired to the Web: A beginner's guide to the Internet'; 'How to search the Web: some search engine tips'; 'A cyber glossary'; and 'Connecting to the Internet in Africa', by Kofi Arthiabah.

Limited quantities are available for free distribution to the African book communities, for copies not for re-sale, and if funds are not available for purchase. To apply for a free copy please write to ABC at the address given below, stating full institution etc. or other details, and purpose for which the copy is required. Others, outside Africa, may purchase the print version at £8.95/$15.00 per copy inclusive of postage (1998 144 pp. ISBN 0952126958; pre-payment is required).

Requests for free copies, and orders, to: African Books Collective Ltd, The Jam Factory, 27 Park End Street, Oxford OX1 1HU, UK
Telephone: +44-1865-726686 Fax: +44-1865-793298
Email: abc@dial.pipex.com

AFRICAN LITERATURE SITES AND AFRICAN LITERARY AND CULTURAL JOURNALS AND MAGAZINES

ADA Magazine
On-line magazine and cultural guide to life in South Africa.
http://www.adamag.co.za/adais.html

Africa Online – African Writer's Series/The African Writer
Presents a variety of news on African writing, including conference announcements, author profiles, and links to organisations.
http://www.africaon-line.com/AfricaOnline/griotstalk/writers/series.html

African Literature Association [single Web page only at this time]
Independent non-profit professional society which exists primarily to facilitate the attempts of a world-wide audience to appreciate the efforts of African writers and artists. Publishes the *ALA Bulletin.*
http://h-net2.msu.edu/~aflitweb/ala.html

African Performance Clearinghouse
Maintained by the African Studies Program at the University of Wisconsin, collects, processes and provides information about performances and tours by African artists in North America.
http://polyglot.lss.wisc.edu/afrst/clear.html

African Postcolonial Literature in English
Brown University; substantial number of links.
http://www.stg.brown.edu/projects/hypertext/landow/post/misc/africov.html

African Writers and their Literature
Obianuju Mollel research project; good links.
http://www.ualberta.ca/~omollel/afwrithome.html

African Writers: Voices of Change
Developed by University of Florida Libraries; with links section to Web sites

that concern African literature, and short biographical profiles of a large number of African writers.
http://www.uflib.ufl.edu/hss/africana/voices.html

AfricArt
Calendar of events, guide, etc.
http://www.ina.fr/AfricArt/Entree/MenuGene.html

Africultures
Forum of information and debate about African cultural expression (In French, updated daily, with monthly condensed version in English.)
http://www.africultures.com/ACCUEIL.htm

Afrique en Scènes
Journal; African music, dance, theatre.
http://www.ina.fr/AfricArt

Afrlit: African Literature Forum
A listserv/on-line forum to promote discussion of works of literature by African authors, including both past and contemporary writers and works in all genres. Visit the Website to subscribe.
http://genesis.acu.edu/chowning/africa/afrlit.htm

Anansi. Fiction of the African Diaspora
Publishes original short fiction and poetry by writers of African descent.
http://aalbc.com/anansi.htm

AOI-zine
Online magazine from the Kennedy Center and which is part of the African Odyssey Interactive Web site; updated weekly to include feature articles, links to new resources, and information about upcoming African arts events.
http://artsedge.kennedy-center.org/aoi/ezine/index.html

ArtThrob
South African art and cultural magazine.
http://www.artthrob.co.za/dec98/images/southwood-peng.jpg

Autores Africanos
Site devoted to Lusophone African writers and poets, with biographical profiles.
http://nicewww.cern.ch/~pintopc/www/africa/africa.htm

Barefoot Press
South African poetry Web site.
http://www.pix.za/barefoot.press/

Blêksem Electric Pamphlet
South African on-line poetry magazine.
http://www.pcb.co.za/bleksem/welcome.htm

Current Writing
South African journal concentrating on the debates surrounding contemporary
and republished texts in Southern Africa, and on the reading of world texts
from a Southern African perspective.
http://www.und.ac.za/und/english/curwrit/

Djembe Magazine
African culture, and cultural news from Africa.
http://www.djembe.dk/index.html

Electronic Seasame
South African literary magazine.
http://www.pix.za/barefoot.press/esesame/esesame.htm

FEMECAmina: une interview avec ...
Interviews with African women writers.
http://www.arts.uwa.edu.au/AFLIT/FEMECamina.html

Francophone African Poets in English Translation
Part of the extensive University of Florida site; see above.
http://www.uflib.ufl.edu/hss/africana/poets.html

Francophone African Women Writers
There are many good links and resources maintained at this University of
Western Australia site.
http://www.arts.uwa.edu.au/AFLIT/FEMEChome.html

Francophone African Writers
Part of the University of Western Australia site above.
http://www.arts.uwa.edu.au/AFLIT/FEMEChomeEN.html#english

Guide du Théâtre en Afrique et dans l'Océan Indien
This useful guide and inventory to African theatre from the publishers of
Afrique en Créations, compiled with the assistance of French cultural centres
in Africa, provides country-by-country listings of theatre activity in Africa, and
gives a summary for each country under four headings: theatre groups or
companies, venues where theatre is performed, festivals and similar events
involving theatre, and programme planners and partners.
http://www.mediaport.net/AeC/Theatre/index.en.html

H-Afrlitcine
The home page of this international electronic discussion group providing
a forum for the discussion and exploration of African literature and
cinema, and which is part of the H-Net family; click on to find out how
to join this mailing list.
http://www.h-net.msu.edu/~aflitweb/

Isibongo
South African on-line poetry journal, and essays, reviews, etc.
http://www.uct.ac.za/projects/poetry/isibongo/isibongo.htm

Mayibuye
African National Congress writers' journal.
http://www.anc.org.za/ancdocs/pubs/mayi9710.html

Mots Pluriel
On-line journal which includes frequent articles on African writing.
http://www.arts.uwa.edu.au/MotsPluriels/MP.html

Organisation of Women Writers of Africa
http://www.owwa.org/

Research in African Literatures
Scholarly journal on all aspects of African oral and written literatures.
http://www.indiana.edu/~iupress/journals/ral.html

Revue Noire
Magazine, African art and cultures etc., English version.
http://antares.rio.net/revuenoire/

South African Poetry Sites on the Net
A site maintained by the South African poet Peter Horn.
http://www.uct.ac.za/projects/poetry/sites.htm

Transition
A leading and influential magazine of African intellectual life, founded in
Uganda in 1961, but now published from the US.
http://web-dubois.fas.harvard.edu/transition/

University of Cape Town Poetry Web
Cape Town and Western Cape poets.
http://www.uct.ac.za/projects/poetry/

Voices from the Gap
African literature.
http://english.cla.umn.edu/lkd/vfg/vfghome

Voices: The Wisconsin Review of African Literatures
http://african.lss.wisc.edu/all/voices.htm

GENERAL RESOURCES FOR WRITERS AND WRITERS' ASSOCIATIONS

African American Online Writers Guild [USA]
http://www.blackwriters.org/

Alternative Press Center
With *Alternative Press Index.*
http://www.altpress.org/

American Society of Journalists and Authors
http://www.asja.org/

Association of Authors & Publishers [USA]
http://www.authorsandpublishers.org/index.html

Authors' Licensing & Collecting Society (ALCS)
With A–Z links to 150 authorship, copyright sites, etc.
http://www.alcs.co.uk/

Authorlink
News, information and marketing service for editors, literary agents, and writers.
http://www.authorlink.com/

Authorworld
Web site for writers devoted to the craft of writing; with on-line directory of publishers and agents.
http://www.authorworld.com/index.shtml

BBC Education – Bookworm
This BBC site offers a great deal of useful news and information, including author interviews, book awards, book programmes, courses and competitions, together with publishing know-how, and tips on how to start writing, and how to get your work noticed and published.
http://www.bbc.co.uk/education/bookworm/

BBC World Service – 1999 BBC African Performance Radio Drama Competition
Details and rules of this competition for the best three new plays for radio, which will be produced and broadcast by the BBC.
http://www.bbc.co.uk/worldservice/africanperformance/

Children's Literature Web Guide
Maintained by David Brown; links, resources, book awards, children's book publishers, and more.
http://www.acs.ucalgary.ca/~dkbrown/

Children's Writing Resource Center
Links, tools, resources, children's book prizes, bookshop.
http://www.write4kids.com/index.html

Copyright & Multimedia Law for Webbuilders & Multimedia Authors
Maintained by University of Iowa Libraries.
http://www.arcade.uiowa.edu/proj/webbuilder/copyright.html

Culturelink. Network of Networks for Research and Cooperation in Cultural Development
Established by UNESCO and the Council of Europe in 1989, the Culturelink Network brings together some 1,000 networks and member institutions from 97 countries in all parts of the world. One of its major objectives is the promotion of regional, interregional and international research projects/joint projects in which most of its members from Europe, Asia, Africa and Latin America participate The site provides access to the 'Cultural Development Database' and the 'Cultural Policy Database', and the review *Culturelink*.
http://www.culturelink.org

Digital Freedom Network
International human rights organisation that publishes censored material on the Internet.
http://www.dfn.org/

Do-It-Yourself Publishing
Some useful tips for the self-publisher; site maintained by Anne Stobbs.
http://www.btinternet.com/~lockwood/gfour.htm

Electronic Poetry Center (EPC)
Serves as a central gateway to resources in electronic poetry and poetics; contains a large number of links, e.g. author libraries, poetry events, lists of poetry magazines and publishers, and there is an on-line directory of poets.
http://wings.buffalo.edu/epc/

Elements of Style
The full text of the classic book by William Strunk, jr, to clear writing in English.
http://www.cc.columbia.edu/acis/bartleby/strunk/

Index on Censorship
The Web site, updated every two weeks, of Writers and Scholars International Ltd, the publishers of the *Index on Censorship*.
http://www.indexoncensorship.org/

Inkspot
This useful site for writers offers market information, tips on improving writing and articles, interviews with professional authors and editors, and

networking opportunities; and also provides a guide to resources for writers on the Internet.
http://www.inkspot.com/

International Black Writers
Encourages and assists in promoting Black writers through workshops and other activities. Publishes *The Black Writer* magazine.
http://lcweb.loc.gov/loc/cfbook/coborg/ibw.html

International Federation of Journalists
http://www.ifj.org/

International Women's Writing Guild
http://www.iwwg.com/

IPL Online Literary Criticism Collection
Over 1,000 critical and biographical Web sites about authors and their works.
http://www.ipl.org/ref/litcrit/

Literary Resources on the Net
Extensive listings of annotated links to the best literary Web sites, especially those covering English and American literatures, together with resources for writers and writing instructors; maintained by Jack Lynch.
http://andromeda.rutgers.edu/~jlynch/Lit/

Organisation of Black Screenwriters, Inc. [USA]
http://www.obswriter.com/

The Poetry Society
Features 'The Poetry Cafe', poetry reviews, information about workshops, events, competitions, links to Web sites of individual poets, Web publications, writers resources, etc.
http://www.poetrysoc.com

Professional Writing Supersite
Writing tools, tips, and resources; how to get published, etc.
http://www.bookdoctor.com/supersite.html

Publishers' and Authors' Message Board
Authors seeking publishers, and *vice versa*.
http://www.InsideTheWeb.com/messageboard/mbs.cgi/mb24867

Pure Fiction
Resources for writers and those aspiring to break into print. Book reviews, author interviews, and lots of good advice plus a large number of links.
http://www.purefiction.com

Resources for Editors
Useful links section from the Society of Editors Tasmania, Inc.; organisations, and associations related to editing, courses, resources for writers, email

discussion lists, on-line magazines, and more.
http://www.tas-editors.org.au/links.html

The Society of Authors
News about activities of The (UK) Society of Authors, grants, book prizes, events, FAQs for new writers, and a good links section.
http://www.writers.org.uk/society/

Society of Children's Book Writers and Illustrators (SCBWI)
http://www.scbwi.org/

Svenska Akademien/Swedish Academy
Find information here about all the Nobel Prize Winners in Literature (and about the laureates in the other four prize categories) by year. Has a searchable archive of all past press releases about Nobel winners, plus biographical profiles, photographs, and Nobel lectures. Also includes facts about the Swedish academy, including its history, members, organisation, and projects.
http://svenska.gu.se/academy.html

toExcel.com
Offers on-demand publishing through the company's Open Publishing Platform. Also good links to writers' associations and groups, courses and workshops for writers, writing programs, and publishing and marketing links.
http://www toexcel.com/

Trace
General writing resources.
http://human.ntu.ac.uk/foh/ems/trace/trace.html

University of Iowa – International Writing Program
http://www.uiowa.edu/~iwp/index.html

University of Wisconsin – Madison Writing Center
Offers instructional materials on academic writing, peer review, grammar and style, documentation styles, and more.
http://www.wisc.edu/writing/Handbook/main.html

Women Writers
Over 1,000 links to women's books and women's writing on-line.
http://womenbooks.com/

World Literature Written in English
The literary quarterly from the University of Oklahoma, devoted to comment on all the major and many of the minor languages of the world.
http://www.nus.sg/NUSinfo/FASS/ELL/wlwe/

Writer's Digest
The Web site of this popular and long-established magazine for writers; updated daily; includes searchable database of writer's guidelines, the 'coolest

places' to get published, products for writers, contests, etc.
http://www.writersdigest.com/about.asp

Writers' Site, The
Includes links to Society of Authors, Writers' Guild of Great Britain, and
National Union of Journalists sites.
http://www.writers.org.uk/

WritersNet
Internet resources for writers, editors, publishers, and literary agents.
http://www.writers.net/

SOME OTHER USEFUL BOOK- AND PUBLISHING-RELATED SITES AND PUBLISHER ADDRESS SOURCES

AcqWeb
The Acquisitions Web is maintained by Vanderbuilt University Library in
Canada and is one of the most comprehensive on-line directories of
publishers' and vendors' Web sites; also with email directory of publishers.
http://www.library.vanderbilt.edu/law/acqs/pubr.html

Acses
Guide to the best deals from on-line bookstores. Calls itself 'The Ultimate
Comparison Shopping Engine'.
http://www.acses.com/

Amazon Internet Bookstore
The leading Internet bookstore, with good search facilities for any type of
book; also many resources for authors and publishers, and literary titbits. And
it ranks sales, enquiries and site hits for over a million titles!
http://www.amazon.com/

Amazon.co.uk
The UK branch of Amazon.com, the major US Internet bookstore. Click on to
the section 'Amazon.co.uk for Authors'.
http://www.amazon.co.uk/

Barnes & Noble
On-line bookstore of this major US bookseller, with current reviews, book
search, etc. and offers of discounted books. Claims to be the world's biggest
bookseller.
http://www.barnesandnoble.com

Bibliography of Books on Writing, Publishing, Marketing and Publicity
On-line bibliography by John Kremer, with links to other book marketing and
publishing resources.
http://www.bookmarket.com/1001bib.html

Blackwell's Online Bookshop
On-line version of Oxford's famous bookshop. 1.5 million titles; good search tools.
http://bookshop.blackwell.co.uk/

Book Information Web site
Devoted to all aspects of the book; large number of links.
http://www.xs4all.nl/~cremers/

The Bookpl@ce
On-line bookshop of the major UK high street chain Dillon's (now owned by Waterstone's). Stocks over 1.5 million books; good search facilities.
http://www.thebookplace.com/

The Bookseller
The major UK book trade journal, with many links to publishers' and retailers' Web sites.
http://www.theBookseller.com

The Book Trust
UK book charity, with listings of literary prizes, book information service, publications.
http://dialspace.dial.pipex.com/town/avenue/ae238/

BookWeb
A miscellany of UK book trade information: publishers, library suppliers, booksellers, wholesales, distributors, book reviews and other links.
http://www.bookweb.co.uk/

Bookwire Navigator
Book-related Internet resources and book industry news, with a very large number of links. A good starting point and one of the most comprehensive on-line information sources for anything related to publishing, editing, writing, designing, or selling books.
http://www.bookwire.com/

Bookworld Companies
All about self-publishing.
http://www.bookworld.com/bwpress.html

Borders.com
Superstore on-line bookshop: books, music, video, children's etc.
http://www.borders.com/

British Council
Publishing and information pages.
http://www.britcoun.org/publishing/index.htm

Center for the Book – Community of the Book Organisations
A useful directory of (primarily US) book-related organisations and

programmes, with full addresses, phone and fax numbers, and email and Web site information where available. The second part of the listing lists organisations under a broad subject index by their main area of activity.
http://lcweb.loc.gov/loc/cfbook/cob4.html

Chicago Manual of Style FAQ
Frequently asked questions on manuscript editing, etc. compiled by the manuscript editing department at the University of Chicago Press, who will also answer individual style questions by email if not covered by the FAQs.
http://www.press.uchicago.edu/Misc/Chicago/cmosfaq.html

Copyright, Intellectual Property, and Publishing on the WWW
Guide to a set of links which provide information on issues of copyright and fair use on the Intenet.
http://139.182.93.107/hypertch/copyright.htm

Culture of Publishing
Oxford Brookes University, Publishing Department, on-line journal maintained by publishing students, including contributions on publishing in developing countries.
http://www.brookes.ac.uk/schools/apm/Publishing/CULTURE.HTM

The Electric Editors
Excellent site with many links and resources for those working in an editorial capacity, or indeed anyone with an interest in preparing the written word for publication. Includes links to dictionaries, style guides, writers resources, etc., and also maintains three mailing lists: EDLine for editorial discussions, LANGline on foreign languages, and Grapevine on computer-related topics.
http://www.ikingston.demon.co.uk/ee/home.htm

The Electronic African Bookworm: A Web Navigator
Part of the Web site of Hans Zell Publishing Consultants. Has almost 1,200 links to some of the best sites on Africa, African studies, African publishing and the book trade, African and Africanist libraries, and resources for writers. It also offers a large number of links to other (not Africa-specific) sites relating to book and journal publishing, library and information science resources on the Internet, search engines and directories, Internet learning materials, and much more. (Also available in a print version; see above.)
http://www.hanszell.co.uk/navtitle.htm

Indiana University Style Guide
Useful clickable links to some 200 common editorial style queries; also editors' and proofreaders' marks and recommended reference works.
http://www.indiana.edu/~iupubs/style95/style95.html

International Board on Books for Young People (IBBY)
http://www.ibby.org/

International Federation of Reproduction Rights Organisations (IFRRO)
http://www.kopinor.no/IFRRO/

International Intellectual Property Association (IIPA)
http://www.iipa.com/

International Publishers Association (IPA)
http://www.ipa-uie.org

International Reading Association
http://www.reading.org/

Internet Book Information Center
http://sunsite.unc.edu/ibic/IBIC-homepage.html

Internet Bookshop
The UK's major electronic bookshop.
http://www.bookshop.co.uk

The Literary Market Place
A major tool of the trade for North American publishing. Subscription-based, but many sections accessible and free of payment.
http://lmp.bookwire.com/

Multicultural Publishing and Education Council (MPEC)
http://www.mpec.org/

New York Times Book Review
With archive of over 50,000 reviews published since 1980; fully searchable. A marvellous resource.
http://www.nytimes.com/books/

Oxford Publishing Services
Services for publishers, authors, NGOs, and research institutes.
http://ourworld.compuserve.com/homepages/JasonOPS/

ParaPublishing
Publishes many useful 'how-to' books and resources on publishing, including self-publishing.
http://www.parapublishing.com/welcome.html

The Publishers Association
UK; with links to PA members and book trade organisations, news and events, market statistics, etc.; and with link to register of consultants and trainers available for training and development projects overseas.
http://www.publishers.org.uk

Publishers Weekly
On-line selections from this major US book trade weekly.
http://www.bookwire.com/pw/pw.html

Publishing News
Weekly on-line journal with 'hot news' about the UK book trade.
http://www.publishingnews.co.uk/

Publishing Training Centre at Book House
Guides to Book House training courses, distance learning, consultancy services, bookshop, career opportunities, etc.
http://www.train4publishing.co.uk/bookhouse/bottom.htm

Small Publishers, Artists and Writers Network (SPAWN)
Offers a variety of information on writing and publishing, with links to research resources, book services, books and articles on writing and publishing, electronic publishing, etc.
http://www.spawn.org/

Society for the History of Authorship, Reading and Publishing (SHARP)
http://www.indiana.edu/~sharp/

Toronto Centre for the Book
http://www.fis.utoronto.ca/research/tcb/index.htm

University of Iowa Center for the Book
With links to a large number of book-related Web sites.
http://www.uiowa.edu/~ctrbook/

Waterstones
On-line bookshop of the major UK retail chain. Search facilities, bestseller lists, book reviews, rare book search, etc.
http://www.waterstones.co.uk

Women in Publishing
UK, with good links, on-line publishing tutorial, and Internet resources, etc.
http://www.cyberiacafe.net/wip/

Women, Ink.
Major international distributor of books on women and development.
http://www.womenink.org/

World Intellectual Property Organisation (WIPO)
http://www.wipo.org/

Worldwide Virtual Library: Literature
Book-related Internet resources.
http://sunsite.unc.edu/ibic/guide.html

Worldwide Virtual Library: Publishers
Publishing-related Internet resources.
http://www.comlab.ox.ac.uk/archive/publishers.html

Writers/Publishers
Maintained by the *Midwest Book Review* this site provides a very substantial

number of links to resources, Web sites, Internet tools, as they relate to publishers and publishing.
http://www.execpc.com/~mbr/bookwatch/writepub/#internet

Zuzu's Petals Literary Resource
Bookstores, on-line books, and related book resources.
http://www.lehigh.net/zuzu/booklink.htm

REFERENCE WORKS/DICTIONARIES

Dict.org
This site offers a quick and painless way to look up the meaning of a word, and which allows you to access dictionary definitions from a set of natural language dictionary databases.
http://www.dict.org/

Information Please
Large, free reference site for searching for facts and statistics, and finding answers in almanacs, encyclopedias and dictionaries.
http://www.infoplease.com/

Internet Public Library
Developed by librarians, this directory contains a very large number of links to general and reference as well as literary resources.
http://ipl.sils.umich.edu/

Logos Dictionary
Freely-accessible and searchable multi-lingual database, including several African languages. The dictionary currently has over 7.5 million entries for all languages. Also has 'Wordtheque' search facility for searching a massive database containing multilingual novels, technical literature and translated texts.
http://www.logos.it/query/query.html

News Resource
Lists links to on-line news sites, including almost 200 listings for Africa. Links are searchable by keyword and location.
http://www.newo.com/news/

Online Reference Works
Dictionaries, thesauri, encyclopaedies, place-oriented references, etc.
http://www.cs.cmu.edu/references.html

Plumb Design Visual Thesaurus
Fascinating interactive thesaurus that can create a web of associations for any word chosen, to form a spatial map of linguistic associations.
http://www.plumbdesign.com/

Reference Works
Good range of links to on-line reference works.
http://digital.net/~klane/ref.html

Research-It!
Look up words in many language tools; translate words to/from various languages; plus library, biographical, geographical and financial tools, and US and Canadian telephone numbers.
http://www.iTools.COM/research-it/

Ultimate Collection of Newslinks
Links to 8,000 newspapers and magazines, including African newspapers.
http://pppp.net/links/news/

UnCover Web 2.0
On-line periodical article delivery service and current awareness alerting service. Provides free access to a searchable database and index to 17,000 English-language periodicals; charges apply for document delivery.
http://uncweb.carl.org/

Voycabulary
This interesting site transforms Web pages into links to dictionary, glossary of thesaurus lookups, and will also translate words into and from several different languages. Simply type in the URL of a Web address you wish to process, then click on any word.
http://www.voycabulary.com/

World Fact Book
Revised and updated every year, and compiled by the CIA, this is a good site for basic factual information on all the countries of the world: geography, people, government, economy, communications, transportation, and military; also provides access to various maps.
http://www.odci.gov/cia/publications/nsolo/wfb-all.htm

World Wide Words
If you are interested in new words this site will be a treat. Records all the latest words or phrases not yet in the dictionaries. Developed by Michael Quinion, the site is updated weekly and you can also join a mailing list to receive all the updates sent to your email address. Other sections cover Questions & Answers, and Weird Words. A great site!
http://www.quinion.com/words/

SOME WEB SITES DEVOTED TO AFRICAN PUBLISHING

African Books Collective Ltd (ABC) The Oxford-based, African-owned book marketing and distribution organisation. ABC's Web site includes the complete on-line catalogue, new title information, the *ABC Newsline*, author profiles, list of members, catalogue request form, and more.
http://www.africanbookscollective.com/

African Publishers' Network (APNET)
Provides details of APNET's mission, projects, activities, training programmes, members, publications, consultant's register, and APNET personnel, etc.
http://www.africanpublishers.org/

Bellagio Publishing Network
An informal association of donors and organisations dedicated to strengthening indigenous publishing and book development in Africa; the site provides on-line access to the informative *Bellagio Publishing Network Newsletter*, with news and reports about publishing activities in Africa, perspectives and commentary, Secretariat reports, book reviews, new publications, and more.
http://www.bc.edu/bellagio

Partners in African Publishing
Edited by Kelvin Smith, this is a useful quarterly newsletter and source of information for publishers and organisations in Europe and Africa and is designed to encourage increased collaboration between partners in the countries of the North and those in the South.
http://www.bookaid.org/resources/partners/cintro.htm

Publishing & Training Resources. Books, Periodicals, Training Materials
On-line version of a very useful reference tool from Book Aid International. Lists a wide range of books and reference material relevant to the needs of publishers in Africa, and which will also be of interest to writers. (Also available in a print version, *see* The Author's Bookshelf.)
http://www.bookaid.org/resources/pubcatpintro.htm

DOCUMENTS

Minimum Terms Agreement

A Minimum Terms Agreement was issued by the UK Society of Authors in 1982, giving a model publishing contract. The Society and the UK Writers Guild continuously negotiate with publishers about the Agreement, and it is revised from time to time. The Agreement is reproduced here however, as a base guideline. The Society publishes a very useful guide to publishing contracts which contains much valuable guidance; and in many ways it is probably more useful for the African writer, given that the guidance given can be interpreted and adapted to the publishing and writing realities of different countries (Society of Authors 1999). The Minimum Terms Agreement referred to in the section on relations with Publishers is reproduced below. It is reproduced by permission of the Society of Authors.

AN AGREEMENT made this   day of
between The Society of Authors and the Writers' Guild of Great Britain cf the one part and   (hereinafter called 'the Publishers') of the other part   WHEREBY IT IS AGREED AS FOLLOWS

A Scope of Agreement

This Agreement contains the minimum terms and conditions to be observed in all contracts ('the contract') between the Publishers and all members of the Society of Authors and all members of the Writers' Guild (any such members being called 'the Author') in respect of any original literary work published in hardcover volume form but excluding the following categories:
1 Illustrated books defined as books which would not have been published save for the illustrations.
2 Technical books, manuals, reference works.
3 Textbooks written for the educational market (as distinct from general books of an academic or instructional nature) .
4 Books involving three or more writers.
5 Plays and Poetry.

B Nature of Agreement

1 The terms and conditions of the contract shall be no less favourable to the Author nor in any way detract from or qualify the terms and conditions specified in Section C hereof.

2   This Agreement may be re-negotiated on either party giving to the other three months' written notice expiring at any time after the fifth anniversary hereof.

3   The contract shall contain the words 'drafted in accordance with the Society of Authors/Writers' Guild Minimum Terms Agreement'.

C Terms of the Contract between the Author and the Publisher

1   *Delivery and Acceptance of the Typescript*

(a)   The Author shall deliver not later than the date specified in the contract one legible copy of the typescript of the work. The contract shall specify the fullest possible details of length, number and type of illustrations, index , etc. The Author shall deliver a script which, in style and content, is professionally competent and fit for publication.

(b)   The Publishers shall notify the Author of any changes required in the script within 30 days. Should the Publishers reject the script on the ground that it fails to meet the specifications in (a) above, they shall within 30 days provide the Author with written notice of not less than 250 words in which the grounds for rejecting the script shall be set out in such a manner as to facilitate arbitration under clause 25 below.

(c)   The Publishers shall not reject the script for any reason other than its failure to meet the specifications in (a) above.

(d)   Should the Author fail to meet the delivery date specified, the Publishers may give the Author six months' notice in writing to deliver the work and should he fail to do so the Publishers shall be entitled to terminate the contract in which event any advance shall be returnable and all rights shall revert to the Author.

2   *Warranty and Indemnity*

The Author shall warrant that the work is an original work, that it has not been published within the territories in which exclusive rights have been granted to the Publishers by the contract, that it does not infringe any existing copyright, and that to the best of the author's knowledge and ability it contains nothing libellous or defamatory.

The Author shall indemnify the Publishers against any loss injury or damage resulting from any breach by the Author (unknown to the Publishers) of the warranty, provided that any legal costs and expenses and any compensation, damages, costs and disbursements shall be paid by the Publishers only on the joint advice of the respective legal advisers of the Author and the Publishers and failing agreement on the advice of Counsel selected and instructed jointly on behalf of the Publishers and the Author. The extent of the Author's Indemnity shall not exceed the total moneys received by the Author under the contract.

3   *Copyright Fees and Index*

(a)   The Publishers shall pay copyright fees for illustrations and/or quotations up to a maximum of £   , any further sum being paid by the Publishers but deducted from the Author's royalties.

(b) If in the opinion of the Author and the Publishers an index is required but the Author does not wish to undertake the task, the Publishers shall engage a competent indexer to do so and the costs shall be shared equally between the Author and the Publishers, the Author's share being deducted from royalties.

4 Licence

The copyright in the work shall remain the property of the Author who shall grant to the Publishers the sole and exclusive right for a period of ten years from the date of the contract or delivery of the script (whichever is the later) to print, publish and sell the work in volume form and to sub-license the rights specified in Clauses 13, 14, 15, 16 and 17(a) hereof as may be agreed in the contract. Except in the case of anthology and quotation rights, if the Publishers wish to enter into any such sub-licence, they shall obtain the consent of the Author (such consent not to be unreasonably withheld or delayed) supplying him with a copy of the sub-licence before it is signed. If the work is in print (as defined in Clause 23(b) hereof) at the end of ten years after delivery of the typescript, the Publishers shall have first refusal to enter into a further contract with the Author.

5 Publisher's Undertaking to Publish

Provided that the work meets the specification in Clause 1(a) above, the Publishers shall publish the work at their own expense and risk in a first edition consisting of the number of copies named in approximate terms in the contract within twelve months (unless otherwise agreed in writing) of delivery of the typescript and any other material specified in accordance with Clause 1. Should the Publishers fail to comply with their undertaking, the advance stipulated in Clause 10 hereof (or any balance unpaid) shall be paid to the Author together with such additional amount as may be awarded under Clause 25 hereof as compensation for such failure by the Publishers.

6 Production

(a) All details as to the manner of production and publication and the number and destination of free copies shall be under the control of the Publishers who undertake to produce the book to a high standard.

(b) The Publishers shall obtain the Author's approval of copy editing, blurb, catalogue copy, number and type of illustrations, jacket design and publication date, such approval not to be unreasonably withheld or delayed.

(c) No changes in the title or text shall be made by the Publishers without the Author's written consent.

(d) Within ten days of publication the Publishers shall inform the Author of the number of copies printed and the number and destination of free copies distributed.

(e) Within thirty days of publication the Publishers shall return to the Author the typescript of the work.

(f) The Publishers shall ensure that the provisions contained in (b) and (c) above are included in any contract for sub-licensed editions of the work in the English language.

7 *Approval of Final Edited Script and Correction of Proofs*

(a) The Author shall be sent for approval a copy of the final edited script at least 14 days before it goes to the printers.

(b) The Author shall be sent two complete sets of proofs of the work and proofs of the illustrations and captions and notes on the jacket. The Author shall correct and return one set of proofs to the Publishers within 14 days. The Author shall bear the cost of proof corrections (other than printers' or Publishers' errors) in excess of 15% of the cost of composition, such cost to be deducted from royalties.

8 *Marketing*

The Publishers shall use their best endeavours to market the work effectively and shall, in particular, despatch review copies at least one month before the publication date, include and describe correctly the work in their catalogue, and do everything they reasonably can to ensure that copies are ready for sale in all leading bookshops by publication day.

9 *Copyright notice and Credit to the Author*

A copyright notice in the form © followed by the Author's name and the year of publication shall be printed on all copies of the work and the Author's name shall appear prominently on the jacket, binding and title page of the work and in all publicity material. The Publishers shall ensure that an identical copyright notice appears in all sub-licensed editions of the work.

10 *Advance*

(a) The Publishers shall pay the Author an advance against royalties which shall be calculated as follows:

(i) On account of the Publishers' own editions: not less than 65% of the Author's estimated receipts from the sale of the projected first printing (if the Publishers' turnover is not less than £   per annum); and

(ii) On account of any rights granted under clauses 13, 14, 15 and 16; a sum additional to that under (i) above, to be negotiated between the Author and the Publishers and to be itemized separately both in the contract and the account statements to be rendered to the Author.

(b) In the case of a non-commissioned work half the advance shall be paid on signature of the contract and half within one year of signature or on publication whichever is the sooner.

(c) In the case of a commissioned work the advance shall be paid either

(i) one third on signature of the contract, one third on delivery of the typescript and one third within one year of delivery of the typescript or on publication whichever is the sooner; or

(ii) one half on signature of the contract and one half on delivery of the typescript.

(d) Except in the case of termination of the contract pursuant to clause 1(d) above, the advance shall be non-returnable and shall be paid in full.

(e) Within ten days of publication the Publishers shall pay to the Author such sum as may be required to bring the advance payment up to the 65% of the Author's receipts from the sale of the entire first printing.

11 *Royalties*

(a) *On home market sales in the UK and Irish Republic and on overseas sales at discounts of less than 45%*
10% of the British published price on the first 2,500 copies, 12½% on the next 2,500 copies, and 15% thereafter.

(b) *On overseas sales (other than to the USA) at discounts of 45% or more)*
5% of the British published price on the first 2,500 copies, 6¼% on the next 2,500 copies, and 7½% thereafter.

(c) *English language editions published overseas (other than US editions)*
The Publishers shall pay to the Author a royalty to be agreed on all copies of any edition in the English language produced and published outside the United Kingdom (other than the USA) either by themselves or by arrangement with another publisher.

(d) Reduced royalties shall not be paid on any reprint unless otherwise agreed in writing.

(e) No proportion of royalties due to the Author shall be reserved against return copies

(f) *Cheap and other hardback editions*
The Publishers shall pay to the Author a royalty to be agreed on any hardback edition published at less than two-thirds of the original published price and also on any 'special' hardback edition under their imprint, e.g. an educational or large print edition.

12 *Remainders and Surplus Stock*

If not less than two years after the first publication the Publishers

(a) wish to sell off copies at a reduced price or as a remainder; or

(b) wish to destroy surplus bound copies

they shall notify the Author accordingly. In the case of (a) the Publishers shall pay the Author 10% of the net receipts and shall give him the option to purchase copies at the remainder price. In the case of (b) the Author shall have the right to obtain free copies within 28 days of the notification.

13 *Paperbacks*

(a) Should the Publishers publish a paperback edition under their own imprint or under that of an associated company they shall pay to the Author on all sales in the home market and overseas including the USA 7½% of the British published price on the first 20,000 copies and 10% thereafter.

(b) Should the Publishers sub-license paperback rights to an independent paperback publisher, all moneys accruing under such sub-licence shall be divided in the proportion 60% to the Author and 40% to the Publishers on the first £5,000 accruing under the sub-licence, and 70% to the Author and 30% to the Publishers thereafter.

14 *Bookclub and Digest Rights*

Should the Publishers sub-license simultaneous or reprint bookclub rights or the right of condensation in volume form they shall pay the Author as follows

(a) On bound copies or sheets sold to the bookclub:

50% of net receipts (being the difference between the sale price and the cost of manufacture) up to £5,000 and 60% on all receipts thereafter. In the event of such a sale the Publishers shall inform the Author of the gross amount received from the bookclub and the cost of manufacture.
(b) On copies manufactured by the bookclub:
    60% of the Publishers' receipts up to £5,000 and 70% thereafter
(c) On copies sold to a bookclub owned or partly owned by the Publishers or one of their associated companies:
    7½% of the bookclub price.

15 *United States Rights*
(a) If the Author grants to the Publishers US rights in the work, they shall make every effort to arrange the publication of an American edition of the work on a royalty basis. The Publishers shall retain not more than 15% of the proceeds from any such edition inclusive of any sub-agent's commission. Should the Publishers fail to negotiate publication of an American edition on a royalty basis, but obtain an offer for an edition at a price inclusive of the Author's remuneration, they shall pay the Author not less than 12½% of their net receipts.
(b) If the Author retains US rights but the Publishers agree to act as his agent for the sale of these rights, US publication shall be covered by a separate contract between the Author and the American publishers. The Publishers shall retain as an agency, commission not more than 15% of the proceeds from any such edition inclusive of any sub-agent's commission.

16 *Translation Rights*
(a) If the Author grants to the Publishers translation rights in the work they shall retain not more than 20% of the proceeds from any foreign-language edition inclusive of any sub-agent's commission,
(b) If the Author retains translation rights but the publishers agree to act as his agent for the sale of these rights, any foreign-language edition of the work shall be covered by a separate contract between the Author and the foreign-language publishers. The Publishers shall retain as an agency commission not more than 20% of the proceeds from any such edition inclusive of any sub-agent's commission.

17 *Subsidiary Rights*
(a) If the Author grants to the Publishers an exclusive licence to handle the following rights on his behalf the Publishers shall pay to the Author the following percentages of the proceeds:
    (i)   Second, i.e. post-volume publication serial rights 80%
    (ii) Anthology and quotation rights 60%
    (iii) Condensation rights 75%
    (iv) Strip cartoon rights 75 %
(b) The following rights shall be expressly reserved for the Author together with any rights not specified above: First serial, one-shot periodical, film and dramatic, TV and radio dramatization, TV and radio readings, reprography, merchandizing, video and sound recording, Public Lending.

18 *Author's Copies*

The Author shall receive on publication 12 presentation copies of the work and shall have the right to purchase further copies at the lowest trade price for personal use. Should a paperback edition be issued under clause 13(a), the Author shall be entitled to 20 presentation copies.

19 *Accounts*

(a) The Publishers shall make up account s at six-monthly intervals in each year and shall render such accounts and pay all moneys due to the Author within three months thereof.

(b) Moneys due to the Author under either Clause 10(a)(i) or Clause 10(a)(ii) shall not be withheld on account of an unearned advance under the other of these two sub-clauses.

Any sum of £100 or more due to the Author in respect of sub-licensed rights shall be paid to the Author within one month of receipt provided the advance under clause 10 a)(ii) has been earned.

(c) Each statement of account shall report the number of copies printed, the number of free copies distributed, the number of copies sold during the previous accounting period, the total sales to date, the list price, the royalty rate, the amount of royalties, the number of returned copies, the gross amount received pursuant to each licence granted by the Publishers, and itemized deductions. Each statement of account shall be accompanied by copies of statements received from sublicensed publishers.

(d) The Publishers shall make no deductions from moneys due to the Author other than those provided for herein. In the event of late payment, the Publishers shall pay interest on moneys overdue at the rate of 3% above the base rate of the major clearing banks.

(e) The Author or his authorized representative shall have the right upon written request to examine the Publishers' books of account in so far as they relate to the work, which examination shall be at the cost of the Author unless errors exceeding 2% of the total sums paid to the Author shall be found to his disadvantage in which case the costs shall be paid by the Publishers.

20 *Actions for Infringement*

If either the Author or the Publishers consider the copyright in the work has been infringed both parties shall join in any legal proceedings and the party initiating such proceedings shall pay all costs and expenses and indemnify the other. Any moneys which shall be recovered in respect of any such infringement of copyright shall after deduction of all costs and expenses be divided equally between Author and Publishers.

21 *Revised Editions*

The work shall not be revised or re-issued in altered or expanded form without the Author's consent. If the Author and the Publishers agree that the Author shall undertake revisions or provide new material for a new edition, this work shall be undertaken subject to an agreed advance against royalties to the Author. No third party shall be engaged to revise or add to the work without the Author's written consent.

2.2 *Assignment*

The Publishers shall not assign the rights granted to them in the contract or the benefit thereof without the Author's written consent.

2.3 *Termination*

(a) If the Publishers fail to fulfil or comply with any of the provisions of the contract within one month after notification from the Author of such failure or if they go into liquidation or have a Receiver appointed, the contract shall automatically terminate and all rights granted by it shall revert to the Author.

(b) If after all editions of the work published under their own imprint are out of print or off the market the Publishers have not within six months of a written request from the Author issued a new edition or impression of at least 1,500 copies (unless a lesser number of copies be mutually agreed) the contract shall terminate and all rights granted shall revert to the Author. The work shall be considered to be out of print for the purposes of the contract if fewer than 12 copies of an edition under the Publishers' imprint are shown to have been sold in any statement of account or if fewer than 50 copies remain in stock.

Termination under (a) or (b) above shall be without prejudice to:

(i)   any sub-licences properly granted by the Publishers during the currency of the contract, and

(ii) any claims which the Author may have for moneys due at the time of such termination, and

(iii) any claims which the Author may have against the Publishers in respect of breaches by the Publishers of the terms of the contract.

2.4 *Advertisements*

The Publishers and the publishers of any sub-licensed edition shall not insert within the work or on its cover or dustjacket any advertisement other than that for their own works without the Author's consent.

2.5 *Disputes*

Any dispute arising in connection with the contract shall be referred to a joint committee composed of a representative of the Society of Authors, a representative of the Writers' Guild and two representatives appointed by the Publishers but not connected with their company, whose unanimous decision shall be binding. Failing unanimous agreement, the dispute shall be referred to a single arbitrator appointed by the above named parties and the decision of the arbitrator shall be binding. Failing agreement on the choice of a single arbitrator, the dispute shall be referred to the London Court of Arbitration under its rules.

2.6 *Option*

The Author shall not grant the Publishers an option or first refusal on any of his future works.

APPENDIX A. PAPERBACK AGREEMENT

Where the work is originally published in paperback form by the Publishers the minimum terms and conditions shall be the same as those set out in the hardcover Agreement except that the following clauses shall be substituted:

Clause 11 Royalties
- (a) *on all sales in the home market and overseas including the USA* 7½% of the British published price on the first 20,000 copies and 10% of the British published price thereafter
- (b) reduced royalties shall not be paid on any reprint unless otherwise agreed in writing
- (c) no proportion of royalties due to the Author shall be reserved against return copies

Clause 13 Hardcover Editions
(a) Should the Publishers publish a hardcover edition under their own imprint or under that of an associated company the Publishers shall pay to the Author the following royalties:
- (i) *on home market sales in the UK and Irish Republic and on overseas sales at discounts of less than 45%*
  10% of the British published price on the first 2,500 copies, 12½% on the next 2,500 copies, and 15% thereafter
- (ii) *on overseas sales (other than the USA) at discounts of 45% or more*
  5% of the British published price on the first 2,500 copies, 6¼% on the next 2,500 copies, and 7½% thereafter
(b) Should the Publishers sub-license hardcover rights to an independent hardcover publisher, all moneys accruing under such a sub-licence shall be divided in the proportion 80% to the Author and 20% to the Publishers.

Code of Practice:
Publishers' Dealings With Authors

The following Code of Practice: Publishers' Dealings With Authors was issued by the Publishers Association, London in 1997 (updated from the earlier issue in 1982). It is reproduced here by permission.

A constructive and co-operative relationship between authors (and the agents and Representatives acting for them) and their publishers is vital to successful publishing. In order to eliminate the causes of any dissatisfaction which may arise, however, perhaps because a title is not the success the author and publisher hoped for or because of misunderstandings of the publishing contract, this Code of Practice attempts to address some of the areas which may lead to avoidable conflict.

The publishing contract must be clear, unambiguous and comprehensive, and must be honoured in both the letter and the spirit.
Matters which particularly need to be defined in the contract include:

- a title which identifies the work or (for incomplete works) the nature and agreed length and scope of the work;
- the nature of the rights conferred, the ownership of the copyright (an assignment or an exclusive licence), whether all volume rights (or part of the volume rights or more than volume rights), and the territories and languages covered;
- the timescale for delivery of the manuscript and for publication;
- the payments, royalties and advances (if any) to be paid, what they are in respect of, and when they are due;
- the provisions for sub-licensing;
- the responsibility for preparing the supporting materials (e.g. indexes, illustrations, etc.) in which the author holds the copyright, and for obtaining permissions and paying for the supporting materials in which the copyright is held by third parties;
- the termination and reversion provisions of the contract.

Should the parties subsequently agree changes to the contract, these should be recorded in writing between them.

The author should retain ownership of the copyright, unless there are good reasons otherwise.

An exclusive licence should be sufficient to enable the publisher to exploit and protect most works effectively. In particular fields of publishing (e.g. encyclo-paedic and reference works, certain types of academic works, publishers' compilations edited from many outside contributions, some translations and works particularly vulnerable to copyright infringement because of their extensive international sale) it may be appropriate for the copyright to be vested in the publisher.

The publisher should ensure that the author who is not professionally represented has a proper opportunity for explanation of the terms of the contract and the reasons for each provision.

The contract must set out reasonable and precise terms for the reversion of rights.

When a publisher has invested in the development of an author's work on the market, and the work is a contribution to the store of literature and knowledge, and the publisher expects to market the work actively for many years, it is reasonable to acquire volume rights for the full term of copyright, on condition that there are safeguards providing for reversion in appropriate circumstances.

The circumstances under which the grant of rights acquired by the publisher will revert to the author (e.g. fundamental breach of contract by the publisher, or when a title has been out of print or has not been available on the market for a stipulated time) should form a part of the formal contract. In addition, a reversion of particular rights that either have never been successfully exploited by the publisher or which are not subject to any current (or immediately anticipated) licence or edition, may, after a reasonable period from their first acquisition and after proper notice, be returned on request to the author, provided that such partial reversions do not adversely affect other retained rights (e.g. the absence of an English language edition should not affect the licensing publisher's interest in a translated edition still in print) and provided that payments made by the publisher to or on behalf of the author have been earned.

The publisher must give the author a proper opportunity to share in the success of the work. In general, the publishing contract should seek to achieve a fair balance of reward for author and publisher. On occasion it may be appropriate, when the publisher is taking an exceptional risk in publishing a work, or the origination costs are unusually high, for the author to assist the publication of the work by accepting initially a low royalty return. In such cases, it is also appropriate for the publisher to agree that the author should share in success by, for example, agreeing that royalty rates should increase to reflect that success.

If under the contract the author receives an outright or single payment, but retains ownership of the copyright, the publisher should be prepared to share with the author any income derived from a use of the work not within the reasonable contemplation of the parties at the time of the contract.

The publisher must handle manuscripts promptly, and keep the author informed of progress. All manuscripts and synopses received by the publisher, whether solicited or unsolicited, should be acknowledged as soon as received. The author may be told at that time when to expect to hear further, but in the absence of any such indication at least a progress report should be sent by the publisher to the author within six weeks of receipt. A longer time may be required in the case of certain works, e.g. those requiring a detailed assessment, particularly in cases where the opinion of specialist readers may not be readily available, and in planned co-editions, but the author should be informed of a likely date when a report may be expected.

It is important, however, for the publisher to know if the manuscript or synopsis is being simultaneously submitted to any other publisher.

The publisher must not cancel a contract without good and proper reason. It is not easy to define objectively what constitutes unsuitability for publication of a commissioned manuscript or proper cause for the cancellation of a contract, since these may depend on a variety of circumstances. In any such case, however, the publisher must give the author sufficiently detailed reasons for rejection.

When a publisher requires changes in a commissioned manuscript as a condition of publication, these should be clearly set out in writing.

In the case of unsolicited manuscripts or synopses, the publisher is under no obligation to give reasons for rejection, and is entitled to ask the author for return postage.

Time

If an author fails to deliver a completed manuscript according to the contract or within the contracted period, the publisher may be entitled (inter alia) to a refund of monies advanced on account. However, it is commonly accepted that (except where time is of the essence) monies advanced are not reclaimable until the publisher has given proper notice of intent to cancel the contract within a reasonable period from the date of such notice. Where the advance is not reclaimed after the period of notice has expired, it is reasonable for the publisher to retain an option to publish the work.

Standard and quality

If an author has produced the work in good faith and with proper care, in accordance with the terms of the contract, but the publisher decides not to publish on grounds of quality, the publisher should not expect to reclaim on cancellation that part of any advance that has already been paid to the author. If, by contrast, the work has not been produced in good faith and with proper care, or the work does not conform to what has been commissioned, the publisher may be able to reclaim the advance.

Defamation or illegality

The publisher is under no obligation to publish a work that there is reason to believe is defamatory or otherwise illegal.

Change of circumstance

A change in the publisher's circumstances or policies is not a sufficient reason for declining to publish a commissioned work without compensation.

Compensation

Depending on the grounds for rejection,
[1] the publisher may be liable for further advances due and an additional sum may be agreed to compensate the author, or
[2] the author may be liable to repay the advances received.
In the former case, the agreement for compensation may include an obligation on the author to return advances and compensation paid (or part of them) if the work is subsequently placed elsewhere.

Resolution of disputes

Ideally, terms will be agreed privately between the parties, but in cases of dispute the matter should be put to a mutually agreed informal procedure (such as that available from the Publishers Association) or, if this cannot be agreed, to arbitration or normal legal procedures.

The contract must set out the anticipated timetable for publication.
The formal contract must make clear the timescale within which the author undertakes to deliver the complete manuscript, and within which the publisher undertakes to publish it. It should be recognised that in particular cases there may be valid reasons for diverging from these stated times, or for not determining strict timescales, and each party should be willing to submit detailed reasons for the agreement of the other party, if these should occur.

The publisher should be willing to share precautions against legal risks not arising from carelessness by the author.
For example: libel. While it remains the primary responsibility of the author to ensure that the work is not libellous – and particularly that it cannot be arraigned as a malicious libel – the publisher may also be liable. Libel therefore demands the closest co-operation between authors and publishers, in particular in sharing the costs of reading for libel or of any insurance considered to be desirable by the parties.

The publisher should consider assisting the author by funding additional costs involved in preparing the work for publication.
If under the contract the author is liable to pay for supporting materials, e.g. for permissions to use other copyright material, for the making and use of illustrations and maps, for costs of indexing, etc., the publisher may be willing to fund such expenses, to an agreed ceiling, that could reasonably be recovered against any such monies as may subsequently become due to the author.

The publisher must ensure that the author receives a regular and clear account of sales made and monies due.

The period during which sales are to be accounted for should be defined in the contract and should be followed, after a period also to be laid down in the contract, by a royalty statement and a remittance of monies due. Publishers should always observe these dates and obligations scrupulously. Accounts should be rendered at least annually, more commonly twice yearly. The publisher should pay the author on request the appropriate share of any substantial advances received from major sub-licensing agreements by the end of the month following the month of receipt (providing monies already advanced have been earned, and proper allowance made for returned stock; allowance may also need to be made if very substantial advances have been outstanding for an extended period of time).

The publisher should be prepared, on request, to disclose details of the number of copies printed, on condition that the author (and the agent) agree not to disclose the information to any other party.

Publishers should be prepared to give authors indications of sales to date, which must be realistic bearing in mind either unsold stock which may be returned by booksellers or stock supplied on consignment.

The publisher must ensure that the author can clearly ascertain how any payments due from sub-licensed agreements will be calculated.

Agreements under which the calculation of the author's share of any earnings is dependent on the publisher's allocation of direct costs and overheads can result in dissatisfaction unless the system of accounting is clearly defined.

The publisher should keep the author informed of important design, promotion, marketing and sub-licensing decisions.

Under the contract, final responsibility for decisions on the design, promotion and marketing of a book is normally vested in the publisher. Nevertheless, the fullest reasonable consultation with the author on such matters is generally desirable, both as a courtesy and in the interests of the success of the book itself. In particular the author should, if interested and available, be consulted about the proposed jacket, jacket copy and major promotional and review activities, be informed in advance of the publication date, and receive advance copies by that date. When time permits, the publisher should consult the author about the disposition of major sub-leases, and let the author have a copy of the agreement on request.

The integrity of the author's work should always be protected.

The author is entitled to ensure that the editorial integrity of the work is maintained. No significant alterations to the work (i.e. alterations other than those which could not reasonably be objected to) should be made without the author's consent, particularly where the author has retained the copyright.

The author who has retained the ownership of the copyright is entitled also to be credited with the authorship of the work, and to retain the ownership of the manuscript.

The publisher should inform the author clearly about opportunities for amendment of the work in the course of production.

The economics of typesetting and printing make the incorporation of authors' textual revisions after the book has been set extremely expensive. Publishers should always make it clear to authors, before a manuscript is put in hand, whether proofs are to be provided or not, on whom the responsibility for reading them rests and what scale of author's revisions would be acceptable to the publisher. If proofs are not being provided, the author should have the right to make final corrections to the copy-edited typescript, and the publisher should take responsibility for accurately reproducing this corrected text in type.

It is essential that both the publisher and the author have a clear common understanding of the significance attaching to the option clause in a publishing contract.

The option on an author's work can be of great importance to both parties. Options should be carefully negotiated, and the obligations that they impose should be clearly stated and understood on both sides. Option clauses covering more than one work may be undesirable, and should only be entered into with particular care.

The publisher should recognise that the remaindering of stock may effectively end the author's expectation of earnings.

Before a title is remaindered, the publisher should inform the author and offer all or part of the stock to the author on the terms expected from the remainder dealer. Whether any royalty, related to the price received on such sales, should be paid is a matter to be determined by the publisher and the author at the time of the contract.

The publisher should endeavour to keep the author informed of changes in the ownership of the publishing rights and of any changes in the imprint under which a work appears. Most publishers will expect to sign their contracts on behalf of their successors and assigns, just as authors will sign on behalf of their executors, administrators and assigns. But if changes in rights ownership or of publishing imprint subsequently occur, a publisher should certainly inform and, if at all possible, accommodate an author in these new circumstances.

The publisher should be willing to help the author and the author's estate in the administration of literary affairs. For example, the publisher should agree to act as an expert witness in questions relating to the valuation of a literary estate.

Above all, the publisher must recognise the importance of co-operation with the author in an enterprise in which both are essential. This relationship can be fulfilled only in an atmosphere of confidence, in which authors get the fullest possible credit for their work and achievements.

[Note: This Code of Practice applies only to agreements whereby an author assigns or licenses an interest in the copyright of a work to a publisher, and does not apply to agreements whereby an author invests money in the publication of a work.]

Reissued: 1997. Copyright © The Publishers Association 1982

Bibliography

Achebe, Chinua 1979. See Ezenwa-Ohaeto 1997.

Achebe, Chinua. 'Interview with Michel Fabre on *Arrow of God*'. *Echoes du Commonwealth*, 5, 1979-80, 7-17.

Achebe, Chinua. *The Trouble with Nigeria*. Enugu: Fourth Dimension Publishers, 1983. London, Ibadan and Nairobi: Heinemann, 1983.

Adcock, Fleur. 'The Thrill of the New'. *Daily Telegraph* (London, 19 September 1995, A7.

Adebiyi, Remi Edwards. 'Passing of a Pioneer Novelist'. *Guardian* (Lagos), 14 June 1997, 11.

Adeniyi, Olayiwola. 'The Double-face Accomplishment'. *Guardian* (Lagos), 30 December 1996 25.

Aidoo, Ama Ata. 'To be an African Woman Writer – An Overview'. In Petersen, ed. 1988, 155-72.

Aidoo, Ama Ata. *Changes*. London: The Women's Press, 1991.

Aihe, Okoh. 'ANA '92: Fury and Fanfare'. *Vanguard* (London), 21 November, 1992, 11.

Altbach, Philip G and Salah M Hassan, eds. *The Muse of Modernity: Essays on Culture as Development in Africa*. Trenton, NJ: Africa World Press, 1996.

Amegatcher, Andrew. 'The Christian Messenger'. *West Africa*, 13 January 1997, 57-61.

Anikulapo, Jahman. 'Dedicating Wole Soyinka's House of Hope'. *Guardian* (Lagos), 25 April 1993, A14-15.

Anikulapo. Jahman. 'Dedicating Soyinka's House of Hope'. *Lagos Life*, 22-28 April 1993, 10.

Anon. 'Hot and Spicy: Growing up in Guyana'. *The Bookseller*, 10 July 1998, 32. (On Oonya Kempadoo's *Buxton Spice*.)

Anyidoho, Kofi. 'Poetry as Dramatic Performance: The Ghana Experience'. *Research In African Literatures*, Vol. 22 no. 2, 1991, 43-55.

Anyidoho, Kofi. '1998 ALA Presidential Address'. *ALA Bulletin* [African Literature Association], Vol. 24 no. 2, 1998, 6-11. 1998 a.

Anyidoho, Kofi. 'Interviewed' by Lee Nichols. *ALA Bulletin* [African Literature Association], Vol. 24 no. 2, 1998, 22-26. 1998 b.

Anyidoho, Kofi. 'Introduction'. *Matatu*, forthcoming.

Appiah, Kwame Anthony. *In My Father's House: Africa in the Philosophy of Culture*. New York: Oxford University Press, 1993.

Ayorinde, Steve. 'Booming Market for the Video'. *Guardian* (Lagos), 1 May 1997, 31.

Bello, Sule and Abdullahi R Augi, eds. *Culture and the Book Industry in Nigeria: Proceedings of NAFEST '83 Seminar*, Lagos. National Council for Arts and Culture, Maiduguri, Borno State, 1993.

Benson, Peter. *Black Orpheus, Transition, and Modern Cultural Awakening in Africa*. Berkeley, CA: University of California Press, 1986.

Bgoya, Walter. 'Autonomous Publishing in Africa: The Present Situation'. *Development Dialogue* (Uppsala), nos 1-2, 1984, 83-97.

Blum, William. *The CIA: A Forgotten History*. London: Zed Books, 1986.

Chakava, Henry. 'An Autonomous African Publishing House: A Model'. *Development Dialogue* (Uppsala), nos 1-2, 1984, 123-31.

Chilemba, Bob. 'Malawi's First Writers' Colony Sprouts'. *This is Malawi* (Lilongwe), July 1996, 16.

Chimombo, Steve. 'Dialogue on Publishing'. *WASI Writer* (Zomba), Vol. 9 no. 3, 1998, 16-18.

Cromhout, Monica. 'Writers Workshop: Offering Other Alternatives'. *African Publishing Review* (Harare), Vol. 5 no. 6 (November/December 1996), 13.

Cunningham, Valentine. 'Unto Him (Her) that Hath: How Victorian Writers Made Ends Meet'. *Times Literary Supplement*, 11 September 1998, 12-13.

Davies, Wendy. 'The Future of Indigenous Publishing in Africa'. Seminar Report. Uppsala: Dag Hammarskjöld Foundation, 1996.

Davies, Wendy. 'African Writers–Publishers Seminar. A Seminar Organised by the African Books Collective and the Dag Hammarskjöld Foundation in Arusha, Tanzania, 23-26 February 1998: Seminar Report'. Uppsala: Dag Hammarskjöld Foundation, 1998.

Dorsey, David. 'African Literary Studies in Cairo'. *ALA Bulletin* [African Literature Association], Vol. 22 no. 4, 1996, 3-17.

Duerden, Dennis. *African Art and Literature: The Invisible Present*. London: Heinemann, 1973.

Duerden, Dennis. 'Broadcasting in Africa'. Unpublished Report to Congress for Cultural Freedom, 1991. [On file in the Harry Ransome Humanities Research Center, University of Texas.]

Duerden, Dennis and Cosmo Pieterse. *African Writers Talking*. London: Heinemann, 1972.

Ehling, Holger. 'Muted ZIBF Reflects Slowdown in Economy'. *The Bookseller*, 14 August 1998, 9.

Ehmeir, Walter. 'Publishing South African Literature in English in the 1960s'. *Research in African Literatures*, Vol. 20 no. 1, 1995, 111-31.

Emenyonu, Ernest. 'Poita Nwana'. In Ogunbiyi, ed. 1988, 9-13.

Evans, Matthew. 'Some Principles of Publishing: A British View'. *Development Dialogue* (Uppsala), nos 1-2, 1984, 113-22.

Ezenwa-Ohaeto. *A Biography of Chinua Achebe*. Oxford: James Currey, 1997.

Fajemisin, Martins Olusegun. 'An APNET Survey of Local Language Publishing'. *African Publishing Review* (Harare), Vol. 4 no. 5, September/October 1995; Vol. 4 no. 6, November/December 1995; Vol. 5 no. 1, January/February 1996; Vol. 5 no. 2 March/April 1996.

Freedman, Jonathan, ed. *The Cambridge Companion to Henry James*. Cambridge: Cambridge University Press, 1998.

Garvey, Anthony. 'When Size Does Matter'. *The Bookseller*, 15 May 1998, 12.

Gbadebo, Tokunbo. 'Author Publisher Relationships: A Publisher's Viewpoint'. In Bello and Augi, 1984, 149-70.

Gérard, Albert. *Contexts of African Literature*. Amsterdam: Rodopi, 1990.

Gibbs, James. *A Handbook for African Writers*. Oxford: Hans Zell Publishers, 1986.

Gibbs, James. 'A Word of Caution'. *West Africa*, 15-21 September 1997, 1469.

Gibbs, James. 'Publishing Hints'. *WASI Writer* (Zomba), Vol. 9 no. 3, 1998, 13-15.

Gititi, Gitahi. Unpublished paper presented at the Conference on Creative Writing in African Languages, London, 12 September 1997.

Gordimer, Nadine. 'The *Classic*: Nadine Gordimer Replies'. *South African Information and Analysis 52*. 1967, 1-2.

Gray, Stephen. 'Literature in Lesotho: Some Reports'. *World Literature Today*, Vol. 72 no. 1, Winter 1998, 49-54.

Greenfield, George. *A Smattering of Monsters*. London: Warner Books, 1997.

Gyamfi, Charles Coffie. 'Soyinka off to London, May Sue Government over Property'. *Guardian* (Lagos), 22 October 1998, 1, 5.

Hare, David. *A Map of the World*. In *Plays 2*. London: Faber, 1997.

Henderson, Bill. *The Publish-It-Yourself Handbook: Literary Tradition and How To*. Yonkers, NY: Pushcart Press, 1973. [Out of print]

Higo, Aig. 'The International Symposium on African Literatures'. In Osofisan *et al.* 1991, 104-10.

Ike, Chuckwuemeka. *To My Husband from Iowa*. Lagos: Malthouse Press 1996.

Ike, Chuckwuemeka, ed. *Directory of Nigerian Book Development*. Awka and Enugu: Nigerian Book Foundation and Fourth Dimension Publishers, 1998.

Isola, Akinwumi. Unpublished paper presented at the Conference on Creative Writing in African Languages, London, 12 September 1997.

Iyayi, Festus 1988. See Osofisan *et al.* 1991.

Izevbaye, Dan. 'Elesin's Homecoming: The Translation of *The King's Horseman*'. *Research in African Literatures*. Vol. 28 no. 2, 1997, 154-70.

Jeffries-Jones, Rhodri. *The CIA and American Democracy*. New Haven: Yale University Press, 1989.

Joyce, James. *A Portrait of the Artist as a Young Man*. New York: Viking, 1961. Chester G Anderson, ed. (Reprinted London: Penguin, 1992. Seamus Deane, ed.)

Kagira, Pacharo. 'Novice Writers Club Still Alive'. *WASI Writer* (Zomba) Vol. 9 no. 3, 1998, 39

Kannan, Lakshmi. 'Sable Shadows at the Witching Time of Night'. In *India Gate and Other Stories*. London: Sangram Books, 1993, 111-36.

Killam, GD, ed. *African Writers on African Writing*. London: Heinemann, 1973.

Kubekron News. (Kubekron, Ghana) Vol. 1 no. 3. December 1994.

Kureishi, Hanif. *Intimacies*. London: Faber, 1998.

Lawal-Solarin, Yinka. 'Publishing in Nigeria'. *African Publishing Review* (Harare), Vol. 6 no. 3, May/June 1997, 10-11.

Leggat, Michael. 'Which Publisher?' *The Author*, Autumn 1997, 96-105.

Limb, Peter and Jean-Marie Volet. *Bibliography of African Literatures*. Lanham, MD and London: Scarecrow, 1996.

Lindfors, Bernth. *Critical Responses to Amos Tutuola*. Washington, DC: Three Continents Press, 1975.

Lindfors, Bernth. *Loaded Vehicles: Studies in African Literary Media*. Trenton, NJ: Africa World Press, 1996.

Lindfors, Bernth. 'A "Proper Farewell" to Amos Tutuola'. In *The Blind Men and the Elephant and Other Essays in Biographical Criticism*. Trenton, NJ: Africa World Press, 1999, 135-46.

Maimane, Arthur. 'Can't You Write About Something Else?' *Présence Africaine* (Paris), no. 80, 1971, 123-26.

Maja-Pearce, Adewale. *Directory of African Media*. Brussels: International Federation of Journalists, 1996.

'Matchet' see Nwagboso, Maxwell 1997.

Mazrui, Ali A. 'Perspective: The Muse of Modernity and the Quest for Development'. In Altbach and Hassan, eds, 1996.

McCartney, Murray. *An Indaba on National Book Policy: The Key to Long Term Book Development*. Harare: Zimbabwe International Book Fair Trust, 1995.

McHardy, Francoise. 'Business as Usual in South Africa'. *The Bookseller*. 10 April 1998, 10.

Morrison, Toni. *Toni Morrison for Beginners* (Shona version). New York, NY: Writers and Readers, 1996. [Out of print]

Moss, Stephen. 'Lauding Art, Not Politics'. *The Bookseller*, 27 March 1998. 27-28. (A consideration of the concept of Commonwealth writing by a recent judge of the Eurasian Region, Commonwealth Writers Prize.)

Mphahlele, Es'kia. 'Interviewed by Richard Samin'. *Research in African Literatures*, Vol. 28 no. 2, 1997, 182-200.

Ngcobo, Lauretta. 'The African Woman Writer'. In Petersen and Rutherford, eds, 1986, 81-86.

Ngugi wa Thiong'o. *Barrel of a Pen: Resistance to Oppression in Neo-Colonial Kenya*. Trenton, NJ: Africa World Press, 1986.

Ngugi wa Thiong'o. *Moving the Centre. The Struggle for Cultural Freedoms*. Oxford: James Currey, 1993.

Nichols, Lee. *Conversations with African Writers: Interviews with Twenty-six African Authors*. Washington, DC: Voice of America, 1981.

Nichols, Lee. *African Writers at the Microphone*. Washington, DC: Three Continents Press, 1984.

Nichols, Lee. Interview with Ngugi wa Thiong'o. 'Lee Nichols' Interview, March 30, Stony Brook'. *ALA Bulletin* [African Literature Association], Vol. 22 no. 2, 1996, 21-25.

Nightingale, Peggy. 'VS Naipaul'. In *International Literature in English: Essays on the Major Writers*. Robert L. Ross, ed. New York: Garland, 1991, 525-34.

Norton, Michael. *The Community Newspaper Kit*. London: Michael Norton, 1975. [Out of print]

Norton, Michael. *The Mural Kit*. London: Michael Norton, 1975. [Out of print]

Norton, Michael. *The Slide Tape Kit*. London: Michael Norton, 1976. [Out of print]

Nwagboso, Maxwell. 'Matchet's Diary'. *West Africa*, 7-13 July 1997, 1077.

Nwoga, Donatus I. 'The *Chi* Offended'. *Transition* (Kampala), no. 15, 1964, 5.

Nwoga, Donatus I, ed. *Rhythms of Creations: A Decade of Oriki Poetry*. Enugu: Fourth Dimension Publishers, 1982.

Nwoga, Donatus I. *Gong and Flute*, Westport, CT: Greenwood Press, 1984, 153-54.

Ofeimun, Odia. 'Postmodernism and the Impossible Death of the Author'. *Glendora* (Lagos), Vol. 2 nos 3-4, 1998, 24-40.

Ogunbiyi, Yemi, ed. *Perspectives on Nigerian Literature: 1700 to the Present*, Vols 1 and 2. Lagos: Guardian, 1988.

Okara, Gabriel. 'African Speech ... English Words'. *Transition* (Kampala), no. 11, September 1963.

Okediji, Oladejo. Unpublished paper presented at Conference on Creative Writing in African Languages. London, 12 September 1997.

Oshunkeye, Shola. 'Poet Osundare Remembers Tutuola, an Unignorable Pioneer'. *Weekend Concord* (Lagos), 12 July 1997, 18.

Osofisan, Femi, Nicole Medjigbodo, Sam Asein and GG Darah. *Proceedings of the International Symposium on African Literatures, 2-7 May 1988, Lagos, Nigeria*. Lagos: Centre for Black and African Arts and Civilisation, 1991.

Osundare, Niyi. 'African Literature Now: Standards, Texts and Canons'. *Glendora Review* (Lagos), Vol. 1 no. 4, 1996, 25-31; Vol. 2 no. 4, 1997.

Paton, JS, ed. *The Grey Ones: Essays on Censorship*. Johannesburg: Ravan Press, 1974.

Petersen, Kirsten Holst, ed. *Criticism and Ideology*. Uppsala: Nordiska Afrikainstitutet, 1988.

Petersen, Kirsten Holst and Anna Rutherford, eds. *A Double Colonization: Colonial and Post-Colonial Women's Writing*. Aarhus: Dangaroo, 1986.

Phiri, Grace. 'Malawian Attitudes'. *WASI Writer* (Zomba), Vol. 9 no. 3, 1998, 39.

Pryor, Felix, ed. *The Faber Book of Letters*. London: Faber, 1988.

Reynolds, Nigel. 'Grief Spurred Brother to Debut Book Success'. *Daily Telegraph*. (London) 14 July 1997.

Ross, Robert L, ed. *International Literature in English: Essays on the Major Writers*. New York, NY: Garland, 1991, 525-34.

Samin, Richard see Mphahlele 1997.

Saro-Wiwa, Ken. *Prisoners of Jebs*. Port Harcourt: Saros International, 1988.

Saro-Wiwa, Ken. 'Eondudekiswahili'. In *Nigeria: The Brink of Disaster*. 1991a.

Saro-Wiwa, Ken. *Nigeria: The Brink of Disaster*. Port Harcourt: Saros International, 1991b.

Saro-Wiwa, Ken. 'Open Letter to Wole Soyinka'. In *Nigeria: The Brink of Disaster*. 1991c.

Saro-Wiwa, Ken. *Pita Dumbrok's Prison*. Port Harcourt: Saros International, 1991d.

Saunders, Frances Stonor. *Who Paid the Piper: The CIA and the Cultural Cold War*. London: Granta Books, 1999.

Schmidt, Nancy J. 'Review of *Directory of African Media*,' *Research in African Literatures*, Vol. 28 no. 2, 1997, 201-2.

Segun, Omowunmi. 'Writing Against Oppression'. An Interview With Niyi Osundare. *C²*, January 1999, 18-19.

Society of Authors, The. *Quick Guide 8: Publishing Contracts*. London: The Society of Authors, 1999.

Soyinka, Wole. 'From a Common Backcloth'. *American Scholar*, no. 32, 1963, 387-97.

Soyinka, Wole. *A Shuttle in the Crypt*. London: Collings/Methuen, 1972a.

Soyinka, Wole. *The Man Died*. London: Collings, 1972b.

Soyinka, Wole. 'Keynote Address'. In Osofisan *et al.*, 1991. 27-31.

Soyinka, Wole. *Ibadan*. London: Methuen, 1994a.

Soyinka, Wole. 'Interview with Chuks Iloegbunam'. *West Africa*, 18-24 July 1994b, 1270-71.

Taylor, Paul. 'Writer in Exile, Revolutionary in Waiting'. *Independent Weekend* (London), 16 September 1995, 3.

Turner, Barry. *The Writers' Handbook 1999*. Basingstoke: Macmillan, 1998.

Unwin, Stanley. *The Truth About Publishing*. London: Unwin/Hyman, 8th edn, 1976.

Veit-Wild, Flora. *Dambudzo Marechera: A Source Book on his Life and Work*. London: Hans Zell Publishers, 1992.

Wali, Obi. 'Dead End for African Literature'. *Transition*. (Kampala), no. 11, September 1963.

Wilkinson, Jane, ed. *Talking with African Writers*. London: James Currey, 1992.

Woolf, Virginia. *A Room of One's Own*. London: The Hogarth Press, 1929 (reprinted as *A Room of One's Own and Three Guineas*. London: Vintage, 1996).

Wren, Robert. *Those Magical Years: The Making of Nigerian Literature at Ibadan, 1948-1966*. Washington, DC: Three Continents Press, 1991.

Writers' and Artists' Yearbook 1999. London: A&C Black, 1999.

Zell, Hans. *The African Book World and Press: A Directory*. 4th ed. Oxford: Hans Zell Publishers, 1989.

Zell, Hans. 'African Journals in a Changing Environment of Scholarly Communication.' *African Periodicals 1996 Exhibit Catalogue*, Harare: SABDET/ ZIBFT, 1996.

Zell, Hans, *et al.*, *A New Reader's Guide to African Literature*. London: Heinemann, 1983.

Zell, Hans and Cécile Lomer. *Publishing and Book Development in Sub-Saharan Africa: An Annotated Bibliography*. London: Hans Zell Publishers, 1996.

Zimbabwe International Book Fair Trust. *Access to Information: Indaba97*. Harare: ZIBFT, 1997.

Index

Index compiled by Derek Copley